Archaeologies of Sexuality

Status, age, and gender have long been accepted aspects of archaeological enquiry, yet it is only recently that archaeologists have started to consider seriously the role of sex and sexuality in their studies.

Archaeologies of Sexuality is the first volume to explore this original archaeological research and meet the challenges of integrating the study of sex and sexuality within archaeology. It presents a strong, diverse body of scholarship, investigating locations as varied as medieval England, the ancient Mayan civilizations, New Kingdom Egypt, prehistoric Europe, prehistoric as well as colonial and Victorian North America, and convict-era Australia. Above all, this work demonstrates that variability in sexual expression is not solely a modern phenomenon. Sexuality has been an important and changing ingredient of human social life for thousands of years.

This pioneering volume will serve both as a valuable reference text for archaeologists pursuing similar studies, and as the essential introduction to sexuality studies for archaeologists who have not explored the topic before.

Robert A. Schmidt and **Barbara L. Voss** are doctoral candidates at the University of California at Berkeley.

Archaeologies of Sexuality

Edited by
Robert A. Schmidt and Barbara L. Voss

London and New York

First published 2000
by Routledge
11 New Fetter Lane, London EC4P 4EE

Simultaneously published in the USA and Canada
by Routledge
29 West 35th Street, New York, NY 10001

Routledge is an imprint of the Taylor & Francis Group

Selection and editorial matter © 2000 Robert A. Schmidt
and Barbara L. Voss; individual chapters © 2000 the contributors

Typeset in Garamond by Florence Production Ltd, Stoodleigh, Devon
Printed and bound in Great Britain by TJ International Ltd, Padstow, Cornwall

British Library Cataloguing in Publication Data
A catalogue record for this book is available from the British Library

Library of Congress Cataloging in Publication Data
Archaeologies of sexuality / [edited by] Robert A. Schmidt and Barbara L. Voss.
    p. cm.
    Includes bibliographical references and index.
      1. Social archaeology.   2. Sex – History.   3. Sex role – History.
    4. Excavations (Archaeology).   5. Material culture.
    I. Schmidt, Robert A., 1953–   II. Voss, Barbara L., 1967–

CC72.4 .A734 2000
930.1′028′5–dc21   00–020504

ISBN 0–415–22365–2 (hbk)
ISBN 0–415–22366–0 (pbk)

Dedicated to the memory of
Robert Daniel Ennis
1946–1998

Contents

II – THE STUFF OF SEX: MATERIAL CULTURE AND SEXUALITY

III – SEXUAL IDENTITIES, SEXUAL POLITICS

IV – THE SEXUAL GAZE: REPRESENTATION AND IMAGERY

CONCLUSION

Figures

Tables

Contributors

Joseph Balicki is a principal archaeologist with John Milner Associates, Inc., whose research experience in Washington, DC, includes excavations in the brothels of Hooker's Division.

Elizabeth Barthold O'Brien is a project architectural historian with John Milner Associates, Inc., who has had a long-term research interest in the history, architecture, and city plan of the United States national capital.

Victor Buchli lectures in the Department of Anthropology, University College London. He writes about Soviet and post-Soviet material culture as well as the archaeology of the recent past.

Eleanor Conlin Casella received her Ph.D. in Anthropology at the University of California, Berkeley and serves as principal investigator for the Ross Factory Archaeology Project. Her archaeological research examines gender identity and power relations within nineteenth-century Australian convict sites. She is currently a Lecturer in Colonial Archaeology at Manchester University.

Margaret W. Conkey is the Class of 1960 Professor of Anthropology and Director of the Archaeological Research Facility at the University of California, Berkeley. She directs a landscape archaeology project, 'Between the Caves' in the French Midi-Pyrénées, and continues to pursue how best to do archaeology as a feminist.

Julia G. Costello is co-owner of a cultural resources management firm in California, specializing in sites of the historic period. She has published widely on her research and has served on numerous professional boards and commissions.

Whitney Davis is the John Evans Professor of Art History at Northwestern University. His recent publications include *Replications: Archaeology, Art History, Psychoanalysis* (1996), *Drawing the Dream of the Wolves: Homosexual Interpretation, and Freud's 'Wolf Man'* (1995) and he was editor of *Gay and Lesbian Studies in Art History* (1994).

Roberta Gilchrist is Professor of Archaeology at the University of Reading, and Archaeologist to Norwich Cathedral. She has written extensively on both gender and medieval archaeology. Her books include *Gender and Archaeology: Contesting the Past* (1999) and *Gender and Material Culture: the Archaeology of Religious Women* (1994).

Sandra E. Hollimon is an anthropology instructor at Sonoma State University and Santa Rosa Junior College. Her research interests include the study of gender and sexuality in Native North American societies, as well as sex differences in health manifested in human skeletal remains.

Rosemary A. Joyce is Associate Professor of Anthropology at the University of California, Berkeley, specializing in ancient Mesoamerican society, and conducts archaeological field work in Honduras.

Lynn Meskell is Assistant Professor in the Department of Anthropology at Columbia University. She currently co-directs the South Saqqara Survey project in Egypt. Her recent volumes include *Archaeology Under Fire* (1998) and *Archaeologies of Social Life: Age, Sex, Class etc. in Ancient Egypt* (1999).

Elizabeth Prine is Assistant Professor of Anthropology at the University of Wisconsin at Oshkosh. Her work focuses on the interstices of archaeology, ethnohistory, and ethnography in the North American Plains, with particular reference to the ways households relate to the larger world.

Gayle Rubin is a Social Science Research Council Sexuality Fellowship Research Program postdoctoral fellow in the History Department at the University of California, Berkeley. She is working to complete a book on San Francisco leathermen.

Robert A. Schmidt is completing his Ph.D. in Anthropology at the University of California, Berkeley. His work focuses upon the intersections of sex, gender, and sexuality in the Mesolithic period of the Baltic region.

Donna J. Seifert is a senior associate with John Milner Associates, Inc. Her special interest in the archaeology of prostitution developed when she co-directed excavations in Hooker's Division, Washington DC's late nineteenth-century red-light district.

Barbara L. Voss is completing her Ph.D. in Anthropology at the University of California, Berkeley. She is currently conducting her dissertation research at the Presidio de San Francisco, a Spanish-colonial and Mexican period military settlement on the central California coast.

Laurie A. Wilkie is an Assistant Professor of Anthropology at the University of California, Berkeley. She received her doctorate from the Archaeology Program at the University of California, Los Angeles in 1994. Her dissertation research explored the construction of African-American identities during and beyond the period of enslavement in Louisiana.

Acknowledgements

Archaeologies of Sexuality began as a conference symposium by the same name which was presented at the 1998 Society for American Archaeology Annual Meeting in Seattle, Washington. The papers contributed to that symposium, and the ensuing dialogues with other archaeologists who attended, form the backbone of this volume. As editors we offer thanks to all the contributing authors for the time and effort they took in writing, and then revising, their contributions.

We would like to thank many colleagues and friends who helped bring this volume to press. Deborah Cohler unwittingly gave us the idea for this project, and throughout she has been generous with her expertise in sexology, feminist studies, and queer theory. Stuart Goodnick provided invaluable moral and tangible support. Will Roscoe's commentary on the original symposium helped to shape the direction of the volume. Gayle Rubin's enthusiasm and common-sense advice kept us on course. Phillip Jeffrey Schmidt and Laurie Binder generously gave important technical assistance. Kathy Sterling gracefully assisted in preparing the manuscript.

At the University of California, Berkeley, Meg Conkey and Kent Lightfoot provided crucial guidance. Our wonderful colleagues at the Archaeological Research Facility encouraged us in innumerable ways. Caren Kaplan and other participants in the Designated Emphasis in Women, Gender, and Sexuality provided an important academic forum for interdisciplinary discussions about sexuality studies.

Finally, we thank Vicky Peters, Catherine Bousfield and many others at Routledge for their patience, guidance, and hard work in bringing this volume to publication.

Chapter One

Archaeologies of sexuality: an introduction

Barbara L. Voss and Robert A. Schmidt

INTRODUCTION

This book is about anthropological archaeology and its emerging contributions to studies of sexuality. Our goal is to foreground sexuality as a subject of archaeological analysis by presenting a number of case studies which focus on the relationship between archaeological data and sexuality in the past. While sexuality has traditionally been absent in archaeological interpretations, the studies in this volume demonstrate that this need not be the case. Archaeological data can – and should – be applied to better understand human sexual expressions throughout history. Because human sexuality touches many, if not all, aspects of culture, archaeological interpretations which include sexuality will provide richer, more nuanced understandings of the past.

Why is a volume like this necessary? Unfortunately, most archaeologists have not addressed sexuality in their research, in large part because of a disciplinary perception that sexuality is outside the purview of archaeology. The challenges are straightforward. Can sexuality be studied historically, and if so, does sexuality leave any material traces? How can we use potsherds, soil stains, animal bones, collapsed walls, or other archaeological data to study sexual identities, sexual activities, and sexual relationships? Yet these challenges – defining cultural variables, and relating material evidence to social behavior – are always present in archaeology. In this sense, perhaps sexuality is no different than political organization, religion, gender, ethnicity, or social ranking – all topics which archaeologists have successfully investigated. What is needed is a recognition that existing theories and methods can also be used to connect material evidence with research questions about sexuality. The case studies in this volume demonstrate that archaeological studies of sexuality are indeed possible, and that such studies can greatly enhance our interpretations of the past.

In this introductory essay, we explore several themes which provide a context for the case studies which follow. First, we address issues of language. What does the term 'sexuality' mean? Next, we define issues which have hindered archaeological studies of sexuality, both in theory and in method. We suggest several guidelines for archaeological investigations of sexuality: some prescriptive and some cautionary. We present an interdisciplinary survey of sexuality studies in sexology, socio-cultural anthropology, physical anthropology, history, classics, and several material disciplines such as art history, material culture studies, geography, and architecture. In summarizing the status of sexuality studies in these fields, we emphasize the approaches, methods, and techniques which may be useful to archaeological research on sexuality. Next, we turn to archaeology itself: how has sexuality generally been treated within archaeological studies? We review the recent emergence of explicit archaeological studies on sexuality over the last decade, and discuss several trends which characterize these studies. Finally, we briefly discuss the chapters that follow, highlighting themes that cross-cut the individual case studies.

THE LANGUAGE OF SEXUALITY

In standard English, the word 'sex' has tangled and ambiguous meanings. According to the *Random House Unabridged Dictionary*, sex refers to being either male or female, to coitus, to eroticism, and to reproduction. These varied meanings are both confusing and revealing, suggesting some of the ways in which anglophone cultures imbricate coitus, genitalia, and gender. 'Having sex' is both an activity and a state of being.

How can we break down these multiple meanings into useful terms which can aid, rather than hinder, research about sexuality? As a first step, we distinguish between biological sex, gender, and sexuality. We take biological sex to refer to the physical and genetic differences of the body which are related to reproduction – for example, genitalia, chromosomal distinctions, hormonal distinctions, and reproductive organs. Gender, as conventionally used in anthropology, refers to the cultural organization of biological sexual differences (Rubin 1975; Vance 1991; but see Butler 1990, 1993a; Fausto-Sterling 1983; Moore 1994: 8–27; and Delphy 1993 for different perspectives on this issue). Sexuality, then, is related to both biological sex and gender, and simultaneously is quite distinct from them.

If sexuality is not encompassed within biological sex and/or gender, then what is it? We employ sexuality to refer to all kinds of sexual relations, including sexual activities, eroticism, sexual identities, sexual meanings, and sexual politics. By sexual activities, we mean what most people think of as 'having sex' – not just coitus and/or orgasm, but the full range of interpersonal and self-stimulatory possibilities. Eroticism is related, but not limited, to sexual activity, including meanings and representations that are intended to arouse sexual interest or that otherwise contain a sexual charge.

Sexual identities, meanings, and politics are more difficult to define. While sexual identities are popularly defined by choice of sexual partner (e.g. heterosexual, homosexual, pederast, etc.), we define them more broadly to include any situation where sexual practices or meanings contribute to the construction of personal or group identity. The term 'sexual meaning' provides a way to discuss how objects or situations reference sexuality; for example, in this volume, Wilkie (Chapter 7) and Meskell (Chapter 14) both consider how childbirth and child-rearing can be infused with sexual meanings in specific cultural contexts. Finally, we define sexual politics as systems which link sexual relations to other power-based cultural relationships and organizations.

While we find these definitions useful in our research, these apparently neat distinctions between biological sex, gender, and sexuality are actually quite problematic. For example, while many feminist and queer studies scholars have used the distinction between biological sex and cultural genders and sexual identities in order to 'dispute the biology-is-destiny formulation' (Butler 1990: 6), this distinction can mistakenly give the impression that biological sex is a blank slate upon which culture inscribes gender or sexuality. It is important to remember that the characteristics which we perceive as biological traits are in fact culturally perceived and selected through gender ideology (e.g. Delphy 1993). Naming a part of the body as 'genitalia' presupposes sexual meaning. It is inappropriate to use biology to separate any aspect of sexuality from culture – a point to which we will return in our discussion of sex essentialism.

Likewise, the relationship between gender and sexuality is not straightforward. As Rubin has argued, in many modern societies it is necessary to separate gender and sexuality analytically to adequately understand either: 'although sex and gender are related, they are not the same thing, and they form the basis of two distinct arenas of social practice' (Rubin 1984: 308). The goal of the archaeologist must be to understand the dynamics of biological sex, gender and sexuality, individually where possible and appropriate, as well as in concert, and to characterize the mechanisms and boundaries of their influences and interactions within the social contexts under investigation. Thus the terms we employ should be situationally chosen and explicitly defined to fit the cultural context and research questions being addressed. They should provide a lexicon which will allow sexuality to become visible, rather than be hidden within narratives of gender and biological sex.

THE ARCHAEOLOGICAL PROBLEM: SEX ESSENTIALISM, SEX NEGATIVITY, THE SEX HIERARCHY, AND LASCIVIOUS TREATMENT OF SEXUALITY

Having defined our terms, we now turn to a central point: why haven't archaeologists usually discussed sexuality in their interpretations of the past? Certainly, no archaeologist would deny that sexual activity happened among the diverse historical populations which we study. But for the most part, sexuality is not explicitly addressed in archaeological research. Before we can begin to develop archaeological studies of sexuality, we must first understand why sexuality has been traditionally neglected.

In her influential article, 'Thinking Sex', Rubin (1984) provides a useful starting point for addressing this question. Rubin identifies several axioms, or ideological formations, within Western discourses which inhibit the development of unbiased investigations of sexuality and the erotic. We have identified four tendencies in archaeological research which parallel the general axioms identified by Rubin. Challenging these underlying axioms is necessary before the project of investigating sexuality in archaeological pasts can begin.

Sex essentialism

The axiom which we believe most greatly influences archaeological research is sex essentialism: 'the idea that sex is a natural force that exists prior to social life and shapes institutions. Sexual essentialism is embedded in the folk wisdoms of Western societies, which consider sex to be eternally unchanging, asocial, and transhistorical' (Rubin 1984: 275). Because of sex essentialism, many archaeologists believe that sexuality is not a cultural phenomenon, and therefore it is treated as a constant rather than as a historical and cultural variable. As a result, archaeologists have usually subsumed sexuality within interpretations of institutions such as marriage or kinship. Sexuality itself has remained unexamined, a biological given which is channeled, but not affected, by culture.

But this position – which is usually implicitly assumed rather than explicitly adopted – is untenable under examination. For example, archaeologists recognize that subsistence practices and foodways are grounded in biological functions, but they would be appalled if anyone suggested that human subsistence practices are therefore unchanging, transhistorical, and pre-social. Even nutritional 'needs' cannot be separated from cultural perceptions and guidelines. So too must sexuality, even in its most biological moments, be understood within a cultural context. Human expressions of sexuality are therefore historical and are an appropriate and productive subject of archaeological investigations. A social constructionist approach to sexuality (discussed below) allows archaeologists to examine the interface between biology and those social, cultural, and historical factors which influence how sexuality has been constructed in the past and present.

Sex negativity

While we believe that sex essentialism is the primary reason why archaeologists have avoided sexuality in their research, sex negativity has also contributed to this lack. 'Western cultures generally consider sex to be a dangerous, destructive, negative force . . . sex is presumed guilty until proven innocent. Virtually all erotic behavior is considered bad unless a specific reason to exempt it has been established' (Rubin 1984: 278). Many scholars are thus hesitant to discuss sexuality in their research, either through personal reluctance or through concern for their careers and social standing (Newton 1993; Vance 1991). Even researchers who are enthusiastic about sexuality studies in archaeology encounter institutional barriers: for example, when choosing the cover art and other illustrations for this volume, we were advised to consider that many countries have legal restrictions on the import and dissemination of sexually-explicit images. Such restrictions pose real barriers to the dissemination of archaeological data and interpretations of sexuality. The effects of both social and legal constraints on sexuality studies have affected archaeology as much as any other discipline.

Sex hierarchies

An outgrowth of sex negativity and sex essentialism is a hierarchical value scale which pervades treatment of sexuality within Euro-American societies. Sex acts are appraised 'according to a hierarchical system' in which monogamous marital sex for the purpose of reproduction has the highest valuation, with other sexual manifestations falling below this pinnacle (Rubin 1984: 279). Within archaeology, the unconscious effect of this value scale is that sexuality, when discussed, is usually only mentioned in reference to heterosexual marriage. When evolutionary theory informs archaeological studies, this hierarchy is modified to emphasize reproductively successful sex acts, because they are the only ones that contribute to the long-term genetic development of the population being studied. Either way, sex hierarchies lead archaeologists to prioritize reproductive heterosexuality, what Abelove has called 'penis in vagina, vagina around penis, with seminal emission uninterrupted' (Abelove 1989: 126), at the expense of non-reproductive and non-heterosexual sexual expressions.

The debilitating effects of sex hierarchies are apparent in archaeological research. Archaeological data viewed through this lens have been distorted to preserve the ideological sex hierarchy valued within dominant Euro-American ideologies. For example, Larco Hoyle has asserted – without supporting evidence – that depictions of same-sex sexual acts on prehistoric Moche and Chimú pottery served as symbolic warnings against engaging in homosexual behavior (Vasey 1998: 412). Likewise, Kauffmann Doig acknowledges that these same ceramics include large numbers (in both the absolute and relative sense) of representations of non-procreative sexual acts, including heterosexual anal intercourse and fellatio, yet he argues that the ceramics' production and use was related to a fertility cult (1979). Our point is not to single out these two studies, but to emphasize that the sexual hierarchy embedded within our cultural background can hinder us from seeing sexual variability in the past. Further, when such sexual variability is uncontrovertibly documented in archaeological evidence, as in the examples above, archaeologists have been likely to generate value-laden interpretations which more accurately reflect their own sexual mores than those of past cultures.

Lascivious treatment of sexuality

While the first three axioms we have discussed have served as barriers to addressing sexuality in archaeological research, a final problem, that of lascivious treatment of sexuality, does not prohibit discussion of sexuality per se. Instead, lascivious treatments of sexuality are used to both trivialize and exaggerate the relationships between sexuality and other aspects of culture. Archaeologists are probably most familiar with this phenomenon in the so-called 'popular press', where it is not uncommon for journalists or authors to isolate individual artifacts or representations and promote them as pornographic. Many readers are also probably familiar with the tourist-driven market for postcards and other merchandise which reproduce archaeologically discovered images of erect penises, breasts, or sex acts.

Yet lascivious treatment of archaeological materials is not limited to the popular market. Most common, perhaps, is the sexualized treatment of representations of nude or partially clothed bodies, which may not have had sexual or pornographic connotations in their original cultural context. For example, some researchers have suggested that the so-called 'Venus figurines' from the European Upper Paleolithic are sensuous representations of female bodies fashioned for the erotic appreciation and arousal of a male audience (Ehrenberg 1989: 37; Dobres 1992b; an egregious example can be found in Collins and Onians 1978). While this is certainly possible, no evidence other than the nudity of the figurines has been advanced to support this theory. Likewise, monographs by Gimbutas (1982, 1989, 1991) and Taylor (1996) assign sexual meanings to archaeological findings such as sculpted bull's heads on the basis of a purported similarity to female genitalia and reproductive organs. When not grounded in archaeological evidence, such interpretations are more likely to titillate present-day audiences rather than promote an understanding of the past.

Guidelines

These four factors – sex essentialism, sex negativity, sexual hierarchies, and lascivious treatment of sexual imagery – have greatly impeded archaeological studies of sexuality. But as the studies in this volume demonstrate, these obstacles are not insurmountable. We propose several measures which archaeologists can adopt to counteract these tendencies:

The social constructionist approach

In order to study sexuality archaeologists must adopt, in some form, the position that sexuality is socially constructed, a product of cultural and historical relationships and ideologies (Rubin 1984: 276–78; Foucault 1975, 1980; Butler 1990). This does not mean that the biological aspects of sexuality should be denied, but rather that the interface between the biological and cultural aspects of sexuality is itself a productive area of study. Archaeology, with its long-term perspective on human history, may be uniquely well-positioned to investigate this interface.

Self-reflexivity

Because of the effects of sex negativity and sexual hierarchies, it is imperative that archaeologists adopt a self-reflexive approach to studies of sexuality. While it is never possible to be completely aware of one's own biases, it is still productive to try to see how one's beliefs and assumptions about sexuality in the present may influence archaeological interpretations of sexuality in the past. We especially note the importance of self-reflexivity in feminist archaeology (e.g. Conkey and Gero 1991: 22; Engelstad 1991; Spector 1993; Wylie 1992) and in post-processual archaeological theory (e.g. Shanks and Tilly 1987; Hodder 1991), and hope that its success in those areas can be equaled in sexuality studies.

Benign sexual variability

Approaching the past with a concept of 'benign sexual variability' (Rubin 1984: 283) presumes that any given culture studied archaeologically will probably include diverse sexual expressions, sexual identities, and sexual ideologies beyond (but certainly including) heterosexual reproductive intercourse. We should not assume that present-day sex hierarchies correspond to the historical meanings or values attached to any particular sexual expression in the past. Rather we should seek to discern such meanings from the evidence at hand.

Contextual analysis

Because lascivious treatments trivialize and distort past sexualities, we urge caution in adopting present-day 'community standards' such as nudity, exposure of breasts or genitalia, or penetration, as evidence of pornographic functions for prehistoric artwork. This is not to suggest that pornographic or erotic intentions are never evidenced in archaeological materials. Rather we contend that the erotic intent of prehistoric and historic imagery should be interpreted on the basis of its production, use, and disposal, contexts which can (and should) be studied archaeologically.

Archaeological studies of sexuality which follow the above guidelines promise to illuminate the social organization of diverse sexual practices within historic cultural contexts. We must always remember that societies and cultures are not monolithic. In some societies, tensions will certainly exist between ideal and actual patterns of sexual behavior, and such tensions may simultaneously differentiate and tie together social subgroups. Ideological celebration, regulation, or suppression of specific sexual practices may occur in any given context, but even vigorous suppression of a particular type of sexual activity may not entirely erase it from the social palette. There will always be a difference between sexual ideologies and lived sexual practices. We must take care to distinguish between them when developing interpretations of archaeological materials.

EVIDENTIAL CONCERNS

The suggestions above, in and of themselves, will go a long way towards enabling archaeologies of sexuality. Yet the issue is also methodological. The question still remains: how can archaeologists investigate sexuality, when sexual activity, in and of itself, rarely leaves material by-products which can be studied through archaeological methods?

There are several ways that this question can be addressed. The first approach might be to respond that sexual activities do indeed contribute to the formation of the archaeological record. For example, there are physical objects ('sex toys') which may have been used in sexual activities (Taylor 1996: 13–18; Panati 1998: 76–80), as well as representations of sexual activity in historic and prehistoric art (e.g. Kauffmann Doig 1979; Montserrat 1996; Kampen and Bergmann 1996; Meskell this volume; Joyce this volume). Particularly well-preserved human remains might even bear physical evidence of sexual activities (Schmidt 1995). But to only accept evidence which meets this 'smoking gun' standard (after Conkey and Gero 1991: 17) would limit investigations of sexuality to certain specific and restricted contexts where such incontrovertible evidence has been or could be found.

Another approach would be to view sexuality in the past as an interconnected aspect of any cultural system, linked to economics, kinship, subsistence, ideology, gender, ranking, ethnicity, and other social systems. Thus, evidence relating to sexuality would be far more accessible, encompassing any archaeological materials which relate to the cultural system as a whole. Of course, methods for identifying sexuality within this larger social web must be developed, perhaps following examples such as Hawkes' ladder of inference (Hawkes 1954), Tringham's chart for middle-range research design (Tringham 1991: 106), or Matthews's approach to identifying social subgroups (Matthews 1995). While this approach is strong in expanding archaeological studies of sexuality, it does presuppose the existence of sexuality as a culturally constructed category in the past. Thus, it prohibits archaeologists from asking the question of whether or not sexuality as a category has always existed.

A third approach to the evidential question might be to re-examine why the question is being asked. Don't all archaeological data contain ambiguities and lacunae which complicate interpretation in the past? Why should studies of sexuality be any different in this regard? Yet it would be a mistake to use sexuality to invalidate the archaeological enterprise. Studies of sexuality may be particularly useful in archaeology precisely because they challenge our assumptions about how and what we know about the past. In fact, we argue that many archaeological interpretations which have ignored sexuality may have misinterpreted archaeological data.

There are no straightforward solutions to these epistemological dilemmas. But the varied approaches which can be used to address evidential concerns about sexuality in the past illustrate one central point: that diverse theoretical and methodological approaches will be needed to address the varied archaeological contexts within which sexuality is embedded. The different tactics used in the case studies presented here demonstrate the strength of theoretical pluralism (Wylie 1996) in developing archaeologies of sexuality. Additionally, archaeologists can turn to sexuality studies in related disciplines as productive sources of inspiration.

SEXUALITY OUTSIDE ARCHAEOLOGY: RELATED DISCIPLINARY DEVELOPMENTS

The issues outlined above – sex essentialism, sex negativity, sex hierarchies, lascivious treatment of sexuality, and evidential concerns – pose significant challenges to archaeologists. But scholars in other disciplines which have rich traditions of studying sexuality have also faced these issues. In the following sections, we consider how researchers in several fields have approached sexuality studies. Our point in this review is to consider how these disciplines have addressed evidential concerns (especially with regard to documenting sexual variability), to identify methods and techniques which could be adopted by archaeologists, and to identify sources of analogy for archaeological interpretation. We also hope that this section will aid other archaeologists in making interdisciplinary connections in their research on sexuality.

Sexology

All modern academic studies of sexuality, including archaeological ones, derive from the body of sexology research which established sexuality as a legitimate topic of academic research in the late 1800s. Sexologists such as Krafft-Ebing (1965 [1886]), Carpenter

(1908), Ellis (1903–1927), Hirschfeld (1991 [1910]), Stopes (1918), Browne (1923), and Kinsey et al. (1948, 1953) were taxonomic in their approach to sexuality, drawing on biological, medical, and sociological practices to organize specific case studies into types of sexual variations.[1] Together, these works are generally attributed with the discursive creation of the sexual categories and sexual identities which dominate present-day political, popular, and academic discussions of sexuality (Katz 1995). The influence of these works in codifying same-sex sexual practices as a sexual identity is particularly notable.

What relevance do these late nineteenth- and early twentieth-century studies have for archaeologies of sexuality? First, they present a critical problem in archaeological research on sexuality: the sexual categories in use today, and indeed, even the separation of sexuality as a distinct arena of research and social discourse, were historically created in the late 1800s (Katz 1995). How, then, can we view sexuality in the past without somehow imposing these modern categories on past cultures? We contend that these sexual categories can be extremely useful heuristic devices for organizing and understanding sexual behavior in the past, but archaeologists must be aware that etic categories[2] such as 'heterosexuality' or 'homosexuality' may have had little meaning for people in the past.

Second, these early sexology studies also highlight the inseparability of sexuality and gender. While some sexologists tried to determine whether gender leads sexuality or sexuality leads gender, their efforts were largely frustrated by the complexity and variability within their data. This suggests that archaeologists, too, would be best served by adopting an integrated approach to gender and sexuality research.

Socio-cultural anthropology

Building on the works of the early sexologists, anthropologists in the twentieth century began to identify and describe cross-cultural variation in sexual behavior as a part of the larger project of discovering and understanding the cross-cultural range of human social behavior. Among the most widely popular and influential early anthropological texts were those which explicitly addressed sexuality, such as Mead's *Coming of Age in Samoa* (1928) and *Sex and Temperament in Three Primitive Societies* (1935), and Malinowski's *The Sexual Life of Savages* (1929). The descriptions and analyses of exotic sexualities in these and other works drew upon taxonomies developed by the early sexologists. Moreover, these pioneering texts often included both implicit and explicit lessons for both the intellectual and moral edification of their contemporary European and American audiences.[3] In comparison, much anthropological work on sexuality from mid-century onwards (see, for example, the cross-cultural work of Broude 1981; Ford and Beach 1951; Frayser 1985; Marshall and Suggs 1971) strove for a more objective, 'scientific' tone which more accurately justifies the public reputation of anthropologists as 'fearless investigators of sexual customs and mores throughout the world, breaking through the erotophobic intellectual taboos common in other, more timid disciplines' even though the field never really lived up to this reputation (Vance 1991: 875).

For archaeologists, the importance of the ways in which anthropologists have framed and wrestled with issues of sexuality can hardly be overestimated. Since the 1920s, anthropologists have recognized that sexuality is not just a 'physiological transaction' but is also a cultural practice, implicated in 'almost every aspect of culture' (Malinowski 1929: xxiii). If, as Willey and Phillips (1958) and Binford (1962) asserted, archaeology is anthropology or it is nothing, then these cross-cultural studies can be used to challenge the archaeological tendency towards sex essentialism. Additionally, anthropology provides a plethora of ethnographically described patterns of sexual variation which may provide models for understanding similar patterns in the past. Recent reviews of anthropological research in sexuality may be particularly helpful in identifying useful studies (Davis and Whitten 1987; Weston 1993). However, archaeologists must also take into account the limitations of ethnographic data and anthropological interpretations. For example, anthropological observers who use sexual categories derived from sexology may seriously misrepresent Native American sexual practices and identities (Jacobs 1997; Roscoe 1995, 1998) and same-sex sexual behaviors have only recently been considered normative objects of study in anthropology (Newton 1993; Vance 1991; Weston 1993). As with any use of direct historical and cross-cultural analogies, it would be dangerous to uncritically apply sexual models derived from anthropology without taking into account the biases of the researcher and the historical context of the research.

Physical anthropology

While cultural anthropology emphasizes the social construction of sexuality, physical anthropology approaches sexuality through the study of human evolution and the interaction between biology and culture. Sexuality is a crucial element in many models intended to explain how humanity developed from its non-human ancestors. Other models in physical anthropology attempt to locate the source of present-day sexual behaviors in ancestral evolutionary developments. Because anthropological archaeologists are heavily influenced by paleoanthropological theories, archaeologists studying the sexualities of anatomically modern humans should be aware of the ways that physical anthropologists engage with issues of sexuality.

An object lesson for archaeologists can be found in the ways that sex hierarchies have influenced physical anthropology. Because physical anthropology is concerned with evolution, it has focused primarily on reproductive physiology and behavior rather than on a broader definition of sexuality (Abramson and Pinkerton 1995a, McDonald Pavelka 1995). As a result, our understanding of primate sexuality – both non-human and human – is based upon 'an adaptationist approach to sex formulated within the context of [Darwinian] sexual selection theory' which 'begins with the *a priori* assumption that sex is enacted for the express purpose of reproduction' (Vasey 1998: 408–409). Yet the simplistic assumption that sexual organs and other physiological traits evolved solely to enhance reproductive functions resembles a hypothetical position that the mouth evolved only for food ingestion, when clearly there are other functions involved (such as breathing, vocalization, and language). Since the 1980s a growing number of studies have demonstrated that members of many animal species generally (Bagemihl 1999), and of many non-human primate species more particularly (de Waal 1989, 1995; McDonald Pavelka 1995; Vasey 1995, 1998), regularly engage in non-reproductive sexual behaviors. Within an evolutionary framework, such non-reproductive sexual behaviors could be seen as adaptive by enhancing social cohesion (e.g. de Waal 1995). Further, both reproductive and non-reproductive sexual behaviors could be motivated by 'mutual sexual attraction and gratification' (Vasey 1998: 416–17; Abramson and Pinkerton 1995a) – a point discounted by adaptationist approaches to sexuality. The point for archaeologies of sexuality is that sex hierarchies in evolutionary theory may inappropriately constrain interpretations of sexual variability.

Another reason for archaeologists to critically examine the treatments of sexuality within physical anthropology is the plethora of 'origin stories' wherein aspects of sexual anatomy, physiology and behavior are employed to explain the development of our species. These origin stories contribute to both sex and gender essentialism (Rubin 1984, Conkey with Williams 1991). The various paleoanthropological theories of human origin that implicate sexuality may seem plausible because they appeal to prevailing notions of 'common sense'. For example, a number of researchers (e.g. Bartholomew and Birdsell 1953; Washburn and Avis 1958; Washburn and Lancaster 1968; and Lovejoy 1981) have argued that the development of stable, heterosexual, monogamous family units was crucial for parental support and training during the unusually long period of dependence of human offspring, so that the 'idea of the pair bond and monogamy thus became established as another hallmark of humanity, essential to maintain the integrity of human social groups' (Zihlman 1987: 12). Other anatomical, physiological and behavioral changes relating to sexuality have been implicated in paleoanthropological models, including loss of estrus leading to 'continuous' sexual receptivity by females; loss of body hair except in sexually meaningful locations; increases in breast size in females as a way to attract males (according to some accounts as mimicry of large buttocks, which were identified as a sexual marker). This latter development has been tied to changes in heterosexual mating positions, i.e. from partners facing the same direction to partners facing each other. Changes in mating positions have also been linked to the change from quadrupedal to bipedal locomotion, such that the posterior display of their genitalia as a signal of sexual receptivity by non-bipedal primate females was no longer physiologically practicable after the development of the upright stance of our ancestors (see Frayser 1985 and Taylor 1996 for discussions of these ideas). It is beyond the scope of this introduction to engage critically with all of these points, but we note that many archaeologists might find recent critiques of these models (Abramson and Pinkerton 1995a; Bentley 1996; McDonald Pavelka 1995; Hager 1997; Zihlman 1997) helpful in deconstructing certain widespread essentialist assumptions about sexuality and human nature.

For archaeologies of sexuality, the most productive engagements with the disciplines of physical anthropology and socio-cultural anthropology will recognize that sexuality is a multiform, variable phenomenon that is multiply determined, the product of both biology and human culture working in mutuality. We underscore the relevance for archaeologies of sexuality of the position taken by Abramson and Pinkerton (1995b: 1) with regard to the effects of the nature/nurture debate upon studies of sexuality: 'What is important, therefore, is not the current sway of the nature/nurture tug-of-war, but the attempt to understand the dynamics of both nature and nurture, individually and in concert, and to delineate the mechanisms and boundaries of their influences and interactions.'

History

While sexological, anthropological, and primatological studies of sexuality have developed primarily through direct observation and participant accounts, historical studies of sexuality rely on textual evidence and thus face different evidential challenges. In this sense, historical studies of sexuality have much in common with archaeological research. The burgeoning historical literature on sexuality can be a rich source of inspiration for archaeological research on sexual identities, sexual practices, sexual communities, and sexual politics, and we have referenced numerous studies here as a starting point for entry into some of the available literature.

Historical studies of sexuality first emerged in the 1960s, in great part as a result of the development of homophile and gay rights movements in England and the United States. Homophile and homosexual activists and academics turned to history as a counter to medical, psychological, and legal discourses which defined homosexuality as deviant, psychotic, or abnormal behavior. Early historical efforts focused on compiling evidence of homosexuality in the past, drawing on both sexology studies (see above) and original research to establish the historical depth (and, in a sense, genealogy) of late twentieth-century lesbian, gay male, and bisexual communities (e.g. Katz 1976; Rowbotham and Weeks 1977; Weeks 1977, 1981). These early works arose within an ongoing political and medical debate about the origin of sexual identities: is homosexuality innate (biologically determined) and thus transhistorical, or are sexual identities contingent upon socio-historical circumstances (i.e. culturally constructed)? The positions held by individual historians in this nature/nurture debate affected, and continue to shape, the research questions asked, the methods used, and even the terms chosen in historical studies of sexuality.

During this same period, lesbian history (or, herstory) emerged as a counterpoint to some 'gay' histories which focused predominantly on male homosexuality. Landmark studies such as Smith-Rosenberg's 'The Female World of Love and Ritual' (1979) brought feminist political theory into historical research on sexuality and demonstrated that the sexual histories of men and women, while intertwined, are by no means identical. In the 1970s and 1980s, considerable research was conducted on biographical studies (Doughty 1982; MacCowan 1982: 254–58; Faber 1980; Wells 1978; Brown 1986) and historic case studies (Roberts 1982; Faderman 1981; Faderman and Eriksson 1980). In the last decade, community-based research projects have flourished (Nestle 1992: 223–29; Kennedy and Davis 1993; Faderman 1991). Lesbian studies have particularly raised the issue of how to discuss and name female sexual desire in an intellectual and social climate which lacks appropriate terms and conventions. These studies have also highlighted the question of 'lesbian attribution' (Vicinus 1989): are women in the past who engaged in passionate same-sex relationships (which may or may not have included genital sex) lesbians, even if they wouldn't have identified themselves as such?

By the mid-1980s and 1990s, the position of sexuality studies as a historical subdiscipline was firmly established with the publication of several comprehensive histories (McLaren 1999; D'Emilio 1983; D'Emilio and Freedman 1988) and the 1990 launch of *The Journal of the History of Sexuality*. Some historical studies of homosexuality pushed into the pre-industrial past (e.g. Boswell 1980, 1994; Brown 1989; Ng 1989; Oaks 1980; Abelove 1989; Trumbach 1990; van der Meer 1994), at times drawing on archaeological evidence to construct sweeping histories of gay and lesbian antiquity (e.g. Grahn 1984). Other researchers began to consider the histories of previously ignored sexual minorities such as sadomasochists (Rubin 1991). Along with lesbian studies, feminist historical studies engaged with sexuality in research on numerous topics, including prostitution (Goldman 1981; Rosen 1982), rape (Lindemann 1984; Davis 1981: 172–201), the intersections between race and sexuality (Davis 1981; Jones 1995; duCille 1993; Gutiérrez 1991) and ways that sexual and reproductive practices are linked to the social control of women (Gordon 1976; Bynum 1992; Dean 1996). Conjugal heterosexuality has become a topic of study in its own right (Stone 1979; Abelove 1989). Most recently, historical studies of both homosexuality and heterosexuality have been complicated by the emergence of transgendered history, which challenges conventional discussions of sexual identity by emphasizing gender identities (e.g. Feinberg 1996; de Erauso 1996).

Although initially many archaeologists, especially those working in prehistoric contexts, might feel otherwise, we believe that these historical treatments of sexuality are particularly applicable to archaeological studies of sexuality. Perhaps the primary lesson to be learned from historical sexuality studies is that sexual diversity in the past is much broader and multi-faceted than conventional historical narratives will allow. In other words, a failure to identify or consider sexualities beyond conjugal heterosexuality is more likely to be a result of the researcher's limited perceptions of the past, rather than an indication of a sexually homogenous past. Moreover, even the contours of conjugal heterosexuality have shifted with changing circumstances. Within the tensions of the nature/nurture debate, many historians have crafted an emerging middle position which posits sexual diversity as a historical continuity while simultaneously foregrounding the historical specificity of the expressions of these diverse sexualities.

Historical studies of sexuality also provide specific contexts and cross-cultural analogies for interpreting archaeological deposits. It is thus not surprising that some of the earliest archaeological studies of sexuality have been conducted in historical contexts where documentary evidence has inspired sexually-oriented interpretations of archaeological findings (see below).

Finally, archaeological research on sexuality can draw from the methods used by historians to counteract the heterocentrist, sexist, and sex-negative biases of the documentary record. Interdisciplinary collaboration, use of previously marginalized sources, retranslations of historical documents, oral histories, community history projects, and innovative combinations of multiple lines of evidence have all been central to historical studies of sexuality (Freedman 1982). For example, Abelove's 'Speculations' (1989) about the rise of penile-vaginal sexual intercourse during the eighteenth century in England is based on a combination of data about industrialization and demographic shifts, and emphasizes correlation, rather than causation, in historical explanation. While archaeologists are faced with data of a physical, rather than documentary nature, these innovative and unorthodox methods will aid in developing archaeological research which foregrounds sexuality.

Classics

For a few members of privileged and well-educated minorities, classical studies have for centuries provided evidence for the existence of sexual regimes, or systems of sexual relations, differing in some fundamental ways from those which have existed in recent European and American history. For example, in the mid-eighteenth century, in work which earned him the reputation of being the first 'modern' historian of ancient art, J. J. Winckelmann envisioned a sexual history of ancient Greece and Rome which he used 'to reconfigure his own erotic imagination' in a way which would come to influence 'an emerging modern sexuality – what came to be called, in the later nineteenth century, "homosexuality"' (Davis 1996: 262). Nonetheless, despite this long history of a sexual undercurrent within classical studies, explicit investigations of sexual regimes in the classical world gained an entirely new level of acceptance and legitimacy within the academic discipline of classical studies through the 1978 publication of *Greek Homosexuality* by K. J. Dover (Halperin 1990: 4). Since then, a variety of authors have explored differing aspects of the constitution of sexual relations in the ancient world (e.g. Boswell 1980, 1994; Halperin 1990; Winkler 1990; and the contributors to Halperin, Winkler, and Zeitlin 1990). As both Winkler (1990: 3–10) and Halperin (1990: 7) have acknowledged, the explanatory power which these new studies display derives from the infusion of an anthropological sensibility into the humanities, i.e. a recognition that, to understand the operation of sexuality in various societies and social contexts in the ancient world, scholars must consider sexual relations as an aspect of cultural relations more generally, and not simply as instances of the operation of an essentialized biological function.

The utility of this body of work for archaeologies of sexuality can be considered in two principal aspects. First, these classical scholars have preceded anthropological archaeologists in the recognition of sexuality as an element of culture, and have investigated sexuality with considerable sophistication. Thus, classical studies of sexuality can provide inspirational examples of how to study a sexual regime fundamentally different from present-day sexual systems. Second, both classics and archaeology are historical disciplines: the evidence which classicists and archaeologists employ is necessarily secondary or indirect (unlike ethnographers, neither classicists nor archaeologists can interrogate their subjects). While texts, rather than material culture, are central to classicists, the evidential resources and concerns of classical scholars and archaeologists tend towards considerable congruence. Thus the ways in which evidence for sexuality in the classical world have been interpreted may further inspire archaeologies of sexuality, both for the sexualities of historical periods where considerable documentary evidence may be available, and for other 'complex society' contexts where texts and visual imagery may be archaeologically preserved.

Art history, material culture studies, geography, and architecture

While sexology, socio-cultural anthropology, physical anthropology, history, and classics all have close institutional ties to anthropological archaeology, a special relationship exists between archaeology and other material studies disciplines. The development of sexuality studies within these fields particularly merits archaeological attention, because the methods and linking arguments used to interpret the sexual meanings of physical objects may apply to both present-day materials and those which are archaeologically documented. For example, archaeologists undertaking sexually oriented studies of prehistoric and historic images might find recent developments in art history useful. Such studies (e.g. Kampen 1993; Kampen and Bergmann 1996; Davis 1998 and chapter 5 this volume) have explicitly expanded the field beyond the study of 'erotic art' to include the analysis of representational practices signifying sexual activity, the erotics of the body, and the ways in which art practice and the resulting imagery 'allows human beings to find and measure themselves as sexual' (Kampen and Bergmann 1996: 1). Likewise the study of material culture in non-archaeological contexts provides inspirations which can inform innovative considerations of artifactual remains. Recent research on 'sex toys' (Maines 1998; Levins 1996; Panati 1998) and Rubin's ground-breaking anthropological study of the props and spatial organization of a leather sex club (1991) show how the material culture of sexual activities can be studied to understand the social construction of sexual practices as well as the formation and development of sexual communities. Other research, such as Wilkie's (1998) study of Mardi Gras beads and the case studies presented in de Grazia and Furlough's *The Sex of Things* (1996), demonstrate the many ways that objects whose form or appearance does not immediately reference sexuality may nevertheless carry significant sexual meaning.

While art history and material culture studies primarily address portable objects, sexuality studies in geography and architecture consider the role of material and symbolic spatial relations in sexuality. Architectural studies have considered the role of buildings and other constructions in constructing and expressing sexual identity and in facilitating, discouraging, or controlling sexual activity (Betsky 1995, 1997; Foucault 1975, 1980; and Sanders 1997). Geographical studies have investigated the connections between spatial relations and coercive sexual behavior, the spatial distributions of sexualized communities, and public displays of sexuality (Bell and Valentine 1995; Colomina 1992; Cream 1993; Dangerous Bedfellows 1996; Duncan 1996; Matthews 1997). Given the strong archaeological emphasis on spatial relationships and architectural remains, the above-cited studies can serve as guides toward applying spatially-organized archaeological data to research questions related to sexuality.

Of course there are many other fields that contribute to interdisciplinary studies of sexuality, such as literature, rhetoric, psychology, medicine, education, and law, and it is likely that archaeologists will find productive interdisciplinary connections outside of the historical, anthropological, and material disciplines reviewed here. The central point of this interdisciplinary survey is that archaeologists are not alone in attempting to use fragmentary data to investigate sexuality. Theories and methods from other fields may aid us in navigating the particular obstacles and bodies of data which archaeological projects on sexuality are likely to encounter.

CURRENT SEXUALITY RESEARCH IN ARCHAEOLOGY

At the beginning of this chapter, we discussed four key issues which have hampered archaeological studies of sexuality: sex essentialism, sex negativity, the sex hierarchy, and lascivious treatment of sexuality. Despite these barriers, in recent years a small corpus of rigorous archaeological research on sexuality has slowly emerged. In the subsections below, we trace these beginnings, considering the foundational works of feminist archaeologists, the emergence of archaeological studies focused directly on sexuality, and current trends in sexuality research.

Foundations: early feminist archaeology

The emergence of feminist archaeology in the mid-1980s (Conkey and Spector 1984; Gero and Conkey 1991) established a firm foundation of critical archaeological research on sex and gender. Prior to feminist interventions, most archaeological studies interpreted the past through a lens of essentialist gender stereotypes which, among other elements, presumed a heterosexual norm, linked men to production and tool making and women to reproduction and child rearing, and identified men as sexually dominant and women as passive sexual objects (see Conkey and Spector 1984: 3–13 and Nelson 1997: 113–29 for further discussion of these points). By challenging these assumptions about men, women, and gender relationships in the past, by calling for renewed rigor in archaeological studies of gender, and by developing new methodological and theoretical approaches for the archaeological study of gendered subjects, feminist archaeologists created the conditions under which archaeological studies on sexuality could emerge.

One important contribution of the earliest feminist research in archaeology is a radical critique of traditional approaches to the sexual (or gendered) division of labor (e.g. Conkey and Spector 1984). Numerous case studies demonstrated the flexibility and variability of gendered divisions of labor (for examples, see Nelson 1997: 85–112) and showed that 'women's work' is shaped by the same range of political, ecological, economic, and social factors which shape men's work (Brumfiel 1991: 243; Wright 1991). Some research has suggested, furthermore, that participation in gendered labor systems or other forms of material culture production may themselves create or define gender (e.g. Lesick 1997; Hollimon 1997), and that gender as we know it may not have existed at all times and in all cultures (Conkey 1991: 87, note 4). By separating gender roles from biological reproduction, these early feminist studies de-centered heterosexual pair-bonding and created possibilities for studying sexuality independently of reproduction. For example, Hastorf's study of food production, consumption, and divisions of labor among the prehistoric Sausa of Peru considers possible connections between food taboos and sexuality (1991: 135).

A second arena of early feminist research in archaeology which has direct bearings on studies of sexuality is an emphasis on social relations, placing interpersonal relations 'at the forefront, substituting these for the more conventional concepts of power politics, governance, and authority' (Conkey and Gero 1991: 15). In particular, feminist researchers focused archaeological attention on the household, emphasizing that 'the analysis of social change at a microscale of the household or co-residential group or family has long been recognized as an essential scale for the study of the social relations of production' (Tringham 1991: 99). Thus archaeologists can use the archaeological record to access the *material context* of those actions and relations and tensions' between individuals in the past (Tringham 1991: 107). Studies in household archaeology have linked archaeological evidence of interpersonal relationships to macroscale research topics such as intensified resource procurement, including the development of agriculture (Brumfiel 1991; Hastorf 1991; Jackson 1991); the formation of the Victorian 'separate spheres' ideology (Praetzellis and Praetzellis 1992; Wall 1991, 1994); and military, capitalist, and colonial ventures (Lightfoot et al. 1996; Brashler 1991; Clements 1993; Spector 1993). These studies demonstrated that research on interpersonal relationships – including sexual acts, sexual relations, and sexual tensions – is neither trivial nor particularistic, but instead is essential to understanding topics ranging from subsistence and settlement systems to imperialist expansion.

A final point relevant to studies of sexuality regards archaeological studies of prehistoric art, especially interpretations of the so-called 'Venus' figurines (such as the famous 'Venus of Willendorf') found at various Paleolithic and Neolithic European sites. Conventionally interpreted in much archaeological discourse as representations of unclothed female bodies, these figurines have variously been seen as by-products of fertility rituals or as evidence of matriarchal, goddess-worshiping cultures (Gimbutas 1982, 1989, 1991; Eisler 1988; Smith 1991). Since the early 1980s, feminist archaeologists have been re-examining these traditional interpretations (for an excellent summary of this literature, see Conkey and Tringham 1995: 212–19). This debate has been particularly important to the development of archaeologies of sexuality because it has introduced feminist theories of representation, the sexual gaze, and the body into archaeological interpretation (e.g. Ehrenberg 1989: 37; Dobres 1992a; Handsman 1991; Nelson 1990). This has led to more sophisticated, empirically-based, and self-reflexive analyses of prehistoric imagery which have emphasized the archaeological contexts and variability between figurines, rock art, and other imagery. Additionally, studies such as Conkey and Tringham's 'Archaeology and the Goddess' (1995) have demonstrated how archaeological evidence can contribute to public debates about the nature of human sexuality.

Emergence: current and forthcoming archaeological research on sexuality

Feminist archaeological studies of the gendered division of labor, the household, and prehistoric art fostered an intellectual climate within which research on sexuality became increasingly possible. Yet early feminist archaeological research rarely addressed the topic of sexuality directly, often because sexuality was considered a function of gender rather than as a distinct aspect of social relations (see Rubin 1984: 309 for a general discussion of this point). Yet as feminist archaeology in the late 1990s slowly shifted to a focus on gender construction and gender variability in the past (see, for example, papers in Moore and Scott 1997), and as interdisciplinary collaboration has increased archaeological awareness of sexuality studies (Schmidt 1997), some archaeologists have begun to explicitly address issues of sexuality in their research. This section traces the emergence of these archaeological studies of sexuality, focusing on prehistoric, culture contact, and historic archaeology.

In studies of so-called 'deep prehistory' (the Pleistocene and early Holocene), investigations of sexuality are still rare, but new research is emerging which focuses on symbolic representations and sexual identities. One central problem in prehistoric studies is the question of when sexuality emerged as an aspect of human culture. Conkey (1991: 87, note 4) has suggested that gender as we know it may not have even existed in Paleolithic Europe; if, as some regional studies suggest, gender differentiation itself could be a relatively recent phenomenon (e.g. McGuire and Hildebrandt 1994), what are the implications for sexuality as a 'distinct arena of social practice' (after Rubin 1984: 308) in deep prehistory? In this sense it is possible that cultural constructions of sexuality could even precede gender in human development – an interesting hypothesis for archaeological testing! While the timing of the emergence of sexuality – and gender – in early anatomically modern human culture may never be known, we suggest that the known development of symbol production 30,000 to 50,000 years ago can be used as a benchmark to suggest when at least the biologically-grounded aspects of sexuality – puberty, genitalia, sexual activity – might have first entered cultural discourse. At the very least, we feel that there is no reason why archaeologists working in the Upper Paleolithic shouldn't consider sexuality when interpreting archaeological remains.

To date, original archaeological research on sexuality in the earliest periods of prehistory have tended to rely upon symbolic representations and images. Yates's (1993) analysis of possible sexual representations in Scandinavian prehistoric rock art questions the conventional interpretation that some of these images represent heterosexual coupling or marriage. Instead, Yates suggests that the images could just as plausibly have represented a homosexual liaison, and calls for a reflexive examination of sexual categories in archaeology. Vasey (1998) has likewise reviewed interpretations of sexual imagery from various prehistoric sites to argue for a greater emphasis on sexual pleasure in interpretations of prehistoric sexuality. Considerable scholarship has also developed on anthropomorphic figurines from Upper Paleolithic, Neolithic, and Mesolithic Europe (see Conkey and Tringham 1995: 212–19), much of which has critically examined representations of genitalia and secondary sex characteristics with the aim of interpreting sexual ideologies and practices. For example, Kokkinidou and Nikolaidou have examined body imagery in early Neolithic figurines to consider a diverse 'iconography of sexuality' (1997: 93) possibly related to symbolic interventions in fertility. Together, these studies suggest that imagery may be one of the most readily accessible lines of archaeological evidence about sexuality in the deep past. Further, they indicate an emerging recognition that the categories used by archaeologists to investigate sexuality must be flexible and diverse if we are to develop the ability to 'see' manifestations of sexuality in the prehistoric past. In addition to broadening interpretations of sexuality beyond heterosexuality (Schmidt 1995, 1997), we must further consider the possibility that the social construction of 'sexuality' as a whole may fluctuate widely (e.g. Meskell, Chapter 14).

Another approach used by some archaeolgists has been to consider the relationship between sexuality and identity in archaeological contexts. Matthews (1995) has argued for a generalized sensitivity to archaeological evidence relating to social subgroups and subcultures, which he has elsewhere suggested could be applied to investigations of an urban male homosexual subculture in ancient Roman society (Matthews 1994). Through examination of controversy regarding the sexual life of the Tyrolean Iceman (Spindler 1994: 173–74), Schmidt (1995) has called for sensitivity to potential variability in sexual practices and identities in prehistory, and has further argued for the relevance of queer theory in archaeological contexts (Schmidt 1997). In North America, research on more recent prehistoric and contact period sites (*c.* 5,000–150 years before present) has focused on variability in sexual and gender identities in Native American populations. The ubiquity of the two-spirit or *berdache* (third/fourth gender) social role in historic Native American cultures has been well-documented ethnographically (Blackwood 1984; Callendar and Kochems 1983; Roscoe 1998). Using the direct historical approach, Hollimon has used analysis of osteological evidence and burial-associated artifacts to identify prehistoric two-spirit burials in Chumash mortuary contexts (1991, 1996, 1997, Chapter 10). Similarly, Whelan (1991) used statistical analysis to measure the correlation between biological sex indicators and mortuary goods from the nineteenth-century Blackdog Burial site in Minnesota, an approach which allowed her to consider the presence of multiple genders, including *berdaches*. In middle Missouri archaeology Prine (1997, Chapter 11) has like-wise considered the process of house construction and architectural variability as archaeological indicators of two-spirit individuals. Together these studies have highlighted the difficulty of defining sexual identity for the purposes of archaeological studies: are *berdaches* defined by their gender, or by their sexual practices, or both? Are two-spirits 'homosexuals' or transgendered 'heterosexuals'? Or, as Roscoe (1998) and Hollimon (Chapter 10) suggest, might the same-sex sexual practices associated with Chumash *berdaches* be related to occupational specialization rather than gender? Archaeological research on North American *berdaches* provides a pressing reminder that sexuality, which many of us associate closely with gender, may be constructed quite differently in other cultural contexts.

Another theme in North American archaeological research on sexuality has developed within culture contact studies on colonial settlements. Based on analyses of household deposits, several researchers have examined the role of interethnic heterosexual relation-ships as a mechanism of cultural exchange between colonizing and indigenous populations in Spanish-colonial Florida (Deagan 1983; McEwan 1991a, 1991b, 1995; Reitz 1990) and Russian California (Lightfoot et al. 1991; Lightfoot and Martinez 1996; Martinez 1994). While these studies have stopped short of exploring colonial sexual interactions outside of co-residential heterosexual relationships or discussing sexual practices per se, they have nonetheless demonstrated the critical role which sexuality can play in cultural change. In all cases these researchers have concluded that participants in interethnic hetero-sexual relationships were responsible for the 'most dramatic adaptations' in both colonial and indigenous cultures (McEwan 1995: 224), and 'may have been at the forefront of both creating and transmitting cultural innovations' (Lightfoot and Martinez 1996: 9) in colonial settings.

Within historical archaeology, explicit research on sexuality has emerged primarily from studies which focused on late nineteenth-century cities, where numerous archaeological investigations have encountered evidence of the seamier underside of urban life (Seifert 1998). The material remains of prostitution, from high-class parlor houses to cell-like cribs (and the deposits associated with them), have been excavated and analyzed to provide a rare window on commercial sex during the Victorian era. One of the first studies in this area was Simmon's study of 'red light ladies' on the North American mining frontier, which uses historical data to develop predictive hypotheses of archaeological patterns related to prostitution (1989: 62–67). Seifert's studies of Washington, DC brothels have been instrumental in revealing how brothel deposits differ from deposits of other working-class households and from other brothel sites (Cheek and Seifert 1994; Seifert 1991, 1994). Costello and Praetzellis directed archaeological research on the historic Los Angeles red-light district with a particular focus on understanding the daily lives of women working in various aspects of the trade, from high-class parlor houses to cribs (Costello and Praetzellis 1999; Costello 1999; The Metropolitan of Southern California forthcoming a and b). This growing archaeological literature on prostitution (continued in this volume by Seifert et al. and Costello, Chapters 6 and 9) has provided an important window into the economics, social relations, and gendered politics of commercial sex. Further, archaeological studies of prostitution have been instrumental in expanding archaeological studies of heterosexuality beyond co-residential (usually married) partners, and have likewise broadened the definition of the 'household' beyond the conjugal family.

While research on nineteenth-century prostitution has been substantial, other sexual topics have received little attention from historical archaeologists. However, there are notable exceptions. Casella's research on a female Tasmanian colony prison (Casella 1999 and Chapter 8) is the first archaeological study we know of to focus explicitly on same-sex sexual relations between women or to consider the material evidence of sexual economies in prison life. Gilchrist's 1994 study of medieval religious women in the British Isles considers the relationship between gender, space, and celibacy (see also Gilchrist, Chapter 4). Surprisingly, to our knowledge there have been no historical archaeological studies which focus on men's sexual experiences, despite the large number of such investigations by historians of the early modern period in Europe; even the aforementioned studies of heterosexual prostitution generally focus on the daily lives of the resident female prostitutes rather than on the experience of male clients (but see Costello, Chapter 9, for an important exception).

Emerging research shows both a continuance and a diversification of the topics and approaches used to address sexuality through the archaeological record. As the first book-length collection of studies focusing explicitly on sexuality, this volume represents a watershed in archaeological treatments of sexual topics. We are also aware of two special journal issues in preparation: one, an issue of *Historical Archaeology* which will publish the papers presented in the 'Sin City' symposium at the January 1998 meeting of the Society for Historical Archaeology (Seifert, personal communication); and two, a special issue of *World Archaeology* entitled 'Queer Archaeologies'. This latter issue brings to the fore a shift currently underway in archaeological approaches to sexuality (see Rubin, Davis, Casella, Meskell, Joyce, and Schmidt, this volume), in that queer theory, 'in its broadest sense as negotiating relational stances against the normative' (Dowson personal communication), rather than feminist theory, is increasingly being taken as a starting point for studies of sexuality.

Trends: sexuality 'in the margins' and the role of text-based evidence

This survey of current and forthcoming research suggests several current trends in archaeological studies of sexuality. Perhaps the most prominent of these is the focus on sexuality 'in the margins': prostitution, fertility cults, interracial relationships, public nudity, homosexuality, third and fourth genders, and religious celibacy. In contrast to the present-day political context wherein conjugal heterosexual sexuality is centered as natural, normal, and morally sanctioned, most archaeological studies of sexuality focus on the deviant, the abnormal, and the perverse. Of course, we argue that these 'marginal' sexualities are in truth central to human sexuality (Butler 1993b; Rubin 1984) – that human sexuality has always been richly textured and varied. But this aside, we believe that there are several reasons why archaeologists have first approached sexuality through what are generally considered 'marginal' sexual practices and identities.

As argued above, conjugal reproductive heterosexuality has been naturalized in archaeological research to the point that it is nearly invisible as an object of knowledge. For example, most archaeological studies take as a given that households are headed by heterosexual couples (Voss in press; but see Tringham 1991 for an important exception). Sexuality is often first seen as a viable research topic when archaeological or textual evidence indicates a departure from these presumed norms, and hence sexuality outside of heterosexual marriage is often the first focus of archaeological research. Additionally, many archaeologists currently conducting research on sexuality are motivated by a desire to bring under-represented sexualities into archaeological discourse and to counter heterosexist biases in archaeological interpretation. Thus, just as feminist archaeology first developed through remedial studies which highlighted women's role in creating the archaeological record, so too, many studies of sexuality are seeking to discover archaeological evidence of non-heterosexual and non-conjugal expressions of sexuality. Finally, archaeology has often been championed as the 'most objective source of information' (Deetz 1977: 160) about subjugated populations such as slaves, workers, the illiterate, and others whose lives are omitted from, or distorted in, the written record. We share the growing sense that archaeology has a unique role to play in chronicling the histories of sexual minorities which are often invisible or misrepresented in documentary evidence and ethnographic accounts.

Given this latter point, the prominence of text-aided studies in archaeologies of sexuality is perhaps confusing. With the rare exception of a few studies on prehistoric imagery, nearly all existing archaeological research on sexuality relies heavily on either archived or archaeologically recovered textual data to support material analyses of sexuality (but see Schmidt, Chapter 12). Such texts, problematic though they may be, play an important role in bringing sexual meanings to bear on the material remains of the past. While some archaeological researchers on gender argued that 'prehistoric contexts presented the greatest methodological challenges to our androcentric thinking' (Gero and Conkey 1991: xii), we do not feel that sexuality studies in archaeology must adopt a similar perspective. Rather, we contend that text-aided archaeology can be a productive point of departure for researchers interested in examining sexuality in deep prehistory. All archaeological interpretations rely on analogies developed in whole or part from texts, whether these texts are historical documents directly related to the site being excavated, deciphered archaeological texts and glyphs, or cross-cultural analogies built on ethnographic and ethno-archaeological studies (Ascher 1961; Gould and Watson 1982; Wylie 1985a, 1995b). Directly grappling with the biases and lacunae in these texts is an important aspect of developing archaeological studies of sexuality (Voss in press), regardless of whether the population being studied is historic or prehistoric.

From tightly reasoned text-aided studies of sexuality, we can also begin to develop methods and comparative contexts which may expand research on sexuality into situations which lack direct documentary evidence. For instance, Seifert et al. (Chapter 6) suggest that because many urban houses of prostitution in the late nineteenth-century United States were not known even to their neighbors, archaeological studies may have excavated parlor houses without realizing it. Thus, research on the remains of known parlor houses may suggest patterns in artifact frequencies which will aid in recognition of undocumented brothels.

ARCHAEOLOGIES OF SEXUALITY

Archaeologies of Sexuality builds upon these previous studies and also marks a turning point in the development of archaeological research on sexuality. While many of the following chapters reflect the trends outlined above, others break new ground. Case studies by Voss, Wilkie, Buchli, and Meskell mark the beginning of critical studies of conjugal heterosexuality in archaeology. Likewise, many of the prehistoric studies in this volume depart from the prior emphasis on prehistoric European art, including investigations of Siberian (Buchli and Schmidt), Mesoamerican (Joyce), and Egyptian (Meskell) prehistory. Finally, this volume reflects the growing influence of queer theory on archaeological studies of gender and sexuality, a point made evident by the contributions of anthropologist Gayle Rubin and architectural historian Whitney Davis, as well as the archaeological case studies contributed by Casella, Prine, Schmidt, Meskell, and Joyce.

In structuring this volume, we chose to group the case studies according to themes which reflect either methodological or interpretive strategies used by the different authors. The first section, 'Where it Happens: Structured Space and Sex', explores the relationship between structured space (architecture, cultural landscapes, cultural geographies) and sexuality. Voss examines archaeological remains of late prehistoric and colonial Californian (AD 1700–1850) architecture to investigate the sexual consequences of missionization on Native Californians (Chapter 2). Rubin's ongoing ethnography of a present-day sexual community employs archaeological methods to delineate urban sexual geographies (Chapter 3). Gilchrist (Chapter 4) examines the relationship between medieval monastic architecture in Britain and the personal celibacy of religious women. Davis, an art historian, uses an archaeological approach to examine representations of homoeroticism and sexual politics at Fonthill Abbey, in late eighteenth-century Britain (Chapter 5). Together, these chapters emphasize the utility of post-structuralist archaeological approaches to spatial analyses of sexuality.

The second section of this volume, 'The Stuff of Sex: Material Culture and Sexuality', focuses on the use of artifacts to investigate sexuality within marginalized communities, especially sex workers, female homosexuals, and post-bellum Southern African-Americans. In a continuation of Seifert's research on nineteenth-century prostitution (Cheek and Seifert 1994; Seifert 1991, 1994), Seifert, O'Brien, and Balicki use comparative studies of artifacts recovered from Mary Ann Hall's brothel in Washington, DC to examine material and economic conditions in the commercial sex business (Chapter 6). Wilkie examines artifacts collected from a well associated with a post-bellum African-American midwife's household (Chapter 7). While these materials would usually be treated as evidence of subsistence and consumer behavior, Wilkie uses oral histories to suggest that the assemblage indicates a connection between sexual medical-magic practices and midwifery practices. Casella (Chapter 8) examines artifacts representing illicit materials to document trade networks associated with convict homosexual relationships at a nineteenth-century convict factory in Australia. The final piece in this section, Costello's 'Red Light Voices' (Chapter 9), is a script about late nineteenth-century prostitution which was developed from three primary sources: artifacts, photographs, and oral histories. Costello's innovative chapter illustrates the power of narrative in presenting archaeological data about sexuality.

The third section, 'Sexual Identities, Sexual Politics', considers the archaeology of sexual identities as well as the sexual politics of archaeology. The first three chapters in this section make visible the histories of third-gender peoples and of homosexual behaviors which have generally been obscured or ignored by conventional archaeological studies. Using mortuary evidence and ethnohistorical studies, Hollimon (Chapter 10) focuses on the role of third gender undertakers in her discussion of sexual identities and occupation in late prehistoric Chumash culture. Prine's study of late prehistoric Hidatsa architecture in South Dakota examines the role of third gender *berdaches* in the construction of homes, and uses statistical correlates of house size and construction methods to identify an archaeologically documented household which may have been headed by a *berdache* (Chapter 11). Schmidt (Chapter 12) uses ethnographic analogies from studies of Siberian shamans to consider the gendered and sexual identities of prehistoric Europeans who have been identified as shamans through mortuary analysis. Buchli (Chapter 13) traces ways that Marxist interpretations of archaeological evidence informed the creation of early Soviet architectural forms which were designed to foster utopian ideals of gender and sexual identities. Together, the chapters in this section demonstrate the intertwined nature of gender and sexuality studies in archaeology.

In the final section of case studies, 'The Sexual Gaze: Representation and Imagery', art, imagery, and representations are employed to explore representations of sexuality and the relationship between archaeologies of sexuality and archaeologies of the body. Meskell (Chapter 14) combines domestic and ritual data from the New Kingdom Egyptian site of Deir el Medina (1500–1100 BC) to demonstrate the integration of sexual imagery with domestic life. Joyce's study of Classic Maya images relates textual, visual, and material discourses to the eroticization of the male body and the public celebration of the homoerotic gaze (Chapter 15). The volume concludes with a closing chapter by Conkey (Chapter 16) which uses a 'Flannery-esque' dialogue between three hypothetical archaeologists to critically review the case studies presented in this volume, and to reflect on the theoretical issues and challenges raised by archaeologies of sexuality.

We wish to emphasize that the topics which structure this volume are not the only possible method of grouping or organizing these chapters. For example, most of the chapters in this volume (not just those in section III) address issues of sexual identity formation and negotiation. Likewise, in addition to Meskell and Joyce, others such as Gilchrist, Davis, Buchli, and Costello draw on imagery and representation as a critical line of evidence in their analyses. We hope that the readers of this volume will view the section themes as entry points into, rather than barriers between, the case studies presented within.

In addition, there are cross-cutting themes in the case studies presented here. Davis, Casella, Hollimon, Prine, Schmidt, and Joyce all focus on the interrelationships between gender and sexuality in social and individual identities. These studies and others in this volume (e.g. Meskell, Gilchrist, and Voss) demonstrate that in many circumstances it would be inappropriate to study gender without considering sexuality, and vice versa. Feminist theory, sexology, and queer theory are best used when jointly deployed to develop archaeological research on topics of sexuality.

Another theme which emerges from these studies is the importance of the body in archaeological studies of sexuality. Whether discussing the confinement of the body (Gilchrist, Voss, Casella), representations of the body (Meskell, Joyce), the body as a source of power and danger (Wilkie), the sale of the body (Costello, Seifert et al.), the remains of the body (Hollimon, Schmidt), and of course bodily sensation (especially Gilchrist, Voss, Costello, Casella, and Joyce), many authors in this volume directly tackle what Montserrat has called 'the growing awareness of the problematic status of the human body, particularly the ancient body' (Montserrat 1998: 1) in archaeology.

Most authors in this volume also consider how sexuality is socially managed in diverse cultural settings. This is particularly apparent in the case studies which focus on institutions such as religious missions (Voss), monasteries (Gilchrist), and prisons (Casella). However, that such cultural mechanisms are always at play is also evidenced by studies such as Wilkie's examination of reproductive medicine, or Hollimon's, Prine's, and Schmidt's explorations of connections between occupation and sexuality. These and other chapters make it apparent that at least many, if not all cultural groups put considerable energy into developing social systems which alternatively promote, repress, channel, and direct different forms of sexual expression (Broude 1981). On the other hand, Davis and Casella provide examples of how archaeology can investigate the ways that individuals resist or play against their culture's sexual norms.

Finally, all of the chapters in this volume confront issues of epistemological certainty in archaeological interpretation. As we have discussed above, sexuality has not been seen as a viable object of archaeological knowledge, much in the way that gender was seen as marginal to archaeology prior to the mid-1980s. Because of this, each author contributing to this volume has had to ask: How do we know what we know about the past? Why is it that sexuality is seen as less knowable than, for instance, status or rank or subsistence? What methods and approaches can be used to move beyond this impasse?

Many of the studies presented here have responded to the evidential challenge through what Rubin (1994: 91–92) has called 'virtuoso empirical work', using conventional archaeological field methods and analyses to successfully evaluate hypotheses within evidential constraints. For example, Seifert uses conventional methods in historical archaeology; Prine uses statistical analysis; Voss undertakes a diachronic review of previous studies; and Casella combines rigorous stratigraphic excavation techniques with spatial analysis of artifact distribution. In some cases, these studies have in turn demonstrated the flawed assumptions that unknowingly bias conventional treatments of archaeological materials. For example, Wilkie suggests that faunal materials which would normally be seen as evidence of subsistence may have actually entered the archaeological record as a by-product of sexual medico-magical rituals. She demonstrates that, without a consideration of sexuality, these faunal remains would be misinterpreted, leading to faulty conclusions about subsistence practices and foodways. Joyce's contextual study of Mayan imagery likewise introduces a new variable – that of male same-sex sexuality and desire – in interpretations of Mayan images which are conventionally analyzed as evidence of political organization. Hollimon's work in this volume and in other studies (Hollimon 1991, 1996, 1997) has similarly challenged conventional approaches to mortuary data. These authors demonstrate that a failure to consider sexuality and sexual diversity may result in misleading interpretations of the archaeological record.

Still other authors have re-examined the objectives of archaeological interpretation. Costello forcefully argues for narrative interpretation as a vehicle to conveying the emotional, economic, and bodily aspects of sexuality in the past. Davis likewise uses architectural data to gain insight into the psyche and life history of an individual's problematic sexuality. Gilchrist also deploys archaeological evidence to examine the personal, interior nature of sexuality. These emphases on the individual and experiential are bold departures from the conventions of archaeological thought. Thus the value of these case studies is heuristic and stems from qualities quite different from those emphasized in more traditional archaeological studies.

Some of the chapters in this volume directly confront the indeterminacy of archaeological evidence in interpretation of past sexualities. Buchli considers the ways that the same sets of data were used to yield differing interpretations of sexuality in the former Soviet Union. His forceful examination highlights the ways in which contemporary sexual narratives are embedded within archaeological interpretations, even if the intentions of the archaeologists are not explicitly sexual. With this in mind, Schmidt underscores the difficulties of constructing interpretations with the paucity of evidence in 'deep prehistory' by applying the direct historical approach in a novel fashion. These studies remind us that all archaeological interpretations, not just those of sexuality, are conditioned by present circumstances and will certainly be challenged by future scholars.

A final theme which many papers in this volume explicitly or implicitly address is the political nature of archaeological research, and the political implications of archaeological studies of sexuality. As Buchli suggests (Chapter 13), archaeologists, at times unwittingly, are always engaged in cultural work. In present-day political debates about sexual issues – from same-sex marriage to statutory rape laws, from prostitution laws to new restrictive divorce laws – participants on all sides reference imagined sexual pasts in order to legitimize their positions. Common quips such as 'Prostitution: the world's oldest profession' and 'Adam and Eve, not Adam and Steve' may seem trite, but they demonstrate that people's perceptions of sexuality in the past influence their expectations of the sexual present. The case studies presented here demonstrate that archaeological research can bring a sense of empiricism to these political debates. While archaeological evidence is often ambiguous, this does not limit us from presenting the data we do have, meanwhile acknowledging the ambiguities inherent in our interpretations so that they do not assume public currency as scientific facts which can 'prove', for example, that monogamous sexual relations are a defining character of human social life (Zihlman 1997).

Together, the archaeologies of sexuality presented in this volume demonstrate two related themes. Archaeology may not simply contribute to, but also lead, studies of human sexuality in an interdisciplinary context. Archaeology alone can provide a truly long-term view of human sexuality which exceeds the bounds of written records, and which represents cultural groups traditionally disenfranchised by history. Simultaneously, for archaeologists, investigations of sexuality are a vehicle for new understandings about the past, not only enriching but also challenging presently accepted assumptions about social organization and cultural change. Thus we see archaeologies of sexuality as relevant both within the discipline of archaeology and to broader discussions about human sexuality.

It is above all these multiplicities – the interrelationship between sexuality and other archaeological inquiries; the plurality of theoretical and methodological approaches used; the relevance of sexuality in the past to many disciplines – which inform this volume. The title of this volume does not simply reflect but wholeheartedly embraces these multiplicities, for we are advocating not a single unified approach, but many interpretations grounded in multi-faceted lines of evidence. It is our hope that archaeologies of sexuality will not be limited to the materials presented herein, but will be extended through future research more broadly than we are presently equipped to imagine.

NOTES

1 Useful summaries and excerpts of these encyclopedic texts can be found in Bland and Doan 1998a and 1998b.
2 The terms *emic* and *etic* refer to the fact that descriptions of cultural forms and meanings will differ based upon who creates the description. An *emic* description would be provided by an enculturated member of a society; an *etic* description is created by an outside observer of a society.
3 For example, Malinowski's (1929) study of sexuality among the inhabitants of the Trobriand Islands primarily addresses heterosexual courtship and marriage, as well as family life; other forms of sexual relations and expression are treated cursorily in a chapter on 'Manners and Morals', wherein the reader is informed about 'the censure of sexual aberrations' which include homosexuality, bestiality, sadism and masochism, fellatio, masturbation, and exhibitionism. However, although Mead's work cited in the text and her other work on sex and gender throughout her career can fairly be characterized as including lessons for moral edification, we do wish to acknowledge that the agenda that Mead brought to her work was not simply a restatement of contemporary moralistic discourses about sexuality, of which Malinowski's work could more fairly be accused. Rather, Mead's work constituted her own explicit cultural and political agenda for reform within American culture (Mead 1972), and thus in this sense at least deserves to be distinguished from the work of Malinowski and others.

REFERENCES

Abelove, H. (1989) 'Some Speculations on the History of Sexual Intercourse during the Long Eighteenth Century in England', *Genders* 6, Fall: 125–30.

Abramson, P. R. and S. D. Pinkerton (1995a) *With Pleasure: Thoughts on the Nature of Human Sexuality*, New York: Oxford University Press.

—— (1995b) 'Introduction: Nature, Nurture, and In-Between', in P. R. Abramson and S. D. Pinkerton (eds) *Sexual Nature, Sexual Culture*, Chicago: The University of Chicago Press.

Ascher, R. (1961) 'Analogy in Archaeological Interpretation', *Southwestern Journal of Anthropology* 17: 317–25.

Bagemihl, B. (1999) *Biological Exuberance: Animal Homosexuality and Natural Diversity*, New York: St. Martin's Press.

Bartholomew, G. A. and J. A. Birdsell (1953) 'Ecology of the Protohominids', *American Anthropologist* 55: 481–98.

Bell, D. and G. Valentine (eds) (1995) *Mapping Desire: Geographies of Sexualities*, London: Routledge.

Bentley, G. R. (1996) 'How Did Prehistoric Woman Bear "Man the Hunter"? Reconstructing Fertility from the Archaeological Record', in R. P. Wright (ed.) *Gender and Archaeology*, Philadelphia: University of Pennsylvania Press.

Betsky, A. (ed.) (1995) *Building Sex: Men, Women, Architecture, and the Construction of Sexuality*, New York: William Morrow.

—— (ed.) (1997) *Queer Space: Architecture and Same-Sex Desire*, New York: William Morrow.

Binford, L. R. (1962) 'Archaeology as Anthropology', *American Antiquity* 28: 217–25.

Blackwood, E. (1984) 'Sexuality and Gender in Certain Native American Tribes: The Case of Cross-Gender Females', *Signs: Journal of Women in Culture and Society*, 10, 1: 27–42.

Bland, L. and L. Doan (eds) (1998a) *Sexology in Culture: Labeling Bodies and Desires*, Chicago: University of Chicago Press.

—— (1998b) *Sexology Uncensored: The Documents of Sexual Science*, Chicago: University of Chicago Press.

Boswell, J. (1980) *Christianity, Social Tolerance, and Homosexuality: Gay People in Western Europe from the Beginning of the Christian Era to the Fourteenth Century*, Chicago: The University of Chicago Press.

—— (1994) *Same-Sex Unions in Premodern Europe*, New York: Villard Books.

Brashler, J. G. (1991) 'When Daddy Was a Shanty Boy: The Role of Gender in the Organization of the Logging Industry in Highland West Virginia', *Historical Archaeology* 25, 4: 55–68.

Broude, G. J. (1981) 'The Cultural Management of Sexuality', in R. H. Monroe, R. L. Monroe and B. B. Whiting (eds) *Hand-book of Cross-Cultural Human Development*, New York: Garland STPM Press.

Brown, J. C. (1986) *Immodest Acts: The Life of a Lesbian Nun in Renaissance Italy*, New York: Oxford University Press.

—— (1989) 'Lesbian Sexuality in Medieval and Early Modern Europe', in M. Duberman, M. Vicinus and G. Chauncey, Jr. (eds) *Hidden from History: Reclaiming the Gay and Lesbian Past*, New York: Meridian.

Browne, S. (1923) 'Studies in Feminine Inversion', *Journal of Sexology and Psychoanalysis* 1: 51–58.

Brumfiel, E. M. (1991) 'Weaving and Cooking: Women's Production in Aztec Mexico', in J. M. Gero and M. W. Conkey (eds) *Engendering Archaeology: Women in Prehistory*, Oxford: Blackwell.

Butler, J. (1990) *Gender Trouble: Feminism and the Subversion of Identity*, New York: Routledge.

—— (1993a) *Bodies that Matter: On the Discursive Limits of 'Sex'*, New York: Routledge.

—— (1993b) 'Imitation and Gender Insubordination', in H. Abelove, M. A. Barale and D. Halpern (eds) *The Lesbian and Gay Studies Reader*, 307–320, New York: Routledge.

Bynum, V. E. (1992) *Unruly Women: The Politics of Social and Sexual Control in the Old South*, Chapel Hill: University of North Carolina Press.

Callender, C. and L. M. Kochems (1983) 'The North American Berdache', *Current Anthropology*, 24: 443–56.

Carpenter, E. (1908) *The Intermediate Sex: A Study of Some Transitional Types of Men and Women*, London: Swan Sonnenschein.

Casella, E. C. (1999) 'Dangerous Girls and Gentle Ladies: Archaeology and Nineteenth Century Australian Female Convicts', unpublished Ph.D. dissertation, University of California, Berkeley.

Cheek, C. D. and D. J. Seifert (1994) 'Neighborhoods and Household Types in Nineteenth-Century Washington, DC: Fannie Hill and Mary McNamara in Hooker's Division', in P. A. Shackel and B. J. Little (eds) *Historical Archaeology of the Chesapeake*, Washington, DC: Smithsonian Institution Press.

Clements, J. M. (1993) 'The Cultural Creation of the Feminine Gender: An Example from 19th Century Military Households at Fort Independence, Boston', *Historical Archaeology*, 27, 4: 39–64.

Collins, D. and J. Onians (1978) 'The Origins of Art', *Art History* 1, 1: 1–25.

Colomina, B. (1992) 'Sexuality and Space', in *Princeton Papers on Architecture*, Princeton: Princeton Architectural Press.

Conkey, M. W. (1991) 'Contexts of Action, Contexts for Power: Material Culture and Gender in the Magdalenian', in J. M. Gero and M. W. Conkey (eds) *Engendering Archaeology: Women and Prehistory*, Oxford: Blackwell.

Conkey, M. W. and J. M. Gero (1991) 'Tensions, Pluralities, and Engendering Archaeology: An Introduction to Women and Prehistory', in J. M. Gero and M. W. Conkey (eds) *Engendering Archaeology: Women and Prehistory*, 3–30, Oxford: Blackwell.

Conkey, M. W. and J. D. Spector (1984) 'Archaeology and the Study of Gender', in M. B. Schiffer (ed.) *Advances in Archaeological Method and Theory*, vol. 7, 1–38, New York: Academic Press.

Conkey, M. W. and R. E. Tringham (1995) 'Archaeology and the Goddess: Exploring the Contours of Feminist Archaeology', in D. C. Stanton and A. J. Stewart (eds) *Feminisms in the Academy*, 199–247, Ann Arbor: University of Michigan Press.

Conkey, M. W. with S. H. Williams (1991) 'Original Narratives: The Political Economy of Gender in Archaeology', in M. de Leonardo (ed.) *Gender at the Crossroads of Knowledge: Feminist Anthropology in the Postmodern Era*, Berkeley: University of California Press.

Costello, J. G. (1999) '"A Night With Venus, A Moon With Mercury": The Archaeology of Prostitution in Historic Los Angeles', in G. Dubrow and J. Goodman (eds) *Restoring Women's History through Historic Preservation*, Baltimore: Johns Hopkins University Press.

Costello, J. G. and A. Praetzellis (1999) 'Excavating L.A.'s Brothels', Venice, CA: Furman Films.

Cream, J. (1993) 'Child Sexual Abuse and the Symbolic Geographies of Cleveland', *Environment and Planning D: Society and Space*, 11: 231–46.

Dangerous Bedfellows (eds) (1996) *Policing Public Sex: Queer Politics and the Future of AIDS Activism*, Boston: South End Press.

Davis, A. Y. (1981) *Women, Race, and Class*, New York: Vintage Books.

Davis, D. L. and R. G. Whitten (1987) 'The Cross-Cultural Study of Human Sexuality', *Annual Review of Anthropology* 16: 69–98.

Davis, W. (1996) 'Winckelmann's "Homosexual" Teleologies', in N. B. Kampen (ed.) *Sexuality in Ancient Art: Near East, Egypt, Greece, and Italy*, Cambridge: Cambridge University Press.

—— (1998) '"Homosexualism", Gay and Lesbian Studies, and Queer Theory in Art History', in M. A. Cheetham, M. A. Nolly and K. Moxey (eds) *The Subjects of Art History*, New York: Cambridge University Press.

de Erauso, C. (1996 [1626?]) *Lieutenant Nun: Memoir of a Basque Transvestite in the New World*, M. Stepto and G. Stepto (trans.), Boston: Beacon Press.

de Grazia, V. with E. Furlough (eds) (1996) *The Sex of Things: Gender and Consumption in Historical Perspective*, Berkeley and Los Angeles: University of California Press.

de Waal, F. B. M. (1989) *Peacemaking Among Primates*, Cambridge: Harvard University Press.

—— (1995) 'Sex as an Alternative to Aggression in the Bonobo', in P. R. Abramson and S. D. Pinkerton (eds) *Sexual Nature/Sexual Culture*, 37–56, Chicago: The University of Chicago Press.

Deagan, K. (1983) 'The Mestizo Minority: Archaeological Patterns of Intermarriage', in K. Deagan (ed.) *Spanish St. Augustine: The Archaeology of a Colonial Creole Community*, New York: Academic Press.

Dean, C. J. (1996) *Sexuality and Modern Western Culture*, New York: Twayne Publishers.

Deetz, J. (1977) *In Small Things Forgotten*, New York: Doubleday.

Delphy, C. (1993) 'Rethinking Sex and Gender', *Women's Studies International Forum*, 16, 1: 1–9.

D'Emilio, J. (1983) *Sexual Politics, Sexual Communities: The Making of a Homosexual Minority in the United States, 1940–1970*, Chicago: The University of Chicago Press.

D'Emilio, J. and E. B. Freedman (1988) *Intimate Matters: A History of Sexuality in America*, New York: Harper and Row.

Dobres, M.-A. (1992a) 'Reconsidering Venus Figurines: A Feminist Inspired Re-Analysis', in S. Goldsmith, S. Selin and J. Smith (eds) *Ancient Images, Ancient Thought: The Archaeology of Ideology*, Calgary, Alberta: The Archaeological Association, University of Calgary.

—— (1992b) 'Re-Presentations of Palaeolithic Visual Imagery: Simulacra and Their Alternatives', *Kroeber Anthropological Society Papers* 73–74: 1–25.

Doughty, F. (1982) 'Lesbian Biography, Biography of Lesbians', in M. Cruikshank (ed.) *Lesbian Studies Present and Future*, Old Westbury, NY: The Feminist Press.

Dover, K. J. (1978) *Greek Homosexuality*, Cambridge, MA: Harvard University Press.

Dowson, T. (personal communication) 1998 'Call for Papers', for Queer Archaeologies, *World Archaeology* 32: 2.

duCille, A. (1993) *The Coupling Convention: Sex, Text, and Tradition in Black Women's Fiction*, New York and Oxford: Oxford University Press.

Duncan, N. (ed.) (1996) *Bodyspace: Destabilizing Geographies of Gender and Sexuality*, London: Routledge.

Ehrenberg, M. (1989) *Women in Prehistory*, London: British Museum Publications.

Eisler, R. (1988) *The Chalice and the Blade*, New York: Harper Collins.

Ellis, H. (1903–1927) *Studies in the Psychology of Sex (6 vols)*, Philadelphia: F. A. Davis.

Engelstad, E. (1991) 'Feminist Theory and Post-processual Archaeology', in D. Walde and N. D. Willows (eds) *The Archaeology of Gender: Proceedings of the Twenty-Second Annual Conference of the Archaeological Association of the University of Calgary*, Calgary, Alberta: University of Calgary.

Faber, D. (1980) *The Life of Lorena Hickok: E. R.'s Friend*, New York: Morrow.

Faderman, L. (1981) *Surpassing the Love of Men: Romantic Friendship and Love Between Women from the Renaissance to the Present*, New York: William Morrow.

—— (1991) *Odd Girls and Twilight Lovers: A History of Lesbian Life in Twentieth-Century America*, New York: Columbia University Press.

Faderman, L. and B. Eriksson (1980) *Lesbians in Germany: 1890's–1920's*, Tallahassee, FL: The Naiad Press, Inc.

Fausto-Sterling, A. (1983) 'The Five Sexes: Why Male and Female Are Not Enough', *The Sciences* April/May 1983: 20–24.

Feinberg, L. (1996) *Transgender Warriors: Making History from Joan of Arc to RuPaul*, Boston: Beacon Press.

Ford, C. S. and F. A. Beach (1951) *Patterns of Sexual Behavior*, New York: Harper and Row Publishers and Hoeber Medical Division.

Foucault, M. (1975) *Discipline and Punish: The Birth of the Prison*, A. Sheridan (trans.), New York: Vintage Books.

—— (1980) *The History of Sexuality, Volume I: An Introduction*, R. Hurley (trans.), New York: Vintage Books.

Frayser, S. G. (1985) *Varieties of Sexual Experience: An Anthropological Perspective on Human Sexuality*, New Haven, CT: HRAF Press.

Freedman, E. (1982) 'Resources for Lesbian History', in M. Cruikshank (ed.) *Lesbian Studies Present and Future*, Old Westbury, NY: The Feminist Press.

Gero, J. M. and M. W. Conkey (eds) (1991) *Engendering Archaeology: Women and Prehistory*, Oxford: Blackwell.

Gilchrist, R. (1994) *Gender and Material Culture: The Archaeology of Religious Women*, New York: Routledge.

Gimbutas, M. (1982) *The Goddesses and Gods of Old Europe*, Berkeley: University of California Press.

—— (1989) *The Language of the Goddess*, San Francisco: Harper and Row.

—— (1991) *The Civilization of the Goddess*, San Francisco: Harper and Row.

Goldman, M. S. (1981) *Gold Diggers and Silver Miners: Prostitution and Social Life on the Comstock Lode*, Ann Arbor: University of Michigan Press.

Gordon, L. (1976) *Woman's Body, Woman's Right: A Social History of Birth Control in America*, New York: Grossman.

Gould, R. A. and P. J. Watson (1982) 'A Dialogue on the Meaning and Use of Analogy in Archaeological Reasoning', *Journal of Anthropological Archaeology* 1: 355–81.

Grahn, J. (1984) *Another Mother Tongue: Gay Words, Gay Worlds*, Boston: Beacon Press.

Gutiérrez, R. A. (1991) *When Jesus Came, The Corn Mothers Went Away: Marriage, Sexuality, and Power in New Mexico, 1500–1846*, Stanford: Stanford University Press.

Hager, L. D. (1997) 'Sex and Gender in Paleoanthropology', in L. D. Hager (ed.) *Women in Human Evolution*, London and New York: Routledge.

Halperin, D. M. (1990) *One Hundred Years of Homosexuality and other Essays on Greek Love*, New York: Routledge.

Halperin, D. M., J. J. Winkler and F. I. Zeitlin (eds) (1990) *Before Sexuality: the Construction of Erotic Experience in the Ancient Greek World*, Princeton: Princeton University Press.

Handsman, R. G. (1991) 'Whose Art Was Found at Lepenski Vir? Gender Relations and Power in Archaeology', in J. M. Gero and M. W. Conkey (eds) *Engendering Archaeology: Women and Prehistory*, Oxford: Blackwell.

Hastorf, C. A. (1991) 'Gender, Space, and Food in Prehistory', in J. M. Gero and M. W. Conkey (eds) *Engendering Archaeology: Women and Prehistory*, Oxford: Blackwell.

Hawkes, C. F. (1954) 'Archaeological Theory and Method: Some Suggestions from the Old World', *American Anthropologist* 56: 155–68.

Hirschfeld, M. (1991 [1910]) *Transvestites: The Erotic Drive to Cross Dress*, M. A. Lombardi-Nash (trans.), Buffalo: Prometheus.

Hodder, I. (1991) *Reading the Past*, Cambridge: Cambridge University Press.

Hollimon, S. E. (1991) 'Health Consequences of Division of Labor Among the Chumash Indians of Southern California', in D. Walde and N. D. Willows (eds) *The Archaeology of Gender: Proceedings of the Twenty-second Annual Conference of the Archaeological Association of the University of Calgary*, Calgary: The University of Calgary Archaeological Association.

—— (1996) 'Gender in the Archaeological Record of the Santa Barbara Channel Area', *Proceedings of the Society for California Archaeology* 9: 205–208.

—— (1997) 'The Third Gender in Native California: Two-Spirit Undertakers Among the Chumash and their Neighbors', in C. Claasen and R. A. Joyce (eds) *Women in Prehistory: North America and Mesoamerica*, Philadelphia: University of Pennsylvania Press.

Jackson, T. L. (1991) 'Pounding Acorn: Women's Production as Social and Economic Focus', in J. M. Gero and M. W. Conkey (eds) *Engendering Archaeology: Women and Prehistory*, Oxford: Blackwell.

Jacobs, S.-E. (1997) 'Is the "North American Berdache" Merely a Phantom in the Imagination of Western Social Scientists?', in S.-E. Jacobs and W. Thomas (eds) *Lang, Sabine*, Urbana and Chicago: University of Illinois Press.

Jones, J. (1995) *Labor of Love, Labor of Sorrow: Black Women, Work, and the Family from Slavery to Present*, New York: Vintage Books.

Kampen, N. B. (1993) 'Ancients and Moderns', *Women's Review of Books*, X, 9, 12.

Kampen, N. B. and B. Bergmann (eds) (1996) *Sexuality in Ancient Art: Near East, Egypt, Greece, and Italy*, Cambridge: Cambridge University Press.

Katz, J. (1976) *Gay American History: Lesbians and Gay Men in the U.S.A.*, New York: Avon Books.
—— (1995) *The Invention of Heterosexuality*, New York: Dutton.
Kauffmann Doig, F. (1979) *Sexual Behavior in Ancient Peru*, Lima: Kompaktos.
Kennedy, E. L. and M. D. Davis (1993) *Boots of Leather, Slippers of Gold: The History of a Lesbian Community*, New York: Routledge, Chapman, and Hall.
Kinsey, A. C., W. B. Pomeroy and C. E. Martin (1948) *Sexual Behavior in the Human Male*, Philadelphia: W. B. Saunders.
Kinsey, A. C. and staff (1953) *Sexual Behavior in the Human Female*, Philadelphia: W. B. Saunders.
Kokkinidou, D. and M. Nikolaidou (1997) 'Body Imagery in the Aegean Mesolithic: Ideological Implications of Anthropomorphic Figurines', in J. Moore and E. Scott (eds) *Invisible People and Processes: Writing Gender and Childhood into European Archaeology*, London: Leicester University Press.
Krafft-Ebing, R. V. (1965 [1886]) *Psychopathia Sexualis*, F. S. Klaf (trans.), New York: Bell Publishing Co.
Lesick, K. S. (1997) 'Re-engendering Gender: Some Theoretical and Methodological Concerns on a Burgeoning Archaeological Pursuit', in J. Moore and E. Scott (eds) *Invisible People and Processes: Writing Gender and Childhood into European Archaeology*, London: Leicester University Press.
Levins, H. (1996) *American Sex Machines: The Hidden History of Sex at the U.S. Patent Office*, Holbrook, MA: Adams Media Corporation.
Lightfoot, K., T. Wake and A. Schiff (eds) (1991) *The Archaeology and Ethnohistory of Fort Ross, California, vol. 1: Introduction*, Berkeley: University of California Archaeological Research Facility.
Lightfoot, K. and A. Martinez (1996) 'Interethnic Relationships in the Native Alaskan Neighborhood: Consumption Practices, Cultural Innovations and the Construction of Household Identities', in K. Lightfoot, A. Schiff and T. Wake (eds) *The Native Alaskan Neighborhood: A Multi-ethnic Community at Colony Ross, vol. 2, The Archaeology and Ethnohistory of Fort Ross, California*, Berkeley: University of California Archaeological Research Facility.
Lightfoot, K., A. Schiff and T. Wake (eds) (1996) *The Native Alaskan Neighborhood: A Multi-ethnic Community at Colony Ross, vol. 2, The Archaeology and Ethnohistory of Fort Ross, California*, Berkeley: University of California Archaeological Research Facility.
Lindemann, B. S. (1984) '"To Ravish and Carnally Know": Rape in Eighteenth-Century Massachusetts', *Signs* 10, Autumn: 63–82.
Lovejoy, C. O. (1981) 'The Origin of Man', *Science* 211, 4,480: 341–50.
MacCowan, L. (1982) 'Lesbian Studies Books', in M. Cruikshank (ed.) *Lesbian Studies Present and Future*, Old Westbury, New York: The Feminist Press.
Maines, R. P. (1998) *The Technology of Orgasm: 'Hysteria', the Vibrator, and Women's Sexual Satisfaction*, Baltimore: The Johns Hopkins University Press.
Malinowski, B. (1929) *The Sexual Life of Savages in North-Western Melanesia: An Ethnographic Account of Courtship, Marriage and Family Life Among the Natives of the Trobriand Islands, British New Guinea*, New York: Readers League of America, distributed by Eugenics Publishing Company.
Marshall, D. S. and R. C. Suggs (1971) *Human Sexual Behavior*, New York: Basic Books.
Martinez, A. (1994) 'Native California Women as Cultural Mediators', *Proceedings of the Society for California Archaeology* 7: 41–46.
Matthews, J. J. (ed.) (1997) *Sex In Public: Australian Sexual Cultures*, St. Leonards, Australia: Allen & Unwin.
Matthews, K. J. (1994) 'An Archaeology of Homosexuality? Perspectives from the Classical World', in S. Cottam, D. Dungworth, S. Scott and J. Taylor (eds), *TRAC 94: Proceedings of the fourth annual Theoretical Roman Archaeology Conference held at the Department of Archaeology, University of Durham, 19th & 20th March 1994*, Oxford: Oxbow Books.
—— (1995) 'Archaeological Data, Subcultures, and Social Dynamics', *Antiquity* 69: 586–94.
McDonald Pavelka, M. S. (1995) 'Sexual Nature: What Can We Learn From a Cross-Species Perspective?', in P. R. Abramson and S. D. Pinkerton (eds) *Sexual Nature/Sexual Culture*, Chicago: The University of Chicago Press: 17–36.

McEwan, B. G. (1991a) 'The Archaeology of Women in the Spanish New World', *Historical Archaeology* 25, 4: 41.

—— (1991b) 'San Luis de Talimali: The Archaeology of Spanish-Indian Relations at a Florida Mission', *Historical Archaeology* 25: 36–60.

—— (1995) 'Spanish Precedents and Domestic Life at Puerto Real: The Archaeology of Two Spanish Homesites', in K. Deagan (ed.) *Puerto Real: The Archaeology of a Sixteenth-Century Spanish Town in Hispaniola*, Gainesville: University Press of Florida.

McGuire, K. R. and W. R. Hildebrandt (1994) 'The Possibilities of Women and Men: Gender and the California Milling Stone Horizon', *Journal of California and Great Basin Anthropology* 16, 1: 41–59.

McLaren, A. (1999) *Twentieth-century Sexuality: A History*, Malden, MA: Blackwell Publishers.

Mead, M. (1928) *Coming of Age in Samoa: A Psychological Study of Primitive Youth for Western Civilization*, New York: Blue Ribbon Books.

—— (1935) *Sex and Temperament in Three Primitive Societies*, New York: William Morrow and Company.

—— (1972) *Blackberry Winter: My Earlier Years*, New York: William Morrow & Company, Inc.

The Metropolitan Water District of Southern California (forthcoming a) 'Historical Archaeology at the Headquarters Facility Project Site, The Metropolitan Water District of Southern California, vol. 1, Draft Data Report: Recovered Data, Stratigraphy, Artifacts, and Documents'. Project Management by Applied EarthWorks, Inc. Co-Principal Investigators: Foothill Resources, Ltd. and Anthropological Studies Center at Sonoma State University. Contributing authors: Julia G. Costello, Adrian Praetzellis, Mary Praetzellis, Judith Marvin, Michael D. Meyer, Erica S. Gibson and Grace H. Ziesing.

—— (forthcoming b) 'Historical Archaeology at the Headquarters Facility Project Site, The Metropolitan Water District of Southern California, vol. 2, Draft Interpretive Report'. Project Management by Applied EarthWorks, Inc. Co-Principal Investigators: Foothill Resources, Ltd. and Anthropological Studies Center at Sonoma State University. Contributing authors: Julia G. Costello, Adrian Praetzellis, Grace H. Ziesing, Judith Marvin, William M. Mason, Michael D. Meyer, Erica S. Gibson, Mary Praetzellis, Suzanne Stewart, Sherri Gust, Madeline Hirn and Elaine-Maryse Solair.

Montserrat, D. (1996) *Sex and Society in Graeco-Roman Egypt*, London: Kegan Paul International.

—— (1998) 'Introduction', in D. Montserrat (ed.) *Changing Bodies, Changing Meanings: Studies on the Human Body in Antiquity*, London and New York: Routledge.

Moore, H. L. (1994) *A Passion for Difference*, Bloomington: Indiana University Press.

Moore, J. and E. Scott (eds) (1997) *Invisible People and Processes: Writing Gender and Childhood into European Archaeology*, London and New York: Leicester University Press.

Nelson, S. (1990) 'Diversity of the Upper Palaeolithic "Venus" Figurines and Archaeological Mythology', in S. Nelson and A. Kehoe (eds) *Powers of Observation: Alternative Views in Archaeology*, Washington, DC: Archaeological Papers of the American Anthropological Association, no. 2.

Nelson, S. M. (1997) *Gender In Archaeology: Analyzing Power and Prestige*, Walnut Creek, CA: Altamira Press.

Nestle, J. (1992) *The Persistent Desire: A Femme-Butch Reader*, Boston: Alyson Publications.

Newton, E. (1993) 'My Best Informant's Dress: The Erotic Equation in Fieldwork', *Cultural Anthropology* 8: 3–23.

Ng, V. W. (1989) 'Homosexuality and the State in Late Imperial China', in M. Duberman, M. Vicinus and G. Chauncey (eds) *Hidden From History: Reclaiming the Gay and Lesbian Past*, New York: Meridian.

Oaks, R. (1980) '"Things Fearful to Name": Sodomy and Buggery in Seventeenth-Century New England', in J. Pleck and E. Pleck (eds) *The American Man*, Englewood Cliffs, NJ: Prentice-Hall.

Panati, C. (1998) *Sexy Origins and Intimate Things: The Rites and Rituals of Straights, Gays, Bi's, Drags, Trans, Virgins, and Others*, New York: Penguin USA.

Praetzellis, A. and M. Praetzellis (1992) 'Faces and Facades: Victorian Ideology in Early Sacramento', A. E. Yentch and M. C. Beaudry (eds) *The Art and Mystery of Historical Archaeology*, Boca Raton, FL: CRC Press.

Prine, E. P. (1997) 'The Ethnography of Place: Landscape and Culture in Middle Missouri Archaeology', unpublished Ph.D. dissertation, University of California, Berkeley.

Reitz, E. J. (1990) 'Zooarchaeological Evidence of Subsistence at La Florida Missions', in D. H. Thomas (ed.) *Archaeological and Historical Perspectives on the Spanish Borderlands East, vol. 2, Columbian Consequences*, Washington, DC: Smithsonian Institution.

Roberts, J. (1982) 'Black Lesbians Before 1970: A Bibliographical Essay', in M. Cruikshank (ed.) *Lesbian Studies Present and Future*, Old Westbury, NY: The Feminist Press.

Roscoe, W. (1995) 'Strange Craft, Strange History, Strange Folks: Cultural Amnesia and the Case for Lesbian and Gay Studies', *American Anthropologist* 97: 448–53.

—— (1998) *Changing Ones: Third and Fourth Genders in Native North America*, New York: St. Martin's Press.

Rosen, R. (1982) *The Lost Sisterhood: Prostitution in America, 1900–1918*, Baltimore: The Johns Hopkins University Press.

Rowbotham, S. and J. Weeks (1977) *Socialism and the New Life: The Personal and Sexual Politics of Edward Carpenter and Havelock Ellis*, London: Pluto Press.

Rubin, G. (1975) 'The Traffic in Women: Notes on the "Political Economy" of Sex', in R. R. Reiter (ed.) *Toward an Anthropology of Women*, New York: Monthly Review.

—— (1984) 'Thinking Sex: Notes for a Radical Theory of the Politics of Sexuality', in C. S. Vance (ed.) *Pleasure and Danger: Exploring Female Sexuality*, Boston: Routledge and Kegan Paul.

—— (1991) 'The Catacombs: A Temple of the Butthole', in M. Thompson (ed.) *Leather-Folk: Radical Sex, People, Politics, and Practice*, Boston: Alyson Publications, Inc.

—— (1994) 'Sexual Traffic: An Interview with Judith Butler', *Differences: A Journal of Feminist Cultural Studies* 6, 2 & 3: 62–99.

Sanders, J. (ed.) (1997) *Stud: Architectures of Masculinity*, Princeton: Princeton Architectural Press.

Schmidt, R. A. (1995) 'AC/DC in BC? Sexual Orientation in Prehistory', symposium paper presented on 5 May, 1995 at the Society for American Anthropology Annual Meeting, Minneapolis, MN.

—— (1997) 'Building a future in the past: the contribution of lesbian/gay/bisexual/transgender studies to archaeology', symposium paper presented on 21 November, 1997 at the American Anthropological Association Annual Meeting, Washington, DC.

Seifert, D. J. (1991) 'Within Site of the White House: The Archaeology of Working Women', *Historical Archaeology* 25, 4: 82–107.

—— (1994) 'Mrs. Starr's Profession', in E. M. Scott (ed.) *Those of Little Note: Gender, Race, and Class in Historical Archaeology*, Tucson: University of Arizona Press.

—— (1998) 'Symposium #66: Sin City', the 1998 Annual Meeting of the Society for Historical Archaeology, Atlanta, GA.

Shanks, M. and C. Tilley (1987) *Social Theory and Archaeology*, Cambridge: Polity Press.

Simmons, A. (1989) *Red Light Ladies: Settlement Patterns and Material Culture on the Mining Frontier*, Corvallis: Anthropology Department, Oregon State University.

Smith, J. C. (1991) 'Gender and the Construction of Reality', in D. Walde and N. D. Willows (eds) *The Archaeology of Gender: Proceedings of the Twenty-Second Annual Conference of the Archaeological Association of the University of Calgary*, Calgary, Alberta: The University of Calgary Archaeological Association.

Smith-Rosenberg, C. (1979) 'The Female World of Love and Ritual: Relations between Women in Nineteenth-Century America', in N. F. Cott and E. H. Pleck (eds) *A Heritage of Her Own*, New York: Simon and Schuster, Touchstone.

Spector, J. D. (1993) *What This Awl Means: Feminist Archaeology at a Wahpeton Dakota Village*, St. Paul: Minnesota Historical Society Press.

Spindler, K. (1994) *The Man in the Ice: The Discovery of a 5,000-Year-Old Body Reveals the Secrets of the Stone Age*, New York: Harmony Books.

Stone, L. (1979) *The Family, Sex, and Marriage in England, 1500–1800*, New York: Harper and Row.

Stopes, M. (1918) *Married Love: A New Contribution to the Solution of Sex Difficulties*, London: A. C. Fifield.

Taylor, T. (1996) *The Prehistory of Sex: Four Million Years of Human Sexual Culture*, New York: Bantam Books.

Tringham, R. E. (1991) 'Households with Faces: The Challenge of Gender in Prehistoric Architectural Remains', in J. Gero and M. W. Conkey (eds) *Engendering Archaeology: Women and Prehistory*, Oxford: Blackwell.

Trumbach, R. (1990) 'The Birth of the Queen: Sodomy and the Emergence of Gender Equality in Modern Culture, 1660–1750', in M. Duberman, M. Vicinus and G. Chauncey Jr. (eds) *Hidden from History: Reclaiming the Gay and Lesbian Past*, New York: Meridian.

Vance, C. (1991) 'Anthropology Rediscovers Sexuality: A Theoretical Comment', *Social Science Medicine* 33: 875–84.

van der Meer, T. (1994) 'Sodomy and the Pursuit of a Third Sex in the Early Modern Period', in G. Herdt (ed.) *Third Sex, Third Gender: Beyond Sexual Dimorphism in Culture and History*, New York: Zone Books.

Vasey, P. L. (1995) 'Homosexual Behaviour in Primates: a Review of Evidence and Theory', *International Journal of Primatology* 16: 173–203.

—— (1998) 'Intimate Sexual Relations in Prehistory: Lessons from the Japanese Macaques', *World Archaeology* 29: 407–425.

Vicinus, M. (1989) '"They Wonder to Which Sex I Belong": The Historical Roots of the Modern Lesbian Identity', in D. Altman, C. Vance, M. Vicinus, and J. Weeks (eds) *Homosexuality, Which Homosexuality?*, Amsterdam: An Dekker.

Voss, B. L. (in press) 'History, the Family, and Household Archaeologies', *Proceedings of the 1997 Chacmool Conference: The Entangled Past-Integrating History and Archaeology*, Calgary, Alberta: The University of Calgary Archaeological Association.

Wall, D. (1991) 'Sacred Dinners and Secular Teas', *Historical Archaeology* 25: 67–81.

—— (1994) *The Archaeology of Gender: Separating the Spheres in Urban America*, New York and London: Plenum Press.

Washburn, S. L. and A. Avis (1958) 'Evolution of Human Behavior', in A. Roe and G. G. Simpson (eds), *Behavior and Evolution*, New Haven: Yale University Press.

Washburn, S. L. and C. S. Lancaster (1968) 'The Evolution of Hunting', in R. B. Lee and I. DeVore (eds) *Man the Hunter*, Chicago: Aldine Publishing Co.

Weeks, J. (1977) *Coming Out: Homosexual Politics in Britain from the Nineteenth Century to the Present*, London: Quartet.

—— (1981) *Sex, Politics and Society: The Regulation of Sexuality since 1800. Themes in British Social History*, London: Longman.

Wells, A. M. (1978) *Miss Marks and Miss Woolley*, Boston: Houghton Mifflin.

Weston, K. (1993) 'Lesbian/Gay Studies in the House of Anthropology', *Annual Review of Anthropology* 22: 339–67.

Whelan, M. K. (1991) 'Gender and Historical Archaeology: Eastern Dakota Patterns in the 19th Century', *Historical Archaeology* 25: 17–32.

Willey, G. R. and P. Phillips (1958) *Method and Theory in Archaeology*, Chicago: University of Chicago Press.

Wilkie, L. A. (1998) 'Beads and Breasts: The Negotiation of Gender Roles and Power at New Orleans Mardi Gras', in L. Sciama and B. Eicher (eds) *Beads and Bead Makers: Gender, Material Culture and Meaning*, New York: Berg.

Winkler, J. J. (1990) *The Constraints of Desire: the Anthropology of Sex and Gender in Ancient Greece*, New York: Routledge.

Wright, R. P. (1991) 'Women's Labor and Pottery Production in Prehistory', in J. M. Gero and M. W. Conkey (eds) *Engendering Archaeology: Women and Prehistory*, Oxford: Blackwell.

Wylie, A. (1985a) 'Putting Shakertown Back Together: Critical Theory in Archaeology', *Journal of Anthropological Archaeology* 4: 133–47.

—— (1985b) 'The Reaction against Analogy', in M. Schiffer (ed.) *Advances in Archaeological Method and Theory*, Orlando: Academic Press.

—— (1992) 'The Interplay of Evidential Constraints and Political Interests: Recent Archaeological Research on Gender', *American Antiquity* 57, 1: 15–35.

—— (1996) 'The Constitution of Archaeological Evidence: Gender Politics and Science', in P. Galison and D. J. Stump (eds) *The Disunity of Science: Boundaries, Contexts, and Power*, Stanford: Stanford University Press.

Yates, T. (1993) 'Frameworks for an Archaeology of the Body', in C. Tilley (ed.) *Interpretive Archaeology*, Providence: Berg.

Zihlman, A. (1987) 'American Association of Physical Anthropologists Annual Luncheon Address, April 1985: Sex, Sexes, And Sexism in Human Origins', *Yearbook of Physical Anthropology* 30: 11–19.

—— (1997) 'The Paleolithic Glass Ceiling: Women in Human Evolution', in L. D. Hager (ed.) *Women in Human Evolution*, London and New York: Routledge.

PART I

Where it happens:
structured space and sex

Chapter Two

Colonial sex: archaeology, structured space, and sexuality in Alta California's Spanish-colonial missions

Barbara L. Voss

The initial act of contact between the mission organization and the Indian was one involving spatial relationships.

Sherburne F. Cook (1943: 73)

The politics of space are always sexual, even if space is central to the mechanisms of the erasure of sexuality.

Beatriz Colomina (1992: 1)

INTRODUCTION

In the last decade, it has become almost axiomatic that sexual politics played a critical role in European colonial ventures throughout the world.[1] The late eighteenth-century colonization of the Alta California coast by Spain was no exception. Although many historians and ethnohistorians have considered sexuality to be an important research issue in Spanish-colonial Alta California (Bouvier 1995; Castañeda 1993b; Castillo 1994b; Cook 1943; Hurtado 1992; Jackson and Castillo 1995; Milliken 1995; Monroy 1990; Sandos 1998), archaeologists have rarely addressed questions of sexuality in their interpretations of colonial-era sites. This is not surprising, as archaeological evidence of sexuality is not always readily apparent (see Voss and Schmidt, Chapter 1). Yet, because sexuality played an important role in the colonization of Alta California's native populations, some consideration of sexuality could be valuable in archaeological studies which are considering culture contact, acculturation, colonial economics, gender relations, and other research domains prominent in Spanish-colonial archaeological research.

In this chapter, I explore possible connections between archaeological research and sexuality studies of Spanish-colonial Alta California. Can archaeologists use the findings of historical research on sexuality to generate a more nuanced reading of the archaeological record? Can archaeological research contribute directly to studies of sexuality during the

Spanish-colonial period? To address these questions, I examine the findings of previous archaeological studies in tandem with sources used by historians and ethnohistorians, including oral histories, mission records, travelers' diaries, sketches, and maps. By drawing on the results of previous research, I aim to demonstrate that archaeological considerations of sexuality need not rely on new field methods or analytic techniques. My goal is not to put forward definite 'answers' about the interplay between colonization and sexuality in Alta California, but rather to introduce new questions into archaeological studies of colonial-period sites.

Such an exploration of new archaeological territory could take many routes. I choose to focus this essay in two ways: first, through an analytic emphasis on spatial relations, as discussed in archaeological, architectural, and historical studies; second, through a geographic focus on the native peoples and colonial settlements within the San Francisco Presidial district (Figure 2.1). Within these parameters, I consider topics related to sexual violence, sexual confinement, and consensual sexual activity. First, however, I provide a brief background of the Spanish-colonial venture in Alta California, including descriptions of sexual mores and values associated with both indigenous and colonial populations, and a discussion of some theoretical tools used in this archaeology of sexuality.

HISTORICAL BACKGROUND: CULTURE CONTACT AND SEXUALITY

Colonization of the California coast occurred relatively late in the history of Spanish America, beginning in 1769 and continuing through the early nineteenth century. Spain held Alta California for five decades (1769–1821). Colonization – and the Mexican period immediately following (1821–1848) – were times of rapid historical and cultural change for California's native peoples.

The San Francisco Presidial district was the northernmost administrative district in Alta California, encompassing coastal and bay shore lands from present-day Santa Cruz to Sonoma County (Figure 2.1). Prior to colonization, the region was occupied primarily by Ohlone, Bay Miwok, Coast Miwok, Patwin, Wappo, and Yokuts groups which resided in tribelets, or village communities.[2] Although there were significant differences between these groups, most ethnographic and archaeological accounts describe Bay area peoples as gatherer-fisher-hunters who used highly developed environmental management techniques to maintain a semi-sedentary, village-based settlement pattern (e.g. Bocek 1991; Levy 1978; Moratto 1984). Population densities were high, averaging four to six persons per square mile, with villages numbering sixty to two hundred people (Milliken 1995: 19–21).

The earliest encounters between Spanish colonists and Bay area tribes occurred in 1769, when the Portolá expedition entered the San Francisco Bay area on horseback. Subsequent expeditions in the early 1770s laid the groundwork for the establishment of colonial settlements (Costanso 1992 [1769]). In 1776, two colonial outposts were founded: the Presidio de San Francisco, a military settlement whose forces both suppressed native resistance to colonization and guarded against attack by other European polities; and Mission San Francisco de Asís, established to aggregate Native Californians and convert them to Catholicism (Costello and Hornbeck 1989). By the early 1800s, a total of six missions were constructed within the San Francisco Presidial district, and most native peoples had either moved to the mission settlements, fled to inland areas beyond colonial control, or died as a result of disease or warfare (Milliken 1995: 219–20).[3]

The process of colonization involved intensive culture contact, in which both indigenous and colonial populations were relocated from their original homelands and brought into

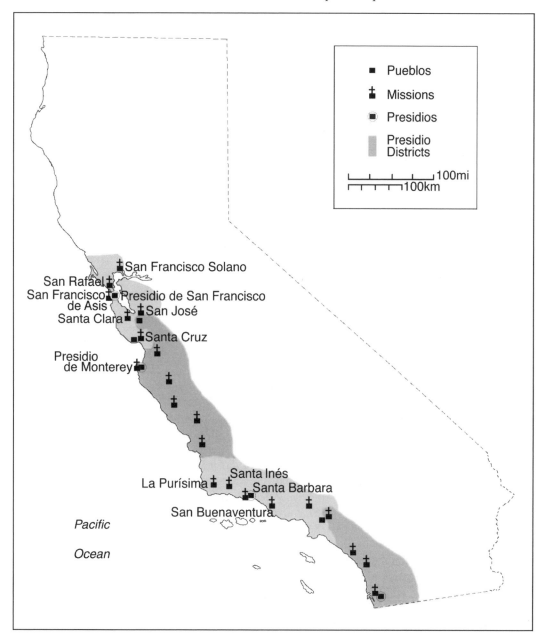

Figure 2.1 Map of missions, presidios, and pueblos in Alta California.
Cartography by Anna Naruta after sources by Fuller (1983) and Wojcik (1978).

close proximity. These new circumstances were devastating to Native Californians and transformed colonial settlers into *Californianos* who were as closely identified with Alta California as with their ancestral homelands. Cultural systems that shaped sexuality were part of these phenomena, and some understanding of the sexual values and practices of the major groups involved is necessary in order to investigate colonial-period sexuality.

Because the colonial immigrants to Alta California were not a uniform group, no unified sexual code existed in colonial Alta California. The most prominent arbiters of sexual morality were the missionaries, the mostly European-born Franciscan priests who were the repository of religious authority within the colony. As stipulated by the marriage canons of the Council of Trent, acceptable sexual practices were limited to two options: reproductive sex within the marriage sacrament, or celibacy (Bouvier 1995: 359; Gutiérrez 1991: 243). Any other sexual activities were mortal sins, and marriage bonds were unbreakable except by death or annulment (Bouvier 1995: 342). However, priests were only a small fraction of the colonial population. Most colonists were military and agrarian settlers who came to Alta California from the present-day provinces of Sonora and Sinaloa, and were of mixed indigenous, African, and Spanish heritage (Forbes 1983; S. Voss 1982). Within secular colonial society, a sexual code which emphasized honor both complemented and contradicted Catholic doctrine: masculine honor accrued through sexual conquests outside the family and through protecting female relatives from dishonorable sexual advances (see Bouvier 1995; Castañeda 1993a, 1993b, 1998; Gutiérrez 1991 and 1993 for more complete discussions of sexual honor). Both religious and secular sexual codes rested upon a heterosexually anchored binary gender system.

Native Californian sexual mores differed sharply from these Spanish-colonial religious and secular norms, and colonists were fascinated and appalled by some Native Californian sexual practices. For example, gender and reproductive capabilities were not necessarily a structuring principle of Native Californian marriages, and marriage was not the only appropriate context for sexual activity (B. Voss, in press). Polygyny and polyandry were both practiced (Milliken 1995: 62). Divorce was freely available, and sexual activity outside of marriage was not stigmatized, although a sense of sexual modesty was important and adultery was discouraged (Levy 1978: 490; Margolin 1978: 81; Ortiz 1994: 111–12, 132, 137–38). Like many other Native American groups (Roscoe 1991, 1998; Whitehead 1981; see also Hollimon and Prine, this volume) Native Californian cultures of the San Francisco Bay area recognized multiple genders, and sexual activity and marriages could occur both across and within gender categories (Williams 1986: 139, 234, 242). Instead of using marriage to regulate sexual activity, most indigenous sexual prohibitions focused on situations when sexual activity would be spiritually detrimental to oneself or others. These included circumstances related to pregnancy, nursing, menstruation, basket making, hunting, ritual dances, and doctoring (Levy 1978: 490; Margolin 1978: 85). Because of these stark differences between colonial and indigenous sexual systems, sexuality was a contentious point of cultural negotiation and domination throughout the colonization of Alta California.

STRUCTURED SPACE, SEXUAL PRACTICES, AND ARCHAEOLOGY

Given that sexuality is important in historical studies of colonial Alta California, what ways might there be to integrate sexuality into interpretations of archaeological findings? Most historians who have written about colonization and sexuality in the Americas have focused primarily on sexual identities, sexual ideologies, and sexual economies in their research (Bouvier 1995; Castañeda 1993b; Castillo 1994b; de Erauso 1996 [1626?]; Gutiérrez 1991; Hurtado 1992; Jackson and Castillo 1995; Riley 1984; Trexler 1995; Williams 1986). Here, I consider sexuality from a slightly different angle: a focus on sexual activity, in and of itself, as a quotidian, or repetitive, cultural practice.

Practice-based approaches to analyses of archaeological data are derived from the works of Pierre Bourdieu (1977), Henrietta Moore (1986), and other anthropologists who have considered how daily activities produce, reproduce, and challenge historically situated social systems. Using practice theory, sexual activities can be framed as processes through which social systems are both enacted and changed. Applying practice theory to sexuality in this way also articulates with branches of North American feminist scholarship which have traced the contours of sexual practices as indices of gender- and race-based power relations (e.g. Bynum 1992; Enloe 1990, 1993; Rosen 1982; Conkey and Tringham 1995). Although there has been considerable disagreement among feminist scholars regarding the social and political implications of specific sexual practices,[4] the centrality of sexual activity as a locus of feminist inquiry is well established. Further, theoretical work in sexuality studies engages the relationship between sexual activity and theories of power in ways which are indebted to earlier feminist discussions of sexuality, and also form part of the emerging field of queer theory (e.g. Abelove 1989; D'Emilio 1983; D'Emilio and Freedman 1988; Foucault 1975, 1990 (1978)).

Given the historical setting of colonial Alta California, a practice-based approach to archaeological investigations of sexuality has theoretical and methodological strengths. A practice-based approach positions indigenous peoples and colonists as knowledgeable actors capable of exercising choice around sexual matters, while acknowledging that these choices were at times severely constrained by sexual politics and mechanisms of sexual control (Moore 1986: xvii). Thus, through a focus on sexual activity, archaeological investigations of sexuality can articulate with studies concerned with resistance to missionization (e.g. Brady et al. 1984; Sandos 1998), the changing status of women (e.g. Bouvier 1995; Castañeda 1988, 1992, 1993b), and the construction of ethnic identities during colonization (e.g. Castillo 1994a; S. Voss 1982). A practice-based approach to archaeological studies of sexuality also draws attention to the shifting locations of sexual activity across both time and space. These spatial and temporal concerns are issues which the archaeological toolbox is uniquely well equipped to address. Existing studies conducted at Spanish-colonial sites in Alta California provide abundant data which document architectural remains and other evidence of structured space. An archaeology of sexuality informed by historical scholarship can read these data to illuminate the shifting contours of colonial-era sexual practices. Simultaneously, a consideration of sexual activity may have explanatory power in interpreting indigenous and colonial architectural strategies.

SEXUAL VIOLENCE AND SETTLEMENT ORGANIZATION

A close examination of the example of colonial-era sexuality demonstrates how sexual activity can influence the organization of space. From the late 1760s through to the early 1800s, rape of Native Californian women by colonial soldiers was pervasive and widespread, creating 'a disturbing pattern of wholesale sexual assault' (Castillo 1994a: 283) across colonized regions. Such rapes were both illegal under secular law and mortal sins under church law; occasionally rapists were prosecuted by Alta California's governors (Monroy 1990: 81). However, sexual violence usually went unpunished because of contradictions between military and legal codes, and because military officials were reluctant to incarcerate the few soldiers under their commands (Castañeda 1993b: 28).

Consequently, rape functioned as an unofficial but widely deployed tactic used in military excursions into Native Californian villages. For example, in 1773, Junipero Serra[5] described one such campaign which occurred near the Presidio of Monterey:

> In the morning, six or more soldiers would set out together . . . on horseback, and go to the distant *rancherías* [Indian villages], even many leagues away . . . the soldiers,

Figure 2.2 *Modo de Pelear de los Indios de Californias* (The Californian Indian Way of Fighting), by José Cardero, an illustrator aboard the *Malaspina* during its 1791 voyage along the California coast. Cardero's drawing illustrates several elements – such as the seclusion of women – mentioned in accounts of indigenous responses to military-oriented sexual violence.
Courtesy of the Bancroft Library, University of California, Berkeley; original at Museo Naval, Madrid.

> clever as they are with their lassoing cows and mules, would catch Indian women with their lassos to become prey for their unbridled lust. At times some Indian men would try to defend their wives, only to be shot down by bullets.
>
> (Castañeda 1993b: 15; Jackson and Castillo 1995: 75)

While Serra's account is anecdotal, the seriousness of interethnic sexual violence in colonial Alta California has been substantiated by numerous historians who have noted the consequential spread of venereal disease and its demographic effects, the role of rape in provoking indigenous rebellions, and the psychological effects of rape on both Native Californians and colonists (Beilharz 1971; Castañeda 1993b, 1998; Castillo 1994b; Cook 1943; Gonzalez 1998; Jackson and Castillo 1995; Monroy 1990). But how can archaeologists participate in studies of sexual violence when rape itself leaves no material traces and is therefore 'archaeologically invisible'? Instead of looking for material signatures of rape, I suggest that archaeologists can benefit from approaches used by feminist geographers who have considered the spatial components of sexual violence in modern communities (e.g. Cream 1993; Duncan 1996; Valentine 1989). Prehistoric and historical archaeological data can then be used to provide new insights into the defensive strategies used by Native Californians and colonial missionaries to reduce sexual violence.

Archaeological studies can also provide a crucial diachronic component to studies of sexual violence on the Alta California frontier. For example, late Holocene (*c.* AD 500–1700) archaeological sites in the San Francisco Bay area provide information about the pre-colonial spatial organization at Native Californian villages. Data from numerous archaeological excavations (Bickel 1976: 351–52; Chartkoff and Chartkoff 1984: 150, 187, 216; Moratto 1984: 272; Nelson 1909: 346) and ethnographic studies (Barrett and Gifford 1971 [1933]: 332; Heizer and Elsasser 1980: 38–41; Johnson 1978: 357–58; Kelly 1978: 417; Levy 1978: 492) indicate that pre-colonial native settlements consisted primarily of several thatched dwellings which were loosely strung along a creek bank or the bay shore. Open-air ramadas, a men's sweathouse, the women's menstrual house, and dance areas were usually located on the periphery of the villages. The intra-site distribution of bedrock mortars, grinding slicks, and artifactual debris at many late prehistoric sites further suggests that food processing, basket making, hide preparation, and other daily work activities were performed outdoors on the periphery of these settlements (Bocek 1991: 76–81; Jackson 1991: 315–17). This latter point is particularly important because several documentary accounts of military rape mention that Native Californian women were working on various tasks on the outskirts of their villages when they were ambushed by soldiers on horseback, taken into the brush or grasslands surrounding the village, and raped (Castañeda 1993b: 15–19; Castillo 1994b: 70–73).

Having reconstructed the general layout of late prehistoric settlements, it is now possible to review colonists' descriptions of Native Californian villages to see how indigenous communities responded to persistent sexual assaults.[6] Father Pedro Font, who traveled through the San Francisco Bay region in 1775, noted of one unnamed village that 'the women were very cautious and hardly left their huts, because the soldiers . . . had offended them with various excesses' (Castañeda 1993b: 18). Of another settlement, Font penned, 'They [the women] all hastily hid in their huts, especially the girls; the men remaining outside blocking the door and taking care that nobody should go inside' (Castañeda 1993b: 18). (See Figure 2.2.) A later account, written in 1797 by Sergeant Pedro Amador, provides a detailed description of the Saclan village of Jussent.[7] The village was composed of three circular clusters of tightly packed thatch houses, each cluster lodging about fifty people. Work areas were located not on the periphery of the village but within protected yards located within the clusters of houses. Further, a series of ditches had been excavated around each housing cluster, forcing Amador and his troops to approach Jussent on foot, without their horses (Milliken 1995: 157).

When compared with archaeological interpretations of late prehistoric settlements, these historical accounts indicate a deliberate reorientation of indigenous architecture and use of space to deter sexual assaults by colonial troops. The gender-specific aggregation of women and girls within a central location and attempts to keep soldiers from entering the village on horseback would have removed Native Californian women from view and prevented soldiers from using their lassos to capture isolated women. Consequently, an explicit consideration of the tactics and methods used in military rapes is necessary to understand changes in architectural strategies in Native Californian villages – changes which are only made apparent through a comparative, diachronic perspective.

Archaeological investigations of military sexual violence in colonial California need not be limited to the use of prehistoric data. Archaeological studies of mission settlements also may provide new insights. Repeatedly, missionaries complained that sexual violence was retarding the spiritual conquest of California, jeopardizing the safety and success of the missions. Because missions relied on a resident military population to deter runaways and

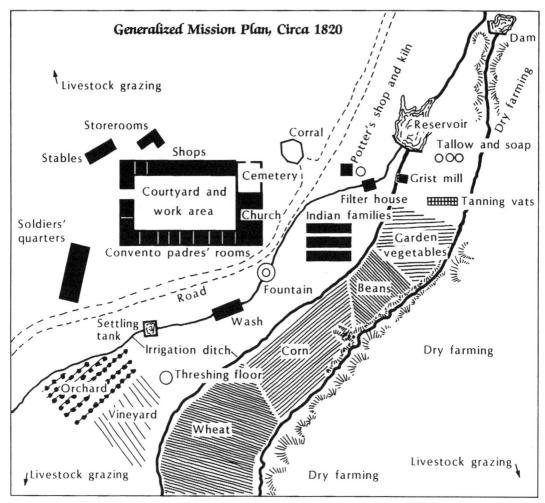

Figure 2.3 Generalized mission plan from Alta California, *c.* 1820 (Costello and Hornbeck 1989: 312). Note the placement of the soldiers' quarters and Indian family housing on opposite sides of the main mission quadrangle.
Reprinted courtesy of Julia Costello.

provide protection against indigenous rebellions, sexual violence occurred not only during military expeditions to indigenous village sites but also against baptized Native Californian women residing in the mission *rancherías*, or neophyte housing areas (Bouvier 1995: 305). As Castañeda (1993b) has documented, priests attempted to reduce sexual assaults in many ways. These included colonial immigration policies which recruited whole families rather than single men, economic incentives to encourage single soldiers to marry Native Californian women, and regulations which prohibited soldiers from leaving the presidios at night or entering native villages without permission.

These policies were largely ineffective (Bouvier 1995; Castañeda 1993b; Hurtado 1992), and historical records indicate that missionaries may have resorted to manipulations of structured space to reduce sexual assaults. Initially, troops assigned to missions in the San Francisco Bay area were housed in the main quadrangle of the mission, next to the priests' residences and the neophyte housing areas (Bouvier 1995: 305). However, the *Informes Anuales*[8] from the 1790s indicate that mission priests ordered the construction of separate military housing outside the main quadrangle of mission within the San Francisco Presidial district (Jackson and Castillo 1995: 152, 155, 160, 162). By the early 1800s, the soldiers' residences were 'always located on the opposite side of the quadrangle from the Indian dwellings' (Costello and Hornbeck 1989: 310) (Figure 2.3). This shift in the location of military housing may be in part a consequence of minimal construction during the early years of colonization, followed by greater specialization of building functions as each mission became more economically viable (Costello and Hornbeck 1989: 310). However, the separation of military housing from neophyte residences at all missions cannot be explained by economic factors alone. In part because of the military's role in sexual assaults, many missionaries came to mistrust military personnel. Changes in the spatial organization of mission settlements might have been one strategy to insulate Native Californian converts from the sexual abuses and secular influence of military settlers. Archaeological studies of military housing areas at mission settlements would be particularly useful in considering this possibility.

SEXUAL CONFINEMENT: THE MONJERÍO

Military housing was not the only aspect of mission architecture which was shaped by the missionaries' attempts to control sexual activity. Perhaps the most obvious attempt to manipulate sexuality through architectural design is seen in the *monjerío*,[9] or women's barracks (Figure 2.4). Located within or immediately adjacent to the main quadrangle of each mission, the *monjerío* was typically a long, narrow adobe room with high walls, small windows, and a single entrance which could be securely locked from the outside. Among baptized Native Californians, all unmarried women and girls were required by mission priests to live in the *monjerío* from late childhood until they married.[10]

In Alta California missions, the *monjerío* was developed from elements of three distinct architectural traditions. The first of these, the religious cloister, originated as part of medieval Catholic theological approaches to sexual sins. This theological framework stressed the need to remove oneself and others from the 'occasion to sin' through the physical separation of the body from temptation (Gilchrist 1994). The second influence was contemporary Spanish domestic architecture, which provided for the seclusion of unmarried daughters in interior rooms and courtyards in order to protect the honor of the family (Gutiérrez 1993: 704). Finally, Enlightenment philosophies of progress and reform embraced architecture as a mechanism for social engineering on a larger scale. These reform movements emphasized that vice was contagious, and architecture was used to separate still-virtuous children from corrupted parents and to segregate the sexes (Markus 1993: 68, 120). In this way, the *monjerío* incorporated not only the religious and paternalistic aims of the mission priests, but also the secular goal of hispanicizing Native Californians. By isolating female children from their kin, the *monjerío* disrupted indigenous adolescent initiation rites, interrupted transmission of cultural lore and technologies, and altered traditional courtship rituals and marriage arrangements (Margolin 1978: 75–76; Milliken 1995: 119, 134–35; Monroy 1990: 59–62; Vallejo 1890: 186–87).

To the mission priests, the *monjerío* was an indispensable tool in curbing sin. The priests were concerned with

> the custom whereby Indian couples looking forward to marriage lived together . . . It constituted a form of fornication [which] was intrinsically evil. But an act that was

Figure 2.4 Reconstructed *Monjerío*, Mission La Purísima Concepción State Historic Park. Completed in the 1950s, the design of this structure was developed from historic descriptions of *monjeríos* at nearby missions; a securable entrance, internal drain, and high, barred windows differentiate this building from other housing constructed for native converts. Photograph by the author.

intrinsically evil could not be permitted by superiors in their subjects. Nor could it be cooperated with. Hence the missionaries found an avenue of escape from their dilemma in the monjerio.

(Guest 1996: 323)

By sequestering unmarried women within the *monjeríos*, the priests could 'safeguard their virginity and help them to prepare for Christian marriage' (Guest 1989: 7). Sexual abstinence was enforced by the priests with the aid of a 'superior', usually an older Native Californian woman or the wife of a colonial military officer (Castañeda 1992: 38). Strict rules of social conduct within the *monjerío* were designed to inculcate Spanish notions of female virginity and family honor into the girls and women, who were confined in the *monjerío* until they were married and released to the supervision of their husbands (Bouvier 1995: 337).

While the missionaries themselves described the *monjeríos* as benign institutions (Engelhardt 1908–1915: 558), other colonial-era writers were more critical. Travelers in colonial California often described the *monjeríos* as unsanitary, penal-like institutions, evidence of Spanish-colonial mistreatment of Native Californians. The Russian explorer Otto von Kotzebue, who visited Mission Santa Clara in 1824, wrote:

We were struck by the appearance of a large, quadrangular building, which, having no windows on the outside, and only one carefully secured door, resembled a prison for state criminals. It proved to be the residence appropriated by the monks, the severe guardians of chastity, to the young unmarried Indian women . . . These dungeons are opened two or three times a day, but only to allow the prisoners to pass to and from church. I have occasionally seen the poor girls rushing out eagerly to breathe the fresh air, and driven immediately into the church by an old ragged Spaniard armed with a stick. After mass, they are in the same manner hurried back to their prison.

(1821: 94–95)

Spanish-colonial military officials, such as Governor Diego de Borica, also criticized the *monjeríos*, noting that the continual confinement of the girls and women caused an unbearable stench and contributed to the rapid spread of fatal diseases (Engelhardt 1908–1915: 550–51; Jackson and Castillo 1995: 48). Historical studies have confirmed Borica's observations, using mission records and other documentary evidence to demonstrate that the *monjerío* system was detrimental to indigenous women's health and contributed to extremely high death rates among young missionized women (e.g. Allen 1998: 14, 92; Bouvier 1995; Castañeda 1998; Cook 1943: 89; Hurtado 1988: 24).

Confinement in the *monjeríos* also transformed native women's youth and adolescence into a period of 'mental and emotional strain' (Cook 1943: 90). Prior to colonization, girls and unmarried women lived with their extended families, were unrestricted in their movements around the village and across the landscape, and were not prohibited from participating in adolescent sexual play and premarital sex. However, under the *monjerío* system, female youth and early adulthood was marked by forced removal from family and kin, confinement, sexual prohibition, and a continuous regime of custodial care which passed from her parents to the priest and finally to her husband.

To most mission priests, secular concerns about forced confinement and ill health were subordinate to their desire to restructure the native sexual practices. The institutional prominence of the *monjeríos* across colonial California demonstrated this. As a key component of the missionization strategy, the *monjeríos* were almost always among the first buildings constructed at each mission (Jackson and Castillo 1995: 81). The *monjerío* system was a durable aspect of the mission institution, surviving initial campaigns for its abolishment after the 1821 Mexican Revolution weakened church control in Alta California. Not until the missions were secularized in 1834 were the *monjeríos* disbanded (Engelhardt 1908–1915: 529).[11]

In addition to colonial documents, Native Californian oral histories and reminiscences of mission life provide another perspective on the effects of the *monjerío* system on indigenous culture. Recounted to and translated by Anglo-American anthropologists and historians in the late 1800s, these accounts often highlight the contrast between official mission policies and the actual practices which occurred. Fernando Librado,[12] a Chumash Indian, related a story he had heard about how one priest at Mission San Buenaventura used the *monjerío* to molest native girls:

The priest had an appointed hour to go there. When he got to the nunnery [*monjerío*], all were in bed in the big dormitory. The priest would pass by the bed of the superior [*maestra*] and tap her on the shoulder, and she would commence singing. All of the girls would join in . . . When the singing was going on, the priest would have time to select the girl he wanted, carry out his desires . . . In this way the priest had sex with all of them, from the superior all the way down the line . . . The priest's will was law. Indians would lie right down if the priest said so.

(Librado 1979: 52–53)

Librado also suggests that in some cases women actively resisted sexual confinement:

The young women would take their silk shawls and tie them together with a stone on one end and throw them over the wall. This was done so that the Indian boys outside the high adobe wall could climb up. The boys would have bones from the slaughter house which were nicely cleaned, and they would tie them on the shawls so that they could climb these shawls using the bones for their toes. The girls slept merely on [woven tule] mats, and there were no partitions or mats hung up inside the room for privacy. The boys would stay in there with those girls till the early hours of the morning. Then they would leave. They had a fine time sleeping with the girls.

(1979: 53)

Librado's accounts illustrate several points which are relevant to archaeological inter-pretations of architecture and sexuality. First, Librado illuminates the difference between the sexual intent of architectural form and the actual sexual practices which occur within that space. In at least one case, the enclosure designed to protect the sexual honor of unmarried women made them even more vulnerable to sexual abuse. In another instance, the ideology of chastity was cleverly subverted by mission residents who were unwilling to let architectural impediments prevent sexual pleasure. Understanding the sexual 'meaning' of specific architectural forms, such as the *monjeríos*, depends on a considera-tion of both overt sexual ideologies and the actual, sometimes covert, sexual practices which may have occurred.

The sexual meanings associated with *monjeríos* were also shaped by sexual practices which happened beyond their confines. Librado's account suggests that indigenous resis-tance to the *monjerío* system included attempts to maintain courtship traditions which incorporated pleasurable sexual relations, often at the risk of corporal punishment and imprisonment. In this light, an association can be made between sexual resistance and other forms of native rebellion (Sandos 1998: 206–207). In 1812, a group of baptized native residents at Mission Santa Cruz attacked and killed the head priest, Padre Quintana, by crushing and removing his testicles (Asisara 1989: 8). Lorenzo Asisara,[13] an Ohlone whose father participated in the attack, related that as soon as the priest was dead, the assassins unlocked the *monjeríos*:

The single men left and without a sound gathered in the orchard at the same place where the Father was assassinated. There was a man there cautioning them not to make any noise, that they were going to have a good time. After a short time the young unmarried women arrived in order to spend the night there. The young people of both sexes got together and had their pleasure.

(1989: 122)

It is informative that, after the priest was dead, the native men and women in Asisara's account chose to have sex outside, away from the *monjerío*, and furthermore chose to do so at the exact site of the priest's highly sexualized death. Together, Librado's and Asisara's accounts illustrate the symbolic and the practical role of structured space in the organization of sexual practices. Simultaneously, these accounts demonstrate that architecture alone could not effect sexual control in the California missions.

These colonial and Native Californian sources suggest that the *monjeríos* are promising locations for archaeological investigations of sexuality: through studies of the *monjerío* system we may unearth direct evidence of the use of architecture to control sexuality as well as indications of indigenous resistance to sexual confinement. However, the history of investigations at mission sites illuminates challenges which archaeologists studying sexuality may face. Remains of *monjeríos* have not yet been identified at any of the six missions located within the San Francisco Presidial district. In other areas of colonial California, only tentative identifications of *monjerío* structures have been made. Webb (1952: 114) describes remains of a sunken tile drain which were used, in conjunction with missionary accounts, to locate the *monjerío* at the Santa Barbara mission.[14] Costello and Gasco's investigations at Mission Santa Inés exposed a similar mortar-and-tile drain which had been installed after the construction of Room I-1, a particularly large enclosure with a tiled floor (Costello and Gasco 1985: 48–49). Noting that historical evidence provides contradictory information about the spatial relationship between the Santa Inés *monjerío* and *convento*, Costello and Gasco postulate that Room I-1 'may have been renovated for use as a monjerio' at some point, but also note that the drain could have been installed not for sanitation but to divert rain water from an adjacent patio (Costello and Gasco 1985: 102). At nearby Mission La Purisima, the restoration of the second site of the mission included a *monjerío*; unfortunately the reconstructed *monjerío* was built without benefit of archaeological research (Joe McCummings, personal communication).[15]

The ambiguities of archaeological findings, the contradictions within the historical record, the multiple uses which any given structure may have served – all of these factors complicate archaeological efforts to study the *monjerío* system. Yet it is not necessary for archaeologists to find a definitive 'smoking gun' (after Conkey and Gero 1991: 11) which will 'prove' that a particular configuration of tile, adobe, and stone served as a location of sexual confinement. We know that each mission maintained a *monjerío* throughout most, if not all, of its occupation. It may be useful to consider, as Costello and Gasco (1985) have done, the various architectural elements (such as sanitation facilities) which might be archaeologically indicative of *monjeríos*. Artifacts or architectural modifications which might indicate resistance to confinement could also be indicative. Such indices, together with documentary evidence, may be sufficient to begin postulating possible locations of *monjeríos* at various mission sites. Alternatively, at some missions it may be that structures used as *monjeríos* are archaeologically indistinguishable from other mission buildings. Even such 'negative findings' could be significant as they may indicate that the degree of architectural elaboration associated with the *monjerío* system varied from mission to mission, perhaps as a result of economic factors or as a reflection of the personalities of individual priests (see Costello 1992 for further discussion of this latter point). Regardless, this examination of the *monjerío* system, as well as the earlier discussion of the placement of military housing (see above), demonstrates that mission architecture reflects not only the religious motives, economic successes, and cultural traditions of Franciscan missionaries, but also the complicated sexual politics operative on the Spanish-colonial frontier.

CONSENSUAL SEX AND DOMESTIC ARCHITECTURE

So far, the main focus of this chapter has been the connection between structured space and sexual coercion, specifically the extremes of rape and enforced celibacy. But can archaeological research also address the role of architecture and structured space in shaping sexual practices between consenting partners? Here again, a rich body of historical research provides a starting point for archaeological explorations. On one hand, mission records chronicle the repression of some kinds of consensual sex; priests issued severe corporal punishments to those who engaged in extramarital sex, divorce, polygyny, polyandry, and sex with same-sex and transgendered partners (e.g. Milliken 1995: 69, 78, 135; Williams 1986: 139), while other historical accounts document the persistence of these practices throughout the colonial period (e.g. Bouvier 1995: 348, 368; King 1994: 206, 223–26; B. Voss, in press). On the other hand, research conducted using marriage and baptismal registers kept at each mission implicitly traces the contours of church-sanctioned consensual sexual practices (e.g. Milliken 1995). Thus, prominent themes of culture contact research, such as acculturation, repression, resistance, and accommodation, surface as central to studies of colonial sexuality.

In this section, I examine some effects of colonization on Native Californian consensual sexual practices. To do so, I consider evidence of household architecture from three contexts: prehistoric settlements in the San Francisco Bay area; late eighteenth-century housing at Mission San Francisco de Asís; and the Santa Cruz Mission Adobe, which was constructed in the early 1820s. In relation to each context, historical and ethnographic sources are placed in dialogue with archaeological findings to explore how the material record can inform interpretations of sexuality. Together, these three examples provide an opportunity to consider diachronic changes and continuities in consensual sexual practices.

Prehistoric household architecture

To understand the implications of missionization on indigenous sexual practices, a consideration of pre-contact contexts is necessary (Lightfoot 1995). Unfortunately, remains of prehistoric architecture are rarely preserved in the San Francisco Bay area. Still, the results of selected archaeological investigations (Bickel 1976: 351–52; Chartkoff and Chartkoff 1984: 188; Moratto 1984: 242; Nelson 1909: 346; Schenck n.d.: 181), when combined with early explorers' accounts (Kroeber 1925: 276) and ethnographic studies (Barrett and Gifford 1971 [1933]: 332; Kroeber 1925: 468; Simmons 1998: 20), suggest certain common characteristics of late prehistoric household architecture. Most structures appear to have been hemispherical or conical dwellings, constructed with a wood frame covered with redwood bark slabs or thatched with tule and grasses. In some cases, houses were semi-subterranean. In general, most dwellings appear to have been 2–4 m in diameter, providing sleeping space for households that ranged from four to ten individuals. Unlike more substantial sweatlodges and dancehouses, domestic architecture appears to have been relatively ephemeral, having a use-life of 2–10 years.

Although this profile of late prehistoric architecture in the Bay area is quite general, there are several points which may be relevant to considering prehistoric sexual practices. First, the ephemeral nature of these structures as well as their construction from readily available materials suggests that prehistoric household architecture may have been very flexible. The size of dwellings appears to vary considerably and dwellings could also have been clustered to fit the size and configuration of each household. As the configuration of households changed as a result of changing sexual relations (e.g. when new households were created through marriage, when a new spouse was brought into an existing marriage, or when households were divided by divorce), household architecture could be modified or replaced to accommodate these new living arrangements. A second point concerns the function of household dwellings themselves. As noted earlier, work and social areas were usually located outdoors away from residential housing areas. Given the relatively small floor space sheltered by these prehistoric homes (approximately 3–12 m^2), such dwellings were probably used primarily for sleeping and storage of personal goods (Kroeber 1925: 468).

This raises several possibilities regarding the geography of late prehistoric sexual activity. Margolin (1978: 81) has suggested that sexual modesty was an important value in Bay area native cultures. If sexual activity was regularly conducted within household dwellings, social conventions may have existed to create a sense of sexual privacy. Whitelaw, in his ethnoarchaeological study of !Kung campsites, has suggested that privacy within and between hunter-gatherer dwellings may be 'symbolic rather than effective' (1994: 225), and that sticks or other visual cues may be used to provide a spatial marker for private space. Perhaps similar strategies may have been used to notionally partition space to create sexual privacy within Bay area prehistoric households.

However, given that most other activities were generally conducted outside of household dwellings, there is no reason to assume that prehistoric sexual activity was confined to interior spaces. The few ethnographic accounts of sexual activity that I could locate all describe couples walking away from their village into areas sheltered by tall grasses, trees, or chaparral (Margolin 1978: 81; Ortiz 1994: 137). Additionally, studies of certain types of petroglyphs in the Bay area, especially cupule-shaped rocks and pecked curvilinear nucleated petroglyphs, suggest that they may have been created through rituals to increase sexual or reproductive power (Fentress 1994: 72; Gillette 1996).[16] Sexual activity near these rock art sites might have been one way to access the power held in the rock outcroppings, and would have also geographically linked sexual practices to spiritual stories and legends which were inscribed on the landscape through oral histories.

At this point, it would be an interpretive leap to make any definitive statements about late prehistoric sexual activities in the San Francisco Bay area. However, the above consideration of available evidence does suggest several observations, namely: (1) that sexual activities, like other activities, were probably not confined to indoor spaces; (2) that outdoor sexual activity may have been preferred at times in order to maintain sexual privacy and to connect sexual activity to geographically based spiritual meanings; and (3) that social conventions may have existed to create symbolic sexual privacy within indoor spaces. In this light, the colonial-era accounts of sexual activity provided by Librado and Asisara (excerpted above) are particularly interesting. Sexual activity within the unpartitioned *monjerío* (Librado 1979: 53) may have been facilitated by the same social conventions which in prehistoric times provided sexual privacy in small household dwellings. Yet, Asisara's account suggests that when possible, the privacy afforded by outdoor sexual activity may have been preferred (Asisara 1989: 122).

Mission San Francisco de Asís

The implications of missionization for indigenous sexual practices can be further explored by considering housing arrangements for baptized Native Californians at Mission San Francisco de Asís, the first mission founded in the San Francisco Bay area. While archaeological research at Mission San Francisco de Asís has been limited because of its urban setting,[17] mission records such as the *Informes Anuales* (translated and summarized in Jackson and Castillo 1995: 152–53), baptismal and marriage records (studied by Milliken 1995) and various travelers' accounts (Milliken 1995: 90; Webb 1951: 12–13) provide an opportunity to examine changes in household architecture during the first decades of missionization (1776–1800).

Milliken's analysis of baptismal records from Mission San Francisco de Asís (1995: 226) indicates that the initial influx of new converts was slow, averaging under fifty baptisms per year between 1776 and 1791. During this period, new mission residents built their own homes in a *ranchería*, or village, adjacent to the mission, using traditional Native Californian methods and materials. While girls and unmarried women were confined to the *monjeríos*, the rest of the mission population lived in homes that were probably very similar to those they had left behind in their villages of birth.

In the early 1790s, the population of Mission San Francisco de Asís exploded, with hundreds of new converts baptized each year (Milliken 1995: 266). Beginning in 1794, the missionaries undertook a concerted effort to replace as much traditional native housing as possible with long, narrow adobe apartment buildings (Jackson and Castillo 1995: 152–53; Milliken 1995: 143). The construction program was so vigorous that colonial military officials rebuked the priests for the harsh labor regime developed to build the new housing. The new adobe apartments were built in front of the main mission chapel, arranged in 'eight long rows of houses, where each family lives apart from the rest' (Langsdorff 1806, as quoted in Webb 1951: 12). Recent archaeological investigations east of the chapel may have exposed remnants of these buildings (Ambro and Holman 1997; Andrew Galvan, personal communication).

Milliken notes that as the mission settlement grew larger in the 1790s, 'the priests were beginning to lose their personal control of the mission communities' (Milliken 1995: 120). In the 1770s and 1780s, priests could use intensive religious instruction and personal relationships with new converts to transmit moral codes of behavior. Once baptismal rates increased, the level of religious instruction before baptism decreased and mission priests could no longer personally supervise the moral conduct of mission residents. The priests' goals of transforming the sexual behavior of the new converts had to be accomplished in different ways. For example, beginning in the 1790s, unmarried Native Californian converts were joined in mass wedding ceremonies, at times to spouses they had barely met (Milliken 1995: 134).

Perhaps the priests' urgency to replace traditional Native Californian houses with adobe apartments was also a strategy to channel consensual sexual activity in directions concordant with Catholic doctrine.[18] Unlike thatch or bark houses, which could be built by household members using readily available materials, the adobe row houses could only be constructed through organized group labor using specialized technologies such as adobe brick and clay tile manufacturing. This transferred the control of residential arrangements from native households to mission priests, who after overseeing and organizing construction then had the sole jurisdiction to allocate individual apartments to couples who had been married in a Christian ceremony. In this way, sanctioned sexual relationships were fixed geographically, where they could be monitored through both formal censuses and casual inspections. Sexual relationships which were forbidden by Catholic doctrine, such as polyandry, polygyny, and same-sex relationships, could thus be denied household status. However, construction of adobe housing at Mission San Francisco de Asís never kept pace with housing needs, and many native converts continued to live in indigenous-style houses as late as the 1820s (von Kotzebue 1821: 77). Those resisting Catholic sexual proscriptions might have chosen not to reside in the adobe row-houses in order to maintain control over household composition.

The Santa Cruz Mission Adobe

The Santa Cruz Mission Adobe is the only surviving example of residential housing for native converts in the San Francisco Presidial district. Constructed in 1824, this building originally was one of three similar adobe structures, each consisting of 15 to 27 apartments

(Allen 1998: 3; Kimbro et al. 1985: 84–89). These apartments housed only a small fraction of the mission population, the majority of which continued to live in traditional
thatch houses throughout the mission period. The inhabitants of the Mission Santa Cruz
Adobe were therefore a select group, probably comprised of long-term mission residents,
skilled craftspersons, and the mission *alcaldes* (trusted native converts who were placed in
positions of authority by mission priests) (Allen 1998: 51; Kimbro 1988: 7). As Allen
(1998: 52) noted, these native residents had to learn 'how to live in these new buildings
that were so dissimilar from the native houses'. Thus the Santa Cruz Mission Adobe
provides a locus to investigate the effects of these new architectural forms on native lifeways, including sexual practices.

In the late 1970s and 1980s, historical, archaeological, and architectural research was
conducted at the Santa Cruz Mission Adobe with the goal of seismically stabilizing the
building and restoring the structure to its late mission/early secularization appearance (Allen
1995, 1998: 31–34; Felton 1987; Kimbro 1987, 1988; Kimbro et al. 1985).[19] The results
of these studies provide a rare window into the spatial patterning of elite native domestic
life at the end of the colonial era in California (Figure 2.5). Excavations and 'vertical
archaeology' of the structure indicated that each apartment consisted of a single rectangular room with a half-loft built in the rafters (Felton 1987: Fig. 3). The apartments were
entered through doors on the exterior connecting corridor, with no connecting passages
between individual apartments. The only other fenestration in each apartment was a single
shuttered window opening to the rear (Kimbro 1987).

Archaeological data from the adobe rooms suggest both continuities and changes in
indigenous uses of space. For example, within each apartment, a central stone hearth was
set into the floor, just as was common in traditional circular houses. However, many
rooms in the adobe also had evidence of secondary fire pits. The arrangement of these
secondary pits did not conform to a set pattern (Allen 1998: 31–37), and suggest innovations in adapting to the light and heat requirements of the rectangular adobe apartment.
Artifactual evidence also indicates that many activities were conducted within the adobe
rooms, including food processing and consumption, stone tool manufacturing, olivella
bead production, and gambling (Allen 1998: 53, 64, 74, 82, 88). While cooking, eating,
and craft production also certainly occurred out-of-doors, especially in the corridor area
adjacent to the adobe (Allen 1998: 64), the indoor location of some subsistence and craft
activities is a significant departure from prehistoric space-use patterns. Even though the
Santa Cruz Mission Adobe assemblage has 'many similarities to assemblages found in
prehistoric California . . . it also reflects the influence of the Hispanic community' (Allen
1998: 89) with respect to spatial organization.

Historical research conducted by Kimbro (1988) on sleeping arrangements at the
Mission Santa Cruz Adobe suggests another arena of colonial cultural influence on native
converts' uses of space. Kimbro suggests that, by the 1820s, some native residents of the
mission had begun to sleep on low sleeping platforms or on beds constructed of wicker-
work and cow hides (Figure 2.6). It is particularly likely that beds were present in
the adobe apartments, because of the high status of the residents, their access to colonial
material goods, and archaeological evidence of their growing cultural identification with
colonial domestic habits. Similarly, the use of *mantas*, or muslin curtains, to screen beds
from view is supported by drawings of elite native residences at other missions in the late
1830s (Kimbro 1988: 6–7, 10).

Together, the growing expansion of daily activity areas to include indoor spaces, and
the evidence for demarcated sleeping spaces through the construction of platforms or beds

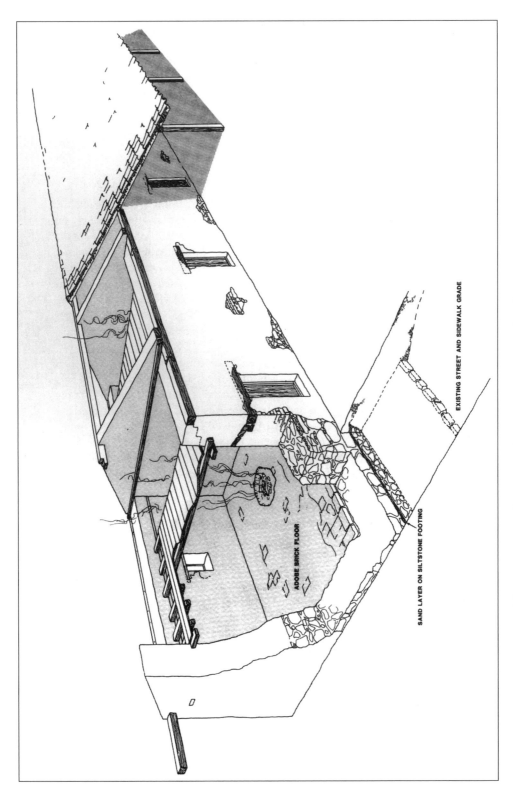

EXISTING STREET AND SIDEWALK GRADE

SAND LAYER ON SILTSTONE FOOTING

ADOBE BRICK FLOOR

Figure 2.5 Santa Cruz Mission Adobe, mission period reconstruction – cut away perspective view. Developed from archaeological and architectural studies. Illustrated by David L. Felton.

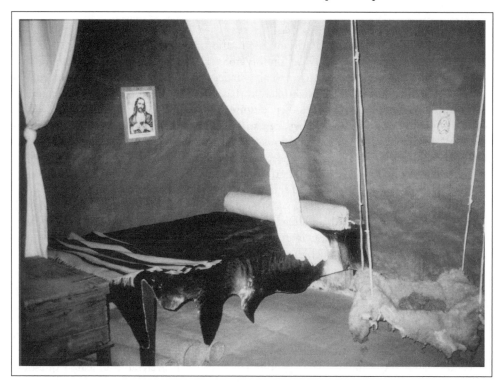

Figure 2.6 Interior of restored apartment, Santa Cruz Mission Adobe. After archaeological research was completed, one apartment in the Santa Cruz Mission Adobe was restored to its mission-period appearance as an interpretive exhibit.
Photograph by the author.

(possibly with screens) in the adobe apartments, suggest a corresponding shift in sexual practices among elite native mission residents. Like food processing, eating, and craft activities, sexual activity may have been in the process of being redefined as a domestic activity which was properly performed indoors, within the household. Relocation of sexual activity indoors undoubtedly disrupted connections between sexual activity and a landscape marked by spiritual and mythical meanings, although it is possible that these connections were maintained through occasional forays outside the mission grounds. Notions of sexual privacy may have shifted from a privacy marked by distance and social conventions to a privacy created by enclosure and visual screening.

This comparative study of domestic architecture at late prehistoric sites, Mission San Francisco de Asís, and the Mission Santa Cruz Adobe suggests that the effects of missionization on consensual native sexual practices were complex and multifaceted. Architectural effects on native sexual practices varied both with the strategies used by individual priests and with the status of native converts within the mission system. Marked by both cultural change and continuity, these sexual transitions were negotiated within the overall sexual repression of the mission system but informed by complicated indigenous responses to shifting conditions of privacy, spatial relations, and spiritual geographies.

CONCLUSION

This chapter began with an exploration of the relationship between archaeological data and sexuality, and it ends on a similarly exploratory note. The above discussions of military rape, sexual confinement, and consensual sexual practices have only touched on some of the complex sexual dynamics which were likely to have been operational during the colonization of the San Francisco Bay area. Yet, despite the limited scope of this project, which focused primarily on the interplay between structured space and Native Californian sexual practices, the above examples have demonstrated that a consideration of sexuality can productively expand interpretations of archaeological evidence. The methods and results of this study have also highlighted analytical strategies which may be useful in further developments of sexuality studies within archaeology: first, an emphasis on locations of sexual activities in time and space; second, a combination of both diachronic and synchronic comparative frameworks; third, an integration of household-level and settlement-level analyses; and finally, the use of multiple lines of evidence, including ethnographic analogies (and documentary sources when available) to construct models of sexual behavior.

To some, these archaeological interpretations of the effects of colonization on Native Californian sexuality may seem frustratingly speculative. While this study has demonstrated that previous archaeological studies can be re-examined with respect to research questions about sexuality, it also suggests the limitations of relying on data developed to address other research questions. As Rubin notes, an anthropology of sexuality must be centered on 'virtuoso empirical work' which avoids 'relying on assumptions, stereotypes, anecdotes, [and] fragments of data' (Rubin 1994: 91–92). Preferably, research questions about sexuality would be integrated into archaeological research designs before excavation and analysis, so that relevant data can be systematically collected. Regardless, interpretations of archaeological findings can play an important and unique role in interdisciplinary sexuality studies, adding material lines of evidence to documentary and ethnographic research.

This study has also shown how research on sexuality can stimulate new directions in archaeological analysis and interpretation. An oft-cited goal of feminist and post-processual archaeological research has been to 'people the past' (e.g. Tringham 1991; Hodder 1991). Archaeological research on sexuality, whether in Spanish-colonial California or elsewhere, forces us to consider the lived experiences of the individual subjects of our research. Sex is individually experienced but culturally shaped. Sexual activity confronts the boundaries between the individual and the social, between the body and culture. Issues of sexual violence, sexual control, sexual privacy, and sexual practice highlight sexuality as a paradoxical locus of pleasure as well as physical and emotional pain. Material remains unearthed through archaeological research can particularly assist in interrogating these paradoxes, leading to a more nuanced understanding of the history of human sexuality.

ACKNOWLEDGEMENTS

I would like to thank Rebecca Allan, El Casella, Julia Costello, Deborah Cohler, Kent Lightfoot, Will Roscoe, and Rob Schmidt, whose careful readings of earlier drafts greatly strengthened this chapter. I would also like to thank Anna Naruta for sharing her cartographic skills, Naomi Schulz for guiding me to important sources at the Bancroft Library, and Julia Costello and Larry Felton for generously permitting reproduction of Figures 2.3 and 2.5. Research conducted for this study was made possible through graduate fellowships from the National Science Foundation and the William and Flora Hewlett Foundation. I am grateful for their support, and, of course, the opinions, findings, conclusions, and recommendations present in this work are those of the author and do not necessarily reflect the views of these organizations.

Notes

1 See, for example, recent studies by Bleys (1995), Enloe (1990, 1993), Gutiérrez (1991), McClintock (1995), Roscoe (1991), Stoler (1991, 1997) and Trexler (1995).

2 The term 'tribelet' was first used by Kroeber (1925) to describe Native Californian political organization. Tribal names, such as Miwok, refer to a regional population sharing related languages; autonomous political groups (tribelets) were smaller, consisting of two or more villages which shared spiritual and political leaders (Heizer 1978: 5) Inter-tribelet political and economic alliances also unified regions both within and across language groups (Field, et al. 1992; Milliken 1995: 21).

3 Comprehensive historical and archaeological accounts of this period can be found in Barker et. al. (1995), Costello and Hornbeck (1989), Milliken (1995), Jackson and Castillo (1995), Skowronek (1998), and Weber (1992).

4 For example, see the wide body of literature on the 'sex wars' of the 1980s (e.g. Linden et al. 1982; Rubin 1984; SAMOIS 1982; Snitow et al. 1983; Vance 1984) as well as more recent works such as Dangerous Bedfellows (1996) and Duggan and Hunter (1995).

5 Serra was the founding priest and the first administrator of the Alta California mission system. This passage is taken from Serra's 1773 *memoria* to Viceroy Buchareli.

6 Unfortunately, very few archaeological studies have investigated colonial-period indigenous villages which were not part of mission, presidio, or ranch settlements; those reports which do exist did not provide enough information to directly reconstruct intra-site spatial organization.

7 Located east of the present-day city of Oakland, Jussent was visited by Amador and his troops during a military expedition to recapture neophytes who ran away from Mission San Francisco (Milliken 1995: 157, 253).

8 Detailed annual reports compiled by the head priest at each mission.

9 Alternatively spelled *monjero, monjerio, monjério, monjería*, and *monjiero* in various documents; loosely translated to mean 'monks' residence' or 'cloister', in Alta California this term and its variants seem to have always referred to barracks for unmarried women only. At a few missions, barracks called *jayuntes* were also established for male bachelors and widowers (Monroy 1990: 61). These may have functioned more like dormitories for unmarried men than supervised cloisters (Engelhardt 1908–1915: 559), although one account (Asisara 1989) suggests that adolescent boys were at times also confined to enforce chastity.

10 The exact age at which Native Californian girls entered the *monjerío* is debated. Historians Englehardt (1908–1915) and Guest (1996) suggest age 11; others suggest an earlier age, nearer to 7–9 years old (Bouvier 1995; Brady et al. 1984: 142; Castañeda 1998; Jackson and Castillo 1995; Monroy 1990). All agree that girls were taken to the *monjeríos* before the onset of puberty.

11 *Reglamento Provisional*, Article 23, Regulation #7 (9 August, 1834).

12 Born in the early 1800s on or near Santa Cruz Island, Librado came of age in the missions and in his later years was interviewed by J. P. Harrington. The passages cited here are taken from an edited compilation of Harrington's notes by Travis Hudson (Librado 1979). Librado attributes these stories about the *monjerío* at Mission San Buenaventura to an Indian sacristan named *Woqoch*, or Old Lucas.

13 Lorenzo Asisara was born in Mission Santa Cruz in 1820, eight years after Quintana was killed. Asisara learned about the event through his father, who was an eyewitness to the assassination. This account was originally transcribed by Bancroft historian Thomas Savage in 1877, and was more recently translated from Spanish to English by Castillo (1989).

14 Fathers Tapis and Lasuen both mention the presence of a sewer at the Santa Barbara *monjerío* for 'corporeal necessities' (Cook 1943: 89).

15 According to Joe McCummings, a ranger at Mission La Purisima State Historic Park, construction of the *monjerío* which stands in the park today was begun by Civilian Conservation Corps (CCC) work crews in the 1930s (see Hageman 1938, 1939; Hageman and Ewing 1991) and

completed by park staff in the early 1950s. Its present location across the mission gardens from the main mission complex is inconsistent with historical documents which place the *monjerío* near the 'shops' building.

16 Fentress bases his associations between cupule rocks and sexual magic largely on Barrett's accounts of a Pomo ritual:

> The sterile pair went to one of these rocks and there first a prayer for fertility was made. Then, by means of a pecking stone, some small fragments were chipped from the sides of one of the grooves or cuppings in its surface. These were then ground to a very fine powder which was wrapped in some green leaves and taken to some secluded spot. Here this powder was made into a paste and with it the woman's abdomen was painted with two lines, one running from the top of the sternum to the pubes, the other transversely across the middle of the abdomen. Some of this paste was also inserted in the female. Intercourse at this time positively assured fertility, due to the magic properties of the rock.
>
> (Barrett 1952, as quoted in Fentress 1994: 72)

Pecked curvilinear nucleated (PCN) petroglyphs are often interpreted as representations of vulvas. Gillette (1996) has found evidence at the Stege Mound and Wildcat Canyon sites that phallic-shaped charmstones may have been 'quarried' from PCN locations, suggesting sexual magic generated by the creation of both penis and vulva from a single stone form.

17 The mission site is located in present-day San Francisco. Renovation of the main mission chapel, the only surviving structure of the mission complex, was accomplished without archaeological studies (Andrew Galvan, personal communication). Limited archaeological investigations were recently conducted during rehabilitation of the Notre Dame School building, the probable location of the mission-era native village. Several adobe foundations and a shell midden also dating to the mission period were identified (Ambro and Holman 1997).

18 I am not suggesting that sexual control was the only motive for this construction boom. A main goal of missionization was to transform Native Californians into Spanish subjects, and encouraging new converts to live in colonial-style dwellings would have been part of this general process. Rather, it is the timing of housing construction which suggests that architecture was also deployed as a proxy for personal moral suasion in sexual (and other) matters.

19 The Santa Cruz Mission Adobe was acquired by the California Department of Parks and Recreation in 1958, which maintains and operates the site as a State Historic Park.

REFERENCES

Abelove, H. (1989) 'Some Speculations on the History of Sexual Intercourse during the Long Eighteenth Century in England', *Genders* 6, Fall: 125–30.

Allen, R. (1995) 'An Archaeological Study of Neophyte Cultural Adaptation and Modification at Mission Santa Cruz, California', Ph.D. dissertation, University of Pennsylvania.

—— (1998) *Native Americans at Mission Santa Cruz, 1791–1834: Interpreting the Archaeological Record*, Los Angeles: Institute of Archaeology, University of California, Los Angeles.

Ambro, R. and M. P. Holman (1997) 'Observations on Recent Archaeological Finds Associated with Mission San Francisco de Asis (Mission Dolores), San Francisco', paper presented at the Society for California Archaeology 31st Annual Meeting, Rohnert Park.

Asisara, L. (1989) 'The Assassination of Padre Andres Quintana by the Indians of Mission Santa Cruz in 1812: The Narrative of Lorenzo Asisara', E. D. Castillo (trans.), *California History* 68, 3: 116–26.

Barker, L. R., R. Allen and J. G. Costello (1995) 'The Archaeology of Spanish and Mexican Alta California', in J. E. Ayres (ed.) *The Archaeology of Spanish and Mexican Colonialism in the American South-west*, Ann Arbor: The Society for Historical Archaeology.

Barrett, S. A. and E. W. Gifford (1971 [1933]) 'Miwok Houses', in R. F. Heizer and M. A. Whipple (eds) *The California Indians: A Sourcebook*, Berkeley: University of California Press.

Beilharz, E. A. (1971) *Felipe de Neve: First Governor of California*, San Francisco: California Historical Society.

Bickel, P. M. (1976) 'Toward a Prehistory of the San Francisco Bay area: The Archaeology of Sites Ala-328, Ala-13, and Ala-12', Ph.D. dissertation, Harvard University.

Bleys, R. C. (1995) *The Geography of Perversion: Male-to-Male Sexual Behavior Outside the West and the Ethnographic Imagination, 1750–1918*, New York: New York University Press.

Bocek, B. (1991) 'Prehistoric Settlement Pattern and Social Organization on the San Francisco Peninsula, California', in S. A. Gregg (ed.) *Between Bands and States*, Carbondale: Center for Archaeological Investigations, Occasional Paper No. 9, Southern Illinois University.

Bourdieu, P. (1977) *Outline of a Theory of Practice*, Cambridge: Cambridge University Press.

Bouvier, V. M. (1995) 'Women, Conquest, and the Production of History: Hispanic California, 1542–1840', Ph.D. dissertation, University of California, Berkeley.

Brady, V., S. Crome and L. Reese (1984) 'Resist! Survival Tactics of Indian Women', *California History* 68, 2: 140–51.

Bynum, V. E. (1992) *Unruly Women: The Politics of Social and Sexual Control in the Old South*, Chapel Hill: University of North Carolina Press.

Castañeda, A. I. (1988) 'Comparative Frontiers: The Migration of Women to Alta California and New Zealand', in L. Schliessel, V. Ruiz and J. Monk (eds) *Western Women: Their Land, Their Lives*, Albuquerque: University of New Mexico Press.

—— (1992) 'Presidarias y Pobladoras: The Journey North and Life in Frontier California', *Renato Rosaldo Lecture Series Monograph* 8: 25–54.

—— (1993a) 'Marriage: The Spanish Borderlands', in J. E. Cook (ed.) *Encyclopedia of the North American Colonies*, New York: Maxwell Macmillan International.

—— (1993b) 'Sexual Violence in the Politics and Policies of Conquest: Amerindian Women and the Spanish Conquest of Alta California', in A. de la Torre and B. M. Pesquera (eds) *Building With Our Hands: New Directions in Chicana Studies*, Berkeley and Los Angeles: University of California Press.

—— (1998) 'Engendering the History of Alta California, 1769–1848', in R. A. Gutiérrez and R. J. Orsi (eds) *Contested Eden: California before the Gold Rush*, Berkeley and Los Angeles: University of California Press.

Castillo, E. D. (1989) '"Editor's Introduction" to The Assassination of Padre Andres Quintana by the Indians of Mission Santa Cruz in 1812: The Narrative of Lorenzo Asisara', *California History* 68, 3: 117–19.

—— (1994a) 'The Language of Race Hatred', in L. J. Bean (ed.) *The Ohlone Past and Present: Native Americans of the San Francisco Bay Region*, Menlo Park, CA: Ballena Press.

—— (1994b) 'Gender Status Decline, Resistance, and Accommodation among Female Neophytes in the Missions of California: A San Gabriel Case Study', *American Indian Culture and Research Journal* 18, 1: 67–93.

Chartkoff, J. L. and Chartkoff, K. K. (1984) *The Archaeology of California*, Stanford: Stanford University Press.

Colomina, B. (ed.) (1992) *Sexuality and Space*, Princeton: Princeton Architectural Press.

Conkey, M. W. and J. M. Gero (1991) 'Tensions, Pluralities, and Engendering Archaeology: An Introduction to Women and Prehistory', in J. M. Gero and M. W. Conkey (eds) *Engendering Archaeology: Women and Prehistory*, Cambridge, MA: Basil Blackwell.

Conkey, M. W. and R. E. Tringham (1995) Archaeology and the Goddess: Exploring the Contours of Feminist Archaeology, in D. C. Stanton and A. J. Stewart (eds) *Feminisms in the Academy*, Ann Arbor: University of Michigan Press.

Cook, S. F. (1943) *The Conflict Between the California Indian and White Civilization*, Berkeley and Los Angeles: University of California Press.

Costanso, M. (1992 [1769]) *Diario del viege de tierra hecho al norte de la California*, Lafayette, CA: Great West Books.

Costello, J. G. (1992) 'Not Peas in a Pod: Documenting Diversity among the California Missions', in B. J. Little (ed.) *Text-Aided Archaeology*, Boca Raton: CRC Press.

Costello, J. G. and J. Gasco, (1985) *Test Excavations in Ten Rooms of the Santa Inés Mission Quadrangle*, Berkeley: Social Process Research Institute, University of California.

Costello, J. G. and D. Hornbeck (1989) 'Alta California: An Overview', in D. H. Thomas (ed.) *Archaeological and Historical Perspectives of the Spanish Borderlands West*, Washington, DC: Smithsonian Institution Press.

Cream, J. (1993) 'Child Sexual Abuse and the Symbolic Geographies of Cleveland', *Environment and Planning D: Society and Space* 11: 231–46.

Dangerous Bedfellows (eds) (1996) *Policing Public Sex: Queer Politics and the Future of AIDS Activism*, Boston: South End Press.

de Erauso, C. (1996) *Lieutenant Nun: Memoir of a Basque Transvestite in the New World*, M. Stepto and G. Stepto (trans.), Boston: Beacon Press.

D'Emilio, J. (1983) *Sexual Politics, Sexual Communities: The Making of a Homosexual Minority in the United States, 1940–1970*, Chicago: The University of Chicago Press.

D'Emilio, J. and E. B. Freedman (1988) *Intimate Matters: A History of Sexuality in America*, New York: Harper and Row.

Duggan, L. and N. D. Hunter (eds) (1995) *Sex Wars: Sexual Dissent and Political Culture*, New York: Routledge.

Duncan, N. (1996) 'Renegotiating Gender and Sexuality in Public and Private Spaces', in N. Duncan (ed.) *Bodyspace: Destabilizing Geographies of Gender and Sexuality*, London: Routledge.

Engelhardt, Z. (1908–1915) *The Missions and Missionaries of California, Vols I–IV*, San Francisco: James H. Barry.

Enloe, C. (1990) *Bananas, Beaches, and Bases: Making Feminist Sense of International Politics*, Berkeley: University of California Press.

—— (1993) *The Morning After: Sexual Politics at the End of the Cold War*, Berkeley: University of California Press.

Felton, D. L. (1987) *Santa Cruz Mission State Historical Park Architectural and Archeological Investigations 1984–1985*, Sacramento: California Department of Parks and Recreation.

Fentress, J. (1994) 'Prehistoric Rock Art of Alameda and Contra Costa Counties', in L. J. Bean (ed.) *The Ohlone Past and Present: Native Americans of the San Francisco Bay Region*, Menlo Park, CA: Ballena Press.

Field, L., A. Leventhal, D. Sanchez and R. Cambra (1992) 'A Contemporary Ohlone Tribal Revitalization Movement: A Perspective from the Muwekma Costanoan/Ohlone Indians of the San Francisco Bay area', *California History* 71, 3: 412–32.

Forbes, J. D. (1983) 'Hispano-Mexican Pioneers of the San Francisco Bay Region: An Analysis of Racial Origins', *Aztlan* 14, Spring: 175–89.

Foucault, M. (1975) *Discipline and Punish: The Birth of the Prison*, New York: Vintage Books.

—— (1978) *The History of Sexuality, Volume I: An Introduction*, New York: Vintage Books.

Fuller, D. L. (1983) 'Missions, Presidios, and Pueblos, 1769–1823' (map) in D. Hornbeck and P. Kane, *California Patterns: A Geographical and Historical Atlas*, Palo Alto, CA: Mayfield Publishing Company.

Gilchrist, R. (1994) *Gender and Material Culture: The Archaeology of Religious Women*, New York: Routledge.

Gillette, D. (1996) 'Revisiting the Stege Mounds in Richmond', paper presented at the Society for California Archaeology 31st Annual Meeting, Rohnert Park.

Gonzalez, M. J. (1998) '"The Child of the Wilderness Weeps for the Father of Our Country": The Indian and the Politics of Church and State in Provincial California', in R. A. Gutiérrez and R. J. Orsi (eds) *Contested Eden: California before the Gold Rush*, Berkeley and Los Angeles: University of California Press.

Guest, F. F. (1989) 'An Inquiry into the Role of the Discipline in California Mission Life', *Southern California Quarterly* 71, Spring: 7.

—— (1996) *Hispanic California Revisited: Essays by Francis F. Guest, O. F. M.*, D. B. Nunis, Jr (ed.), Santa Barbara: Santa Barbara Mission Archive Library.

Gutiérrez, R. A. (1991) *When Jesus Came, the Corn Mothers Went Away: Marriage, Sexuality, and Power in New Mexico, 1500–1846*, Stanford: Stanford University Press.
—— (1993) 'Sexual Mores and Behavior: The Spanish Borderlands', in J.E. Cook (ed.) *Encyclopedia of the North American Colonies*, New York: Maxwell Macmillan International.
Hageman, F. C. (1938) 'Sketch Plan of an Ultimate Development, Mission La Purísima Concepción State Historical Monument, Lompoc', MS on file at University of California, Berkeley Library Map Collection.
—— (1939) *An Architectural Study of the Mission La Purisima Concepcion, California, January 1935 to April 1938*, National Park Service, United States Department of the Interior.
Hageman, F. C. and Ewing, R. C. (1991) *An Archaeological and Restoration Study of Mission La Purísima Concepción: Reports Written for the National Park Service by Fred C. Hageman and Russell C. Ewing*, Santa Barbara: Santa Barbara Trust for Historic Preservation.
Heizer, R. F. (ed.) (1978) *California*, Washington, DC: Smithsonian Institution.
Heizer, R. F. and A. B. Elsasser (1980) *The Natural World of the California Indians*, Berkeley: California Natural History Guides, University of California Press.
Hodder, I. (1991) *Reading the Past*, Cambridge: Cambridge University Press.
Hurtado, A. L. (1988) *Indian Survival on the California Frontier*, New Haven: Yale University Press.
—— (1992) 'Sexuality in California's Franciscan Missions: Central Perceptions and Sad Realities', *California History* 71, 3: 370–86.
Jackson, R. H. and E. Castillo (1995) *Indians, Franciscans, and Spanish Colonization*, Albuquerque: University of New Mexico Press.
Jackson, T. L. (1991) 'Pounding Acorn: Women's Production as Social and Economic Focus', in J. M. Gero and M. W. Conkey (eds) *Engendering Archaeology: Women and Prehistory*, Cambridge, MA: Basil Blackwell.
Johnson, P. J. (1978) 'Patwin', in R. F. Heizer (ed.) *California*, Washington, DC: Smithsonian Institution.
Kelly, I. (1978) 'Coast Miwok', in R. F. Heizer (ed.) *California*, Washington, DC: Smithsonian Institution.
Kimbro, E. E. (1987) *Historical Research of Architectural Details*, Santa Cruz: Gilbert Arnold Sanchez Architects, Inc.
—— (1988) *Furnishing Plan for the Santa Cruz Mission Adobe, Santa Cruz Mission State Historic Park, Santa Cruz, California*, Sacramento: California Department of Parks and Recreation.
Kimbro, E. E., M. Ryan, R. H. Jackson, R. T. Milliken and N. Neuerburg (1985) '*Como la sombra huye la hora*': Restoration Research, Santa Cruz Mission Adobe, Santa Cruz Mission State Historic Park*, Sacramento: Cultural Resource Support Unit, Department of Parks and Recreation.
King, C. (1994) 'Central Ohlone Ethnohistory', in L. J. Bean (ed.) *The Ohlone Past and Present: Native Americans of the San Francisco Bay Region*, Menlo Park, CA: Ballena Press.
Kroeber, A. L. (1925) *Handbook of the Indians of California*, Washington, DC: Smithsonian Institution Bureau of American Ethnology, Government Printing Office.
Levy, R. (1978) 'Costanoan', in R. F. Heizer (ed.) *California*, Washington, DC: Smithsonian Institution.
Librado, F. (1979) *Breath of the Sun: Life in Early California as Told by a Chumash Indian, Fernando Librado, to John P. Harrington, and Edited with Notes by Travis Hudson*, Banning, CA: Malki Museum Press and the Ventura County Historical Society.
Lightfoot, K. G. (1995) 'Culture Contact Studies: Redefining the Relationship between Prehistoric and Historical Archaeology', *American Antiquity* 60, 2: 119–217.
Linden, R. R., D. R. Pagano, D. E. H. Russell and S. L. Star (eds) (1982) *Against Sadomasochism: A Radical Feminist Analysis*, East Palo Alto, California: Frog In The Well Press.
McClintock, A. (1995) *Imperial Leather: Race, Gender, and Sexuality in the Colonial Conquest*, New York: Routledge.
Margolin, M. (1978) *The Ohlone Way: Indian Life in the San Francisco-Monterey Bay Area*, Berkeley: Heyday Books.

Markus, T. A. (1993) *Buildings and Power: Freedom and Control in the Origin of Modern Building Types*, London: Routledge.

Milliken, R. (1995) *A Time of Little Choice*, Menlo Park, CA: Ballena Press.

Moore, H. L. (1986) *Space, Text, and Gender*, Cambridge: Cambridge University Press.

Monroy, D. (1990) *Thrown Among Strangers: The Making of Mexican Culture in Frontier California*, Berkeley and Los Angeles: University of California Press.

Moratto, M. J. (1984) *California Archaeology*, Orlando: Academic Press, Inc.

Nelson, N. C. (1909) 'Shellmounds of the San Francisco Bay Region', *University of California Publications in American Archaeology and Ethnology* 7, 4: 310–46.

Ortiz, B. R. (1994) 'Chocheno and Rumsen Narratives: A Comparison', in L. J. Bean (ed.) *The Ohlone Past and Present: Native Americans of the San Francisco Bay Region*, Menlo Park, CA: Ballena Press.

Riley, G. (1984) *Women and Indians on the Frontier, 1825–1915*, Albuquerque: University of New Mexico Press.

Roscoe, W. (1991) *The Zuni Man-Woman*, Albuquerque: University of New Mexico Press.

—— (1998) *Changing Ones: Third and Fourth Genders in Native North America*, New York: Saint Martin's Press.

Rosen, R. (1982) *The Lost Sisterhood: Prostitution in America, 1900–1918*, Baltimore: The Johns Hopkins University Press.

Rubin, G. (1984) 'Thinking Sex: Notes for a Radical Theory of the Politics of Sexuality', in C. S. Vance (ed.) *Pleasure and Danger: Exploring Female Sexuality*, London: Pandora.

—— (1994) 'Sexual Traffic: An Interview with Judith Butler', *Differences: A Journal of Feminist Cultural Studies* 6, 2 and 3: 62–99.

SAMOIS (ed.) (1982) *Coming to Power: Writings and Graphics on Lesbian S/M*, Boston: Alyson Publications.

Sandos, J. A. (1998) 'Between Crucifix and Lance: Indian–White Relations in California, 1769–1848', in R. A. Gutiérrez and R. J. Orsi (eds) *Contested Eden: California before the Gold Rush*, Berkeley and Los Angeles: University of California Press.

Schenck, W. E. (n.d.) 'The Emeryville Shellmound Final Report', *University of California Publications in American Archaeology and Ethnography* 23, 3: 150–282.

Simmons, W. S. (1998) 'Indian Peoples of California', in R. A. Gutiérrez and R. J. Orsi (eds) *Contested Eden: California before the Gold Rush*, Berkeley and Los Angeles: University of California Press.

Skowronek, K. (1998) 'Sifting the Evidence: Perceptions of Life at Ohlone (Costanoan) Missions of Alta California', *Ethnohistory* 45, 4: 675–708.

Snitow, A., C. Stansell and S. Thompson (eds) (1983) *Powers of Desire: The Politics of Sexuality*, New York: Monthly Review Press.

Stoler, A. L. (1991) 'Carnal Knowledge, Imperial Power: Gender, Race, and Morality in Colonial Asia', in M. di Leonardo (ed.) *Gender at the Crossroads of Knowledge*, Berkeley: University of California Press.

—— (1997) 'Sexual Affronts and Racial Frontiers: European Identities and the Colonial Politics of Exclusion in Colonial Southeast Asia', in F. Cooper and A. L. Stoler (eds) *Tensions of Empire: Colonial Cultures in a Bourgeois World*, Berkeley: University of California Press.

Trexler, R. C. (1995) *Sex and Conquest: Gendered Violence, Political Order, and the European Conquest of the Americas*, Ithaca: Cornell University Press.

Tringham, R. E. (1991) 'Households with Faces: The Challenge of Gender in Prehistoric Architectural Remains', in J. M. Gero and M. W. Conkey (eds) *Engendering Archaeology: Women and Prehistory*, Cambridge, MA: Basil Blackwell, Inc.

Valentine, G. (1989) 'The Geography of Women's Fear', *Area* 21, 4: 385–90.

Vallejo, G. (1890) 'Ranch and Mission Days in Alta California', *Century Magazine* 41, 2: 186–87.

Vance, C. S. (ed.) (1984) *Pleasure and Danger: Exploring Female Sexuality*, New York: Routledge and Kegan Paul.

von Kotzebue, O. (1821) *Voyage of Discovery in the South Seas, and to the Bering Straits, in Search of a North-east Passage*, London: Sir Richard Phillips.

Voss, B. L. (in press) 'History, the Family, and Household Archaeologies', *Proceedings of the 1997 Chacmool Conference: The Entangled Past – Integrating History and Archaeology*, Calgary, Alberta: The University of Calgary Archaeological Association.

Voss, S. F. (1982) *On the Periphery of Nineteenth-century Mexico: Sonora and Sinaloa, 1810–1877*, Tucson: University of Arizona Press.

Webb, E. B. (1951) *The Mission Villages or Rancherias*, Sacramento: California Parks and Recreation Department, Resource Preservation and Interpretation Division Library.

—— (1952) *Indian Life in the Old Missions*, Los Angeles: Warren F. Lewis.

Weber, D. J. (1992) *The Spanish Frontier in North America*, New Haven: Yale University Press.

Whitehead, H. (1981) 'The Bow and the Burden Strap: A New Look at Institutionalized Homosexuality in Native North America', in S. Ortner and H. Whitehead (eds) *Sexual Meanings: The Cultural Construction of Gender and Sexuality*, Cambridge: Cambridge University Press.

Whitelaw, T. M. (1994) 'Order without Architecture: Functional, Social, and Symbolic Dimensions in Hunter-Gatherer Settlement Organization', in M. P. Pearson and C. Richards (eds) *Architecture and Order: Approaches to Social Space*, London and New York: Routledge.

Williams, W. L. (1986) *The Spirit and the Flesh: Sexual Diversity in American Indian Culture*, Boston: Beacon Press.

Wojcik, J. (1978) 'Key to Tribal Territories' (map) in R. F. Heizer (ed.) *Handbook of North American Indians, vol. 8: California*, Washington, DC: Smithsonian Insititution.

Chapter Three

Sites, settlements, and urban sex: archaeology and the study of gay leathermen in San Francisco, 1955–1995[1]

Gayle Rubin

We must then accept these 'moral regions' and the more or less eccentric and exceptional people who inhabit them, in a sense, at least, as part of the natural, if not the normal, life of a city. It is not necessary to understand by the expression 'moral region' a place or a society that is either necessarily criminal or abnormal. It is intended rather to apply to regions in which a divergent moral code prevails, because it is a region in which the people who inhabit it are dominated, as people are ordinarily not dominated, by a taste or by a passion or by some interest ... Because of the opportunity it offers, particularly to the exceptional and abnormal types of man, a great city tends to spread out and lay bare to the public view in a massive manner all the human characters or traits which are ordinarily obscured and suppressed in smaller communities.

Robert E. Park (Park and Burgess 1925: 45–46)

Du temps perdu

Archaeologists routinely utilize ethnographic studies to generate models of human social practice, and productive ways to think about archaeological data. It is far less common for cultural anthropologists to apply archaeological ideas or methods to the study of living populations. Moreover, since archaeology has not been generally known for much professional attention to the details of sexual conduct, ethnographic work on sexually defined communities in the contemporary United States might seem a rather improbable topic to have benefited from tactics borrowed from archaeologists. Nonetheless, my research on a subgroup of homosexual men in San Francisco was significantly shaped by my exposure to archaeology when I was a graduate student in cultural anthropology at the University of Michigan in the early 1970s.

That Michigan anthropology department was an intellectually thrilling place. As Timothy Earle recalls in his preface to *How Chiefs Come to Power*,

> At the University of Michigan in the early 1970s, my professors Kent Flannery, Richard Ford, Roy Rappaport, Marshall Sahlins, Eric Wolf, and Henry Wright taught me to understand the complex interactions among ecology, economy, society and politics. Archaeology graduate students at that time focused on what was to be labeled 'social archaeology' – how to describe the organization of prehistoric human groups and how to explain their social evolution. Prime-mover theories of social adaptation were attacked, as we grappled with the variety, complexity, and specificity of historical sequences from Oaxaca and the Valley of Mexico to Iran, Madagascar, and the Pacific.
>
> (Earle 1997: vii)

From the vantage point of today's more fragmented discipline, the Michigan department circa 1971 seems a paradise of interactivity among the sub-fields. I took courses from many of the same professors, participated in the same heady intellectual environment, and grappled with many of the same questions described by Earle. Yet even then, there was some segregation between socio-cultural anthropology and archaeology. This emergent division was often expressed in geographic terms as a difference between Angell Hall, where the cultural folk had offices and held classes, and the Museum, which was located at the opposite end of the main quadrangle and housed the archaeology labs and classrooms.

However, we graduate students had the luxury of learning from everyone and absorbing ideas from all the various perspectives and approaches. We were still required to take at least one course in each of the four sub-fields. My fascination with archaeology and the quality of the archaeology faculty led me to exceed these requirements. I learned about Mesoamerican and Near Eastern Prehistory from Kent Flannery, Andean Civilizations from Jeff Parsons, and followed up with Henry Wright's seminar on State Formation. These courses and the conversations they generated among my fellow graduate students had a profound, if unlikely, impact on my eventual dissertation topic and subsequent research on San Francisco's gay leathermen.

It would be difficult to understand why this came about without some sense of the state of social science research on gay and lesbian topics at the time. I entered the graduate program in the fall of 1971. This was long before the current deluge of work in queer theory, or in gay, lesbian, bisexual and transgender studies. Outside of medicine and psychiatry, scholarship on such topics was scarce and not readily accessible. I was interested in figuring out some way to study homosexuality, and was especially curious about how homosexuals became concentrated in particular locations, such as Greenwich Village, Provincetown, or Fire Island. Such questions were not easily addressable within the anthropology of the early 1970s. Many hours in the library revealed some serious gaps in the organization of ethnographic interest in homosexual populations.

There was a substantial literature on same-sex contact or cross-gender behavior in non-urban and non-Western societies, particularly in New Guinea and other cultures of the Pacific, among indigenous populations of North America, and in some societies, for example in Africa, where property could occasionally trump anatomy in demarcating sexual or gender roles (Williams 1936; Kelly 1976; Herdt 1981; Evans-Pritchard 1970; Herskovitz 1937; Devereaux 1937; McMurtrie 1914). There was also a tiny but extremely significant literature on the ethnography of urban gay communities in contemporary North America, but most of this was in sociology.[2]

There were two major compendia then available on the anthropology of sexuality, Ford and Beach's *Patterns of Sexual Behavior* (1951), and Marshall and Suggs' *Human Sexual*

Behavior (1971). Ford and Beach were far more tolerant of sexual variety, but their data were largely concerned with traditional societies and they did not appear aware of or interested in organized communities of homosexuals in the United States or other Western societies. By contrast, Marshall and Suggs discussed such gay communities. They noted, 'some homosexuals congregate or regularly visit for residence or recreation specific districts that have shown more tolerance for deviant behavior . . .' and that 'some Western homosexuals have developed entire subcultures, with their own patterned behavior' (1971: 234). However, they went on to state,

> Just as the homosexual advertisements in the *Berkeley Barb* appear with those of the voyeur, the sadist, the masochist, and the fetishist, so it is difficult to interpret such behavioral manifestations as the 'fairy balls', or the transvestite 'beauty contests' of some urban areas as anything more exalted than sociopathic manifestations of personality disturbances *complicated by membership in a pervasive subculture.*
>
> (235; emphasis in the original)

Furthermore, 'medical and psychiatric data together with interpretations by some analysts and by logic indicate that some contemporary Western sexual deviants must be regarded as socially and personally maladjusted, in some cases so very ill as to endanger society' (231). Such comments reflected the prevailing view of homosexuality as a problem better addressed by psychiatry than by anthropology.

In a 1966 essay 'Homosexuality as a Subject of Anthropological Inquiry', David Sonenschein urged anthropologists to study homosexual communities in industrialized countries. 'Among humans,' he noted, 'at least in the Western Urban tradition, homosexual behavior manifests itself in special kinds of culturally distinct groups and artifacts' (1966: 80). Observing that 'anthropologists have ignored homosexuality in Western societies . . .' Sonenschein called for

> the application of an anthropological investigation of homosexuality in contemporary Western society . . . the anthropological approach assumes that homosexual groups and individuals transmit, learn, share, create, and change the content of various forms (such as speech, dress, behavior, artifacts) so as to establish and maintain what can be called a relatively distinct 'culture'. . . . Here, all the interests of cultural and social anthropologists would prevail: social organization, economics, communication, social control and norms, world-views and myths, demography, social and cultural change, material culture, enculturation and socialization . . .
>
> (1966: 77)

It was over thirty years ago that David Sonenschein set out a research program for the anthropological study of homosexuality in contemporary complex, urban societies. With one exception, Esther Newton's *Mother Camp* (1972), hardly anyone was pursuing this research agenda. *Mother Camp* focused on the specialized subgroup of professional female impersonators. In this extraordinary book, Newton's observations of gay community life, social structure, and economics were insightful, original, and provocative. However, for many years, *Mother Camp* stood alone, an exceptional document with no apparent successors or company. Almost a decade passed before more ethnographic work on modern homosexualities began to emerge, and almost two decades before there would be much of an anthropological literature on urban gay communities in the United States (Davis and Whitten 1987; Kennedy and Davis 1993; Lewin 1993; Lewin and Leap 1996; Newton 1993; Weston 1991, 1993).

The scarcity of work on homosexuality is not solely attributable to anti-gay sentiment, although I would not want to underestimate the power of such prejudices. However, the liabilities of doing specifically homosexual research were compounded by several other impedimenta, including the 'sex' problem, the 'North American' problem, and the 'urban' problem. Any research that focused too closely on sexuality was considered somewhat suspect, and some ethnographers even admitted to having data in their field notes which they never published for fear of professional marginalization.

Moreover, there was very little support for doing any research in urban North America apart from studies of ethnic communities or populations of foreign migrants. There are now so many anthropologists working on contemporary urban groups in Western societies that it is sometimes difficult to remember an older hierarchy of anthropological status: thirty years ago, one was often given the impression that 'real anthropologists' studied non-Western and pre-industrial peoples, preferably in some place entirely lacking in electricity or plumbing. Those who studied peasants in Europe, Latin America, or the Near East, could be accepted, if sometimes grudgingly. On the other hand, urbanists were, if not beneath contempt, perhaps latent sociologists.

There were of course long and respected traditions of urban ethnography in sociology, particularly associated with the Chicago school sociologists and their progeny (Bulmer 1984; Fine 1995; Becker 1964, 1973; see also note 4). There were also some anthropologists, such as David Schneider at Chicago, who actively encouraged students to study urban groups.[3] But this was not the case at Michigan. We were blessed with an extraordinary collection of brilliant cultural anthropologists, from whom I was extremely lucky to learn social theory and the passions of ethnographic description. However, they were for the most part disinterested in urban problems, urban theory, or urban research. Virtually all my graduate exposure to thinking about urban societies and how to study them came from two sources: sociologist and historian Charles Tilly, particularly his course on European Urbanization, and the archaeologists.

As it turned out, many of my archaeology professors were vitally interested in urbanism and the role of cities in complex social formations. The archaeologists had to think about cities, albeit ancient and often dead ones. But they knew urban theory and urban geography, and they creatively applied the concepts and methods of those fields to the understanding of ancient cities. They asked what kinds of conditions would facilitate such concentrations of people and resources, and speculated about what impact these places would have had on their surrounding countrysides. Urban theory works as well for Ninevah, Ur, Eridu, Monte Alban, Tenochtitlan, or Cuzco as it does for London, Paris, Berlin, Chicago, or New York. For obvious reasons, archaeological thought was also very spatially focused. Archaeologists were concerned with how space is organized socially, how social relations are reflected spatially, and what spatial arrangements can convey about social ones.

So it was from the archaeologists that I first encountered urban geography, central place theory, settlement patterns, catchment areas, population estimates, migrations and transfers of population, craft wards and occupational or residential specialization. I could not help but think about how these pertained to issues of urbanism and minority sexualities. Clearly, market centers can function for sexuality as well as for grains and vegetables; neighborhood specialization can be as evident for homosexuals or sex workers as for potters or weavers; and regional centers can draw migrants for sexual as well as occupational purposes.

From Charles Tilly I was encouraged to think about the ways urban structure and various forms of political action and mobilization affect one another. It was only years later that I realized that through Tilly and the archaeology faculty, I had been exposed to a refined precipitate of several decades of sophisticated thought about cities, politics, and social structure, which I could then use to think about a different set of problems.[4] I was eventually able to apply these perspectives to my field work among the gay male leather population in San Francisco.

GAY LEATHERMEN AND SOUTH OF MARKET

Leather

'Leather' is a term for a distinctive subgroup of male homosexuals who began to coalesce into coherent communities in the late 1940s. Leather communities appeared first in the major cities of the United States, and later developed in other urban centers and in most industrialized capitalist countries.[5] The leather subculture is organized around sexual activities and erotic semiotics that distinguish it from the larger gay male population.

Leather in this context mostly refers to black leather motorcycle gear. One may easily visualize the imagery of early leather by picturing Marlon Brando in the 1954 film *The*

Figure 3.1 The leather look: portrait of Tony Tavorossi, manager of San Francisco's first leather bar, taken in San Francisco, 1960.
Photograph by permission of R. Michael Photography.

Wild One, wearing jeans, engineer boots, t-shirt, biker jacket, heavy belt, and a Harley cap. 'Leather' was often merged with another category: 'leather/Levi.' In practice pretty much any masculine, working-class attire was acceptable. These modes of dress and their attendant symbolisms came to serve as a marker for a kind of community, a collection of sexual practices, and a set of values and attitudes. In the period after World War II, homosexuals were presumed to be effeminate – fairies, pansies, and queens. Gay men who were masculine in their personal style, and especially those who wanted other masculine men as partners, began to carve out alternative gay social spaces. Many of these men rode motorcycles or wore motorcycle attire (Figure 3.1). As one man later explained to me, 'The motorcycle was the symbol of homosexual masculinity' (Jim Kane interview 1979).

The late 1940s and early 1950s were a formative period, when such men began to congregate with increasing frequency and in greater numbers through private parties and informal networks. These networks achieved a new level of institutional coherence by the mid-1950s with the emergence of leather bars and gay motorcycle clubs. These 'leather' bars were contrasted to 'sweater' bars, a nickname for the establishments which catered to an ostensibly more swishy set. The leather bars and bike clubs were the major institutions of the early 'classic' leather community (Baldwin 1993; Rubin 1994; M. Thompson 1991; Bean 1994).

The leather communities also became the major symbolic and social location in the gay male world for various kinds of 'kinky sex'. By 'kinky sex' I mean primarily activities such as sadomasochism (SM), bondage and discipline, and fetishism. Among gay men, the social organization of sexual sadomasochism and fetishism is generally structured by the idioms of leather and the institutions of leather communities.

Gay male leather, with its singular concatenation of desires, symbolisms, and institutional structures, has been an effective vehicle for establishing sexual identities and communities. In addition, urban gay men tend to be territorial, and leathermen even more so. In New York, for example, most leather sites were located in lower Manhattan along the West Side dock strip or in the nearby meat-packing district. In San Francisco, they have been heavily concentrated in a district called South of Market.

South of Market

> . . . this district represents the most comprehensive paradigm of San Francisco. More than any other neighborhood in the city, South of Market is the part that contains the whole: the one matrix that subsumes unto itself every successive layer of urban identity in the history of the city.
>
> (Starr 1995–6: 370)

Market Street is one of the primary corridors of San Francisco (Figure 3.2). It cuts a sharp diagonal across the city from the Ferry Building to the base of Twin Peaks. The trolley rails along Market Street have long marked a physical and psychological boundary (the Slot) between the area North of Market, where the local centers of political and commercial power are situated, and the predominantly poor and working class area 'South of the Slot' (Averbach 1973; Clark 1987).

South of Market is also one of the oldest, largest, and most diverse neighborhoods in San Francisco (Bloomfield 1995–6; Averbach 1973; Issel and Cherney 1986; Shumate 1988). First settled during the Gold Rush, South of Market has had a predominantly industrial and working-class character since the late nineteenth century. Most of San Francisco's early industries were located here, including iron foundries, boiler works, machine shops,

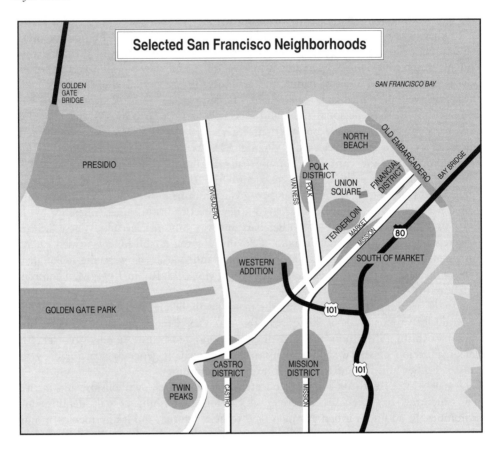

Figure 3.2 Selected San Francisco neighborhoods.
Map by the author.

manufacturers of bullets and shot, breweries, and warehouses. The wharves South of Market were a focus for shipping and shipbuilding. With a few exceptions, the residential population worked in these industries or in other nearby commercial enterprises.

After it was leveled in the 1906 earthquake and fire, South of Market was rebuilt as

> part of San Francisco's commercial downtown. The South of Market, however, did not match North of Market in uses. Here there were no major department stores, fashionable boutiques, banks, or except for the Palace, leading hotels. The owners did not anticipate such high-rent tenants and they built accordingly.
>
> (Bloomfield 1995–1996: 387)

Most of the labor-force that rebuilt San Francisco lived South of Market and much of the housing constructed there after the quake consisted of residential hotels designed to accommodate a population of single, often transient, working men. The proximity to the waterfront and the shipping industry meant that seamen and dockworkers also comprised a good portion of the residential population. World War II brought new populations, especially Chicano, black, and Filipino workers (Averbach 1973: 215). While the ethnic composition of the transient poor changed, the general character of the neighborhood remained relatively stable from the aftermath of the earthquake until the 1950s.

Redevelopment

> This land is too valuable to permit poor people to park on it.
>
> Justin Herman, Executive Director, San Francisco Redevelopment Agency, 1970
> (Hartman 1974: 19)

Dreams of urban renewal promised cleaner, more livable and more prosperous cities to post-war urban planners. In practice, redevelopment throughout San Francisco has often eliminated the areas of low-cost housing occupied by poor and working people, and replaced light industry and wholesale commerce with fancy offices, hotels, restaurants, and convention centers. South of Market was not exempt from this trend, and large sections of the area were approved for redevelopment by the San Francisco Board of Supervisors in 1953.[6] But redevelopment in South of Market did not proceed smoothly or quickly. While final plans for land acquisition and relocation of existing residents were approved in 1966 (Hoover 1979: ix), in 1969 local residents and owners formed an organization opposed to redevelopment and filed the first of many lawsuits which delayed redevelopment and reshaped its ultimate manifestations. During the period of political and legal wrangling, the old neighborhood was significantly dismantled. Housing was demolished and entire streets disappeared. But the construction of new office towers and public buildings awaited the outcome of litigation, so the new neighborhood remained largely unrealized. The hiatus in redevelopment created a vacant or underused urban niche with plenty of empty buildings, both residential and commercial. Rents and land values were cheap. Street life at night was sparse. South of Market became a kind of urban frontier.

The area began to attract artists looking for affordable studio space, musicians in search of practice venues, squatters who occupied the abandoned factories, and gay men. The relative lack of other night-time activity provided a kind of privacy, and urban nightlife that was stigmatized or considered disreputable could flourish in relative obscurity among the warehouses and deserted streets.

Shifting geographies of gay sex

A critical aspect of my research was examining what might, in archaeological language, be termed the 'settlement pattern' of gay sex, especially leather sex, in San Francisco. Tracing the shifting locations of gay sex over time revealed the complex interconnections between the implementation of urban development and redevelopment policies and the geography of gay subcultures, including leathermen.

There had certainly been men engaging in homosexual activities in the old South of Market since its inception as an urban residential and commercial area. A common pattern in which male homosexuals had relationships with masculine 'trade' (i.e. straight-identified men who performed only insertive sex acts) has been well documented in other waterfront and working-class enclaves in late nineteenth- and early twentieth-century US cities (Chauncey 1985, 1994; Corzine and Kirby 1977; Troiden 1974). Research by Allan Berube shows the extent to which gay life in New York and San Francisco overlapped and intermixed with the world of sailors and merchant seamen (1993). San Francisco's Embarcadero was known as a 'tough' gay male cruising area at least as far back as the 1920s (Berube 1993 and personal communication). Berube's research shows that there were also many homosexual seamen who were well integrated into the working-class culture that once dominated the neighborhood. He writes, '. . . before the 1960s, [there] were hundreds of cheap hotels, taverns, lunch rooms, cafeterias, union halls, and the YMCA where maritime and waterfront workers and servicemen hung out and interacted with others outside their worlds.' Berube goes on to explain that these homosexual aspects of waterfront culture 'often attracted gay men from other parts of the city' (Berube 1993: 10–11). These waterfront bars declined, however, in the 1950s and early 1960s as a result of police crackdowns and development of the Embarcadero Center, a massive complex of hotels, office towers, and retail shops (D'Emilio 1983: 182–185; Paul Gabriel personal communication 1997).

As gay sites were driven out of the lower Market and Waterfront, gay occupation increased in the Tenderloin and Polk areas (Willie Walker and Paul Gabriel personal communications 1997; Garber and Walker 1997; Walker 1997). Similarly, the gay presence South of Market shifted westward. It was during the course of the 1960s that the Polk and the Folsom became densely and visibly gay.

Before the emergence of the Castro in the 1970s, the Polk and Tenderloin were the major gay areas of San Francisco. Polk Street became a commercial center. Its variegated gay economy included gay bars and baths, shops that provided gay or sex-related items, and many gay-owned shops which dispensed less specialized goods and services ranging from groceries to antiques. The territories of male hustlers, drag queens, and transsexual sex workers spanned the lower Polk and the adjacent Tenderloin. The Folsom and South of Market drew a different population, the leather crowd. The gay men who began to filter into South of Market in the 1960s were predominantly 'leathermen'.

Folsom Street: The Miracle Mile

> This is the city's backyard . . . An early morning walk will take a visitor past dozens of small business manufacturing necessities; metal benders, plastic molders, even casket makers can all be seen plying their trades. At five they set down their tools and return to the suburbs . . . A few hours later, men in black leather . . . will step out on these same streets to fill the nearly 30 gay bars, restaurants and sex clubs in the immediate vicinity. Separate realities that seldom touch and, on the surface at least, have few qualms about each other.
>
> (M. Thompson 1982: 28)

In San Francisco, leather has been most closely associated with the South of Market neighborhood since 1962, when the Tool Box opened on the corner of Fourth Street and Harrison (see Figure 3.3). In 1964, when *Life* magazine did a story on homosexuality in America, a photograph of the Tool Box interior was spread across the two opening pages (Welch and Eppridge 1964; Fritscher 1991). Despite its enormous fame, the popularity of the Tool Box was short lived. By 1965, it had competition from the Detour and On the Levee, and by 1966, Febe's opened and became the leading leather bar.

The leather scene moved to what would become its Main Street when Febe's and the Stud opened up at the western end of Folsom Street. This inaugurated the era when Folsom became known as the 'Miracle Mile'. The Ramrod, the In Between, and several other bars soon opened along a three-block strip of Folsom Street, establishing a core area that anchored a burgeoning leather economy which continued to develop and expand in the 1970s. By the late 1970s, South of Market had become one of the most extensive and densely occupied leather neighborhoods in the world (Jay 1976; Rubin 1991, 1994, 1997, 1998; M. Thompson 1982; 'San Francisco Gay Life Where It's At' 1977).

By the late 1970s, the Castro was unquestionably the center of local gay politics, but the Folsom had become the sexual center. The same features that made the area attractive to leather bars made it hospitable to other forms of gay sexual commerce. Many of the non-leather gay bathhouses and sex clubs also nestled among the warehouses. South of Market had become symbolically and institutionally associated in the gay male community with sex.

The years between 1966 and 1982 were a period of triumphant expansion for the gay male leather community South of Market. But by the mid-1980s, both neighborhood and community were devastated. By 1987, the institutional infrastructure of leather had undergone substantial attrition, and the South of Market had become a case study in urban succession. Instead of the hordes of gay men en route to the baths and leathermen on the prowl, the Folsom was suddenly filled with the mostly non-gay, non-leather, and evidently heterosexual patrons of the new eateries and music halls (Bean 1988). As an anonymous contributor to the *New York Times* opined:

> Once the rough threatening preserve of welders, wholesalers, butcher supply houses, winos, struggling artists and gay men who dressed in black leather motorcycle outfits and metal studs, Soma [South of Market] has suddenly become fashionable . . . Now the streets are lined with shiny BMWs and Mercedes . . .
>
> ('Off-Beat Rough Toward Chic Very Fine' 1988)

The visible changes in the neighborhood occasioned dozens of articles in the local and even national press celebrating the area's sudden respectability and trendy 'renaissance' (Saroyan 1989). Because many people assumed that AIDS mortality was higher among leathermen than in the general gay population, most commentaries cited AIDS as the cause of South of Market's demographic shifts (Evans 1982; 'The Death of Leather' 1985; Knapp 1983; Robinson 1984; Starkey 1983; T. Smith 1983). However, there are no hard data demonstrating such differential AIDS mortality among gay sexual subpopulations. The belief in greater AIDS mortality for leathermen is unsupported and probably unwarranted; the effects of AIDS on the leather community have been mediated through other factors. The displacement of gay leather South of Market resulted from geographic competition for the area that long preceded AIDS, and from public policy decisions about disease control, as much as it did from AIDS itself (Brandt 1985, 1988; Crimp 1988; Farmer 1992; Fee and Fox 1988, 1992; Levine et al. 1997; Nardi 1988; Patton 1985, 1990; Treichler 1988).

An acrimonious campaign in the early 1980s to close San Francisco's bathhouses and gay sex clubs disproportionately affected the South of Market area, as most of the local sex establishments were closed either by owner initiative or city action between 1983 and 1987. Whether or not bathhouse closures had any appreciable impact on slowing the epidemic is debatable. However, the campaign for closure did result in significant damage to the gay economy South of Market. The combination of abrupt bathhouse closures and pre-existing damage from urban renewal were significant factors in the startling collapse of gay South of Market in the mid-1980s.

In addition to the AIDS-related bathouse closures, redevelopment of the South of Market area had suddenly escalated in the late 1970s after Diane Feinstein became mayor. Feinstein's friendly stance toward development was reflected in an unprecedented building boom and in a marked increase in the pace of 'urban renewal' South of Market. Leather bars in old Victorian houses were not suited to compete with new high-rise, high-rent buildings or even the mid-level eateries and other enterprises that would service them. However, despite these factors, gay South of Market has undergone some significant recovery since the mid-1980s. Although the leather territory has shrunk and continues to be imperiled by aggressive redevelopment, the Folsom is still the main focal point for local leather and remains an international magnet for leather tourism.

ARCHAEOLOGICAL INSPIRATIONS

Time, sites and settlement patterns

As this description of gay settlement South of Market demonstrates, archaeological preoccupations affected my work in several areas: spatial sensibilities, the interest in periodization, the fascination with qualitative shifts in levels of social complexity, and social discontinuities such as the rise and decline of particular social formations. For example, the issue of how chiefdoms or states succeed smaller or less centralized power structures is in some ways similar to the question of how sexual communities with institutional coherence and defined territories emerge from loose networks of individuals with shared inclinations. Archaeologists also think about the opposite process, when certain social formations fail, become smaller and less complex, or become less capable of producing visible evidence of their presence.

I doubt I would have thought of leather periods in terms of formative, classic, and post-classic had I not been exposed to these distinctions in the context of Mesoamerican prehistory; nor would I have approached South of Market and the leather community with a concept such as site distribution. I found the notion of 'site' extremely useful (Figure 3.3). I adapted the 'site' concept to include bars, bathhouses, sex clubs, bookstores, leather shops, cruising territories, and even non-leather businesses heavily patronized by a leather crowd. Some sites have more or less continuous leather occupation for a number of years, despite changes of ownership, business, or name. For instance, site number 14 at 1347 Folsom was the location of the In Between, the Cow Palace Saloon, the bar with no name, the Phoenix, the No Name (official title), the Bolt, the Brig, and the Powerhouse. When such a site ceases to be a location for a leather-oriented use and is permanently occupied by a non-leather or even non-gay business, this may be an indicator of a broader pattern of neighborhood succession. Two sites exemplify such trends: number 8, 1501 Folsom at Eleventh Street, was Febe's for twenty years but in 1986 became a straight rock-and-roll club, The Paradise Lounge. Just across the street, site 26 at 280 Eleventh Street on the corner of Folsom, was The Covered Wagon, the Leatherneck, Dirty Sally's, the Plunge, The Gold Coast, Drummaster/Drummer Key Club, and Dan's Compound. In 1984, this became the Oasis, a straight dance club. This corner, once the heart of the leather territory, now symbolizes the new, non-gay, South of Market entertainment district.

City size and sexual specialization

Archaeological studies are also invariably concerned with the appearance of new social formations, a topic reflected in my research. Why did leather communities first emerge in New York, Los Angeles, Chicago, and San Francisco? From the 1950s until quite recently, the metropolitan areas of New York, Los Angeles, Chicago, and San Francisco have been the four largest in the United States. (The Washington-Baltimore conurbation has now become the fourth largest, bumping the San Francisco Bay area down to the fifth slot.) As I first learned in my archaeology classes, other factors being constant, larger cities typically allow for higher levels of specialization in occupation, commerce, and recreation. Central place theory predicts that larger centers will generally provide a wider variety of goods and services than smaller ones, and that the more specialized the good or service, the less likely that it will be available in smaller regional or local centers.[7]

An excellent example of this process can be graphically seen in Brian Berry's maps of commercial activity in south-west rural Iowa in the 1930s. Berry drew upon a detailed survey that had been conducted on the shopping habits of local farmers, and he mapped the patterns of their responses. These depict 'the very local trade or service areas for goods, services, and facilities that can be provided at small scale and for which consumers were unwilling to travel far, either because of frequency of demand or bulk of the commodity' (Berry 1967: 10). The most locally provided goods included, for example, church services and groceries. Services such as physicians and lawyers were located in the intermediate-sized centers. Shopping for women's coats and dresses tended to concentrate in even larger and fewer sites, as did hospitals. Daily newspapers were the most specialized item (Berry 1967: 10–12 maps). It appears from Berry's maps that some newspapers also came in from unspecified but larger centers east of the region he mapped, and those flow lines probably refer to the Chicago press extending its reach into its regional hinterland.

One might predict a similar relationship between the rarity or specialization of a sexual good or service, and size and type of place in which it will be found. The most specialized sexualities would be more likely to be available in the largest centers serving the broadest regions and greatest populations. The work of two sociologists, Joseph Harry and William DeVall, validates such predictions. Harry and DeVall analyzed the relationships between urban size, and the presence and diversity of gay bars, in the historical and cultural context of North America in the 1970s (Harry 1974; Harry and DeVall 1978). Harry (1974: 240) noted a strong correlation between city size and gay bar specialization: 'institutional differentiation is strongly associated with city size among normal heterosexual institutions, i.e. large cities possess a wider range of establishments and institutions. A similar process of differentiation seems to operate among gay bars'.

Using gay guides of the period, Harry concluded that the number and variety of types of gay bars were directly related to the size of urban areas in the United States in the early 1970s. 'Those bars which are the rarest, such as Black or Leather gay bars are almost exclusively limited to cities of over 500,000 population ...' and, '... since leather costumery and the associated practices of sado-masochism do not appeal to many homosexuals, a city must be of substantial size to support such a bar' (242–44). In their 1978 re-examination of the issue, Harry and DeVall revised the population figure, noting that they 'could find no metropolitan area of less than 1 million population with an exclusively leather bar' (Harry and DeVall 1978: 136–40). Based on such considerations, it is not surprising that the earliest specialized leather facilities emerged first in New York, Los Angeles, Chicago, and San Francisco.

The correlation between size and sexual specialization is of course not an automatic one. First, there were no 'gay bars' in fifteenth century Europe, or colonial North America. In fact, in the United States there were no bars in the contemporary sense until after the repeal of prohibition, when alcohol production, consumption, and distribution became highly regulated and administered by elaborate bureaucracies and urban police (Chauncey 1994; Cavan 1966).

Even given the existence of modern gay bars, other factors such as a tolerant or punitive legal climate, the procedures for obtaining liquor licenses, the location of port facilities or other transportation terminals, or the price of local real estate could all modify the basic expectation of the significance of city size. Nonetheless, the history of leather bar location

South of Market Site Map, 1960-1993

Figure 3.3 South of Market site map, 1960–1993.
Map by the author.

clearly demonstrates that city size and the place of a metropolitan area in regional, national, or international networks of distribution have an important impact on the presence of sexually specialized institutions.

Population estimates and catchment areas

When I was completing my dissertation, a member of my committee asked me a perfectly legitimate question which I had no obvious way to answer. She wanted to know a basic fact which would ordinarily be an easy one to provide: what was the size of my research population? How many of these leather guys were there in San Francisco?

The deceptively simple question was exceedingly difficult to answer for many reasons. In the first place, measuring homosexual populations raises definitional problems. It is difficult for sexual demographers to even agree upon who counts as a homosexual, as the category itself is a slippery one (Kenan 1997). Estimates are often made using assumptions based on Kinsey's work, but there are many ways to interpret the Kinsey data (Kinsey et al. 1948, 1953). Gay rights groups tend to assume that about 10% of the population is predominantly homosexual. Right wing groups opposed to civil equality for homosexual citizens want to minimize the numbers, and argue that only 1% of the United States population is gay. Most census surveys do not measure sexual orientation. The lack of data and the inconsistent definitions make reliable figures difficult to obtain.

On the local level, no one even knows how many homosexual men and women reside in San Francisco, much less how many leathermen live here. The actual city of San Francisco has a total population of roughly 800,000 although that of the surrounding metropolitan area is closer to 6 million. Not all of the homosexuals in the greater metro-politan Bay area live in San Francisco. There are gay, lesbian, bisexual, and transgender households throughout virtually all the residential areas of the greater metropolis. Nonetheless, San Francisco is a magnet, attracting sexually motivated migrants not only from the greater Bay area but also from throughout the western United States, as well as a national and, to a smaller degree, an international population. Thus, homosexuals are disproportionately represented in San Francisco as both permanent residents and tempo-rary visitors, although it is impossible to determine their exact numbers.

It is at least as difficult to count leathermen as it is to count homosexuals. But I was inspired by the creativity with which archaeologists estimate long-vanished populations on the basis of fragmentary data. It seemed to me that one could compare counts of sites in order to make some educated guesses about population proportions, if not absolute numbers. This procedure in turn rested on an assumption that a gay or leather site, such as a bar or cruising area, requires something like a catchment area. Instead of arable land or carrying capacity, a certain population level of potential customers would be necessary to support a 'site' such as a gay bar or street territory.

In the case of a bar, such a population of potential customers would have to be large enough so that the failure of some number of them to regularly patronize the establish-ment would not imperil its financial stability. Furthermore, these customers would have to have sufficient money to spend, certain proclivities to socialize in public drinking establ-ishments, and expectations that such businesses would satisfy various social wants or needs. Most would have to be local, although some individuals might travel great distances to patronize the bar. The exact size of such a population need not be known; an estimate could be inferred. Assuming that the catchment population for each 'site' remained rela-tively constant, simply counting the numbers of establishments should give a relative measure of populations.

I took eleven gay guides from the years 1969 to 1994 and counted the total number of gay sites in San Francisco, the number of leather sites in the city, and the number of lesbian sites. I also counted the non-leather gay sites located South of Market. Like all methods for estimating populations, this technique is methodologically hazardous. Not all gay guides are equally accurate, and criteria for what counts as a gay or leather site are inconsistent between guides (even within guides produced by a single company). The guides themselves evolve, and periodically change their format for presenting their data – they are, after all, intended to assist tourists in finding local recreation rather than academics trying to count queers. Moreover, the repertoire of site types changes over time. While bars were the primary institution of gay social life in the 1950s and early 1960s, the expansion of gay economies in later decades is accompanied by a diversification of gay-oriented businesses. Bars, while still very important, are less central, and by the 1990s, the explosion of phone sex, on-line services, Internet bulletin boards, and sexual chat rooms had further provided alternative opportunities for social contact. It is difficult to know even how to integrate Internet chat rooms with physical locations in 'site' based analyses of population composition.

Finally, how does one determine site 'function' as gay or leather or lesbian? Does a straight-owned laundromat in a gay neighborhood with a large but not exclusively gay clientele qualify as a gay site? Lesbian sites tend to be very different from gay male ones; does one count the local feminist bookstore, where many lesbians can be found although the store itself addresses a larger female population? It is inevitable that counting 'sites' based upon either archaeological data or documents such as gay guides requires constant decisions about what to include or leave out. So the charts that have resulted from my site count should not be regarded as anything more than suggestive. However, the suggestions they make are provocative.

Figure 3.4 shows my calculation of the total number of gay sites, leather sites, lesbian sites, and non-leather sites located South of Market, from 1969 through 1994. Throughout these periods, the proportion of leather sites is consistently 8–12% of the total gay sites. The number of lesbian sites tends to be around 2–6%. And the number of non-leather sites South of Market rises fairly steadily over time, except for a drop in the mid-1980s after the closing of the gay baths and sex clubs.

These relative site frequencies provide fertile ground for hypotheses about the social behavior of different homosexual subgroups. For example, Harry and DeVall estimated a minimum gross urban population of 50,000 would be needed to support a gay bar. This was total urban size, however, and not a figure of how many of those city residents had to be homosexual to support such a bar. Harry and DeVall also caution that using bars to estimate population must take into account

> the size of the available bar clientele, the bar-going propensities of each type, and the propensities of each type of clientele to segregate themselves into separate settings. For example, *because lesbians have lesser bar-going propensities than do gay males, lesbian bars seem fewer in relation to the numbers of lesbians than gay male bars in relation to their numbers.*
>
> (Harry and DeVall 1978: 139; my emphasis)

My own analyses of the San Francisco data concur. The San Francisco bar statistics and my own observations in the field indicate the differences between male and female gay populations in bar-going behavior and the availability of investment capital. For

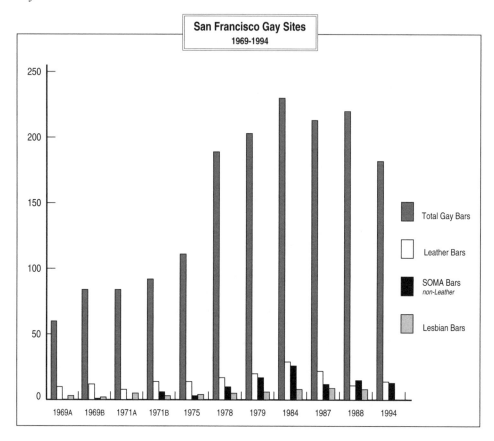

Figure 3.4 San Francisco gay sites, 1969–1994.
Graph by the author.

example, lesbians do not patronize bars as intensively as gay men, and they generally have less access to capital to invest in them. Consequently, a lesbian bar most likely requires a larger population of potential patrons than a gay male bar. By contrast, I would argue that gay leathermen use their bars more intensively than the mainstream gay population, in part because there are fewer alternative institutional formats for the pursuit of a leather-based social life. So it probably takes a somewhat smaller population of leathermen to support a bar than one serving the general gay population.

As Harry and DeVall point out, the qualities which make large cities attractive to gay migrants would give the largest cities that much more appeal for those with more specialized sexual tastes. Consequently, the magnet effect of a city such as San Francisco for gay migration is in all likelihood an even stronger force for gay leathermen. Gay leathermen are probably disproportionately attracted to the largest cities such as San Francisco because those cities are the most likely to support specialized leather institutions. From the frequency of leather bars, and their intensity of use, it is probably reasonable, and even conservative to estimate that the population of leather-oriented gay males in San Francisco may be roughly 10% of whatever is the total gay population.

While the number of lesbian institutions for comparable periods was much smaller, averaging around 4%, the actual lesbian population is probably larger than 4%. In recent years, almost all lesbian bars have disappeared from San Francisco. For a period of time there appeared to be no full-time lesbian bars; at the present time there seem to be only two. This does not indicate a precipitous drop in population or that the lesbian community has been hit by a sudden wave of mortality, dispersion, or social collapse. It has probably resulted from changing patterns of lesbian socializing and the withdrawal of capital from investment in the lesbian bar economy.

The charts in Figures 3.4 and 3.5 show additional trends worth noting. The growth of non-leather gay sites South of Market from 1 in 1969 to 13 in 1994 shows the gradual establishment of South of Market as a major gay neighborhood. By 1984, South of Market had the third largest concentration of gay sites in the city (19%). Only the Castro and Polk Street areas had more gay sites than South of Market. However, by 1988, the percentage of gay sites in South of Market had dropped to only 13%, demonstrating the impact of bathhouse closures in the area. By 1994, the frequency of gay sites in the South of Market area begins to recover (to 15%). Throughout the late 1980s and 1990s, the Castro continues to grow, whereas the Polk area steadily declines as a gay neighborhood.

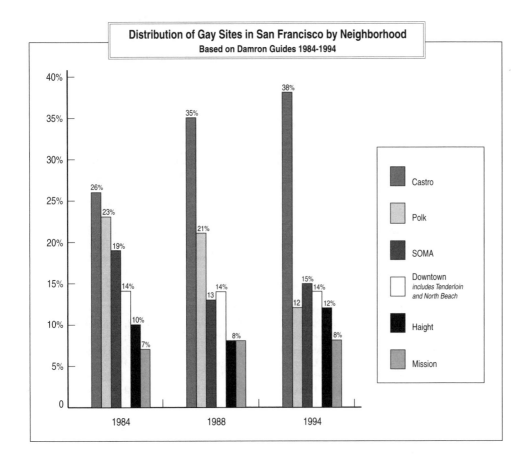

Figure 3.5 Distribution of gay sites in San Francisco, by neighborhood, based on Damron Guides 1984–1994.
Graph by the author.

Conclusion

Settlement patterns, site definitions, population estimates, and catchment areas are but a few of the ways in which my exposure to archaeological concerns and techniques informed this research project on urban gay men. I doubt that my archaeological teachers would have anticipated the uses to which I would put the ideas and techniques I learned in those classes. It may seem a long way from Oaxaca or Teotihuacan to San Francisco's old warehouse and working-class district, from corn cob size to bar patrons, or from craft wards to sexual neighborhoods. Two important lessons may be drawn from my experience. First, the study of sexuality can be done using all the ordinary tools, theories, and methodological armamentaria of the social sciences.[8] Second, the juxtaposition of unrelated fields or unlikely bedfellows can often help thinking about new problems, or approaching problems in new ways. Such experiences are important elements of education, and I treasure those moments in mine.

Notes

1 This essay is based on a talk delivered for a Presidential Symposium on the Place of Archaeology in Anthropology at the Annual Meeting of the American Anthropological Association, November 1996, San Francisco, California. I am deeply indebted to Elizabeth Brumfiel for inviting me to participate in this symposium, as well as for her encouragement and the innumerable conversations in which we have discussed these and other issues over the years. I am immensely grateful to Rob Schmidt and Barb Voss for their patience and determination to have it for this volume, and for their skillful editorial attention. This paper is also intended as an expression of appreciation to my many superb teachers in the department of Anthropology at the University of Michigan in the early 1970s, and to the stellar cohort of fellow graduate students among whom it was my good fortune to land.

2 See Achilles 1967; Hooker 1967; Leznoff and Westley 1967; Mileski and Black 1972; McIntosh 1968; Plummer 1975, 1981; Reiss 1967; Gagnon and Simon 1967, 1970, 1973; Simon and Gagnon 1969; see also Gagnon 1992, Humphreys 1979, Lee 1979, Levine 1979, and Murray 1979.

3 It should be noted that Schneider was Esther Newton's advisor and sponsor for her dissertation, which was published as *Mother Camp*.

4 Several of the key Michigan archaeologists were trained at Chicago. Since urban studies had such a distinguished place in Social Science at Chicago, I have often wondered how much the intellectual environment at Chicago may have contributed to their fluency with urban theory. I was able to get through most of my graduate education before I had ever heard of W. I. Thomas, Robert Park, and Ernest Burgess; it seems unlikely that Chicago students would not have been routinely exposed to their work.

5 See Achilles 1967; Harry 1974; Harry and DuVall 1978; Baldwin 1993; Bean 1994; DeBlase 1993, 1996; Mains 1984; Norwood 1986; Rubin 1991, 1994, 1997, 1998; Schiller 1986; M. Thompson 1991; Vollmer 1981; Brent 1997; Steward 1964; Leathers 1980; Bronski 1990; see also Chester 1996; Falkon 1972; Farren 1984; Finlayson 1990; Goodwin 1989; Gregersen 1969, 1983; Fischer 1977; Grover 1991; Grumley and Gallucci 1977; Harris 1985; Gunn 1994; Janssen 1990; Mariah 1978; McCann 1993; Mizer 1987; Nixon 1996; Rex 1986; Rosen 1986, 1990; Savran 1998; Simpson 1994; Tom of Finland 1992; Townsend 1972.

6 See Hartman 1974, 1984; DeLeon 1992; Redevelopment Agency of the City and County of San Francisco 1952; R/UDAT 1984; Nowinski 1979; Hoover 1979; Port of San Francisco 1997.

7 See Ashworth et al. 1988; Berry 1967; Castells 1979 and 1983; Christaller 1966; Johnson 1967; L. Mumford 1961; Pred 1980 and 1990; C. Smith 1976; Tilly 1974, 1975, and 1990; Winchester and White 1988; see also Groth 1994; Gilfoyle 1992; K. Mumford 1997; Stansell 1986.

8 A similar point was made in Mileski and Black, 1972: 199.

REFERENCES
Books and articles

Achilles, N. (1967) 'The Development of the Homosexual Bar as an Institution', in J. Gagnon and W. Simon (eds) *Sexual Deviance*, New York: Harper and Row.

Apter, E. and W. Pietz (eds) (1993) *Fetishism as Cultural Discourse*, Ithaca: Cornell University Press.

Ashworth, G. J., P. E. White and J. P. M. Winchester (1988) 'The Red-Light District in the West European City: A Neglected Aspect of the Urban Landscape', *Geoforum* 19, 2: 201–212.

Averbach, A. (1973) 'San Francisco's South of Market District, 1858–1958: The Emergence of a Skid Row', *California Historical Quarterly*, 52, 3: 196–223.

Baldwin, G. (1993) *Ties That Bind: The SM/Leather/Fetish Erotic Style*, Los Angeles: Daedalus.

Bean, J. W. (1988) 'Changing Times South of Market', *Advocate* (California supplement), 29 March, 4–7.

—— (1994) *Leathersex: A Guide for the Curious Outsider and the Serious Player*, Los Angeles: Daedalus.

Becker, H. (ed) (1964) *The Other Side: Perspectives on Deviance*, New York: Free Press.

—— (1973) *Outsiders: Studies in the Sociology of Deviance*, New York: Free Press.

Beemyn, B. (ed.) (1997) *Creating a Place for Ourselves: Lesbian, Gay, and Bisexual Community Histories*, New York: Routledge.

Bell, A. P. and M. S. Weinberg (1978) *Homosexualities: A Study in Diversity Among Men and Women*, New York: Simon and Schuster.

Berry, B. J. L. (1967) *Geography of Market Centers and Retail Distribution*, Englewood Cliffs, NJ: Prentice-Hall.

Berube, A. (1990) *Coming Out Under Fire: The History of Gay Men and Women In World War Two*, New York: The Free Press.

—— (1993) '"Dignity for All": The Role of Homosexuality in the Marine Cooks and Stewards Union (1930s-1950s)', paper presented at the conference Reworking American Labor History: Race, Gender, and Class, Madison, Wisconsin.

—— (1996) 'The History of the Bathhouses', in Dangerous Bedfellows (eds) *Policing Public Sex: Queer Politics and the Future of AIDS Activism*, Boston, South End Press.

Bloomfield, A. B. (1995–1996) 'A History of the California Historical Society's New Mission Street Neighborhood', *California History*, Winter.

Brandt, A. M. (1985) *No Magic Bullet: A Social History of Venereal Disease in the United States Since 1880*, Oxford: Oxford University Press.

—— (1988) 'AIDS: From Social History to Social Policy', in E. Fee and D. M. Fox (eds) *AIDS: The Burdens of History*, Berkeley: University of California Press.

Brent, B. (ed.) (1997) 'Special Issue on San Francisco in the Seventies', *Black Sheets*, 12.

Bronski, M. (1990) 'Art and Evidence: Those '50s and '60s Muscle Mags May Be the Future of Gay Male Porn', *Gay Community News* 21 October, 8–9.

Brook, J., C. Carlsson and N. Peters (eds) (1998) *Reclaiming San Francisco: History, Politics, Culture*, San Francisco: City Lights Books.

Brumfiel, E. (1994) *The Economic Anthropology of the State*, Lanham, MD: University Press of America.

Bulmer, M. (1984) *The Chicago School of Sociology*, Chicago: University of Chicago Press.

Castells, M. (1979) *The Urban Question: A Marxist Approach*, Cambridge, MA: MIT Press.

—— (1983) *The City and the Grassroots*, Berkeley: University of California Press.

Cavan, S. (1966) *Liquor License*, Chicago: Aldine.

Chauncey, G. Jr (1985) 'Christian Brotherhood or Sexual Perversion? Homosexual Identities and the Construction of Sexual Boundaries in the World War One Era', *Journal of Social History* 19, Winter: 189–211.

—— (1994) *Gay New York: Gender, Urban Culture, and the Making of the Gay World, 1890–1940*, New York: Basic Books.

Chester, M. (1996) *Diary of a Thought Criminal*, Liberty, TN: RFD Press.

Christaller, W. (1966) *Central Places in Southern Germany*, Englewood Cliffs, NJ: Prentice-Hall.

Clark, T. R. (1987) 'Labor and Progressivism "South of the Slot": The Voting Behavior of the San Francisco Working Class, 1912–1916', *California History: The Magazine of the California Historical Society* 66, 3: 196–207, 235–36.

Corzine, J. and R. Kirby (1977) 'Cruising the Truckers: Sexual Encounters in a Highway Rest Area', *Urban Life* 6, 2: 171–92.

Crimp, D. (ed.) (1988) *AIDS: Cultural Analysis, Cultural Activism*, Cambridge, MA: The MIT Press.

Dangerous Bedfellows (1996) *Policing Public Sex*, Boston: South End.

Davis, D. L. and R. G. Whitten (1987) 'The Cross-Cultural Study of Human Sexuality', *Annual Reviews in Anthropology* 16: 69–98.

Davis, M. (1992) *City of Quartz*, New York: Vintage Books.

Davis, M., S. Hiatt, M. Kennedy, S. Ruddick and M. Sprinker (1990) *Fire in the Hearth: The Radical Politics of Place in America*, London: Verso.

'The Death of Leather' (1985) *San Francisco Focus*, November.

DeBlase, A. F. (1993) 'Leather Concordance', first draft, unpublished manuscript

—— (1996) *Leather History Timeline*, Chicago: Leather Archives and Museum.

Deleon, R. E. (1992) *Left Coast City: Progressive Politics in San Francisco, 1975–1991*, Lawrence, KS: University Press of Kansas.

D'Emilio, J. (1983) *Sexual Politics, Sexual Communities: The Making of a Homosexual Minority in the United States, 1940–1970*, Chicago: University of Chicago Press.

—— (1989) 'Gay Politics and Community in San Francisco Since World War II', In M. B. Duberman, M. Vicinus and G. Chauncey Jr (eds) *Hidden from History: Reclaiming the Gay and Lesbian Past*, New York: New American Library.

Devereaux, G. (1937) 'Institutionalized Homosexuality Among Mohave Indians', *Human Biology* 9: 498–529.

Earle, T. (1997) *How Chiefs Come to Power: The Political Economy in Prehistory*, Stanford: Stanford University Press.

Ellis, H. (1942 [1905]) *Studies in the Psychology of Sex* vol 1, New York: Random House.

—— (1937 [1906]) *Studies in the Psychology of Sex* vol 2, New York: Random House.

Escoffier, J. (1998) *American Homo: Community and Perversity*, Berkeley: University of California Press.

Ethington, P. (1994) *The Public City: The Political Construction of Urban Life in San Francisco, 1850–1900*, Cambridge: Cambridge University Press.

Evans, A. (aka The Red Queen) (1982) 'Milk Milked', *Bay Area Reporter*, 24 November: 6.

Evans-Pritchard, E. E. (1970) 'Sexual Inversion Among the Azande', *American Anthropologist* 72: 1,428–34.

Falkon, F. L. (1972) *A Historic Collection of Gay Art*, San Diego: Greenleaf Classics.

Farmer, P. (1992) *AIDS and Accusation: Haiti and the Geography of Blame*, Berkeley: University of California Press.

Farren, M. (1984) *The Black Leather Jacket*, New York: Abbeville.

Fee, E. and D. M. Fox (eds) (1988) *AIDS: The Burdens of History*, Berkeley: University of California Press.

—— (1992) *AIDS: The Making of a Chronic Disease*, Berkeley: University of California Press.

Fine, G. A. (ed.) (1995) *A Second Chicago School? The Development of a Postwar American Sociology*, Chicago: University of Chicago Press.

Finlayson, I. (1990) *Denim: An American Legend*, New York: Fireside, Simon and Schuster.

Fischer, H. (1977) *Gay Semiotics: A Photographic Study of Visual Coding among Homosexual Men*, San Francisco: NFS Press.

Flannery, K. V. (1976) *The Early Mesoamerican Village*, San Diego: Academic Press.

Ford, C. S. and F. A. Beach (1951) *Patterns of Sexual Behavior*, New York: Harper and Row.

Fritscher, J. (1991) 'Artist Chuck Arnett: His Life/Our Times', in M. Thompson (ed.) *Leatherfolk*, Boston: Alyson.

Gagnon, J. (1977) *Human Sexualities*, Glenview, IL: Scott, Foresman.

—— (1992) 'An Unlikely Story', in B. M. Berger (ed.) *Authors of Their Own Lives: Intellectual Autobiographies of Twenty American Sociologists*, Berkeley: University of California Press.

Gagnon, J. and W. Simon (1967) *Sexual Deviance*, New York: Harper and Row.

—— (1970) *The Sexual Scene*, Chicago: Aldine, Trans-Action Books.

—— (1973) *Sexual Conduct: The Social Sources of Human Sexuality*, Chicago: Aldine.

Garber, E. (*c.* 1990) 'A Historical Directory of Lesbian and Gay Establishments in the San Francisco Bay Area', manuscript on file, Gay and Lesbian Historical Society of Northern California.

Garber, E. and W. Walker (1997) 'Queer Bars and Other Establishments in San Francisco', unpublished data on file, Gay and Lesbian Historical Society of Northern California.

Gebhard, P. H. (1976 [1969]) 'Fetishism and Sadomasochism', in M. S. Weinberg (ed.) *Sex Research: Studies from the Kinsey Institute*, New York: Oxford University Press.

Gero, J. and M. Conkey (1991) *Engendering Archeology: Women and Prehistory*, Oxford: Blackwell.

Gibson, I. (1979) *The English Vice: Beating, Sex, and Shame in Victorian England and After*, London: Duckworth.

Gilfoyle, T. (1992) *City of Eros: New York City, Prostitution, and the Commercialization of Sex, 1790–1920*, New York: Norton.

Gluckman, A. and B. Reed (1997) *Homo Economics: Capitalism, Community, and Lesbian and Gay Life*, New York: Routledge.

Godfrey, B. J. (1988) *Neighborhoods in Transition: The Making of San Francisco's Ethnic and Nonconformist Communities*, Berkeley: University of California Press.

Goodwin, J. P. (1989) *More Man Than You'll Ever Be: Gay Folklore and Acculturation in Middle America*, Bloomington: Indiana University Press.

Gregersen, E. (1969) 'The Sadomasochistic Scene', talk delivered at the 68th Annual Meeting of the American Anthropological Association, New Orleans, LA.

—— (1983) *Sexual Practices: The Story of Human Sexuality*, New York: Franklin Watts.

Groth, P. (1994) *Living Downtown: The History of Residential Hotels in the United States*, Berkeley: University of California Press.

Grover, J. Z. (1991) 'The Demise of the Zippered Sweatshirt: Hal Fischer's Gay Semiotics', *Outlook* 11: 44–47.

Grumley, M. and E. Gallucci (1977) *Hard Corps: Studies in Leather and Sadomasochism*, New York: Dutton.

Gunn, T. (1994) *Collected Poems*, New York: Farrar, Straus and Giroux.

Hall, S. and T. Jefferson (eds) (1991 [1976]) *Resistance through Rituals: Youth Subcultures in Post-War Britain*, London: Harper Collins Academic.

Harris, M. (1985) *Bikers: Birth of a Modern Day Outlaw*, Boston: Faber and Faber.

Harry, J. (1974) 'Urbanization and the Gay Life', *Journal of Sex Research* 10, 3: 238–47.

Harry, J. and W. B. deVall (1978) *The Social Organization of Gay Males*, New York: Praeger.

Hartman, C. (1974) *Yerba Buena: Land Grab and Community Resistance in San Francisco*, San Francisco: Glide Publications.

—— (1984) *The Transformation of San Francisco*, Totowa, NJ: Rowman and Allanheld.

Hebdige, D. (1991 [1979]) *Subculture: The Meaning of Style*, New York: Routledge.

Herdt, G. (1981) *Guardians of the Flutes: Idioms of Masculinity*, New York: McGraw-Hill.

—— (1984) *Ritualized Homosexuality in Melanesia*, Berkeley: University of California Press.

Herskovitz, M. (1937) 'A Note on "Woman Marriage" in Dahomey', *Africa* 10, 3: 335–41.

Hodder, I. (1986) *Reading the Past: Current Approaches to Interpretation in Archeology*, Cambridge: Cambridge University Press.

Hooker, E. (1967) 'The Homosexual Community', in J. Gagnon and W. Simon (eds) *Sexual Deviance*, New York: Harper and Row.

Hoover, C. (1979) 'Introduction', in I. Nowinski *No Vacancy: Urban Renewal and the Elderly*, San Francisco: Carolyn Bean Associates.

Humphreys, L. (1979) *Tearoom Trade: Impersonal Sex in Public Places*, New York: Aldine.

Immel, M. L. (1983) 'Gay Urban Open Space in San Francisco: The Landscape of Liberation', unpublished M.A. thesis, University of California.

Issel, W. and R. W. Cherney (1986) *San Francisco 1865–1932: Politics, Power, and Urban Development*, Berkeley: University of California Press.

Janssen, V. (1990) *The Art of George Quaintance*, Berlin: Janssen-Verlag.

Jay, A. (1976) 'Folsom Street: San Francisco's Leather Lane', *QQ* September/October: 25–27, 44–47.

Johnson, J. H. (1967) *Urban Geography: An Introductory Analysis*, New York: Pergamon.

Katz, J. (1976) *Gay American History: Lesbians and Gay Men in the U.S.A.*, New York: Thomas Crowell.

—— (1983) *Gay/Lesbian Almanac: A New Documentary*, New York: Harper Colophon.

Kelly, R. (1976) 'Witchcraft and Sexual Relations: An Exploration of the Social and Semantic Implications of the Structure of Belief', in P. Brown and G. Buchbinder (eds) *Man and Woman in the New Guinea Highlands*, Washington, DC: American Anthropological Association.

Kenan, S. (1997) 'Who Counts When You're Counting Homosexuals? Hormones and Homosexuality in Mid-Twentieth Century America', in V. Rosario (ed.) *Science and Homosexualities*, New York: Routledge.

Kennedy, E. L. and M. D. Davis (1993) *Boots of Leather, Slippers of Gold: The History of a Lesbian Community*, New York: Routledge.

Kinsella, J. (1989) *Covering the Plague: AIDS and the American Media*, New Brunswick: Rutgers.

Kinsey, A., W. B. Pomeroy and C. E. Martin (1948) *Sexual Behavior in the Human Male*, Philadelphia: W. B. Saunders Company.

Kinsey, A., W. B. Pomeroy, C. E. Martin and P. H. Gebhard (1953) *Sexual Behavior in the Human Female*, Philadelphia: W. B. Saunders Company.

Knapp, D. (1983) 'A 20 Year Cycle', *Bay Area Reporter*, 10 March: 13.

Knopp, L. (1997) 'Gentrification and Gay Neighborhood Formation in New Orleans', in Gluckman and Reed, *Homo Economics: Capitalism, Community, and Lesbian and Gay Life*, New York: Routledge.

Krafft-Ebing, R. V. (1899) *Psychopathia Sexualis*, Philadelphia: F. A. Davis Company.

Kunzle, D. (1982) *Fashion and Fetishism: A Social History of the Corset, Tight-Lacing, and Other Forms of Body Sculpture in the West*, Totowa, NJ: Rowman and Littlefield.

Leathers, R. (1980) 'Two Nations – One Territory: S&M vs. Leather', *DungeonMaster* 5, July: 1–2.

Lee, J. A. (1979) 'The Social Organization of Sexual Risk', *Alternative Lifestyles* 2, 1: 69–100.

Levine, M. P. (1979) *Gay Men: The Sociology of Male Homosexuality*, New York: Harper Colophon.

—— (1992) 'The Life and Death of Gay Clones', in G. Herdt (ed.) *Gay Culture in America: Essays from the Field*, Boston: Beacon.

—— (1998) *Gay Macho: The Life and Death of the Homosexual Clone*, New York: NYU Press.

Levine, M. P., P. Nardi, and J. Gagnon (eds) (1997) *In Changing Times: Gay Men and Lesbians Encounter HIV/AIDS*, Chicago: University of Chicago.

Lewin, E. (1993) *Lesbian Mothers*, Ithaca: Cornell University Press.

Lewin, E. and W. Leap (1996) *Out in the Field*, Urbana: University of Illinois Press.

Leznoff, M. and W. A. Westley (1967) 'The Homosexual Community', in J. Gagnon and W. Simon (eds) *Sexual Deviance*, New York: Harper and Row.

Lockwood, C. (1978) *Suddenly San Francisco: The Early Years of an Instant City*, San Francisco: San Francisco Examiner Publishing.

Lotchin, R. W. (1974) *San Francisco, 1846–1856: From Hamlet to City*, Lincoln: University of Nebraska Press.

Mains, G. (1984) *Urban Aboriginals: A Celebration of Leathersexuality*, San Francisco: Gay Sunshine Press.

—— (1989) *Gentle Warriors*, Stamford: Knights Press.

Mariah, P. (1978) *This Light Will Spread: Selected Poems 1960–1975*, South San Francisco: ManRoot.

Marshall, D. S. and R. C. Suggs (eds) (1971) *Human Sexual Behavior: Variations in the Ethnographic Spectrum*, New York: Basic Books.

McCann, G. (1993) *Rebel Males: Clift, Brando, and Dean*, New Brunswick, NJ: Rutgers University Press.

McClintock, A. (1993) 'Maid to Order: Commercial S/M and Gender Power', in P. C. Gibson and R. Gibson (eds), *Dirty Looks: Women, Pornography, Power*, London: British Film Institute.

McIntosh, M. (1968) 'The Homosexual Role', *Social Problems* 16, 2 Fall.

McMurtrie, D. (1914) 'A Legend of Lesbian Love Among North American Indians', *Urologic and Cutaneous Review* April: 192–93.

Mileski, M. and D. Black (1972) 'The Social Organization of Homosexuality', *Urban Life and Culture* July: 187–202.

Mizer, R. (1987) *Athletic Model Guild: 160 Young Americans Photographed by Robert Mizer*, Amsterdam: Intermale.

Mollenkopf, J. H. (1983) *The Contested City*, Princeton: Princeton University Press.

Moser, C. (1979) 'An Exploratory-Descriptive Study of a Self-Defined S/M (Sadomasochistic) Sample', unpublished Ph.D. dissertation, Institute for the Advanced Study of Human Sexuality.

—— (1988) 'Sadomasochism', in D. Dailey (ed.) *The Sexually Unusual: A Guide to Understanding and Helping*, New York: Harrington Park Press.

Moser, C. and E. E. Levitt (1987) 'An Exploratory-Descriptive Study of a Sadomasochistically Oriented Sample', *The Journal of Sex Research* 23, 3: 322–37.

Mumford, K. (1997) *Interzones: Black/White Sex Districts in Chicago and New York in the Early Twentieth Century*, New York: Columbia University Press.

Mumford, L. (1961) *The City in History*, New York: Harcourt, Brace and World.

Murray, S. O. (1979) 'The Institutional Elaboration of a Quasi-Ethnic Community', *International Review of Modern Sociology*, July–December.

Nardi, P. M. (ed.) (1988) *Perspectives on the Social Effects of AIDS: California Sociologist* 11, 1–2 (Special Issue).

Newton, E. (1972) *Mother Camp: Female Impersonators in America*, Englewood Cliffs, NJ: Prentice-Hall.

—— (1993) *Cherry Grove, Fire Island: Sixty Years in America's First Gay and Lesbian Town*, Boston: Beacon Press.

Nixon, S. (1996) *Hard Looks: Masculinities, Spectatorship and Contemporary Consumption*, New York: St. Martins.

Norwood, J. (1986) 'A Preliminary Examination of Sexual Behavioral Changes in San Francisco's S/M Community Five Years after the Onset of AIDS', unpublished manuscript.

Nowinski, I. (1979) *No Vacancy: Urban Renewal and the Elderly*, San Francisco: Carolyn Bean Associates.

Nye, R. A. (1993) 'The Medical Origins of Sexual Fetishism', in E. Apter and W. Pietz (eds) *Fetishism as Cultural Discourse*, Ithaca: Cornell University Press.

'Off-Beat Rough Toward Chic Very Fine' (1988) *New York Times*, 15 September.

Ortner, S. B. (1973) 'On Key Symbols', *American Anthropologist* 75: 1,338–46.

Ortner, S. B. and H. Whitehead (eds) (1981) *Sexual Meanings: The Cultural Construction of Gender and Sexuality*, Cambridge: Cambridge University Press.

Palen, J. J. and B. London (1984) *Gentrification, Displacement, and Neighborhood Revitalization*, Albany: State University of New York Press.

Park, R. E. and E. W. Burgess (1925) *The City*, Chicago: University of Chicago Press.

Patton, C. (1985) *Sex and Germs: The Politics of AIDS*, Boston: South End Press.

—— (1990) *Inventing AIDS*, New York: Routledge.

Peiss, K. (1986) *Cheap Amusements: Working Women and Leisure in Turn-of-the-Century New York*, Philadelphia: Temple University Press.

Peiss, K. and C. Simmons, with R. A. Padgug (eds) (1989) *Passion and Power: Sexuality in History*, Philadelphia: Temple University Press.

Plummer, K. (1975) *Sexual Stigma: An Interactionist Account*, London: Routledge and Kegan Paul.

—— (ed.) (1981) *The Making of the Modern Homosexual*, London: Hutchinson.

Pred, A. (1980) *Urban Growth and City-Systems in the United States, 1840–1960*, Cambridge: Harvard University Press.

—— (1990) *Making Histories and Construction Human Geographies*, Boulder: Westview.

Read, K. E. (1980) *Other Voices: The Style of a Male Homosexual Tavern*, Novato, CA: Chandler and Sharp.

Reiss, A. (1967) 'The Social Integration of Peers and Queers', in J. Gagnon and W. Simon (eds) *Sexual Deviance*, New York: Harper and Row.

Rex (1986) *Rexwerk*, Paris: Les Pirates Associes.

Robinson, F. (1984) 'A Horror Story and a Challenge', *Coming Up!* April, 10.

Rofes, E. (1996) *Reviving the Tribe: Regenerating Gay Men's Sexuality and Culture in the Ongoing Epidemic*, New York: Harrington Park Press.

—— (1998) *Dry Bones Breathe: Gay Men Creating Post-AIDS Identities and Cultures*, New York: Harrington Park Press.

Rosario, V. (1997) (ed.) *Science and Homosexualities*, New York: Routledge.

Rosen, M. A. (1986) *Sexual Magic: The S/M Photographs*, San Francisco: Shaynew Press.

—— (1990) *Sexual Portraits: Photographs of Radical Sexuality*, San Francisco: Shaynew Press.

Rubin, G. S. (1984) 'Thinking Sex', in C. Vance (ed.) *Pleasure and Danger*, New York: Routledge and Kegan Paul.

—— (1991) 'The Catacombs: A Temple of the Butthole', in M. Thomson (ed.) *Leatherfolk*, Boston: Alyson.

—— (1994) 'The Valley of the Kings: Leathermen in San Francisco, 1960–1990', unpublished Ph.D. dissertation, University of Michigan.

—— (1997) 'Elegy for the Valley of the Kings: AIDS and the Leather Community in San Francisco, 1981–1996', in M. Levine, P. Nardi and J. Gagnon (eds) *In Changing Times: Gay Men and Lesbians Encounter HIV/AIDS*, Chicago: University of Chicago.

—— (1998) 'The Miracle Mile: South of Market and Gay Male Leather in San Francisco 1962–1996', in J. Brook, C. Carlsson and N. Peters (eds) *Reclaiming San Francisco: History, Politics, Culture*, San Francisco, City Lights Books.

Sabloff, J. and C. C. Lamberg-Karlovsky (1974) *The Rise and Fall of Civilizations: Modern Archaeological Approaches to Ancient Cultures*, Menlo Park, CA: Cummings.

'San Francisco Gay Life Where It's At' (1977) *South of Market Special*, Number 4.

Saroyan, W. A. (1989) 'Glory Days South of Market', *San Francisco Chronicle*, 1 January, Review section: 6.

Savran, D. (1998) *Taking It Like a Man: White Masculinity, Masochism, and Contemporary Culture*, Princeton: Princeton University Press.

Schiller, G. C. (1986) *The Pursuit of Masculinity: A Study in Homosexual Sadomasochism*, Ann Arbor: University Microfilms.

Scott, M. (1959) *The San Francisco Bay Area: A Metropolis in Perspective*, Berkeley: University of California Press.

—— (1985) *The San Francisco Bay Area: A Metropolis in Perspective*, second edition, Berkeley: University of California Press.

Shumate, A. (1988) *Rincon Hill and South Park: San Francisco's Early Fashionable Neighborhood*, Sausolito: Wingate Press.

Simon, W. and J. Gagnon (1969) 'Homosexuality: The Formulation of a Sociological Perspective', in R. Weltge (ed.) *The Same Sex: An Appraisal of Homosexuality*, Philadelphia: Pilgrim Press.

Simpson, M. (1994) *Male Impersonators: Men Performing Masculinity*, New York: Routledge.

Smith, C. (1976) *Regional Analysis. Volume I: Economic Systems; Volume II: Social Systems*, New York: Academic Press.

Smith, N. (1996) *The New Urban Frontier: Gentrification and the Revanchist City*, New York: Routledge.

Smith, T. (1983) Letter to the editor, *Bay Area Reporter* 18 August: 8.

Sonenschein, D. (1966) 'Homosexuality as a Subject of Anthropological Inquiry', *Anthropological Quarterly* 2: 73–82.

Stansell, C. (1986) *City of Women: Sex and Class in New York, 1789–1860*, New York: Knopf.

Starkey, R. (1983) *Bay Area Reporter* 14 April: 9.

Starr, K. (1995–1996) 'South of Market and Bunker Hill', *California History* Winter.

Steward, S. M. (as Donald Bishop) (1964) 'Pussies in Boots: The Truth About the Leather Mania', *Amigo* 25.

—— (1991) 'Dr. Kinsey Takes a Peek at S/M: A Reminiscence', in M. Thompson (ed.) *Leatherfolk*, Boston: Alyson.

Stoller, R. J. (1991) *Pain and Passion: A Psychoanalyst Explores the World of S&M*, New York: Plenum.

Stone, L. (1992) 'Libertine Sexuality in Post-Restoration England: Group Sex and Flagellation among the Middling Sort in Norwich in 1706–07', *Journal of the History of Sexuality* 2, 4: 511–26.

Styles, J. (1979) 'Outsider/Insider: Researching Gay Baths', *Urban Life* 8, 2: 135–52.

Taylor, W. R. (1991) *Inventing Times Square*, New York: Russell Sage Foundation.

Thomas, J. M. (1997) *Redevelopment and Race: Planning a Finer City in Postwar Detroit*, Baltimore: Johns Hopkins Press.

Thompson, E. P. (1963) *The Making of the English Working Class*, New York: Vintage Books.

Thompson, M. (1982) 'Folsom Street', *Advocate* 8 July: 28–31, 57.

—— (ed.)(1991) *Leatherfolk*, Boston: Alyson.

Tilly, C. (1974) *An Urban World*, Boston: Little, Brown and Company.

—— (1975) *The Formation of National States in Western Europe*, Princeton: Princeton University Press.

—— (1990) *Coercion, Capital, and European States: AD 990–1990*, Oxford: Blackwell.

—— (1998) *Durable Inequality*, Berkeley: University of California Press.

Tom of Finland (1992) *Tom of Finland*, Koln: Benedikt Taschen.

Townsend, L. (1972) *The Leatherman's Handbook*, New York: The Traveler's Companion, Olympia Press.

Triechler, P. (1988) 'AIDS, Homophobia, and Biomedical Discourse: An Epidemic of Signification', in D. Crimp *AIDS: Cultural Analysis, Cultural Activism*, Cambridge, MA: MIT Press.

Troiden, R. (1974) 'Homosexual Encounters in a Highway Rest Stop', in Goode, Erich, and Troiden (eds) *Sexual Deviance and Sexual Deviants*, New York: William Morrow and Company.

Truscott, C. (1990) 'San Francisco: A Reverent, Non-Linear, Necessarily Incomplete History of the S/M Scene', *Sandmutopia Guardian and Dungeon Journal* 8.

Vance, C. S. (ed.) (1984) *Pleasure and Danger: Exploring Female Sexuality*, Boston: Routledge and Kegan Paul.

—— (1989) 'Social Construction Theory: Problems in the History of Sexuality', in D. Altman, C. Vance et al. (eds) *Homosexuality, Which Homosexuality?*, London: GMP Publishers.

—— (1991) 'Anthropology Rediscovers Sexuality: A Theoretical Comment', *Social Science and Medicine* 33, 8: 875–84.

Vollmer, T. (1981) 'Male Images: The Politics of Gender', unpublished Senior honors thesis, University of California.

Walker, R. (1995) 'Landscape and City Life: Four Ecologies of Residence in the San Francisco Bay Area', *Ecumene* 2, 1: 33–64.

—— (1998) 'An Appetite for the City', in Brook et al. (eds), *Reclaiming San Francisco, History, Politics, Culture*, San Francisco: City Lights Books.

—— (in press) 'Industry Builds the City: Industrial Decentralization in the San Francisco Bay Area, 1850–1940', *Journal of Historical Geography*.

Walker, R. and the Bay Area Study Group (1990) 'The Playground of U.S. Capitalism? The Political Economy of the San Francisco Bay Area in the 1980s', in M. Davis et al. (eds) *Fire in the Hearth: The Radical Politics of Place in America*, London: Verso.

Walker, W. (1997) 'Gay Bars, Bathhouses and Restaurants in San Francisco 1930–1969', unpublished data, charts, and graphs, Gay and Lesbian Historical Society of Northern California.

Walkowitz, J. (1992) *City of Dreadful Delight: Narratives of Sexual Danger in Late-Victorian London*, Chicago: University of Chicago Press.

Waugh, T. (1996) *Hard To Imagine: Gay Male Eroticism in Photography and Film from Their Beginnings to Stonewall*, New York: Columbia University Press.

Weatherford, J. M. (1986) *Porn Row*, New York: Arbor House.

Weightman, B. (1980) 'Gay Bars as Private Places', *Landscape* 24, 1: 9–16.

Weinberg, M. and C. Williams (1974) *Male Homosexuals: Their Problems and Adaptations*, New York: Oxford University Press.

—— (1975) 'Gay Baths and the Social Organization of Impersonal Sex', *Social Problems* 23, 2: 124–36.

Weinberg, M., C. Williams and C. Moser (1984) 'The Social Constituents of Sadomasochism', *Social Problems* 31, 4: 379–89.

Weinberg, T. and G. W. Levi Kamel (1983) *S and M: Studies in Sadomasochism*, Buffalo: Prometheus Books.

Welch, P. and B. Eppridge (photographer) (1964) 'Homosexuality in America', *Life* 26 June: 66–80.

Weston, K. (1991) *Families We Choose: Lesbians, Gays, Kinship*, New York: Columbia University Press.

—— (1993) 'Lesbian/Gay Studies in the House of Anthropology', *Annual Review of Anthropology* 22: 339–67.

White, L. (1990) *The Comforts of Home: Prostitution in Colonial Nairobi*, Chicago: University of Chicago Press.

Williams, F. E. (1936) *Papuans of the Trans-Fly*, Oxford: Clarendon.

Winchester, H. P. M. and P. E. White (1988) 'The Location of Marginalized Groups in the Inner City', *Environment and Planning D: Society and Space* 6: 37–54.

Planning reports and studies

Redevelopment Agency of the City and County of San Francisco (1952) *The Feasibility of Redevelopment South of Market Area*, 1 June.

R/UDAT (Regional/Urban Design Assistance Team) (1984) *South of Market Analysis. San Francisco: Urban Planning and Design Committee of the American Institute of Architects*, printed by Blueprint Services.

Port of San Francisco (1997) *Waterfront Design & Access: An Element of the Waterfront Land Use Plan*, Draft, 7 May.

Interview

Conducted by Gayle Rubin with Jim Kane and Ike Barnes 1979.

Gay guides

(1966) *International Guild Guide*, Washington, DC: Guild Book Service.

(1969) *Guide to the San Francisco Scene*, San Francisco: Hedonic Enterprises.

(1969) *Barfly*, Los Angeles: Los Angeles Advocate.

(1971) *The Timely Gay Bar Guide*, Huntington, Long Island.

(1975) *Barfly*, Los Angeles: Advocate Publications.

(1978) *Bob Damron's Address Book*, San Francisco: Bob Damron Enterprises.

(1978) *The Gay Yellow Pages*, New York: Renaissance House.

(1987) *Bob Damron's Address Book*, San Francisco: Bob Damron Enterprises.

(1987) *The Gay Yellow Pages*, New York: Renaissance House.

(1988) *Bob Damron's Address Book*, San Francisco: Bob Damron Enterprises.

(1994) *Bob Damron's Address Book*, San Francisco: Bob Damron Enterprises.

Chapter Four

Unsexing the body: the interior sexuality of medieval religious women

Roberta Gilchrist

[handwritten: U can't reconstruct find evid for sexual behaviour between 2 people so why it should u (God) :-) understand'g]

> The boundary between the inside and outside, just as much as between self and other and subject and object, must not be regarded as a limit to be transgressed so much as a boundary to be transversed. *[handwritten: what is transversed / lying across]* (Grosz 1995: 131)

An archaeology of sexuality remains an exploratory endeavor, a tentative probing of past experiences, social practices, and classifications of bodily pleasure. Sexuality, however loosely defined, must be understood as a historically created set of values and relationships, rather than a timeless, natural category of existence (Gilchrist 1999). This chapter explores the meaning of sexuality according to the celibacy of medieval religious women. It focuses on the *interior, experiential* qualities of sexuality, as it was expressed through the materiality of space and visual imagery. Through the processes of sensual denial and strict physical enclosure, the sexuality of medieval religious women was turned inside out: sexuality became an interior space, a place of elevated senses and ecstatic states of consciousness. Celibacy, enclosure and contemplation were the avenues through which religious women discovered an intense, profound desire for the suffering body of Christ.

Sources for studying the sexuality of these women include texts, such as monastic rules, devotional guides written for women (by male religious), and very rarely, autobiographical narratives of the mystical visions of religious women. Material sources comprise the art and archaeology of monastic institutions for women, encompassing architecture and evidence for daily life and standards of living. This study concentrates on the experience of religious women from the twelfth to fifteenth centuries, with evidence from medieval Britain placed in a comparative European context. During this time, a woman inspired to a religious vocation might choose between that of the nun, hospital sister, or 'beguine', depending on her class status and regional location. More exceptionally, she might elect the role of the anchoress, who was perpetually enclosed in her cell, symbolically immured in the tomb with Christ. Consideration of the sexuality of these women vividly illustrates the problems inherent in projecting modern sexual categories onto the past, in particular, that personal sexual identity is predicated on intimate sexual activity with another animate individual.

BRIDES OF CHRIST

The numbers and status of medieval women's religious communities varied across north-western Europe. These institutions shared certain fundamental qualities, however, notably their simplicity of architectural planning, their emphasis on enclosure and sexual segregation, and a focus on Eucharistic piety and penitential living.

The majority of nunneries founded in Britain after the Norman Conquest were often poor in comparison with monasteries founded for men. This disparity seems to have resulted from the different social level at which nunneries were founded: over seventy of an approximate total of 130 in England were established by local lords who held neither title nor high office (Thompson 1991: 163). Of the sixty-four Irish nunneries founded between the early twelfth and sixteenth centuries, only seven were established by the higher-ranking Anglo-Normans. In Britain, it is clear that nunneries were established in order to make a more local impact than their wealthier, more political male counterparts (Gilchrist 1994). In contrast, Cistercian nunneries in Germany and France were numerous, some-times powerful, and frequently relatively prosperous. In Denmark, there were twenty-two nunneries and thirty-one male monasteries by 1250, some of which were richer and larger than the female houses; in Norway, there were five nunneries and fourteen monasteries by the same date; while in Sweden there were equal numbers, with six of both nunneries and monasteries for men (Smith 1973). Evidence has been put forward from both England and France to suggest that nuns were held in especially high regard by lay society, contrary to previous historiographical stereotyping. Nuns in Normandy continued to receive gifts and bequests throughout the medieval period (Johnson 1991: 223), and in East Anglia, in eastern England, the personal wills of middle ranking lay-people continued to leave bequests to nuns right up to the Dissolution of the Monasteries (1535–1539), long after they had become disaffected with the wealthier monks and canons (Gilchrist and Oliva 1993: 60–61).

Outside nunneries, religious women found places in medieval hospitals, serving as nursing sisters or servants. In England and Wales there were over 1,100 medieval hospitals founded between the twelfth and the fifteenth centuries. The larger infirmary hospitals were organized along monastic principles, with mixed populations of male and female inmates and staff. Both male and female staff took religious vows, and the women were often concerned particularly with nursing care. A more flexible religious vocation was developed by women in the Netherlands, northern France and the Rhine valley, where informal communities of women banded together and supported themselves through their own labors and by begging for alms. These 'beguinages' prevailed in some areas from the thirteenth century onwards, such as Amsterdam, where fifteen of the eighteen monasteries built within the walls during the fourteenth and fifteenth centuries were semi-monastic communities of women. By this time even the beguines lived in enclosed communities, such as the Great Beguinage at Ghent, enclosed by walls and moats. Historians of monasticism in Britain have assumed until recently that such informal communities of women did not flourish outside continental Europe. While convincing evidence for their existence in East Anglia has been put forward, for the most part religious women in medieval Britain were nuns, hospital sisters, or anchoresses. The most solitary and austere of vocations, that of the anchoress, was favored and supported especially by English laity throughout the Middle Ages. English recluses were predominantly women, particularly from the thirteenth to fifteenth centuries (Warren 1985: 20), and anchoritic literature of the period was directed especially towards women, such as *The Ancrene Wisse* (Salu 1955). Hospital sisters followed a more active, nursing vocation, while nuns and anchoresses shared the contemplative, meditative life that is explored here.

ANIMATE DESIRE

> . . . Interior space, be it of the house or of the body, is a feminine place; for the first
> dwelling-place of man is buried deep in the secret places of women.
> (*Chirurgie* of Henri de Mondeville (1306–1320), quoted in Pouchelle 1990: 130)

Discussions of historical sexuality are generally framed by a concern for tracing sexual preferences between and among individuals, with primacy placed on the physical interaction between human bodies. Studies of ancient sexuality have been permeated by Foucauldian approaches (Foucault 1977) that highlight strategies of *control over* the body, or the *inscription* of sexualized values on the body's exterior (Montserrat 1998: 4; Meskell 1996: 8). There has been an emphasis on the *representation* of sexual identity, or conduct, through images of sexed or sexualized bodies (Kampen 1996). The approaches of feminism and queer theory have added to these considerations the dimension of the 'lived body', through which sexuality is experienced, and categories of sex and gender are created (Butler 1990). A further element is required to unite the exterior and interior qualities of sexuality, one which will move beyond study of sexual representation or inscription to examine how the 'lived body' is produced. The feminist philosopher Elizabeth Grosz has called for a more materialist consideration of the body, one which would examine how the processes of social inscription on the *exterior* surface coalesce to construct a psychical *interior* (Grosz 1995: 104). She proposes that understanding of such sexualized corporeality requires inclusion of the dimensions of time and space (Grosz 1995: 84), the familiar domains of archaeology.

In the case of single-sex communities, such as medieval nunneries or modern prisons (Casella this volume), one might anticipate a culture of same-sex activity. In the medieval example, however, the choice of a communal female life, together with celibacy, was usually voluntary. Entry to a monastic community involved renunciation of all aspects of personal identity, including sexuality, family ties, and social status. The monastic rule used by the majority of communities, that of St. Benedict, warned initiates that 'thenceforward he will not have disposition even of his own body' (McCann 1952: chap. 58). A medieval nun committed her celibacy to the church as a Bride of Christ, beginning with an initiation ceremony that involved adornment in bridal clothes and acceptance of a wedding ring. After having her hair shorn, and donning the identical habit of the nun, she forfeited individuality. The medieval religious woman embraced celibacy as a union with Christ, and her body became their shared, private space (Gilchrist 1994: 18–19).

During the period under consideration, historical sources are silent on the issue of same-sex sexual relations in women's religious communities. Indeed, where transgressions from monastic observances are recorded, for example in the records of bishops' visitations to English nunneries, women are admonished to share the communal sleeping and eating spaces that are specified in the Rule of St. Benedict (Power 1922). Clearly, the impulse for individualism and privacy was a cause for concern, rather than any fear that women sharing communal living areas might engage in homosexual activity. Greater anxiety surrounded the issue of heterosexual relations, since sexual congress with a nun destroyed her virginal celibacy, and involved infidelity with a Bride of Christ. Religious women were expected to guard their chastity fiercely, as conveyed in the twelfth-century tale of the

Nun of Watton, told by a renowned churchman, Aelred of Rievaulx (Constable 1978). This is the (apparently true) story of a young nun, who lived in a 'double house' of monastics of both sexes in Yorkshire in the 1150s or 1160s, who took a monastic brother as her lover. When the other nuns were alerted to her adultery, they beat her, chained her, imprisoned her in a cell, and starved her on bread and water. The male object of her affections was to fare far worse, when the nuns avenged their 'violated chastity' and 'the injury of Christ':

> Some [of the nuns], who were full of zeal for God but not of wisdom and who wished to avenge the injury to their virginity, soon asked the brothers to let them have the young man for a short time, as if to learn some secret from him. The cause of all these evils [i.e. the nun] was brought in as if for a spectacle; an instrument was put into her hands; and she was compelled, unwilling, to cut off the virus with her own hands. Then one of the bystanders snatched the parts of which he had been relieved and thrust them into the mouth of the sinner just as they were befouled with blood.
>
> (Corpus Christi Cambridge MS 139 fols. 149–51;
> quoted in Constable 1978: 208)

This, and other cautionary tales, may have curbed sexual temptation in the nunnery. The celibacy of religious women was enmeshed further in a broad canvas of theological, medical and social discourses surrounding the female body.

Medieval religious and medical traditions characterized women's bodies as more naturally given to sinfulness, requiring taming and containment. Women were regarded as the more physical, lustful, and material side of human nature, contrasting with the more spiritual, rational and intellectual male. Following classical humoral theory, rooted in the works of Aristotle and Galen, medieval medicine proposed that the human body was made up of four basic elements, which also made up the universe: fire, water, earth, and air. Women were regarded as watery and changeable, with a cold, wet humoral balance which contrasted with the hot, dry male (Rawcliffe 1995: 172). The body's interior was generally perceived as a contained, domestic and feminine space: inner, watery, and mercurial, it was in keeping with the proposed phlegmatic humor of women.

Such perceptions of the female body influenced both the expectations placed on medieval religious women, and their own spiritual experience – the 'lived body' of their religiosity. Their innate female corporeality was believed to render them more susceptible to lust and sexual sin. Thus, women were regarded as changeable in disposition and prone to sexual corruption; further, the character of their bodies was considered to be 'interior' by nature. Consistent with these views, monastic authorities demanded the strict physical enclosure of religious women, to ensure the intactness of both their virginity and their mortal souls. From the intact, interior space of their enclosure, the challenge remained for religious women to conquer and contain their physicality. They demonstrated the voracity of their belief through asceticism, a physical denigration of the sensual body. This was achieved through renunciation of sensuous pleasure, including sex, food, freedom of mobility, individual care and adornment of the body. Food, or its denial through extreme fasting, came to have significant religious symbolism to medieval women (Bynum 1987). Women were attributed with a more empathetic response to the suffering and Passion of Christ: the inherent moisture of their own phlegmatic bodies (menstrual blood and tears) was compared with the sacrifice of Christ's blood at the Crucifixion (Robertson 1990: 9). Caroline Walker Bynum has argued influentially that between the twelfth and fourteenth centuries these themes were drawn together, as women developed a special devotion to the Eucharist (Bynum 1987). Focus on the Eucharist and the suffering body of Christ became widespread (Ross 1997), yet seems to have held poignant resonances for religious women. Through the Eucharist, women could consume and absorb the sacrificial body of Christ as symbolic food. At the same time, their own spiritual strength was demonstrated through extreme fasting, which has been termed 'food asceticism' or 'holy anorexia' (Bynum 1987: 87). Denial of sustenance over long periods of time seems to have brought about a heightened emotional state, in which many religious women experienced spiritual visions. These mystical hallucinations were dominated by the blood, heart, wounds, and sacrificial body of Christ, exemplified in the writings of Hildegard of Bingen in the twelfth century, Mechthild of Hackeborn, Hadewijch of Brabant and Mechthild of Magdeburg in the thirteenth century, and Julian of Norwich in the fourteenth century:

> . . . I also saw the bodily sight of the head [of Christ] copiously bleeding. Large drops of blood dripped down from under the crown like pellets – appearing to come from the veins all brownish and red, for the blood was very thick, and as it spread the drops became bright red. When it reached the brows, the drops vanished; nevertheless the bleeding continued until many things were seen and understood. The beauty and vitality, nevertheless, continued with the same loveliness and animation.
>
> (Julian of Norwich *c.* 1373, Colledge and Walsh 1978: long text 7)

Devotional guides written for anchoresses, such as the early thirteenth-century English works *The Ancrene Wisse* (Guide for Anchoresses), *Hali Meidenhad* (Holy Maidenhood) and *Sawles Warde* (The Guardianship of the Soul), together with mystical works written by women themselves, emphasize the role of Christ as Bridegroom and the religious virgin as his bride. These texts convey a highly personal, material dimension, in which the woman's union with Christ is concretely physical and sexually charged (Robertson 1990). In the *Ancrene Wisse*, she receives the Eucharist as her lover:

> After the kiss of peace in the Mass, when the priest communicates, forget the world, be completely out of the body, and with burning love embrace your Beloved who has come down from heaven to your heart's bower, and hold Him fast until He has granted you all that you ask.
>
> (Salu 1955: 14)

She is encouraged to enter the wounds of Christ, and purify herself in his blood: 'Creep into them, in thought. Are they not wide open? And with His precious blood cover your heart' (Salu 1955: 130).

THE GLORIOUS PRISON

In theory, therefore, medieval religious women were expected to be strictly enclosed within their convents and to minimize their contact with the outside world (Schulenburg 1984). By the time the first Cluniac nunnery was founded at Marcigny in 1056, referred to by Abbot Hugh as a 'glorious prison', the concept of enclosure was integral to female monasticism. But it has been argued recently that the degree of enclosure and segregation experienced by religious women has been overestimated, and that in the eleventh to thirteenth centuries there was considerable ease of contact between religious men and women (Berman

1988; Hamburger 1992: 110). In England, there was a certain degree of informality during the early years of Norman monasticism, which, up to the thirteenth century, tolerated cells of religious women placed at Benedictine monasteries of men. This fluidity survived into the later Middle Ages in certain regions, when women were sometimes accommodated in Benedictine monasteries for men in France, Germany, and the Netherlands.

A greater concern for enclosure and sexual segregation was felt in double monasteries, in which architectural mechanisms were developed to ensure separation of male and female communities. Particularly severe were the observances of the French order of Fontevrault, which included eighteen rules for women, all concerning strict enclosure, in contrast to nine for men which related to obedience. At the mother house in Fontevrault the nuns' cloisters were contained within the walls, whereas that of the canons was outside. In the church, two separate choirs were provided in order to facilitate segregation (Simmons 1992: 102–103). In English Gilbertine houses a similar degree of strictness was observed, perhaps to preclude sexual scandals of the kind that surrounded the infamous (Gilbertine) Nun of Watton (above). Two cloisters and two choirs were provided, and food was passed from the nuns' cloister to the canons' through a small turning window approached by a passage from both cloisters. The nuns could only speak to their visiting relatives through a narrow aperture. In houses of the Swedish double order of St. Bridget, buildings of the nuns and canons were placed on opposite sides of a shared conventual church (Nyberg 1965).

Absolute enclosure was observed by anchoresses, religious women who intended to be enclosed perpetually. These women required substantial commitment and financial support from a parish community; they were accommodated in cells attached to parish churches (Figure 4.1), where a servant would have supplied food and removed waste. Given the importance of the Eucharist to religious women, a window or grill provided visibility of the high altar. The anchoress was sometimes buried in her cell after death, and was expected to meditate on the inevitable decay of her own body:

> She should scrape up earth every day out of the grave in which she shall rot . . . the sight of her grave near her does many an anchoress much good . . . She who keeps her death as it were before her eyes, her open grave reminding her of it . . . will not lightly pursue the delight of the flesh.
>
> (Salu 1955: 51)

At the parish church of St. Anne's, Lewes (Sussex), previously known as St. Mary Westout, a female recluse was recorded in 1253, when she was left 5 shillings in the will of Richard de Wych, Bishop of Chichester. Excavation of a cell on the south side of the chancel revealed the remains of a woman's skeleton dug into the foundations. Within a semi-circular recess in the south wall of the church was a squint which slanted towards the high altar; at its base a grave had been tunneled into the sides to allow space for the hands and feet of the skeleton. Below the squint the plaster of the recess continued to the bottom of the grave, which formed the back of the shaped coffin (Godfrey 1928: 166–68). In order to view the high altar through the squint the recluse would have had to kneel daily in her own grave. Such morbid practices were integral to the denigrating qualities of the anchoress's life.

In all female religious institutions some degree of contact between religious men and women was essential, for priests were required for masses and confession. A sacristy was positioned next to the church to store sacred vessels and vestments, and for the priest to robe and disrobe. As a male space, it was necessary to enter the sacristy from outside the

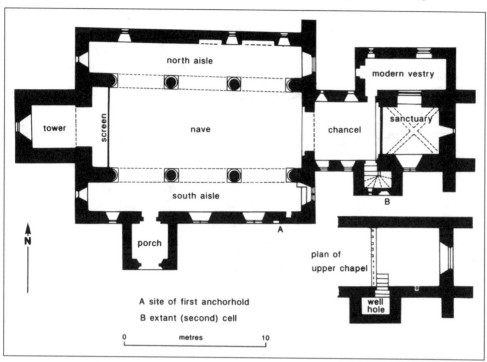

Figure 4.1 Compton parish church (Surrey): ground plan of the medieval parish church showing the position of the extant anchorhold to the south of the chancel (B), and the site of an earlier cell to the south of the nave (A). A squint or aperture would have allowed the anchoress to see the Mass at the high altar.
Illustration supplied by the author.

cloister, with direct access through the precinct. Often this was placed between the church and chapter house, but an entrance in the external wall allowed the priest access to the sacristy without ingress to the nuns' cloister (Figure 4.2). Sacristies became standard in English convent plans by the thirteenth century, just as they disappeared from male houses, or devolved into passageways into the cloister. In several surviving English examples, such as Carrow (Norwich, Norfolk), and Brewood (Shrops.), the sacristy was the most highly ornamented room of the entire convent.

Contrary to our notions of strict enclosure, many convent churches were actually shared with the congregation of a parish church, and church plans developed in accordance with the aim of segregating the two groups. The most common arrangement in Britain was the typical monastic division between eastern conventual choir and western parochial nave. Mechanisms for segregation sometimes developed organically, along local lines, especially where a convent had been founded at the site of an existing parish church. A number of English nunnery churches segregated the two congregations through the provision of parallel aisles, with a screened arcade prohibiting visual contact. This was the practice followed, for example, in the Benedictine communities of St. Helen, Bishopgate, London, and Minster-in-Sheppey (Kent). Parallel aisles were used also to segregate the nuns and canons in Gilbertine double houses, and to divide the male and female communities of many hospitals.

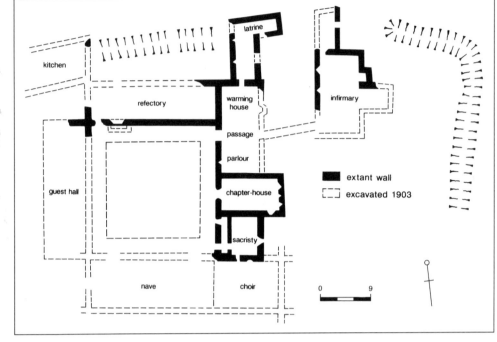

Figure 4.2 The nunnery at Burnham (Berks.) retains a surviving range of buildings and was partially excavated by the antiquary Harold Brakspear (Brakspear 1903). It was founded in 1266 with a simple church (aisleless rectangle), cloister to the north, and sacristy with private access for a priest through a doorway in its eastern wall.
Illustration supplied by the author.

In French convents it was more usual for the monastic choir to be contained in the eastern arm of the church, separated from the nave by a *pulpitum*. Many nunnery churches in Germany, Scandinavia and Britain, in contrast, operated at two levels, and were provided with a gallery-choir in order to achieve adequate sexual segregation. Evidence of galleries in English convent churches can be found at the western end of the church at Aconbury (Herefords.) and the eastern end of the church at Burnham (Berks.). Western galleries were typical in Scandinavian convents, with extant examples at Bosjökloster and St. Peter in Lund in Scania, modern Sweden; and at Roskilde and Asmild in Viborg, Denmark. This solution to the problem of segregation was widespread in German-speaking areas, where western galleries and raised choirs are well known, such as Wienhausen, Chelmno (Kulm, Poland), Adelhausen in Freiburg, and Ebstorf. In some cases special passages were required for the nuns to gain access to their choirs, such as the first-story wall-walks at Marienstern that led from the dormitory to the western choir (Hamburger 1992: 114).

Jeffrey Hamburger has attributed the development of the western gallery-choir to the German tradition of raised crypts and Westwork galleries (1992: 112–113), although their wide geographical distribution may indicate a more ancient origin, possibly even in the galleries or tribunes used to segregate women in sixth-century Byzantine churches. Where convent communities shared their churches with parochial or male religious congregations, there was the possibility that the emphasis on segregation may have diminished the important female connection with the Eucharist. In churches of the English double order of

— What?!

the Gilbertines it is clear that the nuns were unable to witness the moment of transub-stantiation. Parallel aisles were used to separate the male and female communities, with the high altar situated in the canons' church. After the elevation of the host, the sacra-ment was passed through a window to a female sacristan in the nuns' church (Elkins 1988: 141). Caroline Bruzelius has charted the development of choirs in Italian Clarissan houses, noting that their evolution corresponded with the increasing emphasis on Eucharistic devotion. From the fourteenth century, new churches allowed visibility of the altar, while previously the nuns had used western gallery-choirs or lateral chambers which precluded visibility. A highly developed example is that of Santa Chiara, Naples, built early in the fourteenth century, with the choir located directly behind the altar in a retro-choir, with three large grated openings permitting direct sight of the altar and the elevation of the host (Bruzelius 1992: 87).

THE INTERIORITY OF MEDIEVAL RELIGIOUS WOMEN

It has been argued that visual culture would have been central within the enclosed environ-ment of the convent, where the importance of images was enhanced by the nuns' seclusion (Hamburger 1992: 109). The suffering of Christ's body was the pervasive image in texts associated with religious women, with the blood and flesh of the Crucifixion taking on sacramental significance. In rare cases where visual images produced by nuns survive, it is possible to discern the same Eucharistic themes that permeate the writings of the female mystics. Jeffrey Hamburger has studied a group of illuminated manuscripts (dated *c.* 1500) produced at the Benedictine convent of St. Walburg, Eichstätt, Bavaria (Hamburger 1997). These exhibit a childlike, naive quality which shows little awareness of artistic conven-tions outside the nunnery. Hamburger argues that they display a concern with distinctively feminine religious images, such as a blood-drenched Crucifixion and an enclosed garden. Four images in particular convey religious women's mystical concerns with enclosure and the Eucharist: the Symbolic Crucifixion, the Heart on the Cross (Figure 4.3), the Eucharistic Banquet (where a nun and Christ commune inside his heart), and the Heart as House (for the religious woman to reside). Hamburger proposes that these images can only be understood when viewed from the 'inside out, rather than the outside in' (10). He concludes that their scale and choice of subjects reflect an 'interiority', the inwardness and mystical piety of the cloistered life for women.

In English convent architecture, the sacristy, where the Eucharist was housed, was the most embellished room. The imagery in this area was frequently linked to the Eucharist through references to the sacrifice of Christ, including representations of the *Agnus Dei* (the lamb of God), depicted on a corbel at Augustinian Lacock Abbey (Wilts.) in England. In one case, excavations at the site of an English nunnery recovered a carved Sacred Heart, an image that identified with the suffering body of Christ, and which is rarely found in England (Figure 4.4). This piece from Dartford Dominican Nunnery (Kent) is wholly in keeping with the Eucharistic and mystical themes that dominated later medieval female piety: the Sacred Heart was crucial to the visions of Mechthild of Hackeborn, Mechthild of Magdeburg, and Julian of Norwich.

> So He, with great desire, shows her His divine heart. It is like red gold burning in a great fire. And God takes the soul to His glowing heart as the high prince and the humble maiden embrace and are united as water and wine. Then the soul becomes as nothing and is so beside herself that she can do nothing. And He is sick with

Quote with picture —

Figure 4.3 The Heart on the Cross: illumination by a nun of the Benedictine convent of St. Walburg, Eichstätt, Bavaria (dated *c.* 1500). Jeffrey Hamburger has drawn attention to a sequence of visual images produced at this convent that convey themes of enclosure and the Eucharist. He argues that they show the mystical union of Christ with the religious woman: 'Having passed through the wound in Christ's side, the nun enters a metaphorical as well as physical interior' (Hamburger 1997: 138).
Manuscript St. Walburg, Eichstätt, Bavaria. Reproduced from Hamburger, 1997.

love for her, as He ever was, for He neither increases nor decreases. Then the soul says: Lord, You are my comfort, my desire, my flowing spring, my sun, and I am Your reflection.

(Mechthild of Magdeburg, *c.* 1250, quoted in Howard 1984: 179)

Figure 4.4 A Sacred Heart carving excavated from Dartford Dominican
nunnery (Kent) (Garrod 1980).
Reproduced from *Kent Archaeological Review*, courtesy of the Council for
Kentish archaeology. Drawing by Kent Archaeological Rescue Unit.

The themes and images chosen by religious women show a concern with *interiority* –
inner spaces, inner suffering and even the internal organs of Christ – that accords closely
with the 'interior' quality of the female body, and the emphasis on enclosure for female
religious.

COLD COMFORT

While visual images of the Eucharist became central to religious women, other aspects of
their physical lives remained bleak. In comparison with contemporary monasteries for
men, or the manor houses or castles occupied by their secular sisters, religious women
endured a penitential, self-denying existence.

The scale of nunnery architecture is perhaps best assessed through the archaeological
remains of churches. The long tradition of scholarship on the Cistercians, especially, has

led to detailed typologies of the remains of Cistercian convent churches in France (Dimier 1974; Desmarchelier 1982), Germany (Coester 1984, 1986) and, to a lesser extent, England (Nichols 1982). Père Anselme Dimier classified Cistercian nunnery churches in France according to whether the nave had aisles or not, whether the church had transepts, a comparison of the width of the sanctuary in relation to the rest of the church, and the nature in which the east end terminated, whether straight, apsed or with radiating chapels (Dimier 1974; Desmarchelier 1982). Ten plan types were proposed, but the most commonly occurring type seems to have been Dimier's Type 1: the simple rectangle, without aisles, or transept, with nave and sanctuary of the same width, and an eastern end with straight termination. Typically, the French convent churches ranged from 35–50 m in length and 12–13 m in width. Similarly, in the German-speaking regions, the majority of the Cistercian nunneries adopted a simple plan comprising a single vessel, with a certain degree of variation between regions and monastic orders (Hamburger 1992: 112). In Britain, the aisleless rectangle was again the most common arrangement (Figure 4.2), with 62 percent of known convent churches of all monastic orders in England and Wales taking this form; the remaining 38 percent were cruciform churches (Gilchrist 1994: 97). English convent churches could be anywhere from 15 to 50 m in length. These simple, narrow churches were satisfactory for a small community, typically of twelve nuns, with perhaps only a single priest or chaplain (Figure 4.2). Given the liturgical prohibitions placed on nuns, a minimum number of altars was required, and consequently there was little need for additional chapels, transepts, or aisles for later chantries. Many of these churches remained unchanged throughout the Middle Ages. Their simplicity of plan, general absence of embellishment and lack of development or alteration sets them apart from monastic churches for men.

In Britain, it was not unknown for the claustral buildings to be constructed in wood or earth, and for convents to have had relatively unsatisfactory arrangements for hygiene, drainage, and disposal of refuse, all factors considered essential in male establishments. It may be that these were deliberate short-comings, pivotal to the penitential life that many women sought during the twelfth and thirteenth centuries, the time at which the majority of nunneries were founded. Nuns and anchoresses made do with relatively crude systems of sanitation, simple pit latrines that contrasted with the water-flushed lavatories of most male institutions (Gilchrist 1995: 129), while recent excavations have recovered greater quantities of refuse than would be expected of the scrupulous standards of monastic cleanliness (Gilchrist 1995: 145). Poor sanitation may have been one means by which religious women denigrated their bodies. The author of the *Ancrene Wisse* advised them not to take this aspect of their asceticism to extremes: 'Wash yourselves whenever necessary and as often as you wish, and your things as well, Filth was never dear to God, although poverty and plainness of dress are pleasing to him' (Salu 1955).

Such asceticism also extended to diet, which in smaller nunneries seems to have been closer to that of the more affluent peasantry than to the rich fare of monasteries for men; it was cereal-based, consisting largely of bread and pottage (soup), fruit and vegetables, fish, dairy produce, beef, and bacon.

The sites of nunneries were often isolated or inhospitable, frequently placed on islands, causeways, or surrounded by moats, in settings ideally suited to an eremitic calling. Nunneries seem to have been less involved in the reshaping and active management of landscapes than their male counterparts (Gilchrist 1994). English nunneries had more in common with manor houses of the secular gentry than with larger monasteries for men. Both nunneries and manor houses were ordered around open courtyards, often consisting of discontinuous ranges linked by enclosed walkways. The west ranges of many convents functioned as guest accommodation and were modeled closely on manorial halls, with a central hall screened from an upper chamber and divided from the lower service end by a screened passage.

In contrast with the usual arrangement, a significant proportion of nunneries placed their cloisters to the north of the church: in England, over one third of known convents were arranged in this manner (Figure 4.2). Moreover, when mapped, the north cloisters cluster tightly in certain regions, indicating local traditions of meaning associated with religious women (Gilchrist 1994: 128–49). Generally this arrangement did not result from restrictions relating to drainage, water supply, or urban topography, and it may be that the northern region of churches was more suited to religious women. The colder, darker, damper cloister that resulted from a northern situation was perhaps more fitting for the phlegmatic humor of women, and deemed more actively penitential. Further, the north side of churches was associated with traditions in the burial and seating of women, in addition to carrying connotations of the Blessed Virgin Mary. In contemporary depictions of the Crucifixion, Mary's traditional place was at the foot of the cross, on Christ's right hand. When this image was superimposed over the ground-plan of the church (representing the cross), Mary was positioned to the north side. The north cloister may be another aspect of the particular devotion that women showed to images of the Crucifixion.

INSIDE OUT: THE FETISHISM OF MEDIEVAL RELIGIOUS WOMEN

The sexuality of religious women was produced through inversion: all elements of physical sensuality were stripped away, as outward concerns turned inward. Denial of bodily pleasure was not limited to celibacy, but extended to the renunciation of food, cleanliness, warmth, and comfort. Medieval religious women experienced their sexuality through the denigration of their bodies, including an austerity of landscapes, architecture, and quality of daily life. They embraced the enclosure that was imposed on them; indeed, some craved enclosure and suffering in the extreme. Their materiality was forged through enclosure with Christ, their heavenly Bridegroom, in a celebration of the notion of 'interior'. Through their devotion to the Eucharist, Christ's Heart, and Crucifixion, religious women channeled their sexual desire toward the lacerated, crucified, interior body of Christ.

Medieval female religiosity has been characterized as having been steeped in erotic, mystical and maternal imagery (Bynum 1987), a perception which has recently been denounced as a 'rigidly heterosexualized version of their sexuality', by the medieval scholar Karma Lochrie (Lochrie 1997: 181). Lochrie reminds us of the darker side of female mysticism. Women such as Hadewijch of Brabant, Angela of Foligno, and Catherine of Siena described voracious mystical sex, and a narcissistic, violent love for Christ, expressed through withdrawal and death. Shared suffering brought the religious woman ecstatic pleasure, with the most exquisite moments reserved for contemplation of Christ's internal organs, feeding from his sacred wounds, and entry of his body through these wounds – interpreted by Lochrie as homoerotic imagery. However, the desire expressed by religious women was not for another animate individual – either male or female – or for penetration or tactile sensations, but for a sexual encounter capable of overwhelming body, soul, space, and time. Here we glimpse a fetishistic sexuality *experienced* through the suffering body of Christ, an instance of what Elizabeth Grosz has termed 'desire as corporeal intensification':

> One is opened up, in spite of oneself, to the other, not as passive respondent but as co-animated, for the other's convulsions, spasms, joyous or painful encounters

She doesn't discuss what inside of cells looks like

engender, or contaminate, bodily regions that are apparently unsusceptible ... The other need not be human or even animal: the fetishist enters a universe of the animated, intensified object as rich and complex as any sexual relation (perhaps more so than).

(Grosz 1995: 200)

The archaeology, visual culture, and writings associated with medieval religious women allow us an intimate view of their sexualized corporeality. The sexuality of these women was not limited to that *inscribed* by monastic authorities on their *exterior* bodies: theirs was a sexuality experienced deeply and materially. Their distinctive sexuality was *experienced* as *interiority* – the character of the ascetic female body, the conditions of their monastic enclosure, and a profound, perhaps fetishistic, desire for the internal organs of Christ. Churchmen and patrons allowed medieval religious women only limited mobility, religious roles and material conditions of existence. Such limitations were turned inside out, as women joined their suffering and denigration with that of their spiritual Bridegroom, absorbed in a singular, interior sexuality.

REFERENCES

Berman, C. H. (1988) 'Men's Houses, Women's Houses: The Relationship Between the Sexes in Twelfth-Century Monasticism', in A. MacLeish (ed.) *The Medieval Monastery*, St. Cloud: Minnesota.

Brakspear, H. (1903) 'Burnham Abbey', *Records of Buckinghamshire* 8: 517–40.

Bruzelius, C. (1992) 'Hearing is Believing: Clarissan Architecture, 1213–1340', *Gesta* 31/32: 83–92.

Butler, J. (1990) *Gender Trouble: Feminism and the Subversion of Identity*, London: Routledge.

Bynum, C. W. (1987) *Holy Feast and Holy Fast: the Religious Significance of Food to Medieval Women*, Berkeley: University of California Press.

Coester, E. (1984) *Die einschiffigen Cistercienserinnenkirchen West und Süddeutschlands von 1200 bis 1350*, Mainz: Quellen und Abhandlungen zur mittelrheinishen Kirchengeschichte 46.

—— (1986) 'Die Cistercienserinnenkirchen des 12 bis 14 Jahrhunderts', Cologne: *Die Cistercienser Geschichte, Geest, Kunst* (third revised edition): 344–57.

Colledge, E. and J. Walsh (eds) (1978) *A Book of Showings to the Anchoress Julian of Norwich*, Toronto: Pontifical Institute of Mediaeval Studies, Studies and Texts, 35.

Constable, G. (1978) 'Aelred of Rievaulx and the Nun of Watton: an Episode in the Early History of the Gilbertine Order', in D. Baker (ed.) *Medieval Women*, Studies in Church History Subsidia I, Oxford: Blackwell.

Desmarchelier, M. (1982) 'L'architecture des Églises de Moniàles Cisterciennes, essai de classement des différent types de plans (en guise de suite)', *Mélanges à la Mémoire du Père Anselme Dimier présenté par Benôit Chauvin III*, Arbois: Architecture Cistercienne 5 Ordre.

Dimier, A. (1974) 'L'architecture des églises des moniales cisterciennes', *Cîteaux* 25: 8–23.

Elkins, S. K. (1988) *Holy Women in Twelfth-Century England*, Chapel Hill, NC: University of North Carolina Press.

Foucault, M. (1977) *Discipline and Punish. The Birth of the Prison*, A. Sheridan (trans.), London: Allen Lane.

Garrod, D. (1980) 'Important Find from Dartford', *Kent Archaeological Review* 61: 19–20.

Gilchrist, R. (1994) *Gender and Material Culture: the Archaeology of Religious Women*, London: Routledge.

—— (1995) *Contemplation and Action: the Other Monasticism*, London: Leicester University Press.

—— (1999) *Gender and Archaeology: Contesting the Past*, London: Routledge.

Gilchrist, R and Oliva, M. (1993) *Religious Women in Medieval East Anglia: History and Archaeology c. 1100–1540*, Norwich: Centre of East Anglian Studies.

Godfrey, W. H. (1928) 'Church of St Anne's, Lewes: an Anchorite's Cell and Other Discoveries', *Sussex Archaeological Collections* 69: 159–69.

Grosz, E. (1995) *Space, Time and Perversion*, London: Routledge.

Hamburger, J. F. (1992) 'Art, Enclosure and the Cura Monialium: Prolegomena in the Guise of a Postscript', *Gesta*: 108–34.

—— (1997) *Nuns as Artists: The Visual Culture of a Medieval Convent*, Berkeley: University of California Press.

Howard, J. (1984) 'The German Mystic: Mechthild of Magdeburg', in K. M. Wilson (ed.) *Medieval Women Writers*, 153–85, Manchester: Manchester University Press.

Johnson, P. (1991) *Equal in Monastic Profession: Religious Women in Medieval France*, Chicago: University of Chicago Press.

Kampen, N. B. (ed.) (1996) *Sexuality in Ancient Art*, Cambridge: Cambridge University Press.

Lochrie, K. (1997) 'Mystical Acts, Queer Tendencies', in K. Lochrie, P. McCracken and J. A. Schultz (eds) *Constructing Medieval Sexuality*, 180–200, Minneapolis: University of Minnesota Press.

McCann, J. (1952) *The Rule of St. Benedict*, London: Sheed and Ward.

Meskell, L. (1996) 'The Somatization of Archaeology: Institutions, Discourses, Corporeality', *Norwegian Archaeological Review* 29, 1: 1–16.

Montserrat, D. (ed.) (1998) *Changing Bodies, Changing Meanings: Studies on the Human Body in Antiquity*, London: Routledge.

Nichols, J. A. (1982) 'Medieval English Cistercian Nunneries: their Art and Physical Remains', *Mélanges à la Mémoire du Père Anselme Dimier présenté par Benôit Chauvin III*, Arbois: Architecture Cistercienne 5 Ordre.

Nyberg, T. (1965) *Birgittinische Klostergründungen des Mittelalters*, Lund: Bibliotheca Historica Lundensis 15.

Pouchelle, M. (1990) *The Body and Surgery in the Middle Ages*, Cambridge: Polity Press.

Power, E. (1922) *Medieval English Nunneries*, Cambridge: Cambridge University Press.

Rawcliffe, C. (1995) *Medicine and Society in Later Medieval England*, Stroud: Alan Sutton.

Robertson, E. (1990) *Early English Devotional Prose and the Female Audience*, Knoxville: University of Tennessee Press.

Ross, E. M. (1997) *The Grief of God: Images of the Suffering Jesus in Late Medieval England*, Oxford: Oxford University Press.

Salu, M. D. (1955 [1990]) *The Ancrene Riwle*, Notre Dame: University of Notre Dame Press.

Schulenburg, J. T. (1984) 'Strict Active Enclosure and its Effect on the Female Monastic Experience', in J. A. Nichols and L. T. Shank (eds) *Medieval Religious Women 1: Distant Echoes*, 51–86, Kalamazoo, MI: Cistercian Publications.

Simmons, L. (1992) 'The Abbey Church of Fontevrault in the Later Twelfth Century: Anxiety, Authority and Architecture in the Female Spiritual Life', *Gesta* 31/32: 99–107.

Smith, G. (1973) 'De danske nonnekloster indtil ca. 1250', *Kirkehistoriske samlinger*: 1–45.

Thompson, S. (1991) *Women Religious: the Founding of English Nunneries after the Conquest*, Oxford: Clarendon.

Warren, A. K. (1985) *Medieval English Anchorites and their Patrons*, Berkeley: University of California Press.

Chapter Five

The site of sexuality: William Beckford's Fonthill Abbey, 1780–1824

Whitney Davis

This brief chapter is divided into three parts. First, I introduce the erotic and sexual dimensions of William Beckford's neo-Gothic construction of *c.* 1800 in south Wiltshire, about twenty miles from the city of Salisbury: his fantastical residence 'Fonthill Abbey'. My purpose, however, is not to develop a substantive archaeological reconstruction and interpretation of Fonthill Abbey, which no longer exists physically, but rather to comment on the very possibility of such a reconstruction, for which Fonthill Abbey serves as a useful (though not necessarily generally or universally valid) example. In the second part, I review the sources and forensic methods by which the account in the first part – a summary of a large body of complex evidence and argument – might be secured as a so-called 'archaeology of sexuality'. 'Archaeological' analysis proceeds when the thoughts, beliefs, and desires of human subjects must be reconstructed indirectly from deposited material residues. On this view, 'archaeology' is an analytic approach of modern interpretative historicism as it is embodied in disciplines as diverse as philology, art history, and psychoanalysis (see Davis 1997). In the third part, therefore, I comment on the role of the contemporary professional discipline of archaeology (if any), in contributing to the archaeology of sexuality conducted by modern interpretative historicism incarnated in such fields.

So, first: Fonthill Abbey (Figure 5.1). It was built in stages between 1793 and 1812 by the architect James Wyatt for his patron William Beckford (1760–1844), one of the wealthiest subjects in Europe, heir to a vast Jamaican sugar fortune. (For the most recent biographies of Beckford, see Jack 1996 and Mowl 1998, with complete references; for the most extended contemporary descriptions of the Abbey, see Storer 1812, Britton 1823, and Rutter 1823.) Beckford's father, Alderman William Beckford, a famous liberal Lord Mayor of London, had purchased the Fonthill estate in 1745 (Figure 5.2). He built his own earlier house there, on a site beside the lake about three-quarters of a mile to the north-east of the later Abbey (on Rutter's plan [Figure 5.2] it is marked with a small cross), and bequeathed it to his son, who naturally was expected to triumph in society. But in 1784 young William had to flee abroad for a decade after the newspapers exposed his love affair with a young nobleman, William Courtenay, with whom Beckford was purported to have been observed in a moment of intimacy. On his return to England,

Figure 5.1 George Cattermole, *View of the West and South Fronts [of Fonthill Abbey] from the Beacon Terrace*, from Rutter 1823.

Beckford was never able fully to regain his place in society – though he did retain his parliamentary seat and continuously tried to ingratiate himself with successive governments and with the Crown – and for many purposes remained a virtual internal exile. Fonthill Abbey became Beckford's retreat, an enormous house imitating, at least in part, a medieval abbey and baronial hall and bishop's palace (elements of all of which were integrated into Wyatt's designs and Beckford's changing schemes and uses for his construction), erected behind a 'barrier wall' encircling several hundred acres of his father's estate. Here he lived with a handful of European friends (probably also sodomites), a few visitors (chiefly architects and artists employed in the construction and beautification of the Abbey), and servants and workmen, many of whom held him in contempt despite his riches (see especially Alexander 1957, 1962). He was largely shunned by his peers and by the society in which he would otherwise have had a prominent place. For example, despite his extensive patronage of contemporary artists, the Royal Academicians could not bring themselves to invite him to their traditional annual dinner for artists and their friends and admirers. Visitors to the Abbey risked being condemned by the local gentry and inhabitants; Beckford's personal friends sometimes found themselves vilified by local clergymen.

A great deal of study has been devoted to the architectural motifs that Wyatt and Beckford replicated in the Abbey (see especially Brockman 1956, still the most detailed consideration). They included the garden follies typical of the day; specific references to churches and cathedrals of England, such as Canterbury and Salisbury, and of France and Portugal, where Beckford had lived in exile; and exotic references, including literary allusions to Milton's 'Pandemonium' in *Paradise Lost* or to Beckford's own vision of a

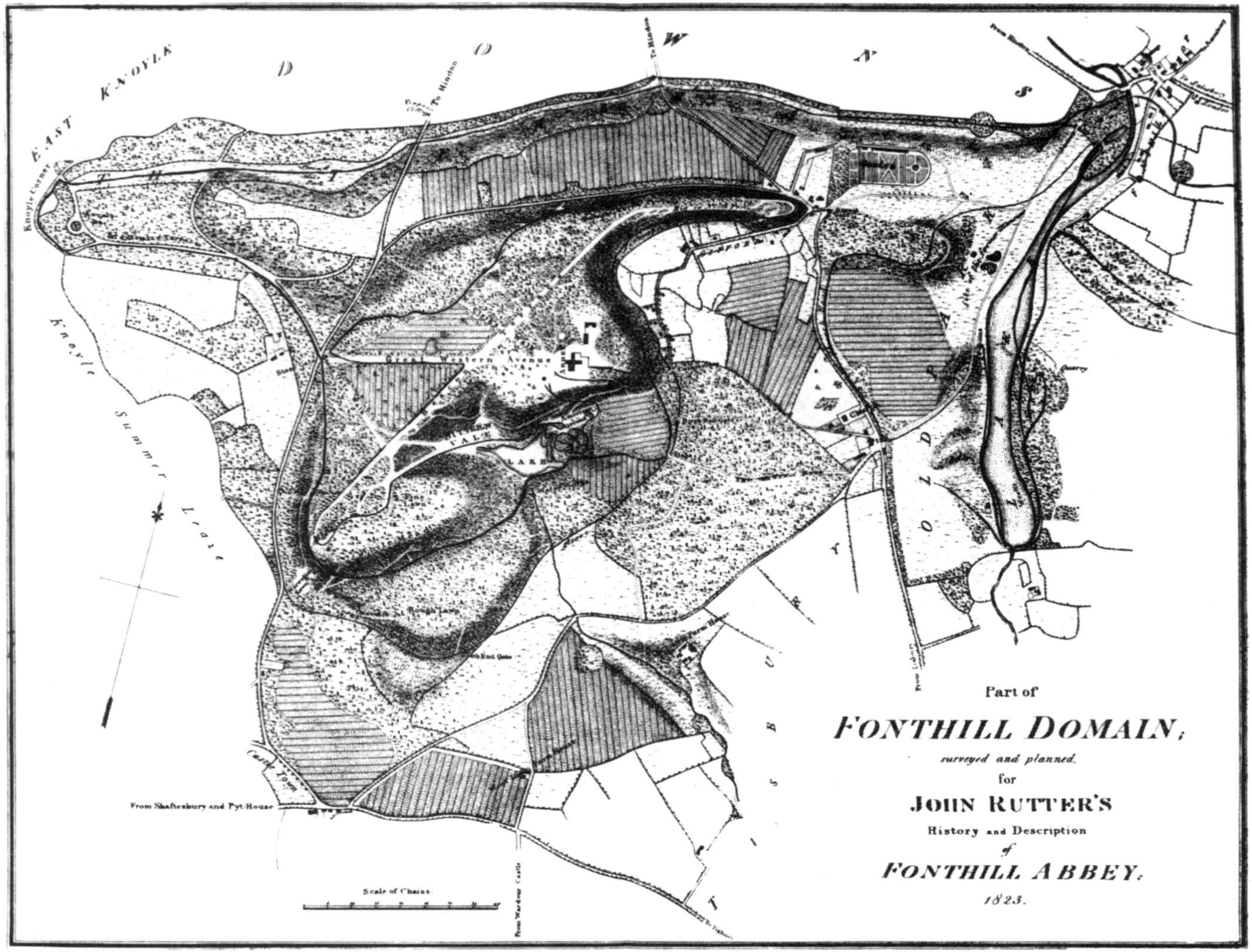

Figure 5.2 [Plan of] *Part of Fonthill Domain*, from Rutter 1823.

semi-legendary Persia embodied in his novelistic fantasy *Vathek* written in 1782 (a useful edition is Beckford 1983, and see generally Parreaux 1960 for Beckford's wide range of allusion). The Abbey in its grounds is now understood to express late eighteenth-century doctrines of the 'picturesque' (a good account is provided by Gemmet 1972); it emphasized individual or even idiosyncratic consciousness, including erotic difference, in opposition to the formality of mind and of sociability represented by the prevalent classical building and garden forms. Important as this general cultural context might be, however, there was also a more specific form of erotic meaning at Fonthill – a structure of 'sexuality' strictly speaking, a material precipitate of the interpersonal and intersubjective history within which someone's specific erotic beliefs and desires had been constituted (for sexuality and intersubjectivity, see Davis 1995).

Fonthill Abbey was architectonically composed to be viewed from a principal ideal vantage point, a hill half a mile south-west of the Abbey where Alderman Beckford had started to build a tower. This vantage point was represented in several contemporary depictions of the building, such as George Cattermole's engraving of the Abbey from the south-west (Figure 5.1), which includes an imaginary viewer seated on the hillside just below the high vantage where the artist-viewer is located. It was recognized by J. M. W. Turner in one of his watercolor pictures of Fonthill Abbey and grounds, exhibited at the Royal Academy in the late 1790s, as a site of interest in its own right; he depicted an imaginary viewer looking towards the place where the ideal viewer of the Abbey, such as we see in Cattermole's engraving, could actually be seated looking at the building. (For Turner's images of Fonthill, see Cundall 1916; Finberg 1909: 1, 122–26.) The principal perspectives towards the Abbey centered on this position. By the same token, the principal viewing possibilities from the Abbey – the vistas one could have standing at its doors or windows – were oriented outwards in that south-westerly direction. Conversely, views to the north and east were barred. As one can see from the ground-plan (Figure 5.3) and section (Figure 5.4) of the Abbey, probably prepared under Beckford's supervision, there was little functional fenestration giving easterly vistas; if there were east windows at all they were, with one exception, screened or blocked. The section shows that the east walls were lined with pictures or cabinets rather than windows, even though the opposite walls were fully fenestrated with vistas towards the ideal center. (This differentiation is most striking on the principal storey [Figure 5.3], where the long south wing, known as 'St. Michael's Gallery', confronts five tall west-facing windows, overlooking the 'Fountain Court' and with views down the 'Great Western Avenue' to the west, with a long unfenestrated eastern wall ranged with bookcases, visible in the section [Figure 5.4]; and where the long north wing, known as 'King Edward's Gallery', confronts seven tall west-facing windows with an unfenestrated eastern wall ranged with bookcases and paintings. On the basement floor, the east-facing windows that are visible in the section [Figure 5.4] were actually false windows.) Outside, to the north and east of the building were located the kitchen gardens, stables and sheds, and workmen's services, all virtually permanent constructions. (They are visible on the estate plan [Figure 5.2] as large structures immediately north-east of the cross identifying the location of the Abbey at the east terminus of the 'Great Western Avenue'.) But the choice to put such functions north-east must have already been determined by the idealization of the south-western orientation (as indicated by the placement of an ideal imaginary viewer [Figure 5.2]). That orientation is, I believe, a function of the sight line that runs south-west to north-east, and which, viewed from the other direction – from 'behind' the Abbey – was a view *from* the north-east towards and over the Alderman's original house, known as 'Splendens', which Beckford's Abbey replaced.

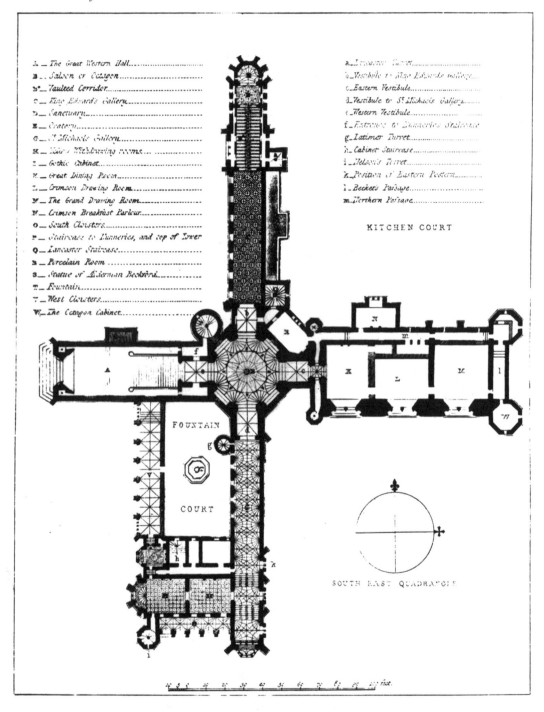

Figure 5.3 *Plan of the Principal Story [of Fonthill Abbey]*, from Rutter 1823.

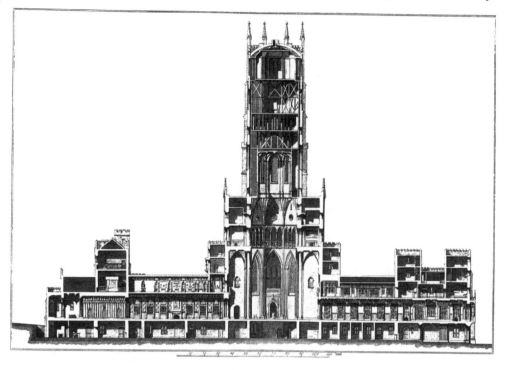

Figure 5.4 *Longitudinal Section [of Fonthill Abbey]. Through the Centre of the Tower Galleries & c. Looking East,* from Rutter 1823.

The Alderman's house had its own history of reorientation and 'behindness'. From two pictures of 1753, showing the first phase of 'Splendens' from the north, and from the south, we learn that the house encased part of an even earlier structure behind it – a manor house built by the Mervyn family in 1566 (see Crowley 1987: 155–69 for complete information on this and many other aspects of the history of the estate). It was seized in 1631 by the Crown, which then passed the property to the Cottingham family, from whom the Alderman acquired the estate: the last Mervyn owner and inhabitant of the house, Mervyn Lord Audley, was executed for committing unnatural crimes with male members of his household, including his own son, in the most famous trial for sodomy in English history before the trial of Oscar Wilde in 1895.

Naturally, the Alderman tried to suppress this unedifying history of the estate and its previous houses and inhabitants when he constructed 'Splendens'; he buried the memory of the previous owners. But his son William reconstituted it as part of the orientation and orienting function of his Abbey. In addition to turning the Abbey completely away from his father's house, which is placed completely 'behind' the Abbey and invisible from it, he brought what was 'behind' the Alderman's house, and rendered invisible by his father, into recognition in the Abbey: he adopted the motto of the Mervyns, 'De Dieu Tout', for his own heraldry and placed it right beside the little entrance door, the only route of physical communication between the 'front' and 'back' of the ideal composition of the Abbey. In the early modern period, sodomy was routinely conceived rhetorically as 'pre-posterousness', as putting ahead or before what should come below or after, inverting the natural order of social relations; we can regard the Abbey as an attempt to construct a place in which the sodomitical identity of the subject – his non-standard historical etiology, however fictional – could be stabilized. (All of these matters – especially the details of the architecture of the Abbey and archaeology of the site – are treated in considerable detail in Davis n.d.)

In turn, Beckford filled the Abbey with an enormous art collection in which many pictures depicted, made visible the fantasy of, the alternative human social and erotic relations that the building might contain. He even went so far as to commission new works of art for the Abbey itself, unfolding a general vision of a homoerotic future that might some day take up the lineage of the homoerotic past (as it had been transmitted, for example, by the Mervyn connection which Beckford explicitly recollected), and repair or replace the erotic frustrations and suppressions of the present day (such as Beckford experienced in his long years of lonely ostracism). Far and away the most ambitious of these efforts was Benjamin West's apocalyptic series based on the Book of Revelation, intended for a room in the Abbey which would contain Beckford's own coffin. In these images, a great and beautiful angel whom West renders as erotically desirable and terrible undoes the hypocrisy of the world and introduces a new or end time – the very event that the Abbey on its hilltop is, as it were, looking out towards and hoping for (for West's work for Beckford, see Hamilton-Phillips 1981, Pressly 1983).

It would take an extremely long article to flesh out these general, schematic, and provisional statements about Fonthill Abbey. In the second part of these remarks, I note the obvious: the sources one would need to use to produce a full documentation, reconstruction, and interpretation are exceedingly diverse. The sources include visual documents, such as contemporary engravings of the Abbey and the Alderman's house that enable us to notice the mutual relation of the two structures. For example, in Turner's engraving of the Alderman's 'Splendens', produced in 1799 and printed in 1800 while the Abbey was still under construction, the artist took care to imagine the tower of Beckford's Abbey rising above the trees in the forest 'behind' – or to the south-west of – the paternal home. In the text written to accompany this depiction, whether it was composed by Turner or by Beckford himself, the fact was noted that the Abbey was designed to 'commemorate the ancient family of Mervyn' (Angus 1800: Pl. 50). As a whole, then, Turner's depiction and the verbal description notify the reader of a highly particular and complex interaction between two constructions, their histories, and their coordinations with one another in an overall framework of viewing. The sources also include the written documents that provide information about the inhabitants, such as the rare pamphlet, of which Beckford owned a copy, describing the sodomy trial of Mervyn Lord Audley. They include the artistic evidence: Beckford's collections and commissions betray some of his ideas about the meaning of human history as related to specific contexts of display in the Abbey. They include, finally, the material evidence as that might be defined by an architectural historian or archaeologist – namely, the architectonics of the building itself, as it can be retrieved from the contemporary plans and sections, and the history of the estate gardens and structures within it. The Abbey itself collapsed in 1825 and everything had largely been cleared away by 1856, when a totally different building was erected for a new owner. Excavation undertaken today would probably not reveal much that is not already comprehensible from the contemporary plans.

What, then, of the role of professional archaeology? With minimal excavated evidence, supposing it were all we had, one could probably infer the existence of the reciprocally defining sight line I have noted and for which any archaeologist used to garden sites or certain civic-public spaces would be on the alert. But it would be difficult to infer the sexual-erotic significance I proposed for it in my initial overview of the meaning of the site – namely, a history in which Beckford seized the sight line towards his father's house from the north-east, 'inverted' it to create a sight line towards his house from the south-east, at the same time blocking any view 'behind' to his father's house and retrieving what was 'behind' that house (namely, the Mervyn house and its history) and making it the entryway into his own. But having achieved that reconstruction, it becomes relatively easy to move, as I did in my initial remarks, toward a reconstruction of intersubjective sexuality. This is largely because such history has been understood, from Winckelmann to Freud to Foucault to present-day cultural studies or queer theory, to involve histories of looking – and of the gaze, a matter there is no need to rehearse here (see Davis 1998), although I do want to underline the homoerotic recognition and refraction of the gaze that Beckford's Abbey apparently staged. But *without* evidence for the possibilities of activating what was and is latently given in the optical situation, in the geometry of the perspectives that might be and perhaps plainly are structured at the site, this account would have a hard time getting off the ground: geometrical optics at a site is not, itself, eroticized interpersonal looking, let alone sexualized fantasy visualization – key components of anything we mean today by 'sexuality'. For the latter we need to know about activities of visually orienting and attending – what the contents of the *upper* storeys of the building, now lost, in combination with the pictorial depictions of it and for it could suggest. So professional archaeologists – even if they agree that opticality is *always* latent in every site and that material deposits at every site *always* say something about the interests and attentions (the desiring gaze) of its users – might still feel that Fonthill Abbey as an example for an archaeology of sexuality is not especially helpful precisely because I have been so dependent on so much evidence which is not ordinarily available to the archaeologist.

My conclusion is a comment about this likely reaction to my overview of the erotic meaning of Fonthill Abbey. One reply to the professional archaeologist's complaint that Fonthill is not usefully representative would simply be: 'So what? Tough luck!' Many socio-cultural facts – not just the facts of eroticism or sexuality – are extremely difficult to document archaeologically and we just might have to say: 'Work harder'. For example, because there is so little use of pictorial evidence or consideration of perspective (the geometrical optics of sites) in archaeology, even in its post-post-processual forms, one cannot be sure that it is even true that Beckford's Abbey is a completely unrepresentative example of what sites, and our sources for interpreting them, might or can afford.

Another more productive response might be – it's been my aim in introducing Beckford's site – to develop the equation I have implicitly employed, in which archaeologically 'sexuality' = opticality + activity + erotic history. More exactly: the given optical dynamic of an assemblage or site (as that can be demonstrated geometrically or inferred from surveying and perspectival analysis of various kinds) plus the record of activity at the nodes and along the lines of that optical quadration (as can be documented or reconstructed archaeologically) is, at least in principle, the trace of a past viewing–visualizing system which was necessarily somewhat eroticized, the precipitate of the socio-cultural formations we call 'sexuality'. (For related considerations, see Davis 1996.) In the equation that, archaeologically, 'sexuality = opticality + activity + erotic history', it is really the final step which is most troublesome and interesting. I have just implied that all looking and all doing is necessarily somewhat eroticized. It is therefore the precipitate of sexuality which can be retrieved archaeologically to the degree that looking and doing have any kind of material residues whatsoever.

Someone might say, of course, that this eroticization of visually attending to the world and to acting or intervening in it, might in some or perhaps most cases be an inflection on the nonerotic trajectory of viewing and doing, so minimal as to be invisible or uninteresting – a quotient that hardly amounts to an archaeology of 'sexuality'. This is just the point, however, I would not want us to concede. 'Sexuality' is precisely not a matter of *types* of people, social relations, or actions; or of *thresholds* of arousal, significance, or value which somehow we must diagnostically identify and 'dig up' archaeologically. To suppose that the erotic orientation of the human agent in his or her world of things and other people is invisible or uninteresting because it fails some typological or barometric test of its presence in the biological or socio-cultural fields is probably to miss innumerable constitutive ways in which being-in-the-world relays erotic fantasy and desire. Almost certainly it is to wish certain 'sexualities' out of existence precisely because their inflection of intention – so modest, so pervasive, perhaps possible only as the barely-there or hardly-visible – apparently has no remains. The archaeology of sexuality should be the material observation of frequencies and distributions – what Gilles Deleuze and Felix Guattari (1987) memorably called 'flows' and 'lines of flight' – that continuously and constitutively bathe the human subject and orient him or her precisely toward their replication, their preservation and enhancement in the quadrations of desire. Instead, probably the main reason we do not have a consensus on the methods of an archaeology of sexuality is due to the sexuality of archaeology – a matter, in other words, for professional and political intervention as much as conceptual and theoretical meditation.

REFERENCES

Alexander, B. (ed.) (1957) *Life at Fonthill: 1807–1822*, London: Rupert Hart-Davis.
—— (1962) *England's Wealthiest Son*, London: Centaur Press.
Angus, W. (1800) *Seats of the Nobility and Gentry in Great Britain and Wales*, Islington, UK: W. Angus.
Beckford, W. (1983) *Vathek*, edited with an introduction by Roger Lonsdale. Revised edition. Oxford: Oxford University Press.
Britton, J. (1823) *Graphical and Literary Illustrations of Fonthill Abbey*, London: Britton.
Brockman, H. A. N. (1956) *The Caliph of Fonthill*, London: Werner Laurie.
Crowley, D. A. (ed.) (1987) *South-West Wiltshire: Chalke and Dunworth Hundreds; A History of Wiltshire*, vol. 13, Oxford: Institute of Historical Research/Oxford University Press.
Cundall, E. G. (1916) 'Turner Drawings of Fonthill Abbey', *Burlington Magazine* 29, 157 (April, 1916): 16–21.
Davis, W. (1995) *Drawing the Dream of the Wolves: Homosexuality Interpretation, and Freud's 'Wolf Man'*, Bloomington: Indiana University Press.
—— (1996) 'Virtually Straight', *Art History* 19: 434–44.
—— (1997) *Replications: Archaeology, Art History, Psychoanalysis*, University Park, PA: Pennsylvania State University Press.
—— (1998) '"Homosexualism", Gay and Lesbian Studies, and Queer Theory in Art History', in Mark A. Cheetham, Michael Ann Holly and Keith Moxey (eds) *The Subjects of Art History*, New York: Cambridge University Press.
—— (n.d.) *Desire in Limbo: Homoerotic Eschatology at William Beckford's Fonthill Abbey*, MS.
Deleuze, G. and F. Guattari (1987) *A Thousand Plateaus*, Brian Massumi (trans.), Minneapolis: University of Minnesota Press.
Finberg, A. J. (1909) *A Complete Inventory of the Drawings of the Turner Bequest*, 2 vols, London: H. M. Stationery Office/Darling & Son.
Gemmett, R. J. (1972) 'Beckford's Fonthill: The Landscape as Art', *Gazette des Beaux-Arts*, 6ème ser., 80: 335–55.

Hamilton-Phillips, M. H. (1981) 'Benjamin West and William Beckford: Some Projects for Fonthill', *Metropolitan Museum Journal* 15: 157–74.

Jack, M. (1996) *William Beckford: An English Fidalgo*, New York: AMS Press.

Mowl, T. (1998) *William Beckford: Composing for Mozart*, London: John Murray.

Parreaux, A. (1960) *William Beckford, auteur de Vathek*, Paris: Nizet.

Pressly, N. L. (1983) *Revealed Religion: Benjamin West's Commissions for Windsor Castle and Fonthill Abbey*, San Antonio: San Antonio Museum of Art.

Rutter, J. (1823) *Delineations of Fonthill and Its Abbey*, Shaftesbury and London: Rutter.

Storer, J. (1812) *A Description of Fonthill Abbey Wiltshire, Illustrated by Views*, London: W. Clarke.

PART II

The stuff of sex:
material culture and sexuality

Chapter Six

Mary Ann Hall's first-class house: the archaeology of a capital brothel

Donna J. Seifert, Elizabeth Barthold O'Brien, and Joseph Balicki

THE FAMILY BUSINESS

Mary Ann Hall was a prostitute and madam who died at the age of 71 with an estate worth nearly $90,000. She was laid to rest in Congressional Cemetery in 1886. Her sister Elizabeth had lived and worked with her in Washington, DC, and her sister Lavinia, who came to care for her in her final illness, may have been married to Henry Colton, a brothel keeper in New York.[1] Both sisters and their mother are also buried in the Hall plot in Congressional Cemetery. It seems that keeping houses was the Hall family business.

Most of what is known about Mary Ann Hall and her business comes from city directories, census records, deeds, tax assessments, and the legal records of the suit filed by her brothers in their attempts to acquire a share of her estate.[2] With the settlement of the suit, interest in Hall's worldly goods ceased – until the Smithsonian's National Museum of the American Indian began planning for the construction of its new museum on the National Mall in Washington, DC. Documentary researchers quickly identified the site as having belonged to long-term property owner and resident Mary Ann Hall and established that her house was a brothel from *c.* 1840–1883. A women's health clinic was located on Hall's property from 1883 until her death in 1886.

To comply with the National Historic Preservation Act,[3] the Smithsonian Institution sponsored historical and archaeological investigations of the Mall museum site, which includes Hall's property as well as some mid-nineteenth-century industrial sites and several lots occupied by working-class residents from the 1870s to the early twentieth century (Figure 6.1).[4] The data recovery excavations focused on 1860s yard surface and midden deposits in the lot adjacent to Hall's but clearly associated with her household. The lot including the midden and the adjacent lots were all vacant at the time the midden accumulated; Hall's household is the only likely source of the deposit. The contents of the midden also support the association.[5] Analysis of the historical and archaeological data gave the research team the opportunity to investigate the business of sex through one high-class house in mid-nineteenth-century Washington, DC.

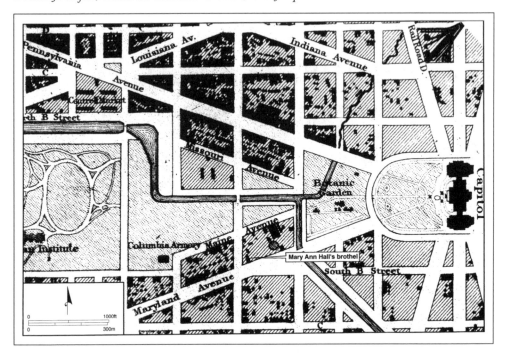

Figure 6.1 Detail of Albert Boschke's *Topographical Map of the District of Columbia Surveyed in the Years 1856, '57, '58, & '59.* This is among the earliest maps showing individual buildings in Washington. Mary Ann Hall's brothel is the long narrow building near the corner of Maryland Avenue and 4½ Street. To the east, the large, circular gas holder of the Washington Gas Light Company and the large rectangular foundry building are also shown on the map.

READING THE RECORD

Prostitution may be impossible to recognize in the archaeological record, but brothels can be identified, particularly with the help of the documentary record. Locations of most brothels were well-known, even identified in guides and marked on maps. *Prostitute* was listed as an occupation in the manuscript population census. Newspaper accounts, police records, and court documents provide information on encounters of the prostitute or madam with the law.

Several recent historical studies analyze the complexity of the practice of prostitution and the social and economic context of brothel life in urban centers of the East. Timothy J. Gilfoyle addressed sex as a consumer commodity in New York (1992), and Marilyn Wood Hill investigated the life and work of prostitutes in New York (1993). Barbara Meil Hobson examined the politics of prostitution (1990). Studies such as these provide the historical archaeologist with a picture of many aspects of brothel life not easily abstracted from the archaeological record. A study contemporary with Mary Ann Hall's time is William W. Sanger's ambitious survey *The History of Prostitution: Its Extent, Causes, and Effects throughout the World*, published in 1858. Sanger reported and interpreted data gathered under his direction through interviews with 2,000 New York prostitutes. Initially designed as a study of the extent of venereal disease among the poor, Sanger drew on his results to support his recommendation for regulation of prostitution to control disease.

Although Sanger's work cannot be used uncritically, it provides the twentieth-century researcher with a mid-nineteenth-century view of the variety of circumstances of the prostitute at the very time Mary Ann Hall's brothel was home and workplace to many women.

Until recently, few studies of the archaeology of the urban brothel have appeared in the literature. It is likely that brothels in cities have been excavated, but not recognized or reported as such, probably because researchers have not known how to recognize them in historical documents or in archaeological assemblages. Brothels are unusual households, but are unusual in a variety of ways, depending on the status of the residents and clients. The archaeological record provides physical evidence of the material culture of brothel life, reflecting the economic status of both residence and place of business.[6]

The brothel was a social and economic institution of the mid-nineteenth-century city. Like other institutions serving a city with a wide range of social and economic circumstances, brothels reflected the disparities within the population. Sex for sale is, of course, the service that defines the brothel. However, the environs, amenities, and providers varied according to the class of the clientele. Mary Ann Hall's first-class brothel clearly served middle- and upper-class patrons. The archaeology of the brothel documents the expensive provisions that Mary Ann Hall selected for use in her establishment.

BROTHELS AND FAMILY HOUSEHOLDS IN WASHINGTON, DC

Several analytical techniques were used to understand the material culture from Mary Ann Hall's brothel, and to compare this brothel artifact assemblage with collections from other brothels and from working-class and middle-class households in Washington, DC. Artifact collections from the 1840s to the 1890s from working-class and middle-class households were selected as well as collections from brothels of three time periods.

The comparative collections represent households occupied between 1844 and 1914 and four household types: middle-class owner, middle-class tenant, working-class tenant, and brothel. The earliest of the comparative collections is from Area D1, Square 373 (Garrow 1982). This collection, from a trash midden deposited between 1844 and 1857, was associated with a single household, probably of the middle class. Two collections associated with middle-class households and dated to the 1850s were selected: Phase 15–3b from Square 530 (Cheek et al. 1996), and Locus 9 from Square 455 (Glumac et al. 1997). All three of these collections are probably earlier than the deposits in Lot 11 from Hall's brothel. However, comparison with these earlier collections helps to place the brothel collection in the context of the material culture of nineteenth-century Washington, DC. The collection from Phase 6a, Square 258, was excavated from the neighborhood historically known as Hooker's Division (Cheek et al. 1991). This collection, from a deposit dating from the 1860s and 1870s, was not assigned to a household type; however, the neighborhood was primarily occupied by working-class tenants during this period. The collection from Lots 15 and 19 on Square 530, which date to the 1860s, were associated with middle-class resident owners (Cheek et al. 1996). The collection from Locus 4, Square 455, associated with an owner-occupant who was a druggist, dates from the 1850s to the mid-1870s (Glumac et al. 1997). Two collections from working-class tenant households on Square 455, Locus 3 and Locus 6, have been combined for this analysis. Together, these collections date from the 1850s to the 1880s. Two collections from working-class tenant households from Square 257–258 have been combined; these collections date from 1870 to 1890 (Cheek et al. 1991). The comparative brothel collections were also from Square 257–258. Two brothel collections were combined to represent the period 1870–1890, and three collections represent 1890–1914. The assemblages from the brothels of three periods exhibit distinctly different patterns, indicating that household function alone does not account for artifact pattern. Collections from all sites were compared using artifact pattern analysis (South 1977). Several groups and classes of artifacts were then examined to study more closely the types of consumer goods used by the brothel inmates and by members of other households.

THE MATERIAL CULTURE OF BROTHEL LIFE

The artifact assemblage associated with Mary Ann Hall's house documents the material advantages of the business. Although historians have questioned contemporary accounts of lavish lifestyles in brothels as exaggerated (Gilfoyle 1998: 5–6), the assemblage from Mary Ann Hall's house confirms that this household's occupants and visitors enjoyed expensive French champagne (Piper Heidseick); meals including high- and mid-priced cuts of beef, pork, and mutton/goat; as well as a variety of wild birds, turtle, and fish. Exotic fruits (such as coconut and brazil nuts) and several types of fruits, berries, and vegetables were also served (Seifert et al. 1998: 123, 193–94). When compared to contemporaneous working-class households in the same neighborhood, the variety, and presence of wild and exotic foods set this household apart.[7] It is likely that these foods were available to both the resident prostitutes and their guests, who probably ordered champagne and light meals, served in private chambers at exorbitant prices (Sanger 1939: 551).

Champagne is noted by William Sanger in his 1858 *History of Prostitution* as the only libation served in first-class houses, known as parlor houses (Sanger 1939: 549) or private brothels (Gilfoyle 1998: 6). The house is also identified as a first-class house in the provost marshal's 1864–1865 list of bawdy houses in Washington, DC. Bawdy houses or public houses were lower-class houses. The fact that Hall's house was known to the provost marshal suggests that it was not one of the truly private brothels – which were often not even known to their neighbors (Gilfoyle 1998: 6). Nevertheless, it was among the best in Washington, according to the provost marshal, who recorded 85, classed as first, second, third, low, or very low (USACE 1884–1865). With 18 inmates, Hall's brothel was also the largest house on the list.

The ceramic assemblage from the excavations also reflects both the class and size of the house (Table 6.1). More than 50 percent of the collection from Hall's brothel is ironstone and porcelain. White ironstone tablewares became popular in the late 1850s, and the high percentage of this ware suggests attention to fashion. The high percentage of porcelain also suggests expenditures for expensive tablewares. While other households in Washington, DC continued to use pearlwares and whitewares, Mary Ann Hall's tables were set with fashionable ironstone and porcelain. The high percentage of porcelain separates this assemblage from all of the contemporaneous Washington collections available for comparison.

Most of the ironstone and porcelain dishes in the brothel collection are white and undecorated. There is little evidence that dishes were purchased as sets; however, similar dishes were apparently selected. Several plates, cups, and saucers are decorated with a gilt band near the rim. There are also several plain white, paneled cups and saucers, a style referred to as Gothic (Wall 1991: 76) that was popular in middle-class family households, particularly for family dining (Wall 1991: 78). The style is thought to have been associated with the private, domestic sphere of the family, separate from the public, commercial sphere of the working world (Wall 1991: 79). However, the Gothic style, interpreted as a symbol of the middle-class, Christian home, the sanctuary of domesticity (Wall 1994:

Table 6.1 Ceramic wares from selected Washington, DC, archaeological sites: types (in percentage) and total numbers

Ware	Sq 530 15–3b	Sq 455 L9	Sq 530 15–3c 19–3	Res C VII, IX (MAH)	Sq 257– 258 6a	Sq 455 L4	Sq 455 L3, L6	Res C III, IV	Sq 257– 258 1, 3a
	1850– 1860	1850– 1870	1860– 1870	1860– 1870	1860– 1870	1850– 1875	1850– 1880	1871– 1886	1870– 1890
Creamware	2.94	6.56	3.34		12.90	2.83	1.56		0.83
Pearlware	35.29	32.19	33.69	0.06	11.60	20.27	16.10	0.35	9.14
Whiteware	37.78	34.69	45.64	11.69	53.60	43.52	50.75	32.09	46.42
Ironstone	2.94	5.94	4.52	29.24	2.90	1.94	7.24	39.57	18.48
Porcelain	2.71	5.00	2.37	26.61	4.80	15.42	5.12	8.29	3.53
Redware	14.25	3.44	5.71	14.91	8.10	6.18	3.31	3.74	10.49
Yellowware	0.45	2.50	1.72	9.32	0.70	2.01	6.85	8.06	1.45
Stoneware	1.58	5.31	2.26	6.60	4.70	5.14	4.69	7.20	9.66
Unid./misc.	2.04	4.38	0.75	1.59	0.90	2.68	4.38	0.69	0.00
n	442	320	929	8,829	766	1,342	5,565	1,736	963

Key:
Square 530, 15–3b; middle-class owner
Square 455, Locus 9; middle-class renter
Square 530, 15–3c, 19–3; middle-class owner
Reservation C, VII, IX; Mary Ann Hall's brothel
Square 257–258, 6a; working-class tenant
Square 455, Locus 4; middle-class owner
Square 455, Locus 3, 6; working-class tenant
Reservation C, III, IV; working-class tenant
Square 257–258, 1, 3a; working-class tenant

160; Fitts and Yamin 1996: 95–96), was also a preferred style in Mary Hall's brothel. Perhaps the Gothic-style ironstone and porcelain tablewares were used primarily by the brothel inmates when they dined by themselves. If Gothic-style dinnerware and teaware truly invoked a feeling of domestic security and morality, surely it would have been an unlikely choice of tableware for entertaining in a high-class brothel. It seems more likely that the gilt-decorated porcelains were used for visitors to the house. In her choices of tablewares and foods, Hall clearly created the elegant environment designed to attract clients with the ability to pay for luxury.

The brothel collection is also unusual in its high percentages of redware, yellowware, and stoneware food-preparation and storage vessels (Table 6.1). These utilitarian wares account for 30 percent of the brothel collection, but only 10 to 19 percent of the comparative collections. The high percentages of two expensive tablewares and three utility wares supports the conclusion that the brothel was preparing and serving meals to a large household of inmates and to clients. The high percentage of kitchen-group artifacts in the brothel collection supports this interpretation as well.

Analysis of vessel forms also provides data useful in understanding household function (Table 6.2). Vessel forms were divided into seven general classes that reflect the functions of ceramics vessels in the household: tablewares, serving vessels, tea and coffee wares, food-preparation vessels, personal hygiene vessels, vessels not associated with food, and unidentified forms.[8]

Table 6.2 Vessel forms from selected Washington, DC, archaeological sites: types (in percentage) and total numbers

Vessel Form	Sq 373 D1	Sq 530 15–3b	Sq 530 15–3c 19–3	Res C VII, IX (MAH)	Sq 257– 258 6a	Res C III, IV	Sq 257– 258 1, 3a
	1844– 1857	1850– 1860	1860– 1870	1860– 1870	1860– 1870	1871– 1886	1870– 1890
Tableware	22.7	22.2	29.10	31.73	13.60	37.68	45.80
Serving	10.5	3.7		15.86	4.20	7.25	5.90
Tea/Coffee	26.5	27.8	25.84	21.81	30.10	20.29	12.40
Food Preparation	10.1	3.7	5.62	13.31	5.40	10.14	5.20
Hygiene	2.5		3.37	3.12	2.70	4.35	
Other	4.2		1.12				1.70
Unassigned	23.5	42.6	34.83	14.16	44.00	20.29	28.80
n	272	54	89	353	73	70	153

Key:
Square 530, 15–3b; middle-class owner
Square 455, Locus 9; middle-class renter
Square 530, 15–3c, 19–3; middle-class owner
Reservation C, VII, IX; Mary Ann Hall's brothel
Square 257–258, 6a; working-class tenant
Square 455, Locus 4; middle-class owner
Square 455, Locus 3, 6; working-class tenant
Reservation C, III, IV; working-class tenant
Square 257–258, 1, 3a; working-class tenant

The percentage of tablewares in the brothel collection is higher than the percentages from the contemporaneous collections, and the percentage of tea and coffee vessels is lower. The most striking difference is in the higher percentages of serving vessels and food preparation vessels. These higher percentages support the conclusion that the brothel was serving a large household and was serving meals to clients. Although relative percentages of tableware, serving vessels, and tea/coffee vessels vary, particularly among the working-class households, no other collection has so many serving and preparation vessels. The high proportion of the tea and coffee vessels from one working-class household in the nearby neighborhood known as Hooker's Division (Phase 6a, Square 257–258) may account for the very low percentage of tablewares; however, the high percentage of tea/coffee vessels suggests that serving tea or coffee may have been unusually important in this household.

Another measure of household expenditures for ceramics is the Miller ceramic index. Analysis of indices provides a means of comparing expenditures among households and assessing socio-economic status. George Miller developed a series of index values for different decorative types and forms, based on price lists used by the English ceramic manufacturers that controlled the ceramic market (Miller 1980, 1991). The index values are based on the cost of the least expensive ware, common creamware. Decorated types were more expensive than plain types, and ironstone and porcelain are more expensive than most of the refined earthenwares (creamware, pearlware, and whiteware). Miller's indices apply to ceramics from 1787 to 1886. Susan Henry developed complementary indices for the late nineteenth and early twentieth centuries, using mail-order catalogues

(Henry 1987). Miller's indices were used in this analysis; Henry's indices were used for the later comparative collections.

Index values are listed by decorative type and year. The mean ceramic date (MCD) of the analytical unit was used to select the appropriate year and value for the ceramics from each collection. Miller's indices include values for few English porcelains (Miller 1991: 15). Values were calculated for each artifact collection first without including porcelains. However, porcelain accounts for 27 percent of the brothel collection. To incorporate the value of porcelain in the collection, a value of 4.00 was assigned to all porcelain, without regard to decoration or vessel size.[9] By incorporating porcelain in the index values for Mary Ann Hall's brothel, the expenditures for ceramics of the brothel can be compared to other households.[10]

The mean index value for the collection from Hall's brothel is the highest value of all the collections (Table 6.3). The value for refined earthenwares is higher than each of the indices from middle-class households; when porcelain is included in all indices, the difference is even more striking. Only the bowl index for the brothel collection is lower than some of the other bowl indices. The high percentage of porcelain and ironstone vessels account for the high individual and mean indices. Thus, the ceramic index values for Mary Ann Hall's brothel indicate a household that spent considerably more on tablewares than contemporaneous working-class and middle-class households.

The archaeological evidence from deposits associated with Mary Ann Hall's brothel reflect a large household that enjoyed many expensive consumer goods and a varied diet. When compared to other family households in Washington, DC, the material culture of the brothel shares many attributes of the middle-class households and clearly exhibits higher expenditures on tablewares and food than the neighboring working-class households.

Table 6.3 Ceramic indices from selected Washington, DC, archaeological sites[1]

Vessel Type	Sq 373 D1	Sq 530 15–3b	Sq 530 15–3c 19–3	Res C VII, IX (MAH)	Sq 257–258 6a	Res C III, IV	Sq 257–258 1, 3a
	1844–1857	1850–1860	1860–1870	1860–1870	1860–1870	1871–1886	1870–1890
Cup & Saucer	2.30/2.79	1.78/2.52	1.24/1.24	3.32/3.57	1.84/1.96	2.20/2.38	1.88/1.98
Plate	2.17/2.17	2.15/2.15	1.59/1.59	2.75/3.18	1.18/1.43	2.03/2.19	1.38/1.79
Bowl	1.43/1.43	3.0/3.0	2.92/2.92	1.77/2.21	1.08/1.08	1.94/1.94	1.44/1.44
Mean Index	2.04/2.23	2.07/2.32	1.73/1.73	2.76/3.18	1.62/1.79	2.06/2.21	1.51/1.75

[1] The first index is calculated for refined earthenwares only; the second index includes porcelain at a value of 4.00.

Key:
Square 530, 15–3b; middle-class owner
Square 455, Locus 9; middle-class renter
Square 530, 15–3c, 19–3; middle-class owner
Reservation C, VII, IX; Mary Ann Hall's brothel
Square 257–258, 6a; working-class tenant
Square 455, Locus 4; middle-class owner
Square 455, Locus 3, 6; working-class tenant
Reservation C, III, IV; working-class tenant
Square 257–258, 1, 3a; working-class tenant

Comparisons among Washington, DC brothels identified no simple brothel artifact signature or pattern. Variation in occupation date and class of house were apparently responsible for differences in the artifact assemblages. All of the brothel assemblages, however, are distinctly different from contemporaneous family households and offer a new view of the life of the working woman in the capital city.

HER STERLING WORTH

When Mary Ann Hall died of a cerebral hemorrhage in 1886, her estate included real estate worth more than $20,000; bonds and securities worth about $67,000; and no debts. A room-by-room inventory, conducted to appraise the value of her house's contents, valued them at $731.20 (DCSC 1886). The *Evening Star* reported her death: 'Departed this life 2 a.m. Friday January 29, 1886, Mary A. Hall, long resident of Washington. With integrity unquestioned a heart ever open to appeals of distress, a charity that was boundless, she is gone; but her memory will be kept green by many who knew her sterling worth' (*Evening Star* 1886).[11] Her impressive monument in Congressional Cemetery is inscribed: 'Truth was her motto; her creed charity for all. Dawn is coming.'

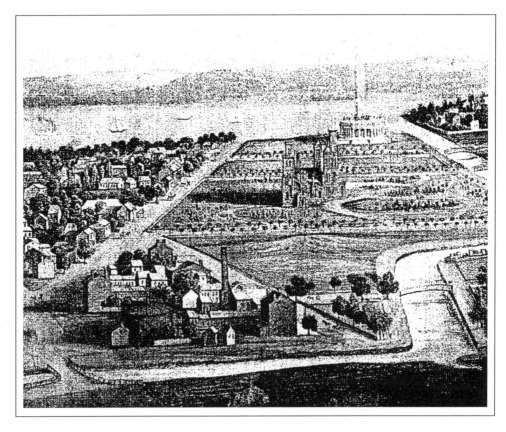

Figure 6.2 Detail of Edward Sachse's 1852 *View of Washington*. The view shows the area west of the Capitol, including the National Mall, the Smithsonian Castle, and the Washington Monument (portrayed as designed, but not as built). Mary Ann Hall's imposing house faces Maryland Avenue, just west of the round Washington Gas Light Company gas holder.

Mary Ann Hall's house, with its elegant furnishings, expensive table service, exotic foods, and exorbitant champagne, located conveniently between the executive and legislative branches of the federal government (Figure 6.2), was one of the best in Washington's *demi-monde*: offering satisfaction for all appetites and pleasing all senses. We may never understand how these women felt or what discomforts they endured – any more than we know these things about their working-class neighbors – but we do know that certain material comforts were indeed part of their lives. And that some, like the 23-year-old prostitute Mary Ann Hall, who built the three-storey house on Maryland Avenue in 1840, were not on the road to ruin, but beginning a life in a prosperous business.

ACKNOWLEDGEMENTS

The authors wish to acknowledge those whose special efforts contributed to the success of the archaeological investigations at the site of Mary Ann Hall's brothel. Dorothy Provine of the District of Columbia Archives located legal documents associated with the settlement of Mary Ann Hall's estate. Petar Glumac of Parsons Engineering Science, Inc., shared data from the excavations of Square 455, undertaken for EDAW, Inc. Justin Estoque, project manager with the Smithsonian Institution's Office of Physical Plant, helped us acquire the Square 455 data and helped us in many other ways throughout the project. The editors of this volume, Barbara Voss and Robert Schmidt, provided several valuable suggestions that helped us refine this paper. To each, we express our appreciation.

NOTES

1 In one of the documents associated with the settlement of Mary Ann Hall's estate, a line describing Lavinia as the wife of Henry Colton was struck out and written over with the word 'single' (DCSC 1886). Henry Colton was a brothel keeper in New York (Gilfoyle 1992: 47), and Lavinia's relationship to Colton, albeit ambiguous, suggests she was also in the business.

2 Brothers John and Basil were each awarded $11,000; sisters Elizabeth and Lavinia received the remaining money and household goods.

3 Section 106 of the National Historic Preservation Act of 1966, as amended, requires that federal agencies take into account the effect of their undertakings on historic properties and afford the Advisory Council on Historic Preservation the opportunity to comment. To comply with this provision of the act, the Smithsonian Institution sponsored identification, evaluation, and data recovery investigations at the Mall museum site during the planning stages of the museum project. The research discussed in this paper was conducted by John Milner Associates, under contract to Venturi, Scott Brown Associates, Inc., for the Smithsonian Institution.

4 Hall's brothel was located within the area of the capital city known as the Island, because it was separated from the rest of the center city by the Washington Canal. By mid-century, the canal had lost whatever charm it may have had and was little better than an open sewer (Press 1984: 54, 56). The Washington Gas Light Company gas holder, a foundry, and a stone yard occupied the other end of the block that included Hall's property. Although proximity to the canal and heavy industry certainly detracted from the neighborhood, amenities were also nearby. West of Hall's house was the Smithsonian Institution, set in its landscaped grounds. To the east, just across the street from the foundry, was the Botanic Garden at the foot of Capitol Hill. Washington, DC, like other eastern cities in the mid-nineteenth-century, exhibited a mix of commercial, industrial, and residential uses within the heart of the city (Hill 1993: 176–77), and brothels were a component of the mix.

There were areas of the city known for their brothels, however, and the Island was one of them. During the Civil War, the provost marshal listed eighteen brothels on the Island, most classed low or very low; only two other first-class brothels are listed on the Island (USACE 1864–1865). The major concentration of brothels during the war was located north of the Mall, between Pennsylvania Avenue and the canal, in the area known as Hooker's Division

(Press 1984: 56). Businesses, industry, and working-class residents also occupied Hooker's Division. In fact, Mary Ann Hall also owned property in Hooker's Division (DCGA 1886–1887), but it was apparently rented to working-class tenants and boarders (USBC 1870, 1880).

5 Historical documents clearly place Mary Ann Hall's brothel on Lot 12. This lot, however, was later occupied by part of a twentieth-century building; thus, the research team expected archaeological deposits on Lot 12 to be disturbed. Excavations did locate building foundations on Lot 12 that date to the brothel occupation, but no preserved artifact deposits. On Lot 11, adjacent to Hall's property, preserved mid-nineteenth-century deposits were found, although the lot was unoccupied at that time. Thus, the deposits must be associated with occupation elsewhere. The only adjacent lot that was occupied at that time was Lot 12, Mary Ann Hall's brothel. Therefore, the most likely source of the household refuse on Lot 11 is the household on Lot 12.

6 The brothel as home and workplace for prostitutes is discussed in papers about the brothels in Washington, DC's Hooker's Division (Seifert 1991, 1994). Although middle-class families separated the public and private spheres, the brothel served as the venue for both functions. Thus, the material remains recovered represent both the consumption patterns of residents and clients and the purchasing decisions of Mary Ann Hall.

7 Phytolith and macrofloral evidence suggests that beans and berries were cultivated on Lot 11, where the midden accumulated, and the brothel may have kept laying hens, either on Lot 11 or in the backyard of Lot 12. Phytolith analyses were prepared by Irwin Rovner, macrofloral analyses, by Leslie E. Raymer and Richard A. Fuss; and faunal analyses, by Lisa D. O'Steen (see Seifert et al. 1998: Appendix VIII, Appendix X).

8 Tablewares are vessels from which food is eaten, such as plates and bowls. Serving vessels are those on which food is brought to the table, such as platters, large bowls, and tureens. Tea and coffee wares include cups, saucers, teapots and coffee pots, sugar bowls, and cream pitchers. The food-preparation class includes all redware, yellowware, and stoneware vessels, including bottles, jugs, crocks, and bowls used in preparing and storing food. Vessels associated with personal hygiene are chamber pots, large water pitchers, and wash basins. Ceramic vessels that are not associated with food, such as vases and lamps, are classed together. Vessels that could not be identified by form or could not be assigned to a class were classified as unassigned. Many of the vessels in each collection could not be assigned to a form class. Vessel-form data were not available for some of the comparative collections.

9 This value is probably conservative. Miller gives index values ranging from 3.4 to 4.0 for undecorated English porcelain plates, and a value of 5.06 for a 5-inch, gold-banded English porcelain plate, the only size vessels with this decoration that he lists (1991: 15). Many of the porcelain vessels in the Hall collection are decorated and were, therefore, more expensive than plain vessels, and larger vessels were more expensive than the smaller ones for which Miller gives index values.

10 Porcelain was included in the original analysis of the ceramics from Area D1, Square 373, at a value of 4.55 (Garrow 1982: 116, 125). Miller's original index values (Miller 1980) were used in the Square 373 analysis; thus, the Area D1 values were calculated using higher values for refined earthenwares (values ranging from 5 to 25 percent higher).

11 Historical documents indicate that a women's health clinic operated on Hall's property between 1883 and 1886, either in the brothel or in one of the smaller buildings on the property (U.S. Senate 1927: 198); perhaps Mary Ann Hall contributed to the support of the clinic. The proprietors of successful, first-class houses often enjoyed a reputation for generosity (Sanger 1939: 554–55; Hill 1993: 222–23). The available evidence suggests that Mary Ann Hall enjoyed a certain respect. Her brothel was just three blocks from the Capitol, so it seems likely that she knew many of the habitués of the hill.

REFERENCES

Boschke, A. (1861) Topographical Map of the District of Columbia Surveyed in the Years 1856, '57, '58, and '59. Drawn by A. Boschke. Engraved by D. McClelland, Washington, DC: McClelland, Blanchard, and Mohun. Map on file, Geography and Map Division, Library of Congress, Washington, DC.

Cheek, C. D., D. J. Seifert, P. W. O'Bannon, C. A. Holt, B. R. Roulette Jr, J. Balicki, G. G. Ceponis and D. B. Heck (1991) *Phase II and Phase III Archeological Investigations at the Site of the Proposed International Cultural and Trade Center/Federal Office Building Complex, Federal Triangle, Washington, DC*, prepared for the Pennsylvania Avenue Development Corporation, Alexandria, VA: John Milner Associates, Inc.

Cheek, C. D., D. J. Seifert, L. J. Galke, E. B. O'Brien and M. J. Wuellner (1996) *Archaeological Data Recovery Investigations at the Site of the Federal Bureau of Investigation, Washington Metropolitan Field Office, Square 530, Washington, DC*, prepared by John Milner Associates, Inc., Alexandria, VA, submitted to TAMs Consultants, Inc., Arlington, VA.

Evening Star (1863–1873) The *Evening Star*, Washington DC. Newspaper on microfilm, Washingtoniana Division, Martin Luther King, Jr, Branch, District of Columbia Public Library, Washington, DC.

District of Columbia General Assessments (DCGA) (1886–1887) General Assessments. Microfilm on file, Washingtoniana Room, Martin Luther King, Jr, Branch, District of Columbia Public Library, Washington, DC.

District of Columbia Supreme Court (DCSC) (1886) Papers relating to the Estate of Mary Ann Hall. On file, District of Columbia Archives, Washington, DC.

Fitts, R. and R. Yamin (1996) *The Archeology of Domesticity in Victorian Brooklyn: Exploratory Testing and Data Recovery at Block 2006 of the Atlantic Terminal Urban Renewal Area, Brooklyn, New York*, report prepared by John Milner Associates, Inc., West Chester, Pennsylvania, submitted to Atlantic Housing Corporation, Brooklyn, New York.

Garrow, P. (ed.) (1982) Archaeological Investigations on the Washington, DC Civic Center Site, prepared by Soil Systems, Inc., under contract to the Department of Housing and Community Development, Washington, DC.

Gilfoyle, T. J. (1992) *City of Eros: New York City, Prostitution, and the Commercialization of Sex, 1790–1920*, New York: W. W. Norton.

—— (1998) Comments on 'Sin City' Panel. Society for Historical Archaeology Conference on Historical and Underwater and Historical Archaeology, Atlanta.

Glumac, P., J. Able, B. D. Crane, D. Hayes and M. Pipes (1997) 'Square 455 (51NW115) Archaeological Data Recovery' (draft), prepared by Parsons Engineering Science, Inc., Fairfax, VA, submitted to EDAW, Inc., Alexandria, VA.

Henry, S. L. (1987) 'Factors Influencing Consumer Behavior in Turn-of-the-Century Phoenix, Arizona', in S. M. Spencer-Wood (ed.) *Consumer Choice in Historical Archaeology*, New York: Academic Press.

Hill, M. W. (1993) *Their Sisters' Keepers: Prostitution in New York City, 1830–1870*, Berkeley: University of California Press.

Hobson, B. M. (1990) *Uneasy Virtue: The Politics of Prostitution and the American Reform Tradition*, Chicago: University of Chicago Press.

Miller, G. L. (1980) 'Classification and Economic Scaling of 19th Century Ceramics', *Historical Archaeology* 14: 1–40.

—— (1991) 'A Revised Set of CC Index Values for Classification and Economic Scaling of English Ceramics from 1787 to 1880', *Historical Archaeology* 25, 1: 1–25.

Press, D. E. (1984) 'South of the Avenue: From Murder Bay to Federal Triangle', *Records of the Columbia Historical Society* 51: 51–70.

Sachse, E. (1852) *View of Washington*, Baltimore: E. Sachse. Print on file, Prints and Photographs Division, Library of Congress, Washington, DC.

Sanger, W. W. (1939 [1858]) *The History of Prostitution*, New York: Eugenics Publishing Company.

Seifert, D. J. (1991) 'Within Site of the White House: The Archaeology of Working Women,' 'Gender in Historical Archeology', *Historical Archaeology* 25, 4: 82–108.

—— (1994) 'Mrs Starr's Profession', in Elizabeth M. Scott (ed.) *Those of Little Note: Gender, Race, and Class in Historical Archeology*, Tucson: University of Arizona Press.

Seifert, D. J., J. Balicki, E. B. O'Brien, D. B. Heck, G. McGowan and A. Smith (1998) *Archaeological Data Recovery, Smithsonian Institution, National Museum of the American Indian, Mall Museum Site*, prepared by John Milner Associates, Inc., Alexandria, VA, submitted to Venturi, Scott Brown and Associates, Inc., Philadelphia, PA, and the Smithsonian Institution, Office of Physical Plant, Washington, DC.

South, S. (1977) *Method and Theory in Historical Archaeology*, New York: Academic Press.

US Army Corps of Engineers (USACE) (1864–1865) 'Bawdy Houses', Provost Marshal's, Department of Washington, 22nd Army Corps, 1864–1865. Document on file, National Archives and Records Administration, Record Group 393, vol. 298, Washington, DC.

US Bureau of the Census (USBC) (1870) *Manuscript Population Census of the United States, 1870*, Washington, DC: US Government Printing Office. Microfilm copy on file, National Archives and Records Administration.

—— (1880) *Manuscript Population Census of the United States, 1880*, Washington, DC: US Government Printing Office. Microfilm copy on file, National Archives and Records Administration, Washington, DC.

US Senate (1927) *Charitable and Reformatory Institutions of the District of Columbia*. Senate doc. 207 69th Congress, 2nd Session. US Government Printing Office, Washington, DC.

Wall, D. (1991) 'Sacred Dinners and Secular Teas: Constructing Domesticity in Mid-19th-Century New York', *Historical Archaeology* 25, 4: 49–81.

—— (1994) *The Archaeology of Gender: Separating the Spheres in Urban America*, New York: Plenum Press.

Chapter Seven

Magical passions: sexuality and African-American archaeology

Laurie A. Wilkie

INTRODUCTION

During the past decade, archaeologists have come to recognize a range of artifacts associated with enslaved African and African-American magical and religious practices (e.g. Brown and Cooper 1991; Ferguson 1992; Orser 1994; Samford 1996; Stine et al. 1996; Wilkie 1994, 1997; Young 1997). These artifacts have been predominantly discussed as evidence of African continuities or acts of resistance against planters. Only a few archaeologists have suggested that these artifacts could have significance as a means of mediating tensions within families and communities (e.g. Franklin 1997; Wilkie 1995, 1997; Young 1997). Archaeologists have ignored the importance of magical and magical-medical practices as means of both controlling and celebrating sexuality and the sexual differences between men and women in African-American communities.

The ethnohistoric record provides one of the most accessible bodies of information regarding sexual magic. However, as I will discuss below, the processes through which these studies were conducted impacts the ways they can be used as sources. Instead, in this work, I will demonstrate how ethnohistory can be used to broaden interpretations of archaeological materials to consider sexuality. In particular, I will demonstrate how weaving together ethnohistoric sources with archaeological materials have enabled me to substantiate a previously unclear connection between medical-magical midwifery and more generalized 'sexual magic'. In doing so, this archaeology of sexuality has placed midwifery into a larger socio-sexual context that goes beyond conventional views that midwifery is somehow related only to women's history. Through the discussion of materials recovered from a late nineteenth- to early twentieth-century African-American midwife's house, I will explore the ways that a consideration of the archaeology of sexuality can enrich our understanding of African-American health and motherhood during this time period. While Lucretia Perryman, the midwife whose materials are to be discussed, practiced her medicine in Alabama, her experiences would not have been unlike those of other African-American midwives working in the South at that time.

I will first provide a cautionary note regarding the potential pitfalls of using ethnohistoric sources related to African-American sexual and magical practices, then present a brief overview of some of the trends and patterns visible in the ethnohistoric record of sexual magic. I will elaborate upon those patterns that I believe to represent part of a larger magical grammar that shaped and influenced how, and what kinds of, material culture were incorporated into spells, potions, and charms associated with sexual magic. Once these parameters are laid out, the discussion will turn its focus to the material culture of midwifery, as recovered from the house area of Lucretia Perryman. In reviewing the material culture and limited ethnographic record of African-American midwifery, it becomes apparent that the magical practices of midwifery are linked to the same belief system that shapes the practices of sexual magic.

THE ETHNOHISTORIC RECORD: CAUTIONS AND CONCERNS

Ethnographies, ex-slave narratives and interviews with conjurers and root doctors (e.g. Botkin 1945; Clayton 1990; Herskovits 1941; Hurston 1990a; Hyatt 1973, 1974; Puckett 1926) are among the early twentieth-century ethnohistorical sources that describe magical practices related to sexual activity as recorded among African-American communities in the southern United States and Caribbean. While useful as a starting point for a discussion of magical practice as related to sexuality, these sources must be viewed with a critical eye. With the exception of Zora Neale Hurston and a small number of black interviewers (Clayton 1990) working for the Works Progress Administration Federal Ex-Slave Narrative Project in Louisiana, the vast amount of the literature related to African-American magical practice has been collected by white men, whose attitudes about African-American sexuality were likely to have been shaped by late nineteenth- and early twentieth-century stereotypes. As such, the ethnographies can be expected to particularly focus upon those aspects of African-American life perceived to be exotic, different, or enhancing stereotypic visions.

As will be further discussed, many spells or charms described in African-American ethnographic and oral historical literature are related to protecting oneself from sexually transmitted diseases or keeping a mate sexually unavailable to another person. Given the sexual violence that characterized the experiences of enslaved men and women, the importance of these spells may have originally been embedded in the desire to protect oneself and one's loved ones from white sexual predators. The importance of these types of spells may be over-represented in the literature as a reflection of the experiences of enslavement and the biases of earlier researchers. In addition, similar sexual magical practices among the Euro-American populations of the rural south are under-represented in the ethnographic literature due to these same researcher biases, since it is clear that white customers were an important component of any African-American conjurer's practice (Wilkie 1996, 1997 in press). While the documented magical spells and their intentions suggest the existence of sexual antagonisms between the two genders in African-American society, these same sources provide little information about the cooperative aspects of African-American conjugal life. Of course, magical practice is in itself a means of mediating tensions in society, and ethnographies conducted with magical practitioners are unlikely to provide much evidence of happy and healthy relationships.

These criticisms of the available source material are not intended to dismiss the possibility of studying African-American sexual magic. Instead, the ethnographic literature should be a starting place to begin to recognize patterns that might inform archaeological interpretations, as the spells available to us are linked to the use and manipulation of specific materials. Once the available record of magical practices related to sexuality is explicitly explored, it becomes apparent that within African-American magical practice, a distinct set of materials and products were used in relation to sexual practice. These materials are recognizable archaeologically. Based upon the analysis of archaeological materials recovered from an African-American midwife's site, I will argue that the magical rituals and elements described in the ethnohistoric literature related to relieving and regulating tension between the sexes represent only one component of African-American sexual magic. Archaeological analysis suggests that these spells were part of a larger magical system that recognized the power of sexual magic in reproduction, women's health, and childcare.

THE ETHNOGRAPHIC RECORD

A review of ethnographic data from the early twentieth-century rural southern United States (e.g. Dollard 1937; Herskovits 1941; Hurston 1990a; Hyatt 1973; Powdermaker 1937) does suggest that African-American magical ideologies recognized two adult genders that corresponded with individuals who would be biologically sexed as either men or women. While sexuality and gender are different social constructs, in rural African-American populations during the late nineteenth and early twentieth centuries, the two are intricately linked. While working in Jamaica, Zora Neale Hurston recorded the practice of sending young brides to be trained in proper positioning and technique for lovemaking, so they could best fulfill their obligations as a wife to their future husbands. As part of this training, young women were also coached in other aspects of wifely and womanly duties (Hurston 1990b). Sexuality was tied to obligations and definitions of male and female genders, with no recognition of homosexuality or transsexuality. Even in accounts of early twentieth-century Mardi Gras celebrations in New Orleans, when cross-dressing for both men and women was used as a way of contesting gender categories in a 'safe' context (e.g. Kinser 1990; Mitchell 1995; Saxon 1988; Wilkie 1998a), these activities were particular to the white, not black, populations.

The ethnographic record also indicates that differences between men and women also existed on the spiritual level. Men and women were magically different from one another. These differences may have been used to the benefit of both sexes or to their detriment. The majority of the ethnographic literature emphasizes the dangerous aspect of female/male interactions. Menstrual blood, semen, urine, hair, and other exuvia were polluting elements to the opposite sex and could be used inadvertently or intentionally to cause harm to another person. Some spells called for the use of the intended victim's bodily fluids, while others required the fluids of the person casting the spell (Wilkie 1997).

As the word is used in the ex-slave narratives, 'hoodoo' describes attempts to control the actions and health of other people (or prevent others from controlling oneself) through the use of potions, charms, and incantations (Botkin 1945; Clayton 1990; Hurston 1990a). Magical practice was often part of a broader cosmological system that sometimes incorporated Christianity or Christian-African syncretized religious traditions (Wilkie 1997). 'Conjures' and 'tricks' are terms used to describe spells, and 'hands', 'tobies', or 'gris-gris', are other terms found in the ethnographic and oral historical record to describe magical charms (e.g. Clayton 1990; Hurston 1990a; Puckett 1926; Tallant 1946).

Charms and spells were used for a variety of purposes, including healing magically caused illnesses, making or breaking a marriage, controlling the actions of others, turning a spell back on its originator, or preventing the casting of spells. Magical cures were often used in conjunction with medicinal cures. For instance, a calabash seed tea with a silver dime boiled in it was used to cure poisoning (Hyatt 1974: 3,126). Similarly, porcupine root, a silver dime, asafetida, and a St. Anthony's medal, worn together in a red flannel bag around the neck, served to prevent disease (Hyatt 1974: 3,135–36). It is impossible to separate the magical from the pharmaceutical in African-American ethnomedical practices for the two were entwined as part of a rich and complex cosmology.

African-American magical practitioners relied most extensively on contagious magic. Contagious magic operates under the belief that associated objects can exert an influence on one another. For instance, the personal property of an individual could be used to exert control over that person. The more intimately connected an object is to a person, the stronger the magical connection. Bath water, pieces of clothing, especially underwear, shoe insoles, hatbands, dirt from a footstep, or a wash-rag are all commonly mentioned ingredients in spells (Haskins 1978; Hyatt 1974; Puckett 1926). The most powerful contagious magical ingredients are any form of exuvia, or body substances. Urine, feces, skin scrapings from feet, earwax, sperm, menstrual fluid, hair (especially pubic hair), and fingernail clippings are all commonly called for in spells.

Inherent in the practice of contagious magic is the recognition that those people in your life with whom you are most intimate are the individuals who have the potential to do you the greatest harm. Family members and sexual partners have greatest access to exuvia. Hyatt, in recording magical spells used by different conjurers, found literally hundreds of spells related to the control of one's mate or lover. Urine, semen, menstrual blood, and pubic hair were all commonly used in spells to control a man or woman's sexual behavior. For instance, a woman's menstrual blood, mixed in her lover's food or drink, once ingested, would leave him impotent with any other woman (1973: 2,501). Burying a woman's exuvia in a teacup near a house doorstep would render her unable to leave (1974: 3,012). Of course, sexual partners were fully aware that spells to bind existed, and in response, a number of spells used to counteract these were also widely employed. Hyatt (1973, 1974) recorded a large number of spells aimed at returning a man's vitality to him.

While many of the magical spells related to interactions between males and females were to spark romance and ensure fidelity, a number of spells also represent outright fear of harm from the opposite sex. Men reported holding a penny in their mouths during intercourse to prevent getting venereal disease from their partners. As a counter-spell, men noted that if a woman held a brass penny in her mouth while a man held a penny in his, the man would receive a worse case of venereal disease (Hyatt 1973: 2,369). Men would also secretly rub a woman's genitals with their own earwax to 'test' her for venereal disease. If she felt a burning sensation, she had tested positive (Wilkie 1997). Likewise, a woman could give a man venereal disease if she rubbed his genitals with earwax and held a silver coin to the roof of her mouth during climax (Hyatt 1973: 2,376). These are just a few of the spells and conjures recorded that are related to the transmission of venereal disease.

As briefly discussed above, the need or desire to cast venereal disease on another may have been exacerbated due to the sexual politics of enslavement. A woman being raped by a slaveholder had limited means of retaliation that would not jeopardize her, her husband, or her children. Punishing her attacker with a sexual disease, which in turn would be transmitted to his family, would be a just vengeance. Despite its possible importance during the experiences of enslavement, it is clear that these particular spells were remembered and still part of the magical arsenal in the early twentieth century. Many of these magical practices have been discussed with the author by informants in Louisiana. The number of tests and preventative measures for sexually transmitted diseases demonstrates a strong sense of distrust that could characterize sexual relationships. It is important to note that these spells were reportedly used by individuals involved in casual sexual relationships, not by married or long-term monogamous couples. Perhaps these spells are best characterized as evidence that sex outside of a committed relationship was perceived as a dangerous pursuit.

Overall, the vast majority of hoodoo spells recorded (e.g. Hyatt 1973, 1974; Puckett 1926; Tallant 1946) dealt with attempts to control the actions of a member of the opposite gender. These spells, which included some of the binding spells described above, in addition to a multitude of others, had counterparts in West Africa and Europe (e.g. Hand 1980; MacGaffey 1986, 1991; Puckett 1926; Herskovits 1941). The resulting magical arsenal most certainly reflects the influences of African, European, and Native American cultural contact and creolization in the New World (Wilkie 1997).

Among the diverse materials incorporated into the magical practices, some elements occurred repeatedly in numerous cures, charms, and spells. In particular, cow feet and hooves, the color blue, Vaseline, perfume, sulfur, hats, coins, and bottles are described over and over in the spells. Hats are mentioned in many spells. A woman wishing to attract a particular man could do so by treating his hatband with perfume (Hyatt 1973: 2,663), while a man wishing to make a woman love him could do so by wearing her hair in his hatband (Hyatt 1973: 1,895). Hats seem to have been important for a number of reasons: they often contain hair or the sweat of the wearer, but also sit on the head, an important center of power within the body. The color blue was often associated with the pursuit or destruction of love. This relationship between the color and emotion may have been related to the association between blue and *Yemalia*, the Yoruban *Orish* who is syncretized in the Diaspora with the Virgin Mary, and strongly associated with motherhood, love, and water (Thompson 1983). Blue candles, blue stone, and blue bottles were all commonly employed in spells that were intended to draw, repel, rekindle, or destroy love (e.g. Hyatt 1973). Blue bottles were also explicitly used in the creation of 'conjure bottles' that were intended to draw or repel love, or to harm a former loved one (Wilkie 1997).

Products such as sulfur, Vaseline, castor oil, and cow feet were associated with many different aspects of sexual magic. Vaseline was a common component of magical cures for male impotency and venereal disease (Hyatt 1973). Cow hooves were used in a variety of sexual spells and medicines. Tea brewed from sulfur and cow hooves was used to take away or restore a man's ability to function sexually. Men may also have used bull's horn, ground and prepared as a tea, to restore sexual function. Sulfur also appeared as a common magical ingredient, in a variety of spells. These magical ingredients were also combined with one another in various spells related to sexuality and reproduction. For example, one cure recorded by Hyatt (1973: 2,026) calls for 'sulfur, Vaseline, castor oil, and blue stone to be boiled together into a salve' to cure venereal disease.

The ethnohistorical data is invaluable, then, as a means of providing insight into magical-medical meanings and uses of commonly available products. In such a way, it is possible to re-evaluate material culture from African-American sites in regard to how they may provide evidence for an archaeology of sexuality. Of course, as in all of archaeology, it is impossible to know exactly what the function of any given artifact may have been. The contents of a single jar of Vaseline could have been bought for use as a hair pomade, used to help cure a bout of impotence, and then used to treat a diaper rash. The acknowledgment that these products may have had sexually-related functions in common along with their other ordinary uses serves to achieve a goal of this volume: that is, promote the recognition that human sexuality is a normal, daily aspect of the human experience.

MAGICAL MIDWIFERY: A CASE STUDY

Although some societies tend to disassociate sexuality and reproduction, and even more so, the state of motherhood and sexuality, such a division is culturally and historically specific. The ethnohistoric literature related to the magic and material culture of sexuality provides a useful framework in which to situate our interpretations of material culture related to African-American midwifery practices so that we can evaluate whether such a division characterized African-American views of sexuality and motherhood. To do this, I will draw upon materials excavated from a midwife's site in Alabama.

In the late summer of 1994, during a grading project in Crawford Park, Mobile, Alabama, six archaeological scatters and features associated with a late nineteenth- to early twentieth-century house site were discovered (Figures 7.1 and 7.2). Unfortunately, most of the shallow deposits were destroyed by grading activities, such that they provided small artifact samples from very questionable contexts. Among the features discovered, however, was a sealed well, filled with domestic refuse. The materials excavated from this well provide the archaeological data for this paper.

Excavation of the well took place as a salvage effort after renovation of the existing park on the lot had begun. The well was excavated in less than ideal conditions, during heavy summer rains. To allow for the recording of a central profile, the interior of the well was bisected and each side was excavated in 10 cm arbitrary levels. At a depth of 70 cm, it was possible to remove collapsed timbers from the upper portion of the well and to define the feature. The well was lined with a wood box, supported by four corner posts, each measuring about 9 cm². The well-box measured approximately 86 cm on its north–south sides and 76 cm on its east–west sides. Excavation continued to a depth of 130 cm. After that point, the excavation was quickly refilling with ground water, and it was unsafe to excavate further. It was also determined that the artifact density had significantly diminished.

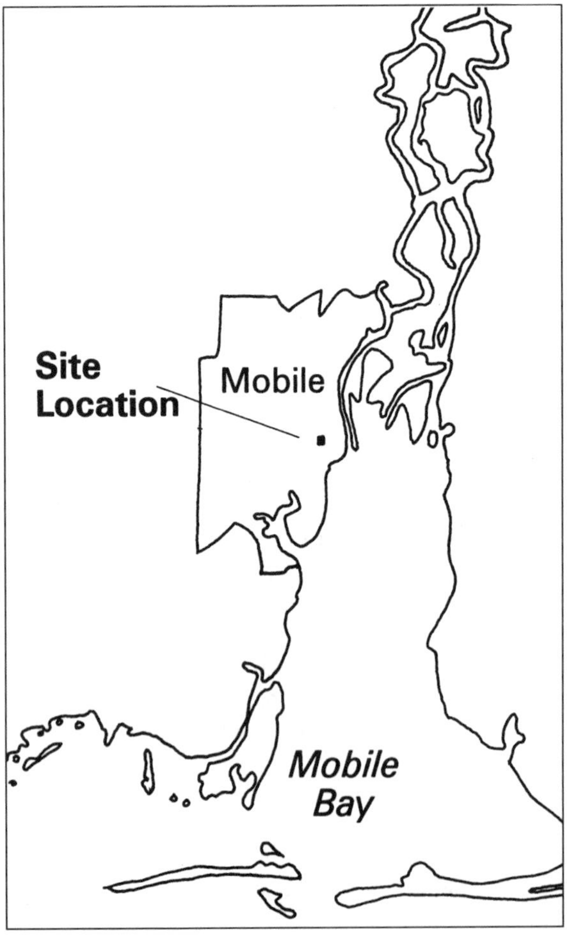

Materials recovered from the well consist of a wide range of domestic materials, including tablewares, decorative ceramics, food and beverage containers, medicine bottles, and a range of other household garbage. Many of the glass beverage containers were recovered whole, facilitating identification. The majority of the ceramics recovered from the well were manufactured during the late 1880s and 1890s; none were manufactured after 1912. When analyzed stratigraphically, the distribution of ceramics did not suggest any particular pattern of deposition. The glass from the uppermost three levels of the well was slightly later than that from the lower levels, indicating an average manufacture date of around 1910,

Figure 7.1 Location of Perryman property within limits of modern city of Mobile, Alabama. The map is oriented to true north.
Illustration by the author.

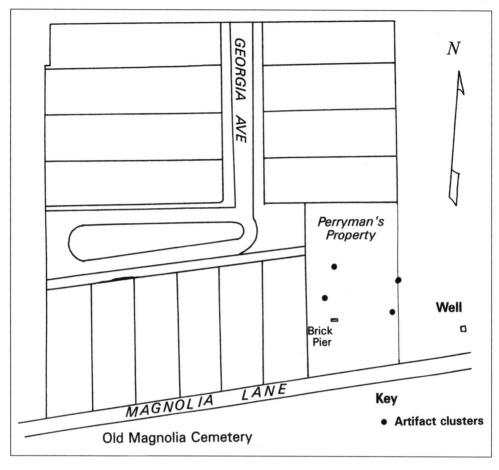

Figure 7.2 North, west and south boundaries of Perryman property, as recorded on August 4, 1921 Mobile County. While mapped as a hard boundary, it is unclear from historical documents whether the eastern boundary represents the limits of the Perryman property or merely the limits of this specific survey. The locations of archaeological features associated with the Perryman family have been superimposed on this map. The Perryman lot, as mapped is 196′ 8″ by 105′.
Illustration by the author.

but the ensuing levels all indicate manufacture between *c.* 1890–1900, corresponding to Lucretia Perryman's time working as a midwife.

Documentary research into the site revealed that the well seems to have been located on a parcel immediately adjacent to a property that had been owned, farmed, and lived on by Lucretia Perryman and her family. Based on a review of county records, it is unclear whether or not the Perrymans owned the land on which the well is situated. A 1921 map drafted to show the extension of Georgia Avenue, if accurately reflecting the boundaries of the Perryman property (Figure 7.2), would place the well beyond the borders of the property. In addition, the 1921 map clearly shows the surrounding property being mapped and cut into lots for future development. A review of city directories and census records clearly indicates that the Perrymans were the only family living on what was known as Gazzam's Lane or Magnolia Lane during this period. Likewise, the well is the only observable source of fresh water for the property. The abandonment, and subsequent filling of the well may reflect the introduction of piped water, but it has not yet been possible to confirm this historically. It was common practice to fill abandoned wells with trash to limit the potential for children or animals falling into them. The Perryman family, therefore, seem to be the only family who could have filled the well.

Based upon census records, Lucretia Perryman was born into enslavement in North Carolina in 1836. She married Marshall Perryman, a Jamaican-born man, and their first child was born in 1853. Together, they moved from North Carolina to Alabama, settling on the outskirts of incorporated Mobile by 1871. Marshall Perryman worked as a store porter, and Lucretia worked at home, raising their children and running their small farming operation until 1889, when she is first listed in the Mobile city directory with the occupation of nurse/midwife (Wilkie 1998b). She continued to hold this position until at least 1907. Perryman's clientele probably included urban and rural families, and white and black families from the lower and middle classes. African-American women had long been the primary providers of midwifery services to the women of the rural south (Matthews 1992), and their techniques and methods would have been familiar and comforting to multiple generations of women, no matter their racial background. What may have differed, however, is the level of cultural meanings that women from differing backgrounds may have recognized or related to before, during, and after the birthing experience.

African-American midwifery has a long history in the United States, with traditions dating back to enslavement and beyond. Midwifery was a unique combination of cultural innovation and conservatism (Wilkie 1998b) that provided for maximum comfort, security, and medical competence for young mothers; unlike obstetricians of the time, who routinely lost patients during childbirth (Mathews 1992). Perryman would have received her training in midwifery as an apprentice to an older, more experienced woman (Wilkie 1998b). Her training would have consisted of overseeing prenatal care, assisting with numerous births and aiding with post-partum care. Once she convinced her mentor of her abilities, she would have been allowed to establish her own practice.

Perryman is not listed in city directories from 1908–1912, probably due to an oversight. In 1907 she is listed as a nurse, but in 1913, when she appears again, she no longer has an occupation. Perryman died in 1917, prior to the period when the state of Alabama began to register, license, and train midwives. The Perryman property was sold to the city of Mobile around 1925 to be converted into a city park (Wilkie and Shorter, in press). The materials associated with Perryman's life as a midwife provide a unique opportunity to study this industry. While Perryman's actual practice as a midwife would have taken her to the homes of her patients, thus presumably leading to the dispersal of some of her midwife's tool kit, other artifacts associated with her practice appear to have been discarded at her home. Therefore, the assemblage provides an opportunity to explore the relationship between the magical practices of sexual tension, as evidenced in the ethnohistoric record, and the magic of sexual harmony, otherwise known as reproduction. Midwifery may not seem directly related to sexuality, but the decoupling of sexuality and reproduction is historically particular to our culture, where the public is shocked by any suggestion that pregnant women could be sexually available or desirable. Such a disarticulation of motherhood, pregnancy, and sexuality is not universal, nor compatible with the physiological experiences of pregnant women.

MATERIAL CULTURE OF MIDWIFERY

African-American midwifery practices are poorly represented in the ethnographic and oral historical literature. African-American midwives were demonized in the early twentieth century throughout the southern United States as a result of a smear campaign instigated by the American Medical Association (Mathews 1992). As a result, midwives came under state-level regulation. Traditional practices were eliminated or driven underground. As a result, few records exist which describe pre-regulation midwifery. Existing records suggest that midwives exclusively treated women and newborns, providing prenatal and neonatal care. Those references that do exist provide some evidence that a magical grammar similar to that which regulated sexual magic may have shaped midwifery practices. Magic was certainly a component of midwifery practice. Campbell (1946: 27) wrote of the period of regulation:

> Nurses have learned to look under the removable lining of the bag. There may be found such things as coins tied into the corners of a hand-kerchief, a piece of rope, a box of snuff, a bottle of homemade tonic or 'bitters', a rabbit's foot, or some other good luck charm.

Material objects like hats, blue glass bottles, castor oil, and Vaseline, products used in magic spells regulating sexuality are men-tioned in regard to childbirth and women's health. For instance, wearing the hat of the baby's father could reduce labor pains for a woman, or blowing in a blue glass bottle could cause the release of a retained pla-centa (Campbell 1946: 35). Vaseline was also used in different midwifery practices, including the repair of collapsed uteruses, and to speed the delivery of afterbirth (Wilkie 1998b). A number of products explicitly named in ethnographies of mid-wifery were recovered archaeologically from the Perryman site.

Ten medicine jars once contained Vaseline (Figure 7.3), which was report-edly used to coat newborns to protect their skin and keep them warm immedi-ately after birth (Coe 1995). Another midwife discussed how, before Vaseline was available, her grandmother used to make an animal-based salve that was used in the vagina to speed delivery (Logan, as

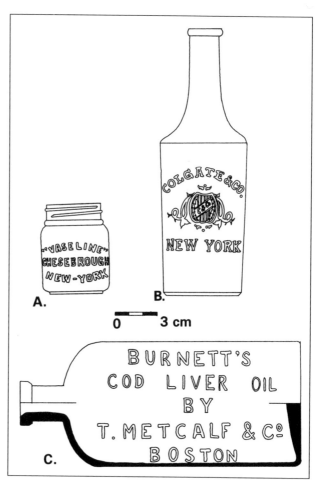

Figure 7.3 Examples of mass-produced commercial medicinal and hygiene products recovered from Perryman well:
A. Vaseline; B. Colgate toilet water/cologne; C. Burnett's Cod Liver Oil.
Illustrations by the author.

told to Clark 1989). By implication then, Vaseline was used this way as well. One bottle of 'Burnett's Cod Liver Oil' and four 'Castoria' bottles were found. Each of these products can be described generically as forms of castor oil (Figure 7.3). Some oral histories mention such cathartics being given to mothers immediately after birth to 'clean the mother out and to heal her up inside' (Coe 1995: 18), while others discuss the use of caster oil to clean the bowels and speed contractions during labor (Logan as told to Clark 1989: 53).

In addition to the medicine bottles, another artifact related to gynecological care was recovered: a white metal vaginal pipe-attachment for a douche kit. Onnie Logan remembered using douching to treat 'fallen ovaries' or 'after-pains' following birth. The patient was first douched with vinegar, then she was wrapped around the middle with an elastic band and her abdomen rubbed with lard or Vaseline, then a medicine-soaked ball of cloth was inserted vaginally and left overnight (Logan, as told to Clark 1989).

While manufactured for one intended use, a review of oral histories and ethnographic accounts related to African-American midwifery suggest that a range of popular commercially produced medicines such as Vaseline, castor oil, and other cathartics were incorporated into the ethnomedical tool kit of midwives. The products incorporated into midwifery practice would have been familiar, and probably, already used, in the households of patients. Several of these products were employed not only in the relief of physical symptoms, but also in the magical treatment of conditions related to procreation and childbirth.

The correlation between the ethnographic literature and the material assemblage is useful in that it demonstrates that the scant ethnographic evidence is reflective of some generalized midwife practices. However, the use of simple correlations between archaeological and documentary data does not necessarily expand our understanding of sexual and reproductive magic. A number of additional artifacts were recovered that suggest a further relationship between the material culture of magic to regulate, and magic to reproduce.

Among the bottles recovered from the site were a minimum of ten 'Sauer's Extracts' bottles. Extracts, such as essence of peppermint, lemon, ginger, and vanilla, were sold as extracts for cooking, as well as employed within medicinal remedies (Schroeder 1971: 790). Peppermint, in particular, one of the more popular extracts sold, was an important ingredient in many traditional African-American magical and medical cures. Peppermint, when used on the hands as a wash, was believed to bring love and friendship to a person (Wilkie 1996). While it is not possible to identify the contents of the extract bottles, peppermint extract was recovered from the site in the form of 'Dr Tichenor's Antiseptic'. Dr Tichenor's active ingredients were peppermint and alcohol. Peppermint was clearly used in spells to draw love, and in turn, may have been important within midwifery. In a similar way, cologne bottles recovered from the site may have served functions in both the secular and spiritual realm. Cologne is often used in spells to repel or attract or to feed charm bags (Hyatt 1973, 1974: 1,885).

Among the artifacts recovered from the site were two pocket knives. Pocket knives, of course, are useful, multi-functional artifacts. Given the midwifery context, however, it is worth considering magical uses of knives. Knives and axes are both described as being placed under mattresses to 'cut' labor pains. They bear magical meanings in other Diaspora contexts as well. Knives and axes, within Santeria and voodoo are strongly associated with the Yoruban male *Orisha Eshu-Elegba* and *Ogun* (Thompson 1983). The use of knives and axes in the context of labor and delivery may also have associations with male power. While the pocket knives recovered from the Perryman site were likely used in a variety

Table 7.1 Identified zooarchaeological remains from Lucretia Perryman's well

Species	Element	NISP*	MNE*
Bos taurus (cow)	cranial fragments	7	1
	mandible fragments	14	2
	teeth	24	10
	vertebrae	7	2
	radii (sawn)	2	1
	distal tibiae (sawn)	3	2
	proximal ulnae (sawn)	1	1
	distal femurs (sawn)	2	1
	rib fragments	3	1
	calcanea	4	4
	scapho-lunars	1	1
	naviculo cuboids	2	2
	astraguli	3	3
	metatarsals	1	1
Sus scrofa (pig)	mandible fragments	3	1
	scapulae	1	1
	humeri	1	1
	phalanges	1	1
Gallus gallus (chicken)	femurs	2	1
Unidentified fish	vertebrae	4	4

* NISP = number of individual specimens. MNE = minimum number of elements present. This measure was used since the assemblage was so fragmentary, and because on many historical sites butchered parts, not entire animals, are represented.

of contexts and for a variety of functions, the possibility that they were also used within Perryman's midwifery practice should not be discounted.

Faunal remains provide some evidence of magical medicine. Almost exclusively, cow elements from the site were drawn from either the head or the lower limbs of the cow (Table 7.1). Scapho-lunars, naviculo cuboids, astraguli, phalanges, and calcanea are found at the lowest extreme of the animals' legs, and provide little in the way of meat. These bones were recovered complete, without evidence of butchering, from the site. As previously discussed, cow hooves are used in other realms of sexual magic related to male sexual function. The presence of these bones in the midwife's site again suggests ties between the magic of sexuality, reproduction, and childbirth. Sulfur is another recurring ingredient in the magic of sexual control and regulation. At least three small chunks of yellow sulfur were recovered from the Perryman site. Again, while the explicit function of these materials cannot be known, the presence of these materials suggests a tie between midwifery and sexual magic.

While it is impossible to assign exclusive functions to materials recovered from archaeological sites, the presence of these artifacts suggests that midwifery may have incorporated a much broader range of magical-medical practices that depended upon the same magical tool kit used by practitioners casting spells to regulate and control sexual behavior. All of these magical-medical cures indicated from the midwifery site incorporated symbols that were strongly connected with regulating sexual activity or treating the consequences of such activity. Childbirth is a condition that results from sexual congress, and as such, seems to be connected to the same magical inventory. There was an important contrast between the magic of sexual control and the magic of childbirth, however. While the magic of sexual control emphasized an adversarial relationship between the sexes, the magic of childbirth used the items to strengthen women during childbirth, and protect them and their children, sometimes through male magic.

Midwives were emphatic that men should not be involved in the actual birth experience (e.g. Susie 1988). Yet, magical tensions between the sexes characterized the practices of other magical mediators in the African-American community. Through the incorporation of magical ritual that used artifacts that symbolically represented male power, or that physically belonged to the child's father, midwives were able to use male magic within the female experience of birth as a healing, rather than divisive, influence. In such a way, midwives were gender mediators who recognized the spiritual and magical implications of the differences between men and women while celebrating these differences. While midwifery as it was practiced prior to the middle of the twentieth century remains an under-documented area of African-American health practice, archaeological materials do suggest that midwives were connected into a broader realm of magical practice that was related to sexuality and reproduction.

CONCLUSIONS

This chapter has attempted to demonstrate how an archaeological consideration of practices and beliefs related to sexuality can enrich our understanding of African-American magical-medical practices. Archaeologists often depend upon the ethnohistorical record to understand African-American magical systems. These resources have limitations, particularly with regard to their portrayal of practices related to love and sexuality. If used in conjunction with archaeological materials, however, the ethnohistoric record can be used to broaden our understanding of practices and attitudes related to sexuality. This archaeology of sexuality has attempted to substantiate a previously unclear connection between magical midwifery practices and other recorded forms of 'sexual magic'. I have suggested that midwifery existed as part of a larger magical-medical system that influenced the way that individuals thought about, defined, pursued, and nurtured love, sexuality, reproduction, and family. While this analysis serves to expand our understanding of 'sexual magic', it also suggests that the practice of midwifery played a central role in the African-American magical-medical system. Instead of being seen as a peripheral avenue of research relevant only to women's history, midwifery should be seen as an important part of the social infrastructure that served to replicate and reinforce the individual's understanding of the social (and sexual) relations that tied her to others.

The archaeological evidence derived from the analysis of midwifery material serves as a balance to the portrait of African-American sexual relations derived from oral history and ethnography alone. A comparison of the portraits of magical practice as revealed by ethnohistoric and archaeological materials demonstrates that love, sexuality, and reproduction were tied together by a complex cosmology in African-American communities of the Deep South during the late nineteenth and early twentieth centuries. This cosmology incorporated magical practices that used male and female spiritual essences as both combined and opposing forces to ensure the stability and health of African-American families. Materially, this magical practice is evidenced by the recurring use of specific magical ingredients.

A complex magical system served as a means for male and female spiritual powers to interact in positive and negative ways. The control and regulation of sexuality and reproduction through magic served as a means of social dialogue between the men and women in African-American communities. Ultimately, magic was used to strengthen family bonds and commitments. Women and men used magic to ensure the faithfulness of their husbands and wives and to ensure that outsiders did not attempt to come between them. The threat of magical harm further served to strengthen a couple's commitment to one another. A philandering spouse, by allowing an outsider access to exuvia, placed his or her entire family at magical risk.

The oppression of enslavement, and the later economic hardships and racial violence of the post-bellum period, placed incredible strains on African-American families. The legacy of slavery continued to shape the experiences of families living and working in the late nineteenth and early twentieth centuries. In the rural post-bellum South, men often traveled for months at a time from their families, following the seasonal round of agricultural jobs (Jones 1992). Distance and limited means of communication strained marriages and disrupted families. Magic provided a means of maintaining some control in unhappy circumstances. While many of the specific recorded magical spells dealt with keeping, gaining, or repelling sexual partners, ultimately all of the spells are about maintaining trust between men and women. Women and men were dependent upon one another for survival, in a physical and spiritual sense. Perhaps this mutual dependence is most clear in the event of childbirth. During the process of birth, the combination of female and male spiritual essences was necessary to preserve the health and safety of baby and mother. Through an understanding of the materials that are related to the magic of sexuality and reproduction, archaeologists will be better equipped to recognize the politics of sexual negotiation and barter in the archaeological record. As this case study has demonstrated, a focused consideration of sexuality will greatly enrich the archaeology of African-American life.

REFERENCES

Botkin, B. A. (ed.) (1945) *Lay My Burden Down: A Folk History of Slavery*, Athens: University of Georgia.

Brown, K. and D. Cooper (1991) 'Structural Continuity in an African-American Slave and Tenant Community', *Historical Archaeology* 24, 4: 7–19.

Campbell, M. (1946) *Folks Do Get Born*, New York: Rinehart and Company, Inc.

Coe, E. (1995) 'Granny Midwives: Grandmother to Nurse Midwives', paper presented at the American Anthropological Association Meetings, Washington, DC.

Clayton, R. (ed.) (1990) *Mother Wit: The Ex-Slave Narratives of the Louisiana's Federal Writers' Project*, New York: Peter Lang.

Dollard, J. (1937) *Caste and Class in a Southern Town*, Madison: University of Wisconsin Press.

Ferguson, L. (1992) *Uncommon Ground*, Washington, DC: Smithsonian Institution Press.

Franklin, M. (1997) *Out of Site, Out of Mind: the Archaeology of an Enslaved Virginian Household, c. 1740–1778*, unpublished doctoral dissertation, Department of Anthropology, University of California, Berkeley.

Hand, W. (1980) *Magical Medicine: The Folkloric Component of Medicine in the Folk Belief, Custom, and Ritual of the Peoples of Europe and America*, Berkeley: University of California Press.

Haskins, J. (1978) *Voodoo and Hoodoo*, Chelsea, MI: Scarbourough House Publishers.

Herskovits, M. (1941) *Myth of the Negro Past*, Boston: Beacon Press.

Hurston, Z. N. (1990a) *Mules and Men*, New York: Harper and Row.

—— (1990b) *Tell My Horse: Voodoo and Life in Haiti and Jamaica*, New York: Harper and Row.

Hyatt, H. (1973) *Hoodoo–Conjuration–Witchcraft–Rootwork*, vol. 3, St. Louis: Western Publishing.

—— (1974) *Hoodoo–Conjuration–Witchcraft–Rootwork*, vol. 4, St. Louis: Western Publishing.

Jones, J. (1992) *The Dispossessed*, New York: Basic Books.

Kinser, S. (1990) *Carnival American Style: Mardi Gras at New Orleans and Mobile*, Chicago: University of Chicago.

Logan, O. (as told to K. Clark) (1989) *Motherwit: An Alabama Midwife's Story*, New York: E. P. Dutton.

MacGaffey, W. (1986) *Religion and Society in Central Africa*, Chicago: University of Chicago.

—— (1991) *The Art and Healing of the Bakongo*, Stockholm: Folkens Museum-Etnografiska.

Matthews, H. (1992) 'Killing the Medical Self-Help Tradition Among African Americans: The Case of Lay Midwifery in North Carolina, 1912–1983', in H. A. Baer and Y. Jones (eds) *African Americans in the South*, Athens: University of Georgia Press.

Mitchell, R. (1995) *All on a Mardi Gras Day: Episodes in the History of New Orleans Carnival*, Cambridge: Harvard University Press.

Orser, C. E., Jr (1994) 'The Archaeology of African-American Slave Religion in the Antebellum South', *Cambridge Archaeological Review Journal* 4, 1: 33–45.

Powdermaker, H. (1937) *After Freedom: A Cultural Study in the Deep South*, Madison: University of Wisconsin Press.

Puckett, N. N. (1926) *Folk Beliefs of the Southern Negro*, Chapel Hill: University of North Carolina Press.

Samford, P. (1996) 'The Archaeology of African-American Slavery and Material Culture', *The William and Mary Quarterly*, third series, 53, 1: 87–114.

Saxon, L. (1988) *Fabulous New Orleans*, New York: Pelican.

Schroeder, J. J. (ed.) (1971) *1908 Sears, Roebuck Catalogue*, Northfield, IL: DBI Books.

Stine, L. F., M. A. Caback and M. D. Groover (1996) 'Blue Beads as African-American Cultural Symbols', *Historical Archaeology* 30, 3: 49–75.

Susie (1998) *In the Way of our Grandmothers: a Cultural View of Twentieth Century Midwifery in Florida*, Athens: University of Georgia Press.

Tallant, R. (1946) *Voodoo in New Orleans*, New York: Pelican.

Thompson, R. F. (1983) *Flash of the Spirit*, New York: Random House.

Wilkie, L. A. (1994) '"Never Leave Me Alone": An Archaeological Study of African-American Ethnicity, Race Relations, and Community at Oakley Plantation', Ph.D. dissertation, Archaeology Program, University of California, Los Angeles.

—— (1995) 'Magic and Empowerment on the Plantation: An Archaeological Consideration of African-American World View', *Southeastern Archaeology* 14, 2: 136–48.

—— (1996) 'Medicinal Teas and Patent Medicines: African-American Women's Consumer Choices and Ethnomedical Traditions at a Louisiana Plantation', *Southeastern Archaeology* 15, 2: 119–31.

—— (1997) 'Secret and Sacred: Contextualizing the Artifacts of African-American Magic and Religion', *Historical Archaeology* 31, 4: 81–106.

—— (1998a) 'Beads and Breasts: The Negotiation of Gender Roles and Power at New Orleans Mardi Gras', in L. Sciama and B. Eicher (eds) *Beads and Bead Makers: Gender, Material Culture and Meaning*, New York: Berg.

—— (1998b) '"Granny" Midwives: Gender and Generational Mediators of the African-American Community', paper presented at the Conference for Historical and Underwater Archaeology, Atlanta.

—— (in press) 'Considering the Future of African-American Archaeology', *Historical Archaeology*.

Wilkie, L. and G. Shorter (in press) *An Archaeological Glimpse of an African-American Midwife's Life: Excavations at 1MB99*, Mobile: University of Southern Alabama Archaeology Facility.

Young, A. (1997) 'Risk Management Strategies Among African-American Slaves at Locust Grove Plantation', *International Journal of Historical Archaeology* 1, 1: 5–38.

Chapter Eight

Bulldaggers and gentle ladies: archaeological approaches to female homosexuality in convict-era Australia

Eleanor Conlin Casella

INTRODUCTION

On 13 December 1848, the Comptroller-General of Convicts in Van Diemen's Land received disturbing news from the Superintendent of Ross Female Factory, a women's prison located in the rural midlands district of this Australian penal colony:

> Last Night about 11 P.M. a disturbance took place in the sleeping apartment of the Crime Class which of course rendered it <u>necessary</u> to enter their room, durring [*sic*] the time that elapsed whilst the keys, which are always in my keeping were being brought over, Mr. Imrie <u>distinctly</u> overheard from the dispute which was then being carried on, that the quarrel arose from some of the women deserting the beds of those to whom they acted in the capacity of men, and taking themselves elsewhere . . . there are some of the women, who by a preter-natural formature, or sometimes by artificial means, are enabled to fill the vile part above described, & who are known amongst their fellow prisoners by a peculiarly significant soubriquet.
>
> (Archives of Tasmania (AOT) Miscellaneous Microfilm (MM) 62/1/11037, original emphasis)

The letter concludes with a request for immediate release of funds for construction of a new block of solitary cells to punish such female inmates for their 'unnatural vices'.

The nature of women's sexuality plays a central role in understanding the life experiences of British women transported to Tasmania during the Australian convict era. While perceptions of the sexual deviance and 'immorality' of female convicts have luridly fascinated colonial diarists, authors, and historians since the establishment of Australian colonies in 1788, most twentieth-century discussions of female convict history have debated the positive versus negative aspects of their sexual experiences (Dixon 1976; Summers 1975; Lake 1988; Aveling 1992). In the last thirty years of historical research, stories of brutal rapes, wife-auctions, drunken whores, and abandoned bastards (Sturma 1978; Hughes 1987; Robson 1965) have been juxtaposed against images of ex-convict wives and mothers quietly settling on rural homesteads and raising the first generation of Anglo-Australians

(Robinson 1985, 1988). Recent research in convict history has moved beyond this moralizing approach by considering the agency of male and female convicts. Exploring their role as active participants in the emerging penal society, these new histories challenge the concept of a disempowered 'criminal class', and instead examine the variety of ways convict men and women worked the system to minimize their disadvantage (Daniels 1993, 1998a; Oxley 1996; Nicholas 1988; Duffield & Bradley 1997).

In her recent book *Depraved and Disorderly*, Australian historian Joy Damousi (1997a) explicity considered the documentary construction of gender roles and female convict sexuality within the penal colonies. She asserted that female homosexuality, a subject that has titillated colonists and historians for two centuries, has yet to be seriously examined, as female heterosexuality, a far more mainstream subject, still occupies an ambivalent historical space. Seeking to transcend the traditional focus on the boundaries and borders confining Australian convicts, Damousi focused her research on 'those moments of transgression that highlighted understandings of sexuality, masculinity and femininity' (1997a: 5). Such moments simultaneously illuminate and challenge the hegemonic struggle for social order by both exploring the margins of acceptable sex/gender roles, and revealing the threatening presence of alternative sexual identities. Drawing on Mikhail Bakhtin's research on the carnivalesque, Peter Stallybrass and Allon White noted that 'transgression becomes a kind of reverse or counter-sublimation, undoing the discursive hierarchies and stratifications of bodies and cultures which bourgeois society has produced as the mechanism of its symbolic dominance' (Stallybrass and White 1986: 200–201). Historian Kay Daniels similarly considered the dangerous social threat posed by convict women's sexuality:

> This internal subculture of the female [convict prisons] simultaneously recreated and mocked elements of the dominant male culture of the colonial society outside. While openly subverting the authority of the convict system which confined them, [the women] not only made a home for themselves within it, but also challenged the concepts of sexuality and gender on which it was based.
>
> (1993: 140)

However, although Daniels and Damousi consider examples of both social and physical 'transgression' of bounded convict landscapes, their historical approach centers on analysis of documentary sources. Adding a necessary material perspective, archaeology provides new evidence for and interpretations of the transgression of sexual and gender roles within Australia's convict era. How did British women transported to the Van Diemen's Land penal colony adapt their sexual roles within the Female Factory prisons? What transgressive sexual relationships were communicated through the material world of these penal sites? Can the shadowy presence of female homosexuality be considered through the material culture of these historic places?

THOSE EXILED TO FURTHEST SHORES

The transportation of convicts to Australia became one of the largest involuntary migrations of European people in modern history. Commencing in 1788 with the arrival of the First Fleet in Sydney Harbour, by the end of Australia's convict era in 1868 approximately 170,000 British men and women had been processed through a vast network of probation stations, hiring depots, hard labor camps, and model prisons across the continent (Hughes 1987). Original settlement concentrated around the New South Wales region of mainland Australia. However, a second penal colony was soon required to accommodate the increasing convict population. In 1803, Van Diemen's Land (present-day Tasmania) was established for that purpose. Within ten years, this distant island became the primary destination for exiled felons. An extensive bureaucratic and institutional infrastructure was rapidly designed to punish and reform the British convicts (Hughes 1987; Robson 1965; Shaw 1966).

Over 12,000 women were transported to Van Diemen's Land between 1803 and 1853, when economic and social forces of the expanding Industrial Revolution caused Britain to cease transportation (Robson 1965; Brand 1990; Kociumbas 1992; Oxley 1996). An extreme demographic imbalance exacerbated the sexual vulnerability of women in the penal colonies; of the 170,000 convicts transported to Australia, less than 15% were women. As economic historian Deborah Oxley statistically demonstrated, the vast majority of these female prisoners had been transported for convictions of petty theft; typically they had supplemented their meager salaries with goods nicked from their domestic employers in Britain (Oxley 1996).

After enduring five months aboard a penal transport vessel, convict women disembarked at Hobart, the colonial capital of Van Diemen's Land (Figure 8.1). Although some women were assigned to private domestic service immediately upon arrival, most convict women spent significant portions of their sentence incarcerated within the Female Factory System, a network of prisons scattered across the island (Brand 1990; Ryan 1995). The name 'factory' was an abbreviation of the institutional title 'manufactory', and referred to the establishments' intended role as Houses of Industry. Upon entry female convicts were assigned to the 'crime class', and incarcerated within a factory for a minimum of six months. While serving this initial sentence, the convicts were supposed to 'reform' through Christian prayer and forced training in acceptable feminine industries, such as sewing, laundry, and cooking. Recalcitrance by any crime class inmate was punished by up to three weeks confinement in solitary treatment cells, accompanied by severe reduction of food rations (Damousi 1997a; Daniels 1993, 1998a). Once they successfully served their probationary period, the 'reformed' women were reclassified into the 'hiring class', and were accommodated within the prison while awaiting assignment to local pastoral properties. Convict women completed their penal sentences as domestic servants for free colonists (Ryan 1995; Oxley 1996; Damousi 1997b: 206). After receiving either probationary 'tickets of leave' or full official pardons, most former convicts took advantage of the colonial gender imbalance to quickly reintegrate into free society. The vast majority of women married, bore children, and then quietly faded from the bureaucratic records of colonial administration (Robinson 1988; Smith 1988; Tardiff 1990).

VISIONS OF FEMALE HOMOSEXUALITY

Within the female factories, the spectacle of female homosexuality was constructed and appropriated through the gaze of male Convict Department officials. A substantial collection of their primary documents exists on this subject, including descriptive letters from factory superintendents, transcriptions of colonial court trials, newspaper accounts, and numerous official reports to and from the Van Diemen's Land Lieutenant-Governor and the British Colonial Office. As Joy Damousi has emphasized:

> An examination of this discussion not only points to the ways in which these concepts shaped understandings of femininity, masculinity and sexuality, but also illuminates

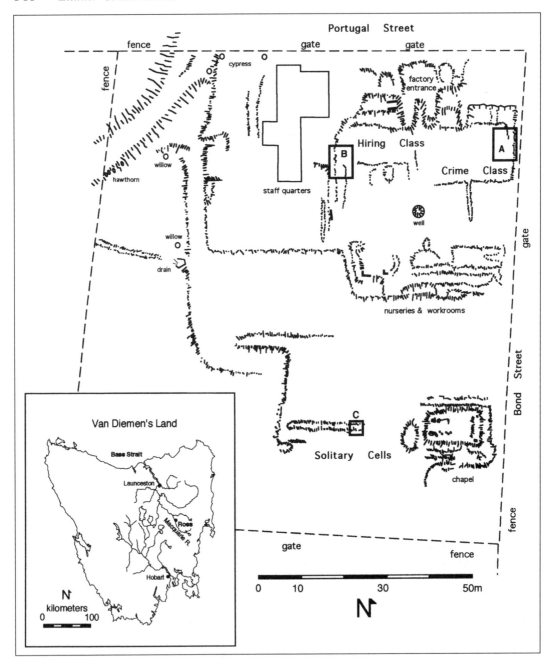

Figure 8.1 Site plan with inset of Van Diemen's Land. Ross Female Factory site features and vegetation. Hatchures indicate surface features; excavation areas are outlined in bold and lettered. Note that excavation area D, a test pit excavated to ascertain natural soil conditions, is located off-site and is not depicted on this map.
Illustration by the author.

the ways in which male observers constructed their own sense of themselves as white, male and middle class in relation to convict women ... Unlike Aboriginal women, who could be dismissed as alien, convict women were the threat from within. There was both a fear and fascination with the unsettling power of the 'other' – in terms of gender and class – embodied in convict women and also in the projection of male sexuality in the eroticisation of these women.

(1997a: 4)

The male authors of these documents used lurid descriptions of female homosexuality to titillate, to shock, to repulse, and to illicit passionate responses within their circle of colonial elites. However, these images were always constructed in relation to masculine sexuality (Casella 1995). In a letter to the Visiting Magistrate, Ross Factory Superintendent Dr Irvine wrote:

... these young girls are in the habit of decorating themselves, cleaning themselves scrupulously, and making themselves as attractive as they can before resorting to the 'man-woman', if I may so style her, on whom they have bestowed their affections: I believe a large proportion of the quarrels which too frequently occur amongst the women ... are occasioned by, or take their rise from disagreements concerning the choice of a pseudo-male, or jealous feelings consequent on some of these disgraceful transactions. To my certain knowledge several disputes have arisen here, from these causes there have been letters intercepted and shown to you, which will prove the warmth and the impetuosity of the feelings excited in the women towards each other, when allied in such unholy bonds.

(AOT MM 62/31/13859)

This perception of homosexual transgression by female convicts communicated their deviance (Creed 1995). 'Normal' Victorian ladies had passionate friendships (Smith-Rosenberg 1985; Vicinus 1989); immoral convicts crossed that boundary and developed sexual relationships (Faderman 1978; 1981). Such transgressive behavior, originally attributed to the moral inferiority of working-class culture (Finch 1993; Peiss 1990; Foucault 1977), soon became medicalized as a biological complication (Chauncey 1983; Foucault 1981; Daniels 1998a, 1998b). The ambiguously gendered sexual behavior of inmates was perceived as a form of transsexuality, with a member of each couple identified as a 'pseudo-male'. In the same letter to the Visiting Magistrate, Dr. Irvine outlined the medically observable characteristics of such 'pseudo-males':

... it is my belief and opinion that these women are often distinguishable by exterior appearance. I mean to say that I think women belonging to the female convict class, who present a masculine appearance, who have a lower voice, and the development of a pair of imperfect moustaches, 'cateris paribus' [*sic*] are very probably belonging to this class [of inverts] ... the 'pseudo-males' in some cases have I believe a preternatural development of an organ peculiar to the female, the 'clitoris' and are thus able to assume partially the functions of a male – in other cases I have learned that artificial substances mechanically secured to the person form the substitute for the male organ.

(AOT MM 62/31/13859)

The point of this letter was not to convey medical knowledge on the anatomy of sexual inversion, but to construct the scientifically observed biological alterity of the female homosexual. Discussing late nineteenth-century research into human sexuality, Lillian Faderman wrote:

> They [congenital inverts] and some of the medical men who work with them, are convinced that [the inverts] are trapped in the wrong bodies. Most are also fixated on the notion that there is 'appropriate' masculine and feminine behavior and that same-sex love is sinful. Thus, if a woman loves a woman, it must be because she is a man.
>
> (Faderman 1981: 317)

The true deviance of 'pseudo-male' inverts would be vulnerably revealed, categorized, essentialized and reformed under the powerful gaze of the medically trained male superintendent of this female prison (Casella 1996). Australian historian Kay Daniels notes that W. Irvine, the Ross Factory Superintendent, was quite a progressive medical doctor for the mid-nineteenth century (Daniels 1998a: 167–69). Although modern social theory traces the origins of the medical gaze into the eighteenth century, the biological identification of female homosexuality became popular with psychologists and sexologists of the *late* nineteenth century (Vicinus 1993). Pioneers such as Krafft-Ebing, Sigmund Freud, Havelock Ellis, Iwan Bloch and Magnus Hirshfeld debated their medical theories of biological transsexualism and homosexual inversions over forty years after Superintendent Irvine pondered the elongated clitorises of his convict inmates.

But regardless of Dr Irvine's modernity, deconstructed visions of female homosexuality remain filtered through the male gaze, reported by male authorities and recorded by male authors. In order to question the everyday transgression of boundaries from the perspective of the female convicts, we must explore the material residue of their presence at the factories. Only through the interdigitation of historical data with archaeological data can we consider the nature of female homosexuality within the convict landscape of Van Diemen's Land.

AN ARCHAEOLOGY OF FEMALE HOMOSEXUALITY

In his 1848 letter to the Comptroller-General of Convicts, Dr Irvine also explained the romantic rituals by which female convicts wooed each others' affections:

> ... the most passionate appeals are frequently made by the women, as contra-distinguished from the pseudo-males, when they have suspected the last named parties of *infidelity* or fickleness; indeed an amount of jealousy seems to be aroused as great as possibly could be if an actual 'male' was in question. Promises, & threats are alike lavished on the objects of their love, & they are habitually in the practice of making numerous presents to their '*lovers*', so that an individual who acts the infamous part of a pseudo male, is most *comfortably* provided for, by the presents bestowed, with every procurable luxury.
>
> (AOT MM 62/31/13859, original emphasis)

What were the luxury goods procured for these romantic seductions? What was the nature of their exchange? Archaeological examination of the Ross factory site provided new perspectives on the material world of these homosexual interactions.

Following extensive alterations to the site and its structures, the male convict station at Ross was converted into the Ross Female Factory. Located on the southern edge of a rural Midlands village of Van Diemen's Land (Figure 8.1), the Ross factory operated from 1848 to 1855, when cessation of British transportation caused the closure of this institution. Since 1995, the Ross Female Factory Historic Site has become the focus of historical, geophysical and archaeological research (Casella 1999). During the Ross Factory Archaeology Project, 105 m^2 were excavated, divided between three different areas of the site: the Crime Class, the Hiring Class, and the Solitary Cells (Casella 1995, 1997) (Figure 8.1). These excavation units investigated archaeological remains from the three different states experienced by female convicts within the penal institution (Casella 1997: 83).

Within the Crime Class and Solitary Cells, we recovered significant amounts of floor and underfloor deposits stratigraphically related to female convict occupation (Casella 1997: 83–84) (Figure 8.2). Besides the wrought ferrous nails, fragments of cheap willow pattern earthenware, window glass, and handmade brick, a substantial amount of olive glass bottle fragments and kaolin clay tobacco pipes were recovered (Table 8.1). While the presence of such recreational materials on most sites would be unremarkable, at the female factories of Van Diemen's Land possession of alcohol and tobacco was strictly forbidden for prisoners. But even according to contemporary documents, the effectiveness of factory rules depended on the leniency of the Matron and turnkeys. In her 1842 deposition to the British Parliamentary Inquiry into Female Convict Prison Discipline, prisoner Mary Haigh described her incarceration at the female factory in Hobart Town:

> I was on my arrival at the Factory searched by Mrs. Hutchinson [the Matron], but not strictly. I could have passed in anything I liked. I was dressed at once in the

Figure 8.2 Solitary cells, facing south, Ross Factory Archaeology Project 1997. Photograph by the author.

Factory clothing and placed in the Crime Class yard where I found two or three of my shipmates who asked me for money and tobacco. I had money and with it I purchased tea, sugar, meat and bread. The meat and bread was brought by the Turnkey from the Cook-House. The tea she obtained from the messenger. Several of the women dealt with her. The work here was carding and spinning. The quantity worked up was a pound and half each day. This took about an hour and a half and then we had the rest of the day to ourselves. The time passed in singing, dancing, playing cards and talking over the different services in the Colony.

(AOT (Colonial Secretary's Office) CSO 22/50)

Later in her deposition, Mary Haigh exposed the rum trade within the factory, explaining how inmates purchased grog through Matron Hutchinson's private servant. Similar evidence of smuggling emerged from the Launceston Female Factory, located in the northern colonial town. In 1841, a letter from inmate Maria Turner was intercepted before reaching her male partner. After declarations of affection and enduring attachment, the letter reminds Steven to remember 'the "tobaco and pipes and . . . a bottle of rum", to be sent "in some way so as [the package] cannot be seen"' (Daniels 1998a: 137). Thus the archaeological presence of both alcohol and tobacco related materials within not only the Crime Class dormitory, but also the floors of the solitary confinement cells suggested the presence of a thriving black market trade of illicit goods throughout the female factory.

'She was damned by wicked indulgence'

Historical and archaeological studies of nineteenth-century institutional life have demonstrated the socially charged nature of alcohol and tobacco consumption. Both practices conveyed intertwined messages of sexuality, gender and class status (DeCunzo 1995). In her reinterpretation of archaeological materials from the American mid-nineteenth century site of Fort Independence, Joyce Clements emphasized the role of conspicuous alcohol consumption in material expressions of masculinity, hierarchical social status, and group solidarity throughout the military institution (1993: 57–60). Similarly, historical archaeologist Kathleen Bond noted in her analysis of the glass assemblage recovered from workers' dormitories at the Boott Mills of Lowell, Massachusetts, that possession and public consumption of alcohol transformed into a rigidly masculine-gendered activity through the nineteenth century with the simultaneous growth of the women's temperance movement and the male-dominated saloon culture (1989: 138). Thus, throughout the Victorian era, public possession and consumption of alcohol became a male-gendered social activity.

In his history of nineteenth-century struggles over regulation of working-class leisure activities in American industrial towns, Roy Rosenzweig explored transformations in the socio-economic geography of alcohol consumption to explain the emergence of male saloon culture (1983). Concerned with maintaining a docile and efficient labor force, industrialists and civic leaders effectively lobbied company-town local councils and state governments to introduce temperance laws limiting the sale and consumption of alcohol to licensed saloons with regulated hours of business. These new town planning and commercial licensing laws effectively criminalized 'kitchen grog shops', or the unregulated and informal taprooms run out of working-class domestic houses. Such 'sly groggies' had provided a main source of income for women within company-towns, particularly for widows, who were economically supported by the working-class community through patronization of her 'speakeasy'. In relocating legal sales from private homes to licensed saloons, lawmakers not only transformed alcohol consumption from a community-oriented social experience to a regulated commercial transaction, they also masculinized the leisure activity, as the presence of women in licensed saloons was legally and socially restricted.

Certainly, within the penal landscape of Van Diemen's Land, strict laws regulated both the exchange of wine and spirits through the colony (Kociumbas 1992), and the conditions under which women could patronize licensed taverns (Oxley 1996; Damousi 1997a). Moral judgments were placed on Australian working-class women who did publicly imbibe:

> A girl's fall away from chastity could result from whatever avenue was required to weaken her hold on her sexual urges. This could be either seduction or alcohol. Thus, to the Victorian social theorist, once a woman had experienced sexual gratification she would be insatiable. The chaste girl fell into prostitution. Giving evidence to an 1887 Commission into Prisons, witness Dr. Jackson testified that 'single women who drank are most likely to gravitate unchecked to the ranks of prostitution.' Examples of this view can be found in most nineteenth century . . . reports which discussed social order, punishment, crime, or alcohol consumption.
>
> (Finch 1993: 45)

Drinking was automatically associated with whoring, a symbolic correlation that both gendered and sexualized the leisure activity. Australian historian Deborah Oxley recently noted:

> In colonial New South Wales the title 'whore' was earned, not by selling sex, but by breaking rules . . . [Nineteenth-century colonist] James Mudie chose his words carefully when he described the women convicts as 'the lowest possible . . . they all smoke, drink and in fact, to speak in plain language, I consider them all prostitutes.' Convict women were damned because they did not behave like ladies nor [*sic*] sober workers . . . They got drunk, they smoked, they gazed back and they spoke in lewd ways their critics thought reserved for men.
>
> (1997: 93)

Thus, while tobacco was issued to male convicts as a reward for exemplary behavior, smoking was considered a masculine activity, and female convicts were strictly forbidden this indulgence (Walker 1980: 270; Ritchie 1971: 83). Within the convict economy of Van Diemen's Land, tobacco thus constituted a potent currency of illicit exchange (Walker 1980: 270; Maxwell-Stewart 1997: 148). Lauren Cook and Mary Beaudry commented on the class and gender identities communicated through consumption of tobacco:

> The middle classes disapproved of smoking in public. What is more, middle- and upper-class smokers were male (middle- and upper-class women could not smoke in public without gaining a reputation for loose behavior), whereas both men and women of the working classes smoked.
>
> (Beaudry 1993: 93)

In her study of the nineteenth-century working-class households and brothels of Washington, DC's Federal Triangle, Donna Seifert interpreted the specific consumption of tobacco through kaolin clay pipes as a distinctly masculine activity, since working-class women preferred smoking tobacco through rolled cigarettes (Seifert 1991: 99; Peiss 1986: 99). Within convict-era Australia, pipe smoking was the most common method of tobacco consumption. Although urban hotels and pubs frequently supplied patrons with kaolin pipes, these objects were typically associated with male Irish laborers (Gojak 1995: 12; Walker 1980: 270–71). The archaeological presence of alcohol bottles and tobacco pipes, both masculine gendered artifacts, within the Crime Class dormitory and solitary treatment cells, suggests that while obtaining 'every procurable luxury' for their 'pseudo-male' lovers, the female convicts communicated their class identity, while effectively transgressing both gender and sexual social boundaries.

'Doing trade': the sexual economy of a prison

Since 1980, the Ross factory has been designated as a protected heritage site, managed through the Tasmanian Parks and Wildlife Service. Recycling of structural materials and pastoral use of the property during the late nineteenth and twentieth centuries reduced the Ross site to an open field. Today, the original Staff Quarters constitute the only factory structure to survive in a modified, yet architecturally intact, form (Figure 8.1). Within the field, topographical features delineate subsurface remains of the factory. The main compound of the Ross prison lay immediately east of the Staff Quarters. The entrance gates, sandstone Crime Class and Hiring Class dormitories, and a variety of storerooms and offices were located in the northern half of the rectilinear compound. A hospital, workrooms, a well for laundry water, and a locked wool store were contained in the southern half. The extreme demographic gender imbalance and sexual vulnerability of women in Van Diemen's Land caused many convicts to fall pregnant out of wedlock during assigned domestic service on rural pastoral properties. When discovered by the authorities, these women were returned to the female factories as punishment for their 'wanton' sexual practices (Damousi 1997a: 113–27). Nurseries were added to the southern half of the Ross main compound to accommodate the children of factory inmates.

During excavation of the Ross Female Factory, convict-related deposits were recovered from two of the four research areas (Casella 1997, 1999). Within Area A (Figure 8.1), the Crime Class dormitory interior contained underfloor deposits that had accumulated below the wooden floorboards during the female factory occupation period. Historical sources dated the completion of the block of twelve Solitary Cells within Area C to 1851 (Scripps and Clark 1991: 12). Built explicitly to architecturally discourage homosexual encounters between female inmates (AOT MM 62/1/11037), these sandstone solitary confinement cells contained sunken earth floors, a startling architectural feature found in no other punishment cells of convict-era Australia (Kerr 1984). Due to a combination of post-depositional impacts and differences in the use of the structure, significant underfloor deposits were not recovered from remains of the Hiring Class dormitory of Area B. Area D consisted of a sterile test pit opened off-site to examine the natural stratigraphic soil profile (Casella 1997).

Table 8.1 presents data on the frequency of illicit objects recovered from the underfloor deposits of the Crime Class dormitory, and the earthen floors of the Solitary Cells. Olive glass bottles, the most common container for wine, beer and gin during the nineteenth century, were specifically selected as a material representation of alcohol consumption because an insufficient number of diagnostic shards of clear glass were recovered to differentiate between vessels for alcoholic spirits (most commonly whisky) and food containers. In Table 8.1, the presence of kaolin clay tobacco pipe fragments and olive glass bottle fragments is demonstrated in terms of total weight (in grams) and percentage by weight of the total artifact fabric category. The minimum number of vessels (MNV) present in each context was also calculated, and is presented within this table.

Table 8.1 Distribution of olive bottle glass and clay tobacco pipes, Ross Factory Archaeology Project

	Crime Class	*Solitary Cells*
Total glass assemblage	2,751 g	406 g
Olive glass alcohol bottle fragments	1,529 g (55%)	312 g (77%)
Minimum number of vessels	15	10
Total ceramic assemblage	4,416 g	1,547 g
Kaolin clay tobacco pipe fragments	23 g (0.5%)	74 g (5%)
Minimum number of vessels	5	10
Total area excavated	48 square meters	16 square meters

Results of this analysis suggest that in terms of both relative frequency and MNV counts, more illicit materials existed within the Solitary Cells than the Crime Class dormitory. A greater estimated number of kaolin clay tobacco pipes were found within the excavated Solitary Cells; these forbidden objects also comprised a higher percentage of the overall ceramic assemblage recovered from cell interiors. While a greater minimum number of olive glass bottles were recovered from the Crime Class dormitory, three times more area had been excavated in this region than in Area C. Therefore, while a larger number of illicit grog bottles were recovered from the Crime Class underfloor deposits, they occurred much less frequently than within the Solitary Cells. Comprising 77 percent of the glass assemblage from Area C, olive bottle glass constituted only 55 percent of the glass recovered from Area A.

These results could have been affected by such factors as occupation density, differential preservation of the material record, and depositional processes. The Crime Class dormitory, located within the main compound of the prison site, experienced a significantly higher occupation density than the Solitary Cells. Such intensive use of the Crime Class would naturally result in a higher amount of general occupation debris, lowering the relative frequency of illicit objects. However, given that three times more area was excavated in Area A, the MNV counts demonstrate that illicit objects appeared much more frequently within Area C. Despite lower occupation density, alcohol bottles and tobacco pipes were more frequently deposited within the Solitary Cells.

The overall weight of ceramic assemblages could have been affected by the presence of terracotta bricks within the Crime Class dormitory. During laboratory analysis of the Ross collection, artifacts were cataloged by fabric type. Ceramics included earthenwares (including clay pipes), stonewares, porcelain, and terracotta (including bricks). Since the Solitary Cells were of sandstone construction, less brick structural debris was cataloged within the ceramic assemblage, causing an increased relative frequency for the kaolin clay tobacco pipe fragments recovered within Area C. Again, the MNV data demonstrates larger minimum number of pipes independent of the assemblage weights.

Another possible bias within the Table 8.1 data might have resulted from recycling and reuse of bottle glass within Areas A and C. Historical documents record the violent social landscape of the female factories (Daniels 1998a; Damousi 1997a). Given the common occurrence of vicious threats, inmate fights, and prison riots, the thick olive glass of empty grog bottles probably provided an efficient raw material for the manufacture of bladed weapons. Such recycling activities would have a small effect on the deposition of olive glass bottles in both the Crime Class and Solitary Cells, one that would have slightly altered the amount of olive glass recovered from the Ross site.

But regardless of these considerations, the overall pattern of use can be discerned by comparatively examining both MNV estimates and weight frequencies within the context of relative excavation size. More tobacco pipes and alcohol bottles were deposited within the Solitary Cells than inside the Crime Class dormitory. No existing documentary sources describe how illicit materials were physically transported into the Ross Solitary Cells. Although archaeological evidence for increased prohibited activities could merely reflect the lack of alternative pastimes within these dark, isolated, damp, 4×6 ft. cells, a social explanation of these activities can also be interpreted through consideration of the sexual economy that operated within the female factories.

In her 1997 book, Joy Damousi described a frenzied 1842 revolt at the Launceston female factory, the convict prison located in the northern colonial town (Figure 8.1). This particularly violent riot became infamous for its demonstration of 'a remarkable degree of unity and solidarity amongst the women' (1997a: 82). Kay Daniels linked the origins of this rebellion to a steadfast sexual relationship between two long-term inmates, Catherine Owens and Ellen Scott (1998a: 147–48, 155–56). After seizing control of the prison for two days, the 185 women of the Crime Class were finally subdued when fifty prisoners from the adjacent male convict barracks were enlisted to restore order to the institution. Testimony to a court of the Convict Department later revealed that the prison revolt had been provoked by Ellen Scott who had been enraged by the prolonged solitary confinement of her lover, Catherine Owens. These two women were identified by the Convict Department as 'ringleaders', as habitual and recalcitrant offenders with long and violent records of recidivism. Both occupied central nodes of the convoluted knot of black market networks that operated throughout the factories of Van Diemen's Land. Their penal conduct records documented frequent sentences of solitary confinement for possession of forbidden substances, particularly alcohol.

As places of ultimate punishment, the Solitary Cells were architecturally fabricated to discipline repeat offenders, typically women located at the apex of the underground sexual economy of the female factories. The higher frequencies of tobacco- and alcohol-related materials within the Ross factory Solitary Cells probably reflects the flourishing of illicit trade within this edifice of confinement and punishment. While under solitary sentence, the factory 'incorrigibles' continued to maintain their access to black market activities, relieving the monotonous boredom, cold, and hunger of disciplinary confinement with a pipe and a bottle. Thus, data from Table 8.1 archaeologically suggests that while inmates of the Crime Class actively engaged in homosexual and economic 'trade', the most potent covert paths of this penal world led directly to the Solitary Cells. As inmate Mary Haigh noted in her 1842 deposition to the Parliamentary Committee of Inquiry, 'I have been in the dark Cells. That is bad punishment but even there Tea Sugar etc [*sic*] can be obtained . . .' (AOT CSO 22/50).

'SHE SAID IT WAS NO SIN': ON MOTIVATIONS AND REPERCUSSIONS

Severe consequences accompanied the discovery of homosexual interaction between inmates. Accusations of 'unnatural vice' were followed by official inquiries and prisoner interrogations in order to identify those who initiated the sexual activity, and to determine the extent of their sexual networks. Guilty parties were dispersed among the three

Van Diemen's Land factories, and subjected to extended periods of solitary confinement, reduced rations, and increased surveillance (AOT MM 62/1/11037; AOT MM 62/25/11876). Furthermore, all occurrences of this stigmatized sexual activity were permanently lodged on the inmate's conduct records (Tardiff 1990; Daniels 1998a: 176). Since the Convict Department used these bureaucratic documents to judge the moral character of an inmate, such notation had the potential to impact future evaluations of a woman's petitions for assigned employment, marriage, criminal pardon, or child custody.

Given these sobering consequences, why did convict women engage in homosexual activity within the female factories? Homosexuality might have presented women with an effective means of minimizing their disadvantage. Survival within the penal colony required strong bonds between incarcerated convicts for transmission of necessary goods and information. 'Women's networks and subculture were sites of an exchange for their colonial survival knowledge and skills, as well as an opportunity for women to reject the passivity and modesty of ideal femininity' (Damousi 1997b: 210). As earlier quotes have demonstrated, homosexual relationships between the female convicts provided a potent transfer site for both subversive information and illicit 'gifts'. In 1842, prisoner Mary Haigh explained to the Parliamentary Committee of Inquiry:

> The women named the bad services and advised each other not to go to them. Services where women are well kept and clothed, but coerced are considered bad situations, and those in which women are allowed to do as they please are held to be good ones. Women learn in the Factory at what houses they can obtain liquor on the sly and those houses at which shelter is to be obtained when they abscond.
>
> (AOT CSO 22/50)

All sexual relationships, particularly those within institutional environments, can take on more negative aspects. Female convict homosexuality was no exception. Close ties between female prisoners were essential for self-protection within the female factories – protection from the male overseers, superintendents, or turnkeys, and some other female prisoners. In the same deposition to the Parliamentary Committee, Mary Haigh informed on her fellow inmates:

> In the Factory are found several women known by the name of the 'Flash Mob' who have always money, wear worked caps, silk handkerchiefs, earrings and other rings. They are the greatest blackguards in the building. The other women are afraid of them. They lead the young girls away by ill advice.
>
> (AOT CSO 22/50)

In 1851, Ross factory inmate Margaret Knaggs described her interactions with prisoner Agnes Kane to the Campbell Town District Police Magistrate – sexual interactions that could be contextually interpreted as harrassment, seduction, or both:

> . . . she used to follow me about everywhere to prevail upon me to let her do something to me, that she would show me the way. I told her I did not want to do any thing of the Kind . . . That sort of conversation is common among 6 or 7 of the women in the building. On Wednesday 10th April I was in the Water Closet, Agnes Kane wanted me to let her come to me, she had often asked me before, she tried to put her hand under my clothes but I would not let her . . . she wanted to argue.

I walked away because I knew she was after me, because she used to follow me and ask me to sit down with her, and walk with her. I would not because I heard she had the name of being bad behaved & spoken – I used to shun her. I did not let her destroy me. I did not give her the opportunity. If I did she would. She told me she had six or seven girls and they liked her, that I had no courage in me or I should do it – I told her I would not have that sin upon me – she said it was no sin . . .

(Mitchell Library of Sydney (ML) 111 15163/2)

Although we must recognize the predatory nature of some prison sexual interactions, many involved in homosexual relationships must have also enjoyed some physical pleasure or emotional comfort, providing a basic motivation for their dangerous transgressions. In an 1843 letter to Lord Stanley, the British Colonial Secretary, Lieutenant-Governor Eardley-Wilmot noted that the factory inmates 'have their Fancy-women, or lovers, to whom they are attached with quite as much ardour as they would be to the other sex, and practice onanism to the greatest extent' (AOT Governor's Office (GO) 25/11). Ultimately, the ambivalent nature of convict homosexuality paralleled the ambiguities of female heterosexuality, and reflected the generally ambiguous nature of female sexuality within convict-era Van Diemen's Land.

To better understand the intricate social world of the female factories, we must explore the subtle dynamics of convict women's sexuality. Traditionally, historical approaches to this controversial subject have portrayed these women as either depraved opportunistic whores, or pathetic victims of colonial misogyny. Recent historical work has begun to challenge these stereotypical icons, by documenting the variety of ways convict women actively worked the system to minimize their disadvantage. Such research has exposed the complex sexual relationships and social networks developed by convict women within the female factory prisons. By using these document-based studies to contextualize the material culture excavated from the Ross factory, homosexual aspects of these sexual relationships can be archaeologically interpreted. Differences in the distribution of illicit materials between the convict dormitories and solitary punishment cells can be interpreted as reflecting a sexual economy within this convict world. Convict women transgressed nineteenth-century constructions of feminine sexual identity through possession of masculine-gendered luxuries, and through the homosexual activity that underlay these illicit exchanges. By interweaving documentary and material data sources, we can begin to transcend conventional images of convict sexuality, and explore the situational, ambiguous and often contradictory nature of nineteenth-century female homosexuality.

ACKNOWLEDGEMENTS

My archaeological research has greatly benefited from recent work on female convicts by a number of Australian historians. I would like to thank Lyndall Ryan, Deborah Oxley, and Kay Daniels for their comments on earlier drafts of this manuscript. Joy Damousi has been a particularly brilliant source of intellectual inspiration, humor, and emotional support. Don Ranson and Angie McGowan of the Tasmanian Parks and Wildlife Service helped create the Ross Factory Archaeology Project; Chris Tassell and Elspeth Wishart of the Queen Victoria Museum and Art Gallery provided necessary logistic support throughout the research program. The Riggall Family of Sommercoates Property and the Tasmanian Wool Centre of Ross generously provided accommodation and local support. The Ross Factory Archaeology Project was funded through grants from the Wenner-Gren

Foundation for Anthropological Research and the University of California Pacific Rim Research Program. Data analysis was supported by an Educational Fellowship through the American Association of University Women. Finally, I want to thank Barb Voss and Rob Schmidt for encouraging us to adventure into a new intellectual landscape.

REFERENCES

Primary sources

Archives of Tasmania (AOT), Miscellaneous Microfilm: MM 62/1/11037: 11 December 1848. Letter from Superintendent W. J. Irvine, MD to J. S. Hampton, Comptroller-General of Convicts.

Archives of Tasmania (AOT), Miscellaneous Microfilm: MM 62/25/11876: 8 May 1849. Letter from Visiting Magistrate R. P. Stuart to J. S. Hampton, Comptroller-General of Convicts.

Archives of Tasmania (AOT), Miscellaneous Microfilm: MM 62/31/13859: June 1850. Report from Superintendent W. J. Irvine, MD to Visiting Magistrate R. P. Stuart.

Archives of Tasmania (AOT), Colonial Secretary's Office: AOT CSO 22/50: 1841–1843. Report of the Committee of Inquiry into Female Convict Prison Discipline.

Archives of Tasmania (AOT), Governor's Office: AOT GO 25/11: 2 November 1843. Letter from Lt. Governor Eardley-Wilmot to Lord Stanley, Secretary of State for the Colonies.

Mitchell Library of Sydney (ML), Tasmanian Papers 111 15163/2: Trial of Prisoner Agnes Kane for Assaulting Prisoner Margaret Knaggs on 10 April 1851.

Secondary sources

Aveling, M. (1992) 'Bending the Bars: Convict Women and the State', in K. Saunders and R. Evans (eds) *Gender Relations in Australia: Domination and Negotiation*, Sydney: Harcourt Brace Jovanovich.

Beaudry, M. (1993) 'Public Aesthetics versus Personal Experience: Worker Health and Well-Being in 19th-Century Lowell, Massachusetts', *Historical Archaeology* 27, 2: 90–105.

Bond, K. (1989) 'The Medicine, Alcohol, and Soda Vessels from the Boott Mills Boardinghouses', in M. Beaudry and S. Mrozowski (eds) *Interdisciplinary Investigations of the Boott Mills, Lowell, Massachusetts*, vol. 3. Cultural Resources Management Study, No. 21. Boston: National Park Service, North Atlantic Regional Office.

Brand, I. (1990) *The Convict Probation System*, Hobart, Tasmania: Blubber Head Press.

Casella, E. (1995) '"A Woman Doesn't Represent Business Here": Negotiating Femininity in 19th Century Colonial Australia', in M. D'Agostino, E. Prine, E. Casella and M. Winer (eds) *Kroeber Anthropological Society Papers* no. 79, Berkeley, CA: Kroeber Anthropological Society.

—— (1996) '". . . one or two globular lamps made of glass": Archaeology and the Cultural Landscapes of Tasmanian Convictism', in S. Ulm, I. Lilley and A. Ross (eds) *Australian Archaeology '95: Proceedings of the 1995 Australian Archaeological Association Annual Conference*, Tempus, vol. 6. St. Lucia: Anthropology Museum, University of Queensland.

—— (1997) '". . . a large and efficient Establishment": Preliminary Report on Fieldwork at the Ross Female Factory', *Australasian Historical Archaeology* 15: 79–89.

—— (1999) 'Dangerous Girls and Gentle Ladies: Archaeology and 19th Century Australian Female Convicts', unpublished Ph.D. dissertation, Department of Anthropology, University of California, Berkeley.

Chauncey, G. (1983) 'From Sexual Inversion to Homosexuality: Medicine and the Changing Conceptualization of Female Deviance', *Salmagundi* 58/59: 114–46.

Clements, J. (1993) 'The Cultural Creation of the Feminine Gender', *Historical Archaeology* 27, 4: 39–64.

Creed, B. (1995) 'Lesbian Bodies: Tribades, Tomboys and Tarts', in E. Grosz and E. Probyn (eds) *Sexy Bodies: The Strange Carnalities of Feminism*, London: Routledge.

Damousi, J. (1997a) *Depraved and Disorderly*, Cambridge: Cambridge University Press.

—— (1997b) 'What Punishment will be Sufficient for these Rebellious Hussies? Headshaving and Convict Women in the Female Factories, 1820s–1840s', in I. Duffield and J. Bradley (eds) *Representing Convicts*, London: Leicester University Press.

Daniels, K. (1993) 'The Flash Mob: Rebellion, Rough Culture and Sexuality in the Female Factories of Van Diemen's Land', *Australian Feminist Studies* 18: 133–50.

—— (1998a) *Convict Women*, St. Leonards, NSW: Allen and Unwin.

—— (1998b) 'Convict Women – the View from Van Diemen's Land', in I. Terry and K. Evans (eds) *Hobart's History: the First Two Hundred Years*, Hobart: Professional Historians' Association of Tasmania.

DeCunzo, L. (1995) 'Reform, Respite, Ritual: An Archaeology of Institutions: the Magdalen Society of Philadelphia, 1800–1850', *Historical Archaeology* 29, 3: 1–68.

Dixon, M. (1976) *The Real Matilda*, Melbourne: Penguin Books.

Duffield, I. and J. Bradley (eds) (1997) *Representing Convicts*, London: Leicester University Press.

Faderman, L. (1978) 'The Morbidification of Love between Women by Nineteenth-Century Sexologists', *Journal of Homosexuality* 4: 73–90.

—— (1981) *Surpassing the Love of Men*, New York: W. M. Morrow.

Finch, L. (1993) *The Classing Gaze*, St. Leonards, NSW: Allen and Unwin.

Foucault, M. (1977) *Discipline and Punish*, Harmondsworth: Penguin Books.

—— (1981) *The History of Sexuality, Volume 1: An Introduction*, Harmondsworth: Penguin Books.

Gojak, D. (1995) 'Clay Tobacco Pipes from Cadmans Cottage, Sydney, Australia', Society for Clay Pipe Research Newsletter 48: 11–19.

Hughes, R. (1987) *The Fatal Shore*, London: Collins Harvill.

Kerr, J. S. (1984) *Design for Convicts*, Sydney: Library of Australian History.

Kociumbas, J. (1992) *The Oxford History of Australia, Volume 2: Possessions 1770–1868*, Melbourne: Oxford University Press.

Lake, M. (1988) 'Convict Women as Objects of Male Vision: An Historiographical Review', *Bulletin of the Centre for Tasmanian Historical Studies* 2, 1.

Maxwell-Stewart, H. (1997) 'Life at Macquarie Harbour', in I. Duffield and J. Bradley (eds) *Representing Convicts*, London: Leicester University Press.

Nicholas, S. (1988) *Convict Workers*, Cambridge: Cambridge University Press.

Oxley, D. (1996) *Convict Maids*, Cambridge: Cambridge University Press.

—— (1997) 'Representing Convict Women', in I. Duffield and J. Bradley (eds) *Representing Convicts*, London: Leicester University Press.

Peiss, K. (1986) *Cheap Amusements: Working Women and Leisure in Turn-of-the-Century New York*, Philadelphia: Temple University Press.

—— (1990) '"Charity Girls" and City Pleasures: Historical Notes on Working-Class Sexuality 1880–1920' in E. DuBois and V. Ruiz (eds) *Unequal Sisters*, New York: Routledge.

Ritchie, J. (ed.) (1971) *Evidence to the Bigge Reports*, vol. II, Melbourne: Melbourne University Press.

Robinson, P. (1985) *The Hatch and Brood of Time*, Melbourne: Oxford University Press.

—— (1988) *The Women of Botany Bay*, Melbourne: Penguin.

Robson, L. L. (1965) *The Convict Settlers of Australia*, Carlton: Melbourne University Press.

Rosenzweig, R. (1983) *'Eight Hours for What We Will': Workers & Leisure in an Industrial City 1870–1920*, New York: Cambridge University Press.

Ryan, L. (1995) 'From Stridency to Silence', in D. Kirkby (ed.) *Sex, Power and Justice*, Melbourne: Oxford University Press.

Scripps, L. and Clark, J. (1991) 'The Ross Female Factory', unpublished historical report for the Department of Parks, Wildlife and Heritage, Tasmania, Australia.

Seifert, D. (1991) 'Within Sight of the White House: the Archaeology of Working Women', *Historical Archaeology* 25, 4: 82–108.

Shaw, A. G. L. (1966) *Convicts and Colonies*, London: Faber and Faber.

Smith, B. (1988) *A Cargo of Women*, Sydney: Sun Books.

Smith-Rosenberg, C. (1985) 'The Female World of Love and Ritual', in C. Smith-Rosenberg (ed.) *Disorderly Conduct*, New York: Oxford University Press.

Stallybrass, P. and White, A. (1986) *The Politics and Poetics of Transgression*, Ithaca: Cornell University Press.

Sturma, M. (1978) 'Eye of the Beholder: The Stereotype of Women Convicts 1788–1852', *Labour History*, 34.

Summers, A. (1975) *Damned Whores and God's Police*, Melbourne: Penguin.

Tardiff, P. (1990) *Notorious Strumpets and Dangerous Girls*, Sydney: Angus and Robertson.

Vicinus, M. (1989) 'Distance and Desire: English Boarding-School Friendships', in M. B. Duberman, M. Vicinus and G. Chauncey, Jr (eds) *Hidden from History: Reclaiming the Gay and Lesbian Past*, New York: New American Library.

—— (1993) ' "They Wonder to Which Sex I Belong": The Historical Roots of the Modern Lesbian Identity', in H. M. Abelove, M. A. Barale and D. M. Halperin (eds) *The Lesbian and Gay Studies Reader*, New York: Routledge.

Walker, R. (1980) 'Tobacco Smoking in Australia, 1788–1914', *Historical Studies* 19, 75: 267–85.

Chapter Nine

Red Light Voices: an archaeological drama of late nineteenth-century prostitution

Julia G. Costello

INTRODUCTION

The Archaeology

In the spring of 1996, archaeologists working in Los Angeles discovered a parlor house's six-seater privy, densely filled with artifacts reflecting a decade of prostitution. The location was the 4.3-acre site of the proposed Headquarters Facility building of the Metropolitan Water District of Southern California. Adjacent to the Union Station Passenger Terminal and directly across Alameda Street from El Pueblo de Los Angeles (birthplace of the modern city), this vicinity was known to contain archaeological evidence of historic Spanish, Mexican, Anglo-American, and Chinese populations. The excavations, documentary research, and analysis of findings was directed by the author, of Foothill Resources, Ltd., and by Adrian and Mary Praetzellis, of Sonoma State University.

When the 1930s' asphalt parking lots and underlying fill were removed, most of the nineteenth-century ground surface was found to be intact. There were building foundations, miscellaneous architectural remains, and old backyards pockmarked with trash pits, outhouse holes, and wells. Seventeen of these 'hollow features' were filled with dense caches of artifacts that could be related to individual households or events, and nearly 40,000 individual artifacts related to the nineteenth-century development of Los Angeles were recovered. One such cache came from a line of six privy holes serving a parlor house at 327 Aliso Street, the place of business and residence of a madam's working women. When the privies were abandoned for a sewer hook-up in 1901, the brothel was also refurbished. Within months, the conveniently open backyard privy vaults were filled with household cullings forming an extraordinary collection of nearly 2,000 objects documenting more than a decade of parlor house activities. These were the actual items purchased, used, and discarded by prostitutes, pimps, and johns: the material culture of prostitution (Figure 9.1).

Also recovered during excavations were six artifact-filled privies, each associated with a contemporary blue-collar residence in the same neighborhood. Contrasts between the parlor house and the residence collections in the numbers and types of items relating to personal, domestic, and household use, highlighted the unique lifestyle of the brothel residents.

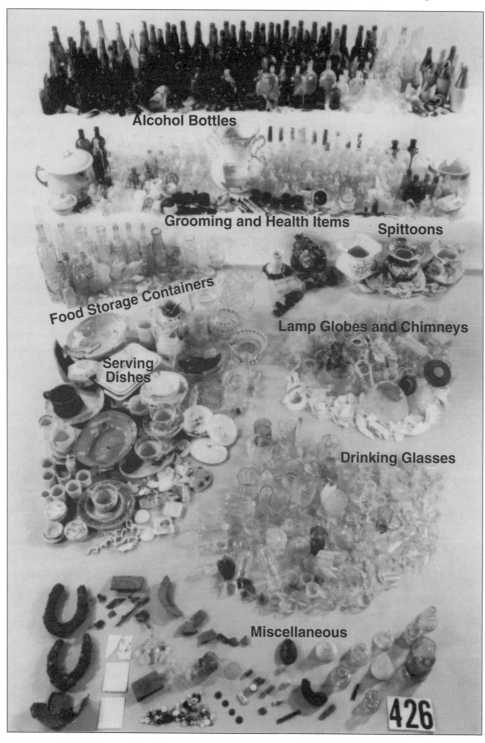

Figure 9.1 Parlor house artifacts. Artifacts recovered from the six-seater privy behind 327 Aliso Street, Los Angeles: the nearly 2,000 items reflect parlor house operations between *c.* 1888 and 1901. Reprinted by permission of the Metropolitan Water District of Southern California.

Differences are particularly noticeable in the quality of table settings, types of eating and serving vessels, quantities of tumblers and stemware, and types of decorative furnishings. Prostitutes' dressers were filled with remarkable quantities and varieties of beauty creams, cures for venereal disease, conception preventatives, and pain-numbing tinctures of opium and morphine. Recovery of artifacts from a nearby privy associated with crib prostitutes was comparatively meager, reflecting their spartan quarters. Analyses and interpretations of the artifactual data and extensive documentary research are included in two report volumes and several academic articles (The Metropolitan Water District of Southern California, forthcoming a; The Metropolitan Water District of Southern California, forthcoming b; Costello 1999).

These findings from the Los Angeles parlor house and work on other archaeological sites associated with prostitution (Cheek et al. 1991; Cheek and Seifert 1994; Seifert 1991, 1998; Simmons 1989; Spude 1999) have increased our understanding of life in the *demi monde*. Are there archaeological 'patterns' of sexuality? Yes. The business of sex – prostitution – can indeed be identified by both the quantities and qualities of specific types of artifacts. The marketing, material culture rewards, and health depredations are all recorded in the archaeological record.

But we can move still closer to the participants in this historical drama. While most documentary sources on nineteenth-century prostitution consist of observations made by reformers and health workers, and of police and court records documenting illegalities and violence, there are some exceptions. Historic photographs and, more rarely, a few transcripts and letters preserving first-person accounts, have allowed faces and voices from the past to be seen and heard in the present.

Storytelling, drama, and archaeology

Use of fictional narrative by archaeologists appears to be coming of age. Among the first, and perhaps still the most impressive, efforts is *Dance of the Tiger: A Novel of the Ice Age*, by Björn Kurtén (1980). One of Europe's finest evolutionary paleontologists, Kurtén explains why, after a lifetime of prestigious publications, he felt compelled to write a novel about prehistoric peoples:

> In the last three decades, it has been my privilege to be immersed in the life of the Ice Age. More and more, I have felt there is much to be told that simply cannot be formulated in scientific reports. How did it feel to live then? How did the world look to you? What were your beliefs? Above all, what was it like to meet humans not of your own species? That is an experience denied to us, for we are all *Homo sapiens*.
>
> (1980: xxiii)

The book's introduction is written by Stephen Jay Gould, who supports Kurtén's arguments for 'storytelling':

> . . . Let me, as a scientist, make a claim that may seem curious. I believe that Kurtén's novel is a more appropriate place than the professional literature itself for discussing many of the truly scientific issues that swirl about the Neanderthal–Cro-Magnon debate . . . [these stories] probe the range of alternatives; they channel thought in to the construction of testable hypotheses; they serve as tentative frameworks for the ordering of observations . . .
>
> (Gould in Kurtén 1980: xvii–xviii)

And, just as importantly: '. . . I know, as abstract intellectual propositions, the theories that Kurtén discusses. But Kurtén has taught me something by giving them a human face' (xix).

As anthropologists, more and more modern archaeologists are striving to expose the human face behind our data. Ruth Tringham humanized her research of Neolithic European villages (Tringham 1991) while Janet Spector has spun a fictional context for a bone awl discovered on a North American Indian site (Spector 1993). Historical archaeologists, closer in time to the people they are studying, have embraced this new medium with enthusiasm (Praetzellis 1998; Praetzellis and Praetzellis 1998). 'Red Light Voices' can be counted among these efforts to provide faces for the past, but with an important variation: the dialogue text is not made up, but is itself primary data edited to tell a story.

The inspiration for scripting historic dialogue comes from the work of award-winning dramatist and Stanford professor, Anna Deavere Smith. Smith bases her performances on actual current events or crises, constructing her dialogues from taped interviews which she conducts with the real-life players. These people are the creators of the 'events', and Smith believes that an understanding of 'what happened' is best achieved through hearing the stories of the individuals involved. Her tapes and verbatim transcripts are her data, presented as edited but unadulterated testimony.

> Sometimes there is the expectation that inasmuch as I am doing 'social dramas', I am looking for solutions to social problems. In fact, though, I am looking at the process of becoming something. It is not a result, it is not an answer. It is not a solution. I am first looking for the humanness inside the problems, or the crises. The spoken word is evidence of that humanness.
>
> (Smith 1996: 12A)

Here is the same goal held by the storytelling archaeologists: to arrive at a deeper understanding of past events by humanizing them. However, Smith's method of dramatization does not require a fictionalized voice; the historic characters can speak for themselves. Dialogue is simply treated as another available data set (Costello 1996, 1998).

For prostitution in the United States *c.* 1900, two unique sources of first-person dialogues exist. The first consists of transcribed interviews conducted by Al Rose in the 1960s with elderly prostitutes, pimps, and johns once active in the red light district of Storyville, New Orleans (Rose 1974: 147–65). While Rose presents these interviews as being typical of participants in the district, he cautions that these individuals were also unusual in being alive, healthy, and mostly financially comfortable nearly fifty years after the district closed. 'The fate of many of Storyville's inhabitants, and even many of its patrons, was not always so happy' (Rose 1974: 147). The second primary source is a lengthy set of letters written by prostitute Maimie Pinzer between 1910 and 1922, to a prominent Boston lady (Pinzer 1977). Pinzer's words and thoughts are preserved in this chronicle of her 'fall' from a middle-class immigrant family and of her life as a prostitute in the north-eastern United States.

'Red Light Voices' tells a story of prostitution through the words of these participants, illustrated by artifacts and photographic images from Los Angeles. For the script, the testimonies of five Storyville personalities and that of Maimie Pinzer have been edited and paired in three Acts to simulate dialogues: Act I between two johns; Act II between two prostitutes; and Act III between a pimp and a prostitute who were born into 'the business'. The topics chosen for the 'discussions' address activities documented by the artifacts: those related to food preparation and consumption, drinking, health, grooming, and hygiene.

The script adds a human face and voice to our analysis, and encourages the reader not just to view the past from the present, but to take this opportunity to step inside.

SCRIPT: *RED LIGHT VOICES*[1]

Act I: Men Talk
Rene: From an upper-class New Orleans family, a regular brothel customer
Lew: A blue-collar, railway worker and frequent brothel customer

Act II: The life
Lola: An immigrant from Cuba and parlor house prostitute (her dialogue is reproduced as it was originally transcribed to preserve her ethnic character)
Maimie: Maimie Pinzer, from a middle-class background, became an independent prostitute

Act III: Family business
Violet: Born in a brothel, she worked in the family business before marrying and raising a family
Marc: Born in a brothel, he became a successful pimp

Narrator: 'Red Light Voices' tells a story of prostitution in the United States in about 1900. Recent archaeological excavations in the Los Angeles red light district unearthed a treasure trove of artifacts from a 1901 parlor house. All of the objects used to illustrate this dialogue come from that collection.[2] The script of the presentation is not made up. These are the actual words of people who worked in or frequented brothels. The photographs are historic images of turn-of-the-century prostitutes and brothels in Los Angeles.

Act I: Men talk
Narrator: Rene, a gentleman from an upper-class family, and Lew, a railroad worker, are comparing notes on their experiences in brothels.
Rene: My father took me [to my first brothel]. I'm sure he had the tacit approval of my mother, since in those days, at least in our group, people were always worried about the effects on the brain of masturbation and seemed to think it was safer to expend semen in some rented woman.

   They were also afraid of venereal diseases, but had the superstitious belief that this could be avoided by a process they described as 'being careful'. Well, I learned all my father could teach me about 'being careful' and I later spent a fortune with doctors to control the ravages of both gonorrhea and syphilis – and so did he. My father really died from the effects of syphilis – although that's not what it said in his lengthy obituary . . .
Lew: (*sympathetic*) I think the girls could diagnose clap better than the doctors at that time. She'd have a way of squeezing . . . if there was anything in there, she'd find it. Then she'd wash it off with a clean wash cloth. They had little washstands. She'd fill the basin with water and put in a few drops of purple stuff – permanganate of potash, it was – they didn't have Lysol in those days – then she'd wash you with it.
Rene: Lulu White, herself, greeted us after we'd been announced . . . she was . . . laden with diamonds worn not selectively but just put on any place there seemed to be an inch to accommodate them. She wore a red wig that hardly pretended to be

Figure 9.2 Aliso Street in the Red Light District. Los Angeles, *c.* 1899, looking west on Aliso Street, the brothel at No. 327 is on the right, just east of the two-story, brick, 'Farm Wagons' building.
Courtesy University of Southern California, Regional History Center.

natural in color [and] . . . she smelled overpoweringly of perfume . . . The instant we stepped inside that door, it became apparent that, though ornate, the taste reflected in the furnishings and decor was just miserable. There was just too much of everything . . .

Imitation Renaissance tapestries and wall hangings of particularly muddy color hung everywhere. The oriental rugs, possibly actually *from* the Orient, were thick but shoddy imitations of the luxurious pile and color for which the East is famous . . . the main parlor [was] a melange of parquet flooring and rugs, overstuffed and overcarved furniture and more ill-selected 'art' and sculpture.

Lew: (*impressed, missing the point*) Naturally, as a wage laborer, I couldn't afford those luxury palaces . . . but there were little parlor houses . . . Some say the cribs went from twenty-five cents to a dollar, the parlor houses a dollar to two and the mansions from five to fifty dollars. The real truth is, though, that an evening in any house, no matter what the going rate was reported to be, always cost you just as much as you had in your pocket.

Those places were organized to take all your money. Let's say you went into a so-called two-dollar house. Well, you couldn't very well sit down in the parlor without buying a little wine or at least putting some change in the player piano. It would cost you usually a couple of dollars before you even got around to the business you came for. Clever girls, once they got you in a boudoir, would always offer little 'extra' services, for 'extra' prices, naturally – and you'd pay! Things are not

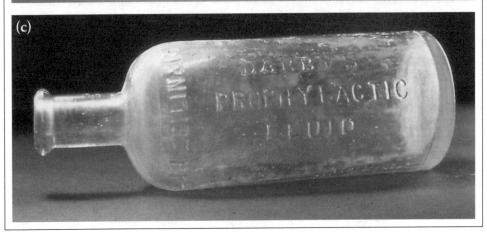

easy to resist at such times. Of course, they never tried to sell you anything *afterwards*. They were smart enough to know that the man leaving is not the same man as the man entering.

I heard that Grace Hayes had a pet raccoon that was trained to pick the pockets of her customers. If that isn't true it's the only story I know about ways to take your money in the District that wasn't . . .

Rene: Off and on, I patronized those District houses for about twelve years. Only, however, because it was convenient. It took much time and trouble to seduce the young ladies of our social circle. Though I sometimes took the time and trouble . . . it was difficult to make the effort with the District so near.

Lew: When you first went in the house, why there'd be the girls, maybe three or four dressed up to kill – in ball gowns and things like that. They were young girls, mostly – and usually good-looking ones. The player piano only had *fast* tunes. It seemed like everything they did was fast, especially take all your money . . .

Well, the girls would dance with you as long as you kept on feeding the box . . . after a couple of dances you'd take her or *she'd* take *you* upstairs to a small 'boudoir' . . . You wouldn't believe how fast those girls could get their clothes off. Usually, they'd leave on their stockings and earrings, things like that. A man usually took off his trousers and shoes . . . I'll tell you, five minutes was a long time to spend in one of those rooms.

In fact, from the time you'd come in the front door of the house until you'd be back out on the banquette hardly ever took more than fifteen minutes! And there you'd be, standing on the banquette without a cent in your pocket, and no place to go but maybe home. And that would be the last place in the world you'd want to go.

Act II: The Life

Narrator: Maimie Pinzer, an Anglo independent prostitute, and Lola, a Latina prostitute who worked in an upscale parlor house, talk about their time in the business.

Maimie: I was thirteen . . . prior to my father's death, we had a general servant in the house, and a laundress and scrubwoman who came, each two days in the week. After his death, I was given it all to do but the laundress's work – and I did it very poorly, and always only after receiving severe whippings . . .

After a violent scene with my mother . . . I went to the city, and there got a regular job in a department store, at $5.00 a week, though I was only past thirteen years old. I was a 'saleslady' – and this store, to this day, is quite the place for men to come during the afternoon hours to make 'dates' for the eve. I found I could stay away from dinner, and go along with some boys, and come home and tell some sort of story – and that it was accepted, due to the five dollars I was bringing home . . .!

Of course, the inevitable thing happened. Some young chap took me to his room; and I stayed three or four days before I put in an appearance in the neighborhood of my home. As I neared our house, a man spoke to me by name, and told me he was a 'special officer' and that he had a warrant for my arrest . . .

Figure 9.3 Medicine and health artifacts. Examples of health-related items found in the Los Angeles parlor house deposits: (a) embossed pharmacy bottles; (b) syringes, infusion douches, and a breast pump; (c) one of nine quart-size bottles of Darby's Prophylactic Fluid. All reprinted by permission of the Metropolitan Water District of Southern California.

Figure 9.4 Cosmetics and selling sex. Items related to grooming comprised a large portion of the Los Angeles parlor house artifacts: (a) perfume bottles, mostly from France (reprinted by permission of the Metropolitan Water District of Southern California); (b) two crib prostitutes in their windows (LA Daily Times, December 2, 1903); (c) toilet waters, perfumes, colognes, creams, and tooth paste containers (see opposite) (reprinted by permission of the Metropolitan Water District of Southern California).

Figure 9.4 (*continued*)

Lola: May Spencer, she's Dago, you know . . . she's take me in her house . . . I coo'n't speak no Eenglish. She's treat me better than my mawtber, May Spencer. People says she rooeen't me, May Spencer. She din' rooeen't me! I was *puta* [whore] at home befor' I come dees country . . . Home, I din' have fine clothes, I din' have mawney, I din' have nawthing but goo-for nawting hawsban' mak' me work for heem. I start to work for May Spencer when I'm seexteen years.

Maimie: I knew that I didn't want to be bad. But I didn't see what else I should do if I didn't find some way of earning my keep . . . you know, I've told you how hard I looked for work. Well I did, in a halfhearted sort of a way and with the feeling: 'Oh! what's the use' – for I didn't propose to get up at 6.30 to be at work at 8 and work in a close, stuffy room with people I despise, until dark, for six or seven dollars a week! When I could spend an afternoon with some congenial person and in the end have more than a week's work could pay me . . . then what do girls do? . . . I don't know exactly what they do, unless they resort to living as I did formerly; or perhaps marry; or if they do work, are laundresses, potato peelers, scrubwomen . . .

Lola: I get up each day, t'ree, faw in de afternoon . . . We eat downstair – ees no dining room, ess keetchen weet' roun' table – we eat. Seex, sometime seven, eight *muchachas*. Si, coffee, French bread. I am de younges', but de oldes' maybe twenny-wan, two. May Spencer may be thirty-fi . . . We do nawthing till maybe seven o'clock.

We take bath. May Spencer have two bathtubs. Piazza don' have two bathtubs . . . We dress always party clothes. I hav' nine party dress, two street dress. Den,

Figure 9.5 Cribs in Los Angeles. Cribs were one-room cubicles where prostitutes solicited business from the front window, as is this crib prostitute near Alameda Street in 1898. Courtesy Department of Special Collections, Charles E. Young Research Library, UCLA.

pues, we seet een our room. Later, maybe eight o'clock, downstair de bell she's ring. We go, all de girls, we go downstairs, because when de bell she's ring, ees because a man you know – a cawstomer hees cawm een . . .

Maimie: I decided to marry – and thought I could use Albert's simplicity of manner and appearance, and my tricky brain, to make it possible for him to do something beside pound nails . . . [However], when I saw how useless trying to use him to earn any more than a bare, meager livelihood was, I gave up in disgust; and . . . I began to use what charms I might possess to make it possible to have a few of the luxuries which had become necessities.

Lola: We drink wine wee theem . . . De piano player he play . . . We try to dance weet' man . . . Aft' while, de man he peek out wheech girl he gon' take, you know, for upstairs – an' dey go. Eef ees me, we go to nex' floor . . . I have room weet all kin' Mexican t'ings. Ees sombreros, you know, mantillas, serapes, all dees t'ings. I nevair

Figure 9.6 Parlor room serving dishes. Quantities of expensive porcelain dishes (a) and fancy glassware (b) distinguished the Los Angeles parlor house serving ware from that of its residential neighbors. Reprinted by permission of the Metropolitan Water District of Southern California.

see such t'ings at home [in Santo Domingo], but May Spencer, she teenk good idea for my room . . .

I take off my party dress. . . I exameen hees, heem, you know, to see he has not de clap. I wash heem weet' dat medeecene stoff. I lay on de bed, an' he do what he want. Ees nawthing, you know – maybe wan, two minute . . . I take de mawney, at lees fi' dollair an I go downstair . . .

Maimie: (sisterly) I must tell you that to contract the worst of the dread diseases – syphilis – one has to have a broken place on the skin, and only so can it enter the system . . . I've always been very careful of infection when such conditions prevailed. But the other and minor trouble – gonorrhea – is contracted in a dreadfully innocent and easy manner sometimes. By the use of a towel it can be gotten . . . I became expert on these things, and was criminally ignorant before.

Lola: Mos' I take t'ree, faw men upstair every night. Saturday, Sawnday, fi', seex, seven. Mardi gras, I don' know . . . Maybe t'ree o'clock in de mawning, we eat. Ees good *comida* in May Spencer house. Ees always bes' meat, fruit, vegetables – all you wan'.

Maimie: At times, I would go all over the thoughts that passed through my mind . . . and would decide that I would keep my word to myself and cut it out. Of course, the attending luxuries that go with loose living I did not want to give up. [However], summed all up, it is anything but a pleasant road to travel; and I saw how the few luxuries did not make up for the indignities offered me . . .

Act III: Family business

Narrator: Violet and Marc were born into District life.

Violet: I was born in 1904 in the wintertime. I was a 'trick' baby. That means my father was just one of them johns that paid my mother for a fuck. I was born upstairs, like in the attic of Hilma Burt's house . . . A lot of kids was born in that attic and in the Arlington attic and other places like that. There was a midwife used to come for all the girls who got caught. Why do people think whores can't have kids?

Marc: My old lady – it wasn't no secret – was a whore . . . I don't know who my ol' man was. Just another trick, you know. Anyway, the ol' lady died in 1903 from the clap. One day I come back to the place from school . . . – you surprised? You had to go to school: it was the law – and she was missin' . . . I never seen her again. I didn't try to see her at the hospital, because I always been afraid of them places – and anyhow, I didn't specially feel like seein' her.

Violet: I read in a book one time about one of the houses that was selling a mother and daughter combination for fifty dollars a night. The man that wrote the book acted like that was some kind of a freak act or something. Well, you can write the truth is that I remember fifty combinations like that and I was one myself, and I know two girl friends, both still living, that were in the same kind of an act.

Marc: Well, I didn't have much education, but I wasn't stupid. And I see how these broads was with money and I begin to understand how all these big-shot pimps got all those broads workin' for 'em and them guys buy their selves diamonds and sharp clothes and like that . . . Well, you know, by the time I was seventeen I had eight broads turnin' tricks for me. Later on, I [bought] a whorehouse of my own . . . an' spent some money fixin' the inside. I found out you have to spend some money to make any. In 1902, I must have had an average of thirty women all the time.

Violet: The . . . year the district closed down . . . I had money saved and I got a job. I was always high priced . . . because I was a novelty, and I didn't hang around long

Figure 9.7 Life in the district. Life in the Los Angeles red-light district included socializing between prostitutes, johns, pimps, and other red-light district residents. Decorative tumblers and whiskey bottles from the Aliso Street parlor house represent the social drinking which accompanied this business.
Reprinted by permission of the Metropolitan Water District of Southern California.

enough to get wore out. I got a job as a waitress. Yes, I still turned a few tricks, but after I started goin' with my husband, I cut all that out ... My mother moved into a crib in the French Quarter and kept on until she got too old. I was lucky, I never got the clap and, so far as I know, neither did my mother. You know what! She's still livin'! ... Her head don't work right no more. But she gets around. She lives in her own place and does her own cookin' ...

Marc: I don't care that I made mine pimpin' ... I was in business like anybody else, and I run it good. Better than the rest of 'em. I wasn't no lush. I didn't take dope an' I didn't gamble. What's wrong with that? The rest of 'em is all gone. Some just got broke and disappeared. Some let whiskey, an' dope get 'em. I know three what killed their selves and two that got knifed to death by their broads. A lot of 'em got put in jail for different things. Mostly for tryin' to stay in the same business after it became illegal. But I saved my money and I'm still here. The rest of them guys is gone – but I'm still here.

Violet: All my three girls is older now than I was when I quit the business, and I don't see that they're much better off than I was at their age. I know it'd be good if I could say how awful it was and like crime don't pay – but to me it seems just like anything else – like a kid who's father owns a grocery store. He helps him in the store. Well, my mother didn't sell groceries.

The end

Acknowledgements

Permission to reprint excerpts from Al Rose's interviews with Storyville informants Rene, Lew, Lola, Violet, and Marc, was kindly provided by Rex Rose, Executor of the Al Rose Estate.

Notes

1 'Red Light Voices' was first presented at the Annual Meeting of the Society for Historical Archaeology in Atlanta, Georgia, in January 1998 (in the session 'Archaeologists as Storytellers' organized by Mary Praetzellis) it was performed by Julia Costello and Judy Tordoff. Its second staging, at the Annual Meeting of the Society for American Archaeology, in Seattle in March 1998, was performed by Julia Costello and Adrian Praetzellis (in the session 'Archaeologies of Sexuality' organized by Barbara Voss and Robert Schmidt). In two subsequent performances, at the Society for California Archaeology annual meeting in Sacramento in April 1999, and at the Institute of Archaeology at UCLA in May of 1999, Costello, Tordoff, and Praetzellis all performed together.
2 The views expressed in this writing are solely those of the author and do not represent the views of the Metropolitan Water District of Southern California.

References

Cheek, C. D., D. J. Seifert, P. W. O'Bannon, C. A. Holt, B. R. Roulette, Jr, J. Balicki, G. A. Ceponis and D. B. Heck (1991) *Phase II and Phase III Archeological Investigations at the Site of the Proposed International Cultural and Trade Center/Federal Office Building Complex, Federal Triangle, Washington, DC*, prepared for the Pennsylvania Avenue Development Corporation, Alexandria, VA: John Milner Associates, Inc.

Cheek, C. D., and D. J. Seifert (1994) 'Neighborhoods and Household Types in Nineteenth-Century Washington, DC: Fannie Hill and Mary McNamara in Hooker's Division', in P. A. Shackel and B. J. Little (eds) *Historical Archaeology of the Chesapeake*, Washington, DC: Smithsonian Institution Press.

Costello, J. G. (1996) 'The Smell of Bread Fresh from the Oven . . .', paper presented at the Annual Meeting of the Society for Historical Archaeology, Bakersfield, CA, performed by Julia Costello and Judy Tordoff.

—— (1998) 'Bread Fresh from the Oven: Memories of Italian Breadbaking in the California Mother Lode', in 'Archaeologists as Storytellers', *Historical Archaeology* 32, 1: 66–73.

—— (1999) '"A Night With Venus, A Moon With Mercury": The Archaeology of Prostitution in Historic Los Angeles', in G. Dubrow and J. Goodman (eds) *Restoring Women's History through Historic Preservation*, Baltimore: Johns Hopkins University Press.

Kurtén, B. (1980) *Dance of the Tiger: A Novel of the Ice Age*, Berkeley: reprinted by University of California Press (1995).

The Metropolitan Water District of Southern California (forthcoming a) 'Historical Archaeology at the Headquarters Facility Project Site, The Metropolitan Water District of Southern California, vol. 1, Draft Data Report: Recovered Data, Stratigraphy, Artifacts, and Documents', unpublished Mitigation Monitoring Report. Project Management by Applied EarthWorks, Inc. Co-Principal Investigators: Foothill Resources, Ltd. and Anthropological Studies Center at Sonoma State University. Contributing authors: Julia G. Costello, Adrian Praetzellis, Mary Praetzellis, Judith Marvin, Michael D. Meyer, Erica S. Gibson, and Grace H. Ziesing.

—— (forthcoming b) 'Historical Archaeology at the Headquarters Facility Project Site, The Metropolitan Water District of Southern California, vol. 2, Draft Interpretive Report. Project Management by Applied EarthWorks, Inc. Co-Principal Investigators: Foothill Resources, Ltd. and Anthropological Studies Center at Sonoma State University. Contributing authors: Julia G. Costello, Adrian Praetzellis, Grace H. Ziesing, Judith Marvin, William M. Mason, Michael D.

Meyer, Erica S. Gibson, Mary Praetzellis, Suzanne Stewart, Sherri Gust, Madeline Hirn, and Elaine-Maryse Solair.

Pinzer, M. (Maimie) (1977) *The Maimie Papers*, R. Rosen (ed.), Old Westbury, NY: Feminist Press in cooperation with the Schlessinger Library of Radcliffe College.

Praetzellis, M. (1998) 'Archaeologists as Story Tellers #2', session at the Annual Meeting of the Society for Historical Archaeology, Atlanta.

Praetzellis, A. and M. Praetzellis, (eds) (1998) 'Archaeologists as Storytellers', *Historical Archaeology* 32, 1: 1–96.

Rose, A. (1974) *Storyville, New Orleans*, Birmingham: University of Alabama Press.

Seifert, D. J. (1991) 'Within Site of the White House: The Archaeology of Working Women', *Historical Archaeology* 4: 82–108.

—— (1998) 'Sin City', session at the Annual Meeting of the Society for Historical Archaeology, Atlanta.

Simmons, A. (1989) 'Red Light Ladies: Settlement Patterns and Material Culture on the Mining Frontier', *Anthropology Northwest*, no. 4. Anthropology Department, Oregon State University, Corvallis.

Smith, A. D. (1996) Stagebill: *Twilight: Los Angeles 1992*, conceived, written, and performed by Anna Deavere Smith; directed by Sharon Ott. Berkeley Repertory Theater, at the Marines Memorial Theater, San Francisco.

Spector, J. D. (1993) *What This Awl Means: Feminist Archaeology at a Wahpeton Dakota Village*, St. Paul: Minnesota Historical Society Press.

Spude, C. H. (1999) 'Predicting Gender in Archaeological Assemblages: A Klondike Example', in G. Dubrow and J. Goodman (eds) *Restoring Women's History through Historic Preservation*, Baltimore: Johns Hopkins University Press.

Tringham, R. (1991) 'Households With Faces: the Challenge of Gender in Prehistoric Architectural Remains', in J. M. Gero and M. W. Conkey (eds) *Engendering Archaeology: Women and Prehistory*, Cambridge: Basil Blackwell.

PART III

Sexual identities, sexual politics

Chapter Ten

Archaeology of the *'Aqi*: gender and sexuality in prehistoric Chumash society

Sandra E. Hollimon

The examination of sexuality in the prehistoric record is a subject that until recently has received very little attention on the part of archaeologists (see Schmidt, this volume). One approach is to assess the ramifications of gender upon sexuality (and *vice versa*), and specifically to investigate the intersection of these two interdependent aspects of social identity. In this paper, I discuss the organization of gender, sexuality, and labor among the Chumash of the Santa Barbara Channel area in coastal southern California (Figure 10.1).

THE CHUMASH

Prehistorically, the Chumash displayed a level of complexity unusual for non-agriculturists (Arnold 1992; Johnson 1988; Kroeber 1925). During late prehistoric times, this society was characterized by a simple chiefdom-level political organization that integrated densely populated coastal villages (Arnold 1987). These villages were supported by a maritime subsistence economy, and extensive trade networks that relied, in part, upon the ocean-going plank canoe, or *tomol* (C. King 1990; see below).

Chumash society was dominated by the political/religious organization known as *'antap*, whose members included local hereditary chiefs, economic elites, and members of specific craft guilds (Blackburn 1975: 13, 1976: 237). At least twelve *'antap* officials dwelled in every major village, and often participated in rituals in widely scattered locations. The *'antap* organization acted as an integrative mechanism throughout Chumash territory, in that chiefs, other political officers, shamans, and economic elites were obligatory members of a wide-reaching religious society, responsible for economic redistribution at large ceremonies, among other duties (Blackburn 1976: 236–37).

The prehistory of the Santa Barbara Channel area has been divided into three periods (C. King 1990). Recent calibrated radiocarbon samples have revised the dates of these periods: Early (7500–2600 BP), Middle, (2600–850 BP) and Late (850–218 BP) (Arnold 1992: 66). While the first documented European contact with the Chumash occurred in AD 1542 during the Cabrillo expedition, the Historic Period began after AD 1782, when the Chumash were forced into the Spanish missions established throughout their territory (see Costello and

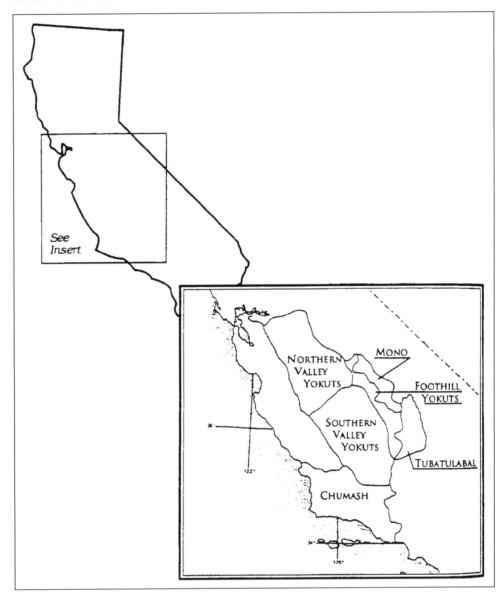

Figure 10.1 Location of the Chumash and their neighbors.
Illustration by the author.

Hornbeck 1989: 323–24). During this time, the Chumash experienced demographic and social collapse, with a tremendous upheaval of traditional lifeways and social practices following the imposition of a new religion (Roman Catholicism), a new subsistence base (agriculture and animal husbandry), and a new residential pattern (mission barracks). (See Hudson 1980; Johnson 1989; Walker and Johnson 1992, 1994; Walker et al. 1989.)

The most extensive source of Chumash ethnographic information was collected by John P. Harrington of the Smithsonian Institution, beginning in 1912. His consultants' descriptions of the *'antap* organization, the *'aqi*, occupational guilds, and other aspects of Chumash culture are important sources regarding this native California society, and are used in this discussion in conjunction with archaeological data to elucidate prehistoric circumstances.

Recent research in the prehistory of the southern California coast has focused on the role of environmental perturbation, such as elevated sea temperature (e.g. Arnold 1992, 1997; Arnold et al. 1997) and terrestrial drought (e.g. Raab 1996; Raab and Bradford 1997; Raab and Larson 1997) in the evolution of organizational complexity. The impact of environmental deterioration and resulting subsistence stress on human populations have been advanced as explanations for the emergence of elite managers among the prehistoric people of the area. The relative importance of specific environmental factors (viz. drought vs. sea temperature rise) is not the main concern of the present discussion; rather, the role of labor organization in the development of Chumash society is informed by these sources.

This chapter introduces the possibility that late prehistoric forms of labor organization, such as craft guilds, may have been influenced by the structure of the society of under-takers, and that this professional association may pre-date others described in the Chumash ethnohistoric and ethnographic literature. The people who performed undertaking and other funerary rites in Chumash society were called *'aqi*, and this term inextricably links gender, labor, and sexuality in the definition of this category. The occupation/gender known as *'aqi* can be examined within the framework of gender diversity in other Native North American groups.

NATIVE NORTH AMERICAN GENDER DIVERSITY

Unlike gender systems that identify sex/gender primarily on the basis of external genitalia and sexual object identification, Native American gender markers place greater emphasis on supernatural endowment, preference for types of work, and temperament, attributes not generally recognized in European-derived systems (Jacobs et al. 1997; Roscoe 1987; Whitehead 1981; Williams 1986). In addition, ethnographic evidence from North America and Asia suggests that it is the liminal experience that is important in marking 'super-numerary' genders (Fulton and Anderson 1992; Jacobs and Cromwell 1992; Miller 1982; Thayer 1980). In contrast to European-derived systems that consider gender permanent and immutable, many cultures view gender as temporary and flexible (Bolin 1996; Jacobs and Cromwell 1992). The Chukchi of Siberia recognize seven genders that can be adopted at any time in a person's life, and the transformation need not be permanent; some of these alterations are specifically said to occur when shamans enter trance states or perform particular ceremonies (Jacobs and Cromwell 1992: 51; see also Balzer 1996).

Recent research concerning the intersection of gender and sexuality in Native North American societies has focused debate on the relationship between sexual orientation and gender identification (see Jacobs et al. 1997; Lang 1998; Roscoe 1998). Does sexual orien-tation follow gender identity, or vice versa? In many regards, this is still an open question. However, in the Chumash case, it appears that non-procreative sexual activity is critical in the identification of the *'aqi* gender, and that these aspects are inextricably linked to the undertaking occupation (Hollimon 1997; see below).

'AQI GENDER, LABOR, AND SEXUALITY

The Chumash gender system at the time of missionization apparently included culturally defined categories of women, men, and a third gender, *'aqi* (also *'axi*), identified by indige-nous and non-indigenous sources as biological males who adopted certain aspects of women's clothing and work (Hollimon 1997: 173). In addition, several ethnographic accounts indicate that the undertakers were 'old women' (Blackburn 1975: 271; L. King 1969: 50), suggesting that post-menopausal women could also be identified as *'aqi*.

According to available ethnographic and ethnohistoric evidence, the Chumash lacked a linguistically marked female gender category analogous to the *'aqi*. During Catholic confession, Chumash women were asked if they had ever 'sinned' with a woman, but no term for female homosexual was given in either a Chumash language or Spanish (Beeler 1967: 52–53). It is possible that no such role existed at the time of European contact, or during the nineteenth and twentieth centuries when the majority of ethnographic work with the Chumash was accomplished. Alternatively, such a role may have existed, but was more subtle than that of the *'aqi*, or it may not have constituted a true gender category that was recognized by the Chumash or the ethnographers (see Cromwell 1997: 128 for a discussion of the 'invisibility' of female gender variation).

Perhaps the *'aqi* gender consisted of liminal culturally defined women (or non-men), in the sense that they were non-reproductive females or biological males without offspring. As biologically non-reproductive individuals, male-bodied third gender persons were also socially recognized as *'aqi*.

It is possible that women were considered to be 'gender-modified' as *'aqi* only when performing specific tasks, or after menopause (Hollimon 1997: 183). Female persons who performed undertaking duties may not have been considered normative women while doing this work (Will Roscoe, personal communication 1994). Perhaps a person's gender was modified by this work that entailed spiritual contact with another realm (see above for Siberian examples (Jacobs and Cromwell 1992: 51; Balzer 1996)). After completing mortuary duties, a person might return to one's 'original' gender (Hollimon 1997: 182).

The ethnographic data indicating that undertakers underwent a secret initiation rite supports the idea that *'aqi* comprised a gender apart from men and women, 'a status as a distinct and autonomous category of personhood' that existed on a par with the genders of woman and man (Roscoe 1994: 364; see also Roscoe 1991: chap. 5). The initiation rite of the Mohave (Colorado River) third gender (*alyha:*) marked a transition not from male to female, but from boy to *alyha:*, and this was a shift not just in age but in gender status (Roscoe 1994: 362). As such, an initiating rite for *'aqi* undertakers might have simultaneously marked a passage between childhood and adulthood, analogous to puberty rites for boys and girls, and a formal recognition of membership within an occupational guild.

The spiritual mandate for undertaking in Chumash society apparently derived from the gender/reproductive status of the *'aqi*. I have suggested elsewhere that life, death, and the afterlife were gender-associated concepts in Chumash cosmology (Hollimon n.d.a). Life was apparently conceptualized in two main aspects: earthly abundance and fertility were associated with femaleness, and sunlight was a product of the male deity of Sun. Death was a male-associated concept, that was also brought by Sun. The journey to the afterlife (*Šimilaqsa*) was a series of encounters with female supernatural entities, and was facilitated by *'aqi* mortuary practitioners (Hollimon n.d.a). Perhaps the mediation between death and the afterlife, and between human and supernatural realms, was entrusted by the Chumash to individuals who could not be harmed by symbolic pollution of the corpse, and who were no longer (or never had been) capable of giving birth (see Claassen 1992: 149–52; Hollimon 1997, n.d.a).

The ethnographer J. P. Harrington's consultant Maria Solares expressed some confusion regarding the gender of Chumash undertakers. She apparently could not reconcile the fact that the terms for undertaker (said to be 'old women') and male homosexual were synonymous (L. King 1969: 50). This confusion about the gender of *'aqi* can be explained when one considers the symbolic importance of procreation in Chumash cosmology. What do male-bodied persons who are not culturally identified as men have in common with post-menopausal women? Their sexual activity does not result in conception and birth. It is this facet that appears most important in terms of identifying the gender of *'aqi* persons, as well as the spiritual mandate for their work in handling the dead (see Poole 1996 for a discussion of the relationships among procreative symbolism, gender, and ritual in Papua New Guinea).

One gloss of the term *'aqi* was given as 'arse-fucker' (although probably intended to mean anal receptive), and others included homosexual and undertaker (L. King 1969: 48). Based on extensive ethnographic surveys of Native North American gender systems, as well as contemporary ethnographic data from North and South America, it appears that the categories of men and non-men (women, third gender males, *berdache* [sic], etc.) are defined on the basis of penetration and reception (see Callender and Kochems 1983; Lang 1997; Roscoe 1987, 1994; Thomas 1997; Williams 1986). For example, men are culturally defined as people who penetrate with the penis, while non-men are those who are penetrated by men (e.g. Bolin 1996; Callender and Kochems 1986; Devereux 1937; Jacobs et al. 1997; Kulick 1997; Roscoe 1994; Williams 1986: 95–99; perhaps the Chumash euphemism of a man 'getting into the canoe', that is, performing intercourse with a woman, reflects this principle [see Blackburn 1975: 208]). Based on this evidence, it seems unlikely that male-bodied *'aqi* would have been the inseminators of women, and therefore would not have 'fathered' children.

The contemporary Euro-American categories of sexuality, such as hetero-, homo-, and bisexual, are inapplicable to Native American gender systems such as that of the Chumash. Relations between people of the same biological sex did not necessarily imply that these individuals belonged to the same gender, rendering these labels meaningless (see Lang 1996: 188 and 1997: 102–107; Thomas 1997: 167–68). Despite this inapplicability, the Spanish missionaries questioned native neophytes about same-sex sexual behavior, translating their *confesionario* into native California languages (Katz 1976: 287; see also Guerra 1971). The Spanish asked Chumash men if they had ever had intercourse with a man, or with a homosexual (*'aqi* in Ventureño Chumash, *joya* in Spanish; see Roscoe 1995: 201–204 for a discussion of the use of the term *joya* in Alta California).

Ironically, in one instance, the term *'aqi* was glossed as 'celibate medicine man' (Yates 1957: 38), simultaneously emphasizing supernatural power on the one hand, and denying sexual activity on the other. It is my contention that in this gloss, celibacy was mistakenly conflated with sexual activity that did not produce offspring. Obviously, non-procreative sexual activity is not the same as a complete absence of sexual practices.

CHUMASH GUILDS

The discussion of sexuality in Chumash society has bearing on the development of guilds, in that the *'aqi* may have provided a model of labor organization that pre-dated other ethnographically or ethnohistorically documented forms. The mechanism of inheritance of guild membership, in the absence of biological procreation, and its implications, are discussed below.

At the time of European contact, Chumash society contained a number of economic, ritual, and political positions that could be considered examples of craft or occupational specialization, such as the one comprised of plank canoemakers and owners. Archaeological evidence, including burial associations, suggests that professional guilds existed in pre-contact times (Arnold 1987: 19–22, 1992: 68, 73–74; Hudson et al. 1978: 153). These elite *gremios*, such as 'The Brotherhood of the *Tomol*' (plank canoe), restricted access to materials, knowledge, ritual paraphernalia, and esoteric information necessary for the manufacture of particular goods and performance of services (Arnold 1987: 20; see also Blackburn 1975: 51).

It could be argued that Chumash undertakers also comprised a professional guild. Undertakers were paid for their services with bead money, baskets, and any goods that were left by the graveside (L. King 1982: 74); overpayment of the *'aqi* was considered to be a good omen for the deceased's journey to the afterlife (L. King 1969: 50). Other evidence that this was a specialization comes from ethnographic data stating that undertakers did no other work and were respected for their duties (L. King 1969: 47; see also Arnold 1987: 19–26, Blackburn 1975: 52ff., 1976, and T. F. King 1978 for descriptions of Chumash occupational specialists).

Although a name for the guild has not been identified (perhaps *'aqi* was the name of the guild), guild status is suggested by the fact that undertakers belonged to a secret, initiating society (L. King 1982: 74; see also Roscoe 1994: 346–47 for a discussion of '*berdache* [*sic*] priesthoods' among other Native North American groups). In this respect, undertakers resembled other Chumash guilds and the religious/political society known as the *'antap*. Esoteric knowledge and ritual paraphernalia and materials were not accessible to the entire Chumash population; only initiated members of these groups had access to these commodities. Blackburn (1976: 236) describes the 'baptism' of *'antap* members as children, and specifically refers to a period of apprenticeship during which they learned the esoteric language, sacred songs and dances that were integral components of Chumash rituals.

The detailed knowledge necessary for *tomol* construction was similarly restricted, and imparted only to specially trained assistants who served as apprentices to master builders (Hudson et al. 1978: 41; Arnold 1992: 71). The *'altomolich* (canoemakers) '. . . have learned how to do it under older men', and, 'an old canoemaker would have his helpers and he would allow no one else around' (Hudson et al. 1978: 40).

Inheritance of guild membership

At least one Chumash guild based its membership on heredity. The Brotherhood of the *Tomol* was comprised of people who inherited their status as canoemakers and owners (Hudson et al. 1978: 153–55). Another Chumash guild, that of sinew-backed-bowmakers, may have operated along the same lines. Guild members were called 'relatives', while non-members were referred to as 'non-relatives'. However, it appears that fictive kinship may have been established when a person wished to purchase a bow. The individual would approach a guild member, ask to join, and if allowed, would be called a convert or relative (Hudson et al. 1978: 153). Therefore, it appears that guild membership was available for purchase, and that fictive kinship was maintained among members who were not actually related consanguines or affines, giving the *gremios* a 'kinship veneer' (Hudson et al. 1978: 155).

Despite the emphasis on kin-based inheritance of social, economic and/or political status, there are several descriptions in the ethnohistoric and ethnographic literature of instances where succession was not based on kinship. For example, one source indicated that upon the death of an *'antap* member, candidates for replacement would be nominated and elected by the remaining members (Hudson et al. 1977: 22). Additionally, an *'antap* official could choose his or her successor before death. 'This person can be anyone that will be competent, whether a relative or not . . .' (Hudson et al. 1977: 21). In such cases, a relative of the deceased did not automatically inherit the position.

A description of chiefly succession reiterates this point. During the 1860s, a Chumash chief abdicated his position, as he was too poor to fulfill his ceremonial and administrative responsibilities. At a meeting of other chiefs from throughout the region, a woman named Pomposa was appointed *wot* (chief). While she was related to the chiefly lineage through her grandfather, she was not in the direct line of succession (Blackburn 1976: 241). Pomposa's election as *wot* highlights the possibility of other forms of succession of important ritual and political positions in Chumash society.

Perhaps the undertaking guild operated in a similar manner. Certain ethnographic information indicates that the 'office' of undertaker was passed from mother to daughter (L. King 1969: 47–48). These data can be interpreted in a number of ways. First, it is possible that the *'aqi* were actually female-bodied, that they married and/or had children during their pre-menopausal years. Perhaps such a person could be identified as *'aqi* later in life, after menopause. Any daughters who were interested would inherit the specialization, possibly serving apprenticeships, and assuming the position of undertaker after their reproductive years had passed.

In this scenario, it is possible that the gender of these individuals was modified while performing undertaking tasks, such that an individual might be socially defined as a woman during the majority of her life, and was only a member of the ''*aqi* gender' during burial rituals, or perhaps after menopause (Will Roscoe, personal communication 1994). After completing mortuary duties, the undertaker might return to his or her 'original' gender (Hollimon 1997: 182; see also Jacobs and Cromwell 1992).

Alternatively, we could assume that the *'aqi* were third gender male individuals who were in some ways identified socially as women. In this scenario, adoption or fictive kinship could establish familial ties among individuals who were not biologically related, such as the previous example of the bowmakers. It is also possible that *'aqi* included both post-menopausal (or non-reproductive) women, and third gender males.

Support for this idea comes from the ethnographic record of neighboring groups, such as the Mono, and from other areas of North America, which suggest that a young person's early interest in occupational specialization was critical to the identification of third gender status (Callender and Kochems 1983; Kessler and McKenna 1978; Whitehead 1981). The Mono appear to have had an institution similar to the *'aqi*, in which third gender persons and/or women were the undertakers (Hollimon 1997). In this society, the undertaker's dream helper or spirit guide was a dead person, explaining the corpse handler's lack of fear of the dead, as well as a supernatural mandate for the work (Gayton 1948: 236). Similarly, the Yokuts indicated that undertakers 'grew up that way, with a desire to get rid of the dead' (Gayton 1948: 168).

Given that a youngster's interest in professional specialization was most likely noted by his or her natal family, it is possible that this person was 'apprenticed' to an undertaker and may have been adopted by that individual. Maria Solares told the ethnographer J. P. Harrington that the undertakers 'did nothing else from the time they were little girls' (L. King 1969: 47), and an oral narrative describes an *'aqi* who had 'followed this occupation from youth on up' (Blackburn 1975: 271). Archaeological support for this information comes from a tentative identification of an *'aqi* burial from Santa Cruz Island. A relatively young (18 years) male skeleton showed evidence of advanced degenerative arthritis in the area of the spine where females normally showed this pathological condition. It is possible that this individual incurred repeated stress on the spine from the use of a digging stick while excavating graves, and had been doing so for a considerable time prior to death (Hollimon 1996: 206).

Adoption is described in several Chumash oral narratives, including an example with an individual that bears many resemblances to an *'aqi*, in that he expresses no sexual interest in women and boasts about his ability to manufacture tools that are usually associated with women's work (Blackburn 1975: 154). This form of fictive kinship might explain otherwise contradictory ethnographic information which indicated that *'aqi* were women who never married, yet the occupation descended from mother to daughter (L. King 1969: 47–48; of course, the birth of children did not always require formal marriage). Blackburn (1975: 50) suggests some matrilineal inheritance of goods and statuses among the Chumash, based on descriptions in oral narratives. Ritual services, such as the administering of *Datura* during the boys' initiation, could be owned (Blackburn 1975: 51). If an undertaker had no biological offspring, an older person ('mother') might take a younger person ('daughter') under her/his wing, ensuring that the office would be inherited.

Given that it is unlikely that *'aqi* persons were the inseminators of women, the *'aqi* may have gained children by marriage to a divorced or widowed man who had children of his own. Two points argue against such an interpretation. First, it was apparently the woman who was usually the custodial parent following divorce (Blackburn 1975: 57). Second, there are no instances of marriage recorded for mission period *'aqi* (called *joyas* in Spanish documents), nor are any marriages mentioned in the ethnographic literature, although this pre-contact practice may have been significantly disrupted by the Spanish padres (John Johnson, personal communication 1997). In fact, only negative evidence is provided, in that Harrington was told that *'aqi* never married (L. King 1969: 47–48). It seems most likely that male-bodied *'aqi* maintained fictive kinship with their 'children'.

Additional support for the existence of fictive kinship comes from ethnographic evidence of other Native North American groups. Roscoe (1994: 346–47) discusses the group identification and coordinated activities of *berdaches* [*sic*] among the Hidatsa, Crow, and Timucua, in which these persons were socially recognized as belonging to a distinct class, often fulfilling ceremonial or religious functions. In an interesting parallel to the Chumash, a late sixteenth-century engraving by De Bry (based on Le Moyne's original drawing) depicts Timucua 'hermaphrodites' who are working collectively to bury the dead and were specifically stated to be acting as a group (Lorant 1946; Roscoe 1994: 347). This group identity apparently has persisted into modern times, such that a fictive 'sisterhood' has been described among third gender males in Pueblo (White 1980: 100) and Shoshoni (Hall quoted in Lang 1997: 106) societies; Williams (1986: 94), discussing the Pueblo case, states, '*berdaches* [*sic*], with their sense of sisterhood, are in essence a fictive kin group'.

This fictive kinship may have also been a feature of the Chumash *'aqi*. The acknowledgment of a person's status as *'aqi* may have simultaneously been an indication of occupation, non-procreative sexuality, guild membership, fictive family membership, and spiritual endowment. This may have operated in a similar manner to the identification of an *'antap* society member, or *tomol* 'brother'; a person's acknowledged status entailed implications about wealth, political power, and social deference (see Blackburn 1975, 1976).

Distribution of guild members

Unlike craft specialists tied to specific and locally available resources (e.g. shell bead manufacturers or coastal canoemakers [Arnold 1992]), undertakers would have been required occupational specialists in every community. While there may have been entire villages devoted to the manufacture of specialized items in the Chumash area prior to European contact (see Arnold 1987, 1992), with high percentages *per capita* of specialists, the *'aqi* would have been numerically rare in a village but geographically widely dispersed throughout the territory. Fages, a Spanish chronicler, indicated that in large coastal Chumash villages, up to three *'aqi* would be resident (Heizer and Whipple 1971: 259; see also Gayton 1948: 106–107 for a discussion of population size and distribution of undertakers among the neighboring Yokuts).

During the mission period, a number of individuals were identified as *joya* (= *'aqi*) in baptismal records. These documents give the natal village of all entries, as well as information about marriages and offspring. Johnson's (personal communication 1997) research on these records documents a number of *joyas* from several villages in Chumash and adjacent territory. One person came from Piru in Tataviam territory and was recorded at Mission San Fernando. The 1803 records at Mission La Purisima document a 50-year-old who came from the village of *Nomgio* (modern Gaviota). The 1803 census at Mission Santa Barbara records a 54-year-old who came from the village of *Siuxtun* (modern Santa Barbara), and the 1819 record from the same mission shows a 33-year-old who was originally from the village of *Cajats* on Santa Cruz Island. These records, limited as they are, demonstrate the widespread distribution of *'aqi* throughout Chumash and neighboring territories, unlike other specialists who were tied to particular resources that were locally available. The distribution of *'aqi* more greatly resembles the members of the *'antap* society, who were found widely dispersed throughout the Chumash area.

'ANTAP SPECIALIZATIONS

The organization of the *'antap* religion comprised an overlapping of economic, political and religious elites in Chumash society; membership was compulsory for the *wot* (chief) and his or her family, and was probably mandatory for *'altomolich* (canoemakers) and other high-status occupational specialists as well (Blackburn 1976: 236–37; Hudson et al. 1978: 156). As such, this religious/political network served to integrate various social and economic aspects of Chumash society throughout a far-flung territory, organizing the *gremios* that cross-cut localized affiliations and had a kinship-based charter (Blackburn 1975: 10, 1976: 236–37).

The ritual practitioners of the *'antap* society were specialists who maintained esoteric knowledge, songs, dances, and language appropriate to specific tasks or duties. One official, the *liwimpshut* or 'custodian of the algebra', was an expert in treating skeletal ailments and divining information from human and animal bones (Hudson et al. 1977: 25, 101, note 29). Others specialized in administering *Datura* to adolescent boys, naming children, interpreting astrology, curing with herbs, making rain, collecting information for the *wot*, and acting as symbolic or actual executioner, among other tasks (see Hudson and Underhay 1978: chap. 2).

It is possible that the specialization of *'antap* officials was a late development in the religion, but that an incipient form of the society existed prior to the Late or Historic Periods (see below). Perhaps the specializations within the *'antap* organization mirrored occupational specializations in the larger Chumash society during the Late and Historic Periods.

Integration of *'aqi* and *'antap*

For a comparative model of such an integrated ritual/political network, it is possible to turn to the ethnographic literature of the neighboring Yokuts and Mono people. Gayton's

(1930) classic study of the 'unholy alliance' between Yokuts chiefs and shamans (and perhaps other ritual specialists) most likely is a close parallel of the Chumash situation (Blackburn 1976: 233). Gayton's (1948: 106) consultants stated that if there were not enough undertakers available, the Yokuts chief could appoint women to help the undertaker, and that all these people were referred to as *tono'cim* (undertaker/third gender). Among the Chumash, dancers and singers were kept on payroll by the *wot* (Blackburn 1976: 237), and it may be that the *'aqi* were similarly 'salaried' by the chief, in addition to the fee paid by the deceased's family for burial.

As important ritual practitioners, *'aqi* were most likely consulted by *'antap* officials when scheduling the periodic mourning ceremony that brought together people from throughout Chumash territory, and even beyond (see Blackburn 1976: 237). Indeed, descriptions of the activities of the Yokuts *tono'cim* at the periodic mourning ceremony closely parallel that of the 'poisoner' in Chumash rituals. The Yokuts undertakers would symbolically capture audience members as hostages, and extract payment for their release, despite their already liberal payment (Kroeber 1925: 500–01); according to popular Chumash belief, the *'antap* practitioner called *'altipatushwu* would select a wealthy person from a rich and populous village, and begin to poison him/her months before the mourning ceremony, extorting payment for a cure (Blackburn 1976: 237–38). The chief paid the poisoner a percentage of the mourning ceremony 'take' or popular contribution, in the event of the victim's death (Blackburn 1976: 238).

These similarities are indicative of the widespread distribution of comparable religious beliefs throughout south-central California (Hudson and Blackburn 1978: 225). In addition to the twelve *'antap* members in each sizeable Chumash village, the society existed on the provincial level (Blackburn 1976: 236; Hudson and Underhay 1978: 29), and even cross-cut linguistic boundaries (Hudson and Blackburn 1978: 238; Hudson and Underhay 1978: 27, 32). The virtually identical terminology used to identify ritual specialists throughout the region lends support to this conclusion, and suggests panethnic interaction in ceremonial contexts (Hudson and Blackburn 1978: 240).

Given the apparent religious connections between the Chumash and their neighbors, it is possible to consider the *'aqi* in light of information from other groups in the south-central California region. The descriptions of third gender undertakers among the Yokuts, Mono, and Tubatulabal are remarkably similar to those of the Chumash (Hollimon 1997). It is possible that these various societies shared fundamental ideas about the disposal of the dead, and the importance of entrusting this duty to those with the proper supernatural endowment. These people were apparently those whose sexual activity did not result in procreation, a hallmark of spiritual capability in the cosmology of peoples throughout the region (see Hollimon n.d.b).

ANTIQUITY OF THE *'ANTAP* SOCIETY AND THE *'AQI* GUILD

There is some controversy with regard to the age and evolution of the *'antap* organization. According to the available ethnographic and ethnohistoric information, Hudson et al. (1977: 4, 11) concluded that the society was a protohistoric phenomenon, dating no earlier than the sixteenth century AD. In part, they base this conclusion on the similarities between some *'antap* beliefs and Christianity, a situation that apparently was paralleled in the *Chinigchinich* religion of the Luiseño; these religions may be indigenous responses to the imposition of Catholicism (Hudson et al. 1977: 4).

In contrast, some archaeological studies have concluded that ritual specialists were present and socially recognized during the Early Period. Mortuary studies, such as those of Late (L. King 1982: 455–61) and Historic Period (Martz 1984: 484) mainland cemeteries have documented burials with fairly clear *'antap* associations (Hollimon 1990: 140, 146). These inclusions, such as turtle shell rattles, wands, and quartz crystals, have also been documented in Early, Middle, Transitional, and Late Period cemeteries on Santa Cruz Island (Hollimon 1990: 153).

The presence of recognized burial areas with systematic treatment of the dead has been documented among Early Period sites in the Santa Barbara Channel area, *c.* 7500–2600 BP (C. King 1990: 28, 95). While variations in burial treatment exist in Early Period cemeteries (C. King 1990: 95), this evidence suggests a well-established mortuary program, presumably integrated with incipient eschatological concepts that were greatly elaborated by the Late/Historic period (see Blackburn 1975: 32–33; Hudson and Blackburn 1978: 246).

Material correlates of craft specialization have been documented in the Santa Barbara Channel area, such as the tools and by-products associated with the manufacture of drills, plank canoes, and shell beads (see Arnold 1987: 31–33, 1992). The presence of items associated with these specializations has been found in mortuary contexts throughout the Chumash region. Burials suggesting distinct statuses in Chumash society occur during all prehistoric periods. Those with accompaniments suggesting craft specialization are more common during the Late Period than during earlier times. This may be due to the relative ease of identifying paraphernalia associated with particular specializations that have been documented ethnographically or ethnohistorically, such as canoe planks and bead-making tools (see Hollimon 1990: 153).

In contrast to craft specializations, in which a material item is produced, the occupational specialization of undertaking featured a tool kit whose items were not unique to the profession. Digging-stick weights and basketry impressions could be associated with food gathering, as well as with grave digging. On this basis alone, the existence of the undertaking professional guild is difficult, if not impossible, to identify unambiguously in the archaeological record.

While it may be impossible at present to establish the antiquity of the *'aqi* guild through specific material correlates, other forms of archaeological data may provide evidence of this specialization. In a study of several hundred burials from Santa Cruz Island, many male burials were found to contain either digging-stick weights or basketry impressions, but only two included both artifacts that may be indicative of the undertaker's tool kit. One is dated to the Early Period, and the individual was about 18 years old at the time of death (Hollimon 1996: 206). A male burial from a Middle Period (*c.* 2600–80 BP) site on Santa Cruz Island displays a pattern of spinal arthritis characteristic of Early Period females, despite the relatively young age (about 18 years) of the individual (Hollimon 1996: 206; Walker and Hollimon 1989: 176).

When considering the markers of status in burial contexts from this region, it must be kept in mind that the majority of the deceased's property was destroyed, either at the time of death, or at a periodic mourning ceremony. This is based on cosmological beliefs about the tendency of the dead to remain around their belongings, rather than departing for *Šimilaqsa*, or the Land of the Dead (Hollimon 1997, n.d.a; L. King 1969). The burial accompaniments in Santa Barbara Channel area graves likely reflect more about the loved ones of the deceased than about the deceased him/herself (see L. King 1982).

Possible exceptions can be inferred from documentary evidence about the Brotherhood of the *Tomol*. Hudson et al. (1978: 154) discuss the two types of property belonging to members of the *gremio*: personal property, and property belonging to the Brotherhood as a corporate entity. The latter could include knowledge, tools, and other aspects relevant to the construction and use of canoes; sacred medicines, herbs, charms and other ceremonial paraphernalia to ensure supernatural aid; and possibly a financial share, in the form of bead money, in the economic activities undertaken by the *gremio* (Hudson et al. 1978: 154). This type of property would revert back to the *gremio* upon the death of a brother, and would be distributed to a new member upon acceptance into the guild (Hudson et al. 1978: 154).

Several sources indicate that canoe effigies, and other forms of personal property, were buried with *tomol* guild members (L. King 1969: 51). The *tomol* itself was either burned whole (Heizer 1955: 156), or knocked to pieces and then burned (L. King 1969: 51). Canoe planks have been recorded in numerous burials (Hollimon 1990: table 15, after Kohler 1977). These data suggest that the status of a Chumash craft specialist may be marked in a mortuary context, unlike 'average' persons, whose grave accompaniments were most likely the belongings of relatives (see Arnold 1987: 235; L. King 1982; Martz 1984). Perhaps the basketry fragments and digging-stick weights of *'aqi* could be included in their graves, either as personal property marking guild membership, or as tokens of esteem from other guild members.

Caution in the interpretation of mortuary remains must still be exercised, however. For example, the presence of a canoe drill in the burial of a Middle Period female (Hollimon 1990: 142) may indicate either that she was a 'brother' in the *tomol* guild, or that she was related to someone who was, who then placed this implement in her grave.

If, as several analyses suggest, the status of occupational specialist was indeed one that was symbolically important in Chumash society (see L. King 1982; Martz 1984), then the undertaking profession might be similarly marked in a mortuary context. Support for this inference has been described in the examples of biological males buried with elements of the undertaker's tool kit.

ANTIQUITY OF OTHER GUILDS

Archaeological, ethnographic, and ethnohistoric information indicate that Chumash professional guilds, if not craft specializations, were a Late Period phenomenon (*c.* post-80 BP). Archaeological evidence of possible craft specializations, with designated manufacturing sites, centralized control over resources and finished products, and high volume and standardization of production (see Arnold 1987: xiii–xiv), may date to the Middle or even Early Periods (Michael Glassow, personal communication 1990). It is possible that some craft specializations, such as steatite object manufacture, were operating at lower levels of intensity than those that have been documented at Late Period sites (see Arnold 1987, 1992; Munns and Arnold 1991).

The presence of professional guilds per se appears to be limited to the Late Period. For example, the *tomol* was apparently invented about 1,500 years ago, during the Middle Period, but canoe paraphernalia in burial contexts is limited to the transitional time between the Middle and Late Periods, in excess of 500 years later (see Hudson et al. 1978; Hollimon 1990: 160; L. King 1982; Martz 1984). Perhaps this reflects the development of the *tomol* guild during the ensuing era, which restricted access to canoe-related knowledge and paraphernalia, and the concomitant social recognition that members were set apart from the rest of the populace.

Burial inclusions of caches of microliths, associated with the manufacture of beads, are also primarily found in Late Period graves (Hollimon 1990: 160), perhaps indicating that individuals belonging to a formal organization, such as canoe- or bowmakers, were present only during the Late Period (see Arnold 1992: 73–74). It should be noted, however, that there are burials containing caches of unworked *Olivella* shells (raw material for beads) in Early Period Santa Cruz Island graves (Hollimon 1990: 153–54; see also table 12 for a list of material indicators of various statuses documented ethnographically and ethnohistorically).

Evolution of guilds

The lack of clear archaeological indicators of the *'aqi* and other occupational specialists limits the assessment of the timing and precise nature of the formation of guilds in Chumash society. However, informed speculation about the evolution of specialists' organizations is warranted.

It is possible that the *'aqi* were among the first occupational specialists in prehistoric Chumash society. As noted above, burial inclusions associated historically with *'antap* ceremonialism have been found in Early Period sites in the Santa Barbara Channel region. The evidence that has led to a preliminary identification of an *'aqi* burial also comes from an Early Period cemetery. It may be that the earliest form of the *'antap* religion was coterminous with the formation of the undertaking guild.

Without doubt, the need to dispose of the dead was a ubiquitous requirement throughout the area during all prehistoric periods. It could be argued that the elaboration of beliefs in the *'antap* religion were, in part, a result of contact with other belief systems, such as Catholicism (see p. 179–80). However, it seems likely that the established burial program evident at least by the beginning of the Early Period reflects some fundamental belief about the ultimate disposition of the dead. The detailed descriptions of the journey to *Similaqsa* (see Hollimon n.d.a) may have been developed relatively late in Chumash prehistory, but minimally, the burial program suggests that there was an acknowledgment of an afterlife in some form.

If the specializations within the *'antap* organization were part of a larger trend toward economic, ritual and political specialization in Chumash society, then an antecedent form of specialization, and perhaps a template for later forms, could be found among the *'aqi*. The aspects of fictive kinship, geographical distribution, and integration of *'aqi* functions with *'antap* organization (in whatever form) may have served as models for other guilds that were in place by the Late and/or Historic Periods, such as the Brotherhood of the *Tomol*.

DECLINE OF THE UNDERTAKING GUILD

The activities of the *'aqi* surely were impacted by the Spanish missionary effort in the Chumash region. Perhaps most profoundly, the institution of Catholic burial programs and designated mission cemeteries would have usurped the traditional responsibilities of the *'aqi*. The imposition of Catholic practices, in combination with a tremendously high death rate among mission populations (Walker and Johnson 1992, 1994) would undoubtedly have contributed to the disintegration of the guild. For example, historic period sources describe grave digging by normative men, and the abolishment of indigenous funerary practices by the Spanish padres (Hudson 1980: 73–76).

Another aspect of the *'aqi*, to which the Spanish paid great attention, was cross-dressing among male-bodied persons (see Heizer and Whipple 1971: 259; Hemert-Engert and Teggart 1910: 137). This presumably would not have been tolerated within the mission system, although there is no information about the sartorial circumstances of the *joyas* identified in mission documents. One of Harrington's consultants, Maria Solares, indicated that Fernando Librado *Kitsepawit* (died 1915) was *'aqi* (L. King 1969: 47–48), although her identification may have been an intended insult based on personal animosity (Johnson, personal communication 1995). If the lifelong bachelor was an *'aqi*, he did not cross-dress, or provide Harrington with any information to indicate that he was an undertaker (see Hudson 1980, Hudson et al. 1977).

CONCLUSION

The examination of sexuality in the archaeological record is one means of addressing the dynamics of pre-contact Chumash society. This chapter has discussed various lines of evidence, including ethnohistoric information about third gender occupational specialization. These data suggest that sexuality and gender were important organizing principles in Chumash society before the mission period, and that they influenced many aspects of ritual and labor, and may have served as a model for other forms of occupational specialization.

I have suggested that the organization of undertakers, a role that encompassed non-procreative sexuality, gender identification, occupational specialization, and supernatural power, was one that may have pre-dated other forms of labor organization in the Santa Barbara Channel area. Specifically, the occupational guilds documented in the ethnographic and ethnohistoric literature may have had the undertakers' society as a model for their formation. The geographic distribution of undertaking guild members, their integration with the *'antap* society, and fictive kinship of the non-reproductive *'aqi* have been suggested as templates for the formation of later guilds, such as the Brotherhood of the *Tomol*.

While it is an open question whether gender classification follows sexual orientation or vice versa, it should be noted that the archaeological examination of sexuality must include the study of gender also. The assumption that the sexual repertoire of prehistoric societies was limited to 'heterosexual' relations is an idea that must be questioned. The possibility of gender diversity in prehistoric cultures should be considered alongside the examination of sexuality. While archaeological evidence of specific sex acts may be virtually impossible to recover, it is possible to view sexuality in terms of its organization, symbolism, and its articulation with larger social systems, such as kinship and marriage, division of labor, and ritual (Roscoe, personal communication).

Similarly, the interpretation of material culture must take these perspectives into account to fully understand the function of particular objects in these integrated and embedded systems. For example, the baskets used by Chumash women to collect, store, and process food may look identical in style to the ones used by *'aqi* to dig graves. Similarly, the weights placed on digging sticks used to harvest bulbs and roots might be identical to those used by *'aqi* to excavate graves.

However, these artifacts functioned in very different ways, as prescribed by Chumash culture. The undertakers' baskets had to be unused, and after digging the grave, were then given to the *'aqi* as a form of payment. This is consistent with the belief that ordinary people and their property must not come in contact with the corpse or grave, because of their supernatural power and potential for harm. If a woman's food processing basket, as a life-giving or life-sustaining symbol, were to be used in a context of death, this might entice the deceased's spirit to remain, rather than completing its journey to the afterlife.

Following this argument, a basket or digging-stick weight that had been used to excavate a grave could never be returned to a function related to food, because it had been in contact with the potentially harmful power of the corpse. Without this consideration of the undertaker's tool kit, we might immediately assume that all basket fragments and digging-stick weights are merely food-related items.

This example demonstrates the need to consider issues relating to gender and sexuality in the examination of material culture from archaeological contexts. As researchers dealing with past societies, we must ask questions such as, 'when is a basket not just a basket?' in order to reach a fuller, richer understanding of these cultures. Given that sexuality, in some form or other, is a human universal, we must address these variables if we hope to understand the lives of prehistoric peoples in all their aspects.

REFERENCES

Applegate, R. (1977) 'Native California Concepts of the Afterlife', in T. Blackburn (ed.) *Flowers of the Wind: Papers on Ritual, Myth and Symbolism in California and the South-west*, Socorro: New Mexico: Ballena.

Arnold, J. E. (1987) *Craft Specialization in the Prehistoric Channel Islands, California*, Berkeley: University of California Press.

—— (1992) 'Complex Hunter-Gatherer-Fishers of Prehistoric California: Chiefs, Specialists, and Maritime Adaptations of the Channel Islands', *American Antiquity* 57, 1: 60–84.

—— (1997) 'Bigger Boats, Crowded Creekbanks: Environmental Stresses in Perspective', *American Antiquity* 62, 2: 337–39.

Arnold, J. E., R. H. Colten and S. Pletka (1997) 'Contexts of Cultural Change in Insular California', *American Antiquity* 62, 2: 300–18.

Balzer, M. M. (1996) 'Sacred Genders in Siberia: Shamans, Bear Festivals, and Androgyny', in S. P. Ramet (ed.) *Gender Reversals and Gender Cultures*, London: Routledge.

Beeler, M. S. (1967) 'The Ventureño Confesionario of Jose Senan, O. F. M.', *University of California Publications in Linguistics* 47: 1–79.

Blackburn, T. C. (1975) *December's Child*, Berkeley: University of California.

—— (1976) 'Ceremonial Integration and Social Interaction in Aboriginal California', in L. J. Bean and T. C. Blackburn (eds) *Native Californians: A Theoretical Retrospective*, Socorro, New Mexico: Ballena.

Bolin, A. (1996) 'Traversing Gender: Cultural Context and Gender Practices', in S. P. Ramet (ed.) *Gender Reversals and Gender Cultures*, London: Routledge.

Callender, C. and L. M. Kochems (1983) 'The North American Berdache', *Current Anthropology* 24: 433–56.

—— (1986) 'Men and Not-Men: Male Gender-Mixing Statuses and Homosexuality', in E. Blackwood (ed.) *The Many Faces of Homosexuality*, New York: Harrington Park.

Claassen, C. (ed.) (1992) *Exploring Gender Through Archaeology*, Madison, Wisconsin: Prehistory Press.

Costello, J. G. and D. Hornbeck (1989) 'Alta California: An Overview', in D. H. Thomas (ed.) *Columbian Consequences, vol. 1: Archaeological and Historical Perspectives on the Spanish Borderlands West*, Washington: Smithsonian.

Cromwell, J. (1997) 'Traditions of Gender Diversity and Sexualities: A Female-to-Male Transgendered Perspective', in S. Jacobs, W. Thomas, and S. Lang (eds) *Two-Spirit People: Native American Gender Identity, Sexuality and Spirituality*, Urbana: University of Illinois Press.

Devereux, G. (1937) 'Institutionalized Homosexuality of the Mohave Indians', *Human Biology* 9, 7: 498–527.

Fulton, R. and S. W. Anderson (1992) 'The Amerindian "Man-Woman": Gender, Liminality and Cultural Continuity', *Current Anthropology* 33, 5: 603–610.

Gayton, A. H. (1930) 'Yokuts-Mono Chiefs and Shamans', *University of California Publications in American Archaeology and Ethnology* 24: 361–420.

—— (1948) 'Yokuts and Western Mono Ethnography II: Northern Foothill Yokuts and Western Mono', *University of California Anthropological Records* 10: 2.

Guerra, F. (1971) *The Pre-Columbian Mind*, London: Seminar.

Heizer, R. F. (1955) 'The Mission Indian Vocabularies of H. W. Henshaw', *University of California Anthropological Records* 15, 2: 85–202.

Heizer, R. F. and M. A. Whipple (eds) (1971) *The California Indians: A Source Book*, Berkeley: University of California Press.

Hemert-Engert, A. and F. J. Teggart (eds) (1910) 'The Narrative of the Portola Expedition of 1769–1770, by Miguel Costanso', *Publications of the Academy of Pacific Coast History* 1, 4: 91–159.

Hollimon, S. E. (1990) 'Division of Labor and Gender Roles in Santa Barbara Channel Area Prehistory', unpublished Ph.D. dissertation, University of California, Santa Barbara.

—— (1996) 'Sex, Gender and Health Among the Chumash: An Archaeological Examination of Prehistoric Gender Roles', in J. Reed (ed.) *Proceedings of the Society for California Archaeology* 9: 205–08.

—— (1997) 'The Third Gender in Native California: Two-Spirit Undertakers Among the Chumash and Their Neighbors', in C. Claassen and R. Joyce (eds) *Women in Prehistory: North America and Mesoamerica*, Philadelphia: University of Pennsylvania Press.

—— (n.d.a) 'Death and Gender in Chumash Cosmology and Ritual: Archaeological Implications and Interpretations', paper presented at the meetings of the American Anthropological Association, Washington, DC, 1997.

—— (n.d.b) '"Berdaches", Giants, and Cannibals: Depictions of Gender and Humanness in Native North American Myths', paper presented at the 14th International Congress of Anthropological and Ethnological Sciences, College of William and Mary, August 1998.

Hudson, T. (ed.) (1980) *Breath of the Sun: Life in Early California as told by a Chumash Indian, Fernando Librado Kitsepawit to John P. Harrington*, Banning: Malki Museum Press.

Hudson, T. and T. Blackburn (1978) 'The Integration of Myth and Ritual in South-Central California: The "Northern Complex"', *Journal of California Anthropology* 5, 2: 225–50.

Hudson, T., T. Blackburn, R. Curletti and J. Timbrook (eds) (1977) *The Eye of the Flute: Chumash Traditional History and Ritual as Told by Fernando Librado Kitsepawit to John P. Harrington*, Santa Barbara: Museum of Natural History.

Hudson, T., J. Timbrook and M. Rempe (eds) (1978) Tomol: *Chumash Watercraft as described in the Ethnographic Notes of John P. Harrington*, Socorro, New Mexico: Ballena.

Hudson, T. and E. Underhay (1978) *Crystals in the Sky: An Intellectual Odyssey Involving Chumash Astronomy, Cosmology and Rock Art*, Santa Barbara: Museum of Natural History.

Jacobs, S. and J. Cromwell (1992) 'Visions and Revisions of Reality: Reflections on Sex, Sexuality, Gender and Gender Variance', *Journal of Homosexuality* 23, 4: 43–69.

Jacobs, S., W. Thomas and S. Lang (eds) (1997) *Two-Spirit People: Native American Gender Identity, Sexuality and Spirituality*, Urbana: University of Illinois Press.

Johnson, J. R. (1988) 'Chumash Social Organization: An Ethnohistoric Perspective', unpublished Ph.D. dissertation, University of California, Santa Barbara.

—— (1989) 'The Chumash and the Missions', in D. H. Thomas (ed.) *Columbian Consequences, vol. 1: Archaeological and Historical Perspectives on the Spanish Borderlands West*, Washington: Smithsonian.

Katz, J. (1976) *Gay American History*, New York: Thomas Y. Crowell.

Kessler, S. and McKenna, W. (1978) *Gender: An Ethnomethodological Approach*, New York: Wiley.

King, C. D. (1990) *Evolution of Chumash Society: A Comparative Study of Artifacts Used for Social System Maintenance in the Santa Barbara Channel Region before AD 1804*, New York: Garland.

King, L. B. (1969) 'The Medea Creek Cemetery (LAN-243): An Investigation of Social Organization from Mortuary Practices', *UCLA Archaeological Survey Annual Report* 11: 23–68.

—— (1982) 'Medea Creek Cemetery: Late Inland Patterns of Social Organization, Exchange and Warfare', unpublished Ph.D. dissertation, University of California, Los Angeles.

King, T. F. (1978) 'Don't That Beat the Band? Nonegalitarian Political Organization in Prehistoric Central California', in C. L. Redman, M. J. Berman, E. V. Curtin, W. T. Langhorne, Jr, N. M. Versaggi and J. C. Wanser (eds) *Social Archeology: Beyond Subsistence and Dating*, New York: Academic Press.

Kohler, L. (1977) 'Evidence for the Chumash Plank Canoe', *Pacific Coast Archaeological Survey Quarterly* 13, 3: 61–75.

Kroeber, A. L. (1925) *Handbook of the Indians of California*, Washington: Smithsonian.

Kulick, D. (1997) 'The Gender of Brazilian Transgendered Prostitutes', *American Anthropologist* 99, 3: 574–85.

Lang, S. (1996) 'There is More Than Just Women and Men: Gender Variance in North American Indian Cultures', in S. P. Ramet (ed.) *Gender Reversals and Gender Cultures*, London: Routledge.

—— (1997) 'Various Kinds of Two-Spirit People', in S. Jacobs, W. Thomas and S. Lang (eds) *Two-Spirit People: Native American Gender Identity, Sexuality and Spirituality*, Urbana: University of Illinois Press.

—— (1998) *Men as Women, Women as Men: Changing Gender in Native American Cultures*, J. L. Vantine (trans.), Austin: University of Texas Press.

Lorant, S. (1946) *The New World*, New York: Duell, Sloan and Pearce.

Martz, P. C. (1984) 'Social Dimensions of Chumash Mortuary Populations in the Santa Monica Mountains Region', unpublished Ph.D. dissertation, University of California, Riverside.

Miller, J. (1982) 'People, Berdaches, and Left-Handed Bears: Human Variation in Native America', *Journal of Anthropological Research* 38: 274–87.

Munns, A. and J. E. Arnold (1991) 'The Organization of Shell Bead Production on California's Northern Channel Islands', paper presented at the 56th Annual Meeting of the Society for American Archaeology, New Orleans.

Poole, F. J. P. (1996) 'The Procreative and Ritual Constitution of Female, Male, and Other: Androgynous Beings in the Cultural Imagination of the Bimin-Kuskusmin of Papua New Guinea', in S. P. Ramet (ed.) *Gender Reversals and Gender Cultures*, London: Routledge.

Raab, L. M. (1996) 'Debating Prehistory in Coastal Southern California: Resource Intensification Versus Political Economy', *Journal of California and Great Basin Anthropology* 18, 1: 64–80.

Raab, L. M. and K. Bradford (1997) 'Making Nature Answer to Interpretivism: Response to J. E. Arnold, R. H. Colten and S. Pletka', *American Antiquity* 62, 2: 340–41.

Raab, L. M. and D. O. Larson (1997) 'Medieval Climatic Anomaly and Punctuated Cultural Evolution in Coastal Southern California', *American Antiquity* 62, 2: 319–36.

Roscoe, W. (1987) 'A Bibliography of Berdache and Alternative Gender Roles among North American Indians', *Journal of Homosexuality* 14: 81–171.

—— (1991) *The Zuni Man-Woman*, Albuquerque: University of New Mexico Press.

—— (1994) 'How to Become a Berdache: Toward a Unified Analysis of Gender Diversity', in G. Herdt (ed.) *Third Gender, Third Sex*, New York: Zone Books.

—— (1995) 'Was We'wha a Homosexual? Native American Survivance and the Two-Spirit Tradition', *GLQ* 2: 193–235.

—— (1998) *Changing Ones: Third and Fourth Genders in Native North America*, New York: St. Martin's.

Thayer, J. S. (1980) 'The Berdache of the Northern Plains: A Socio-religious Perspective', *Journal of Anthropological Research* 36: 287–93.

Thomas, W. (1997) 'Navajo Cultural Constructions of Gender and Sexuality', in S. Jacobs, W. Thomas and S. Lang (eds) *Two-Spirit People: Native American Gender Identity, Sexuality and Spirituality*, Urbana: University of Illinois Press.

Walker, P. L. and S. E. Hollimon (1989) 'Changes in Osteoarthritis Associated with the Development of a Maritime Economy Among Southern California Indians', *International Journal of Anthropology* 4, 3: 171–83.

Walker, P. L. and J. R. Johnson. (1992) 'Effects of Contact on the Chumash Indians', in J. W. Verano and D. H. Ubelaker (eds) *Disease and Demography in the Americas*, Washington: Smithsonian.

—— (1994) 'The Decline of the Chumash Indian Population', in C. S. Larsen and G. R. Milner (eds) *In the Wake of Contact: Biological Responses to Conquest*, New York: Wiley-Liss.

Walker, P. L., P. Lambert and M. J. DeNiro (1989) 'The Effects of European Contact on the Health of Alta California Indians', in D. H. Thomas (ed.) *Columbian Consequences, vol. 1: Archaeological and Historical Perspectives on the Spanish Borderlands West*, Washington: Smithsonian.

White, E. (1980) *States of Desire: Travels in Gay America*, New York: E. P. Dutton.

Whitehead, H. (1981) 'The Bow and the Burden Strap: A New Look at Institutionalized Homosexuality in Native North America', in S. B. Ortner and H. Whitehead (eds) *Sexual Meanings: The Cultural Construction of Gender and Sexuality*, Cambridge: Cambridge University Press.

Williams, W. (1986) *The Spirit and the Flesh: Sexual Diversity in American Indian Culture*, Boston: Beacon.

Yates, L. (1957) 'Fragments of the History of a Lost Tribe', *University of California Archaeological Survey Report* 38: 36–39.

Chapter Eleven

Searching for third genders: towards a prehistory of domestic space in Middle Missouri villages

Elizabeth Prine

INTRODUCTION

Berdaches, or Two Spirit people,[1] were Native Americans whose identity combined some of the gender characteristics associated with men with some of those associated with women. 'Gender' in this case refers to the culturally and socially constructed identities and actions that are commonly associated with biological sex. For instance, the gender category 'woman' generally coincides with the biological category 'female', while biological 'males' are typically gendered as 'men'. A Two Spirit's biological sex could be either male or female, but berdaches' genders were neither those of men nor those of women – they were something unique and different, a third and a fourth gender.

Given the two-gendered traditions of most contemporary cultures, the existence of genders other than women and men is anthropologically intriguing. One area of interest has been berdaches' sexuality. Were they homosexual, heterosexual, bisexual, or abstinent? Given the cultural diversity of indigenous North America, it is not surprising that little consensus exists as to this question (see, for example, Epple 1998 and Roscoe 1998 for very different perspectives on the question). Research on berdaches and their sexuality is complicated by Two Spirits' simultaneous ubiquity and invisibility in the past – while Roscoe (1998: 7) has found ethnohistorical references to berdaches for some 155 Native American tribal groups, to date his biography of We'wha (1991) and his collection of biographical essays on other Two Spirit people (1998) are the only lengthy discussions published about individual berdaches. Work by other authors has explored berdache life from a broadly cross-cultural perspective (e.g. Callender and Kochems 1983; Fulton and Anderson 1992; Whitehead 1981), through ethnohistoric and ethnographic case studies (Epple 1998; Hauser 1990), and through anthropological film (Beauchemin et al. 1991). These studies share basic agreement in some areas, such as the definition that anatomically male and female berdaches in fact existed and that they did indeed comprise socially recognized genders. Yet the studies disagree on other fundamental questions, such as the sexuality and cultural meanings associated with Two Spiritedness.

Given the confusion arising from pan-Indian research on berdaches, these questions are perhaps best answered through close readings of the ethnographic, historic, and archaeological records. This chapter is such a study, in this case of Hidatsa berdaches. It focuses on ways to connect evidence from these three subdisciplines of historical anthropology in order to elucidate the ways archaeologists might envision sexuality in the past. While archaeologists of protohistory are often fluent in the historic documentation of their era and locale, our main concern is with the material remains of the cultures in question. Sexual behavior is for the most part non-material; biologically speaking, sexual activity requires no exclusive space or artifacts, although it often occurs in conjunction with such due to the cultural expectations of the individual(s) involved. Sexual identity-making and other sexualized activities occur today in a variety of places and with a variety of accoutrements; a contemporary ethnoarchaeologist of sexuality might find it quite difficult to disentangle the symbol systems inherent in Americans' sexual behaviors, let alone those of our sexual identities. If it is difficult to use ethnoarchaeological data to approach sexuality within our own culture in a definitive way, how then can we approach past sexuality with archaeology? It seems a difficult task, even provided that we narrow the fields of time, cultural affiliation, and gender considerably to nineteenth-century Hidatsa berdaches. Before moving to archaeological data, however, problems concerning the relations between archaeological theory, archaeological evidence, and sexuality must be addressed.

THEORIZING SEXUALITY AND ARCHAEOLOGY

Archaeologists are students of material culture. Because our work relies on material culture, we tend to follow the 'ladder of inference' defined by Hawkes (1954) and reiterated by Binford (1962): that archaeological methods produce more data on technology than on economics, more on economics than on social organization, and more on social organization than on symbol systems. We presume we can move from the lower rungs of the ladder to a higher level via a chain of evidence. For instance, we might interpret a stone blade first as evidence of a particular sequence of flintknapping (after Crabtree 1974), and then as evidence of a subsequent activity, like cutting grain or meat (after Tringham et al. 1974). These are fairly straightforward deductions given the current state of technological scholarship in archaeology. Attempts at moving beyond blade manufacture and use push us to the limits of inference, for in suggesting a richer picture of the past – in attempting to envision *who* made or used the blade – we find ourselves on the slippery slope of presupposition. In this case, our starting presumptions about whether tool production and food processing are the domains of a single or of different demographic groups would certainly lead us to multiple constructions of the past (see Wylie 1991 for a discussion of the roles of gender preconceptions in constructions of the past; the relation between archaeologists' internalization of contemporary gender roles and the visual imagery we produce has been especially well deconstructed, e.g. Moser 1992a, 1992b).

What of sexuality? Can archaeologists find it as we 'find' tool production techniques? For the purposes of this paper I define sexuality as sexual behaviors and sexual identity as their enactment in the public and private realms. In this definition I draw on practice theory – the idea that the repeated daily activities that individuals enact constitute a set of practices or habits indicative of the nature of the human experience in a particular cultural–historical milieu (Bourdieu 1977; Foucault 1970; Giddens 1979, 1984). This approach demands that one examine the routines and anomalies of daily life for evidence relating to the subject at hand – in this case, sexually-charged identity-making behavior.

For the most part, practice theory was designed by and for scholars working with living people such as Bourdieu's bourgeoisie (1984) or with well-documented historical events such as Foucault's infamous legal cases (1977). In its first widely disseminated application within anthropology, Henrietta Moore (1986) used practice theory to demonstrate that the material and symbolic production of Marakwet gender and space are so dialectically interconnected as to be barely intelligible when viewed separately. Notably, early practice theorists' work appeared in translation at a moment when some archaeologists were becoming concerned that New Archaeology's highly quantitative approaches ignored some nuances of the human condition (cf. Hodder 1982, 1985; Leone 1982, 1984; Miller and Tilley 1984).

A major concern of processualism has been to clarify the relation between evidential and inferential statements (Binford 1967, 1978; Gould and Watson 1982; Raab and Goodyear 1984; Schiffer 1972, 1984; Watson 1984; Watson et al. 1971). Many post-processualists have also worked to clarify this relation by identifying and problematizing so-called 'hidden' (in the sense of 'hiding in plain sight') sources of bias in archaeological scholarship. In prehistory, gender research has been especially productive in this arena (cf. Conkey and Spector 1984; Conkey and Williams 1991; Gero and Conkey 1991; Wylie 1982a, 1982b, 1985, 1992a, 1992b). In historical archaeology, research on gender, class, and race have all exposed 'hidden' agendas in either the present or the past (e.g. Ferguson 1992; Hall 1995; Markell et al. 1995; McGuire and Paynter 1991).

Despite the fact that our data sources are quite different from those of the early practice theorists, a number of archaeologists feel that approaches based on practice theory can enrich our understandings of the past (e.g. Bender 1992, 1993; Conkey 1991; Dobres and Hoffman 1994, 1999; Johnson 1989, 1991, 1993, 1996). Although the confrontational dynamic of academic discourse has not encouraged processualists and post-processualists to collaborate on specific problems, the use of practice theory nonetheless allows us to tighten the synthetic relation between deductive and inductive reasoning – it allows us to move between processualist and post-processualist views, between quantitative measurements and symbolic meanings, and between particularism and generalization within a given cultural context precisely because it requires us to look at the repetitive behaviors that both theoretical genres cite as evidence. While more humanistic methodologies will probably never outweigh more quantitative approaches to archaeology (nor, in my opinion, should they), they can open archaeologists' minds to alternative explanations for the material record – an important component of any study that attempts to move from the etic to the emic.

Practice theory may provide an opening for archaeological considerations of sexuality. It has already been tested in some archaeological studies of gender. Early gender research was predicated not on the idea of 'finding' men or women in the archaeological record but on allowing ourselves to 'see' them there, as Conkey and Gero make clear in their introduction to *Engendering Archaeology*:

> An engendered archaeology refuses to be limited to exploring only those aspects of the past that have been deemed 'testable' and insists, moreover, that other programs have in fact proceeded from a strongly developed theoretical position (e.g. systems theory) that itself was assumed and never subjected to a testing cycle. In this regard, gender inspections are perhaps on firmer ground than most theoretical paradigms, including systems theory, since the 'seeing' of either systems or gender in the archaeological record is a non-empirical vision. At least there is empirical evidence for women

while arguments about whether or not 'systems' are meaningful analytical units are less easily settled.

(1991: 21)

Simply put, the authors contributing to *Engendering Archaeology* worked from the presumptions that women in fact existed in the past, and that they were a substantial demographic group. They did not presume that a lack of 'women's things' meant an absence of women. Instead, they presumed that culture was as complicated in the past as it is now, that social diversity occurred in the past as today, and that it was time to include women (and other genders) in our representations of the past.

This seems to be a logical starting point for an archaeology of sexuality as well. Although the cognitive leap from gender to sexuality is fairly substantial (see Voss and Schmidt, this volume), archaeologists studying sexuality can frame questions about sexuality using similar presumptions: that culture has always been complicated, that a variety of sexualities existed in the past as they do now, that they may have been expressed in a variety of ways (or left unexpressed), and that it is time to include this understanding of past diversity in our research. If we follow the tenets of good research by making our presumptions and evidentiary links clear, our conclusions about the past should withstand criticism.

FRAMING THE VIEW: HIDATSA ARCHAEOLOGY AND ETHNOHISTORY

This chapter focuses on the behavior of a group of post-contact Native Americans; given the commercial interests of many historic observers and the material nature of the archaeological record, investigations of protohistoric cultures' economic activities (and hence, a large part of their day-to-day routines) are fairly straightforward. This is not to say that our understanding of protohistory is complete or conclusive. This is particularly true regarding sexuality, as those who recorded historical commentary on indigenous sexual practices and sexual identities generally had a stake in controlling and/or exploiting them.

Scholars of the contact period generally use a tripartite scheme to categorize Euro-American colonizers: the colonizers were missionaries, members of the military, or civilians. The historical literature on colonial missionization and military exploits is simultaneously eloquent and disturbing, and often reveals instances of rape and other forms of sexual control (see, for example, Voss, Chapter 2). Civilian colonizers were also concerned with indigenous sexuality, although many studies indicate that colonial elites framed the subject in ways which focused on controlling sexual behavior within their own, colonial, communities rather than among Native peoples. For instance, sixteenth- and seventeenth-century public preoccupation with Native men's supposed rapaciousness was clearly used as a tool for controlling colonial women's sexual behavior (e.g. Kestler 1990; Kolodny 1975; Smith 1990 discuss how the rhetoric of interracial rape continues to be used to control women's behavior). During the same period, anti-miscegenation laws were enacted to disenfranchise the children born to Native American women who had intercourse with colonizing men. In this case the point was not to control the colonizers' sexual behavior, but rather to prevent the economic 'dilution' – or equalization – that might have accompanied a diffusion of estates had mixed-race children been seen as legal heirs of white men (cf. Frederickson 1981). Thus our historical documentation of the sexual practices and sexual identification-making of colonial period Native America was for the most part written by people who neither understood, nor cared to learn, how the behavior they observed fitted

into a larger cultural milieu. As a result, history has had little to contribute to our understandings of sexuality in colonized cultures.

Archaeologists have also had little to say about Native American sexuality in the past.
In large part this has been a developmental problem – archaeologists have understandably
given basic questions of cultural chronology and delimitation precedence over research on
social identities of any kind. Research on past sexuality has been hindered more thoroughly than developmental limits might suggest, however, by archaeologists' focus on
index artifacts. This supposition holds that we cannot discuss sexuality until and unless
we find irrefutable artifactual markers of (in this case) berdaches. However, given the difficulties of reading sexuality in (or into) the ethnohistoric and archaeological records, we
must at this point look not for archaeological indices of berdaches, but for 'openings' in
archaeological contexts which might allow us to include Two Spirits and their sexuality
in our visions of the past. We can begin such an investigation by considering what is
known of the Hidatsa and Hidatsa Two Spirit people, or *miati*.

Painting the background: general contexts

The Hidatsa lived in palisaded villages along the Missouri River in North Dakota from the
fifteenth through the nineteenth centuries AD (see Figure 11.1; Ahler et al. 1991; Wood
1980). They and their neighbors, the Mandan, occupied the social and locational nexus of
the northern Plains' vast pre- and protohistoric exchange network, which Euro-American fur
traders later employed to connect urban centers such as Saint Louis to the fur-producing hin-
terlands (Wood 1974, 1985). Because of their central role in Euro-American commercial
activities, the Hidatsa have an especially extensive and well-known historic record (e.g.
Chardon 1932; Culbertson 1952; Larpenteur 1933; Maximilian of Wied–Neuwied 1966
[1843]; Smith 1980; Tabeau 1939; Wood and Thiessen 1985). Hidatsa culture history is also
well understood because of archaeological investigations sponsored by the Smithsonian
Institution's River Basin Surveys, an enormous salvage archaeology effort in operation from
1945 to 1969 (e.g. Cooper 1958; Hartle 1960; Lehmer 1954, 1971; Roberts 1960). In addition, the National Park Service conducted inventory- and mitigation-related excavations at the Knife River Indian Villages National Historic Site, the location of the three major historic period Hidatsa villages, in the 1970s and 1980s (e.g. Ahler and Swenson 1985; Ahler and Weston 1981, Ahler et al. 1980; Thiessen 1993a, 1993b, 1993c, 1993d).

What does ethnographic and archaeological research tell us about proto-
historic Hidatsa life? Oral traditions hold that the Hidatsa were invited to the region when a foraging party sighted a group of Mandan Indians on the opposite bank of the Missouri (Beckwith 1930). The Mandan were established village horticulturists, and subsequently

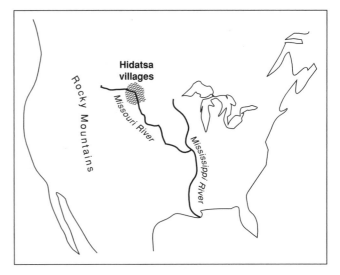

Figure 11.1 Location of the Hidatsa villages.
Illustration by the University of Wisconsin Oshkosh
Instructional Resources Center.

invited the Hidatsa to move to the region upriver in order to establish villages and gardens of their own. Arriving in three waves between about 1400 and 1600, the three linguistic divisions of the Hidatsa (the Awaxawi, Awatixa, and Hidatsa-proper) eventually settled in separate fortified villages in the grassy uplands at the confluence of the Knife and Missouri Rivers (Wood 1980).

First contact with Euro-Americans was established in the eighteenth century (Smith 1980). Contact was followed by a series of epidemics and a general heightening of inter-tribal raiding, which had long been endemic to the Plains (for an overview see Owsley and Jantz 1994; on warfare see Albers 1993; on epidemics and their effects, see Hanson 1983, McGinnis 1990). In the late eighteenth and early nineteenth centuries, the Mandan relocated to the Knife River vicinity. They had suffered particularly high losses from the smallpox epidemic of 1780–1781 and moved proximally to the Hidatsa in order to maximize protection from raiding parties (Hanson 1983). In 1845, the Hidatsa and Mandan consolidated their five independent villages into a single new town, Like-a-Fishhook village, next to the trading post at Fort Berthold (Smith 1972). The Arikara, rival villagers from areas further down the Missouri, joined the Hidatsa and Mandan at Like-a-Fishhook in 1862. Native holdings in the area have since been known as the Fort Berthold Reservation, home of the Three Affiliated Tribes. The three tribes stayed at Like-a-Fishhook until the reservation was allotted in the 1880s, when the village was abandoned in favor of individuated farmsteads (Meyer 1977).

Archaeologists and ethnohistorians assume that many of life's daily routines remained more or less the same for the Hidatsa from the 1400s through the 1800s. During the warmer months, from about March through November, extended matrifocal families lived together in large dome-shaped earthen homes at the villages on the Missouri River. In the harshest winter months, each village's population dispersed as extended families settled in hamlets in the river bottoms, where trees provided shelter and fuel. The hamlets were rebuilt at new locations each year (flooding destroyed them each spring), while the villages remained in use over centuries (Maxidiwiac 1921; Wilson 1934).

According to ethnographic sources (e.g. Maxidiwiac 1921), the Hidatsa practiced a division of labor informed by both gender and age. Women farmed corn, beans, and squash in nearby river-bottom gardens; their work provided the people with their staple foods. Women were also responsible for building and maintaining homes, cooking, leather and hide production (skinning, tanning, and making finished goods), and the rituals associated with agricultural production, migratory birds (especially waterfowl), and healing (Maxidiwiac 1921; Wilson 1917). Men focused on hunting, raiding, defense, and the rituals associated with these activities; older men also gardened small plots of ceremonial tobacco (Bowers 1992; Wilson 1924, 1928). Children were a valued part of the family and began to help their parents in adult activities at around the age of 10 or 12; grandparents were responsible for much of the routine care of younger children (Goodbird 1914; Maxidiwiac 1921; Wilson 1917).

According to Bowers (1992), the Hidatsa reckoned kinship matrilineally and lived matrilocally. Polygyny was the rule, and typical households comprised a group of senior spouses (several co-wives and their husband), their daughters, their daughters' husbands and children (if any), and the senior group's unmarried sons. Marriage was accomplished through inter-family negotiations or elopement; the former was preferred and resulted in a mutual gift exchange between the families of the marrying couple. Daughters were usually married according to birth order, and the eldest daughter's husband was treated as a preferential spouse for younger daughters – providing, of course, that the first marriage was working well. If not, marriages were easily dissolved, with the woman or women involved removing the husband's belongings from their residence and the husband returning to his natal home.

Wilson's main informant, Maxidiwiac (also known as Buffalo Bird Woman; see Maxidiwiac 1921, Wilson 1917), stated that food production and raiding were the major status activities for women and men respectively, and that many ceremonial and ritual events surrounded each. During warm weather, women worked attending their crops and enlarging their fields; additional time was spent preparing food for winter storage, making pottery, and processing animal hides. A successful woman was a good housekeeper and highly productive. Her goods were used to pay the ritual specialists who officiated at public rituals such as the NaxpikE, or Sun Dance, thereby enabling her male relatives to participate in the events and enhance their spiritual power. Older women were often amongst those officiating such rituals, and also engaged in a variety of women-centered ritual events that ensured agricultural success (Bowers 1992). Whether the majority of the participants were female or male, these public rituals ensured community, familial, and personal well-being (Harrod 1995).

Individual men also engaged regularly in private vision quests to seek spiritual guidance, power, and fortitude. Vision questing is an intensely stressful event both physically and psychologically, involving fasting and ritualized self-injury. While most men sought connection with spiritual beings through vision questing, the men who were Guardians of the several Spirit Bundles were under particular obligation to do so. According to the Hidatsa, Spirit Bundles are living entities who must be ceremonially nourished and protected; the fate of the Hidatsa was, and according to some still is, inextricably tied to the Bundles' well-being (see Meyer 1977: 206–207). The Bundles – collections of sacred materials presented to Guardians during their vision quests – in turn provide for the welfare of the people. Traditionally, each Bundle has a single Guardian who is responsible for Bundle care. Bundle Guardianship is passed from each Guardian to one of his sons or brothers, and has been among the most prestigious roles a man can play in traditional Hidatsa culture. As I discuss below, the limited number of these prestigious positions may have contributed to the creation of individual Hidatsa berdaches.

Like vision questing, men's most prestigious non-ritual activity, raiding, also conjoined the physical with the spiritual and peril with power. While ritualized warfare has a long history on the Plains, raids conducted by small parties of ten to twenty-five men began in earnest following the post-contact spread of horses (McGinnis 1990). The success of a raid was measured not in the number of enemies killed or couped, but in the safe return of all members of the raiding party. Leaders were expected to seek spiritual guidance through vision quests and to heed the directives of the spirit beings they encountered. Those leaders whose raiding forays resulted in loss of (Hidatsa) life also lost their authority; the community presumed that a failed leader had displeased one or more spiritual entities and that those entities would not discriminate between the transgressors and their followers (see Bowers 1992 for extensive discussion of the conjunctions of spiritual and raiding activities).

Some question remains as to whether the gendered and age-graded division of labor was as strict as early twentieth-century informants conveyed. Maxidiwiac's descriptions of life in her girlhood, for instance, were probably influenced by her membership in an elite family and by Gilbert Wilson's oddly juxtaposed roles as anthropologist and Presbyterian minister (see Gilman and Schneider 1987). Both contexts might have caused Maxidiwiac, or her son and translator Good Bird, to gloss or omit certain practices (berdaches, for instance, are not discussed in Wilson's work; see Prine 1996, 1997). There is no evidence for either Maxidiwiac or Good Bird embellishing their descriptions of Hidatsa life, however – their information correlates closely to the descriptions produced later by Bowers (1948, 1950, 1992), who relied on other informants. Certainly the Hidatsa material record reflects the kind of highly conservative culture often associated with strict divisions of labor. For instance, archaeological research indicates that there is only subtle (albeit important) material differentiation between the Hidatsa subgroups, and that the only major techno-logical changes that occurred in 500 years of occupation on the Knife River were those induced by Euro-American trade goods (see Prine 1998).

The equivocal nature of ethnographic and historical data can be frustrating, but these data are certainly no more or less misleading or difficult to deal with than the fragmentary evidence with which all archaeologists work. Maxidiwiac's descriptions of nineteenth-century life may be especially productive for archaeological studies of Hidatsa life, as they provide a rare emically-defined model against which to test germane archaeological data. The idealized behavioral codes of Euro-American colonizers are of course widely available to historical archaeologists (see Falk 1991), but few such models exist for in-digenous cultures. Such a model is particularly intriguing as it relates to Hidatsa Two Spirits; as I describe below, one of the defining characteristics of *miati* was their role as innovators. As the archaeological, ethnographic, and historical records all agree that Hidatsa material and behavioral cultures were quite conservative, specific types of innovations may be one way to discern the presence of berdaches at Hidatsa archaeolog-ical sites.

Adding depth to the background: Berdaches

I will limit my discussion of berdaches in Hidatsa culture to those of the third gender/male biology, as I have found no descriptions of fourth gender/biologically female Hidatsa berdaches to date. The historic record includes a number of clues to *miati* cultural roles, including their sexuality. William Clark recorded what appears to be the earliest written account of these individuals during the Voyage of Discovery's 1804–1805 overwintering near the Knife River. His diary entry of 22 December 1804 notes that 'a number of Squars womn & men Dressed in Squars Clothes Came with Corn to Sell to the men for little things' (Clark in Moulton 1993: 260). Later, in the entries of *Fort Mandan Miscellany*, Clark mentions that '"a punishment for boys too fond of women" is to Dress and perform the Duties of Women during Life', including sexual duties (Clark, quoted in Moulton 1993: 486; Ronda 1988: 130–31, however, believes Clark conflated generalized trans-gendered behavior with specifically sexual behavior).

Washington Matthews, an Army staff surgeon posted near the Hidatsa in the 1870s, recorded the next published comment on Hidatsa berdaches' sexual preferences in his *Ethnography and Philology of the Hidatsa Indians*:

> mi á ti, *n. fr.* mia; a man who dresses in woman's clothes and performs the duties usually allotted to females in an Indian camp. Such are called by the French Canadians 'berdaches'; and by most whites are incorrectly supposed to be hermaphrodites.
>
> (1877: 191)

Matthews' reference to hermaphrodism probably reflects his medical perspective and an interest in clarifying for readers that *miati* were in fact males rather than intersexed indi-viduals. James Owen Dorsey essentially repeated Matthews' description in his Bureau of American Ethnology report on Siouan cults:

The French Canadians call those men berdaches who dress in women's clothing and perform duties usually allotted to women in an Indian camp. By most whites these berdaches are incorrectly supposed to be hermaphrodites. They are called *miati* by the Hidatsa, from mia, a woman, and the ending, ti, to feel an involuntary inclination, i.e. to be impelled against his will to act the woman. See the Omaha mi^nquga, and Kansa mi^nquge, and the Dakota winkta and winkte.

(1894: 516–17)

Contrary to Dorsey's interpretation that *miati* were impelled against their will, Matthews defines the suffix *ti* as 'denoting readiness or desire to perform an action; to be about to' (1877: 203). This kind of 'internal compulsion' is a far different motivation for *miati* behavior than that which Dorsey describes. When conjoined, the Clark, Matthews, and Dorsey texts imply that Euro-American observers recognized *miati* through their cross-gender behavior and appearance, and perhaps their sexual interactions with men.

Two twentieth-century ethnographers worked extensively with the Hidatsa. Both worked with elders who had experienced life prior to the reservation era. Gilbert Wilson conducted his fieldwork from 1909 to 1918; his published work does not mention berdaches, probably because his role as preacher outweighed his role as anthropologist in his informants' and translators' eyes and influenced their accounts (Prine 1996). Alfred Bowers worked with the Hidatsa and Mandan during the 1920s, and says literally nothing regarding berdache sexual preferences, although his accounts of Hidatsa Two Spirits are otherwise quite informative.

In his ethnography, Bowers (1992) suggests that berdaches had a central role in Hidatsa life because of their direct links to two very powerful deities, Village–Old–Woman and Woman Above. Village–Old–Woman is one of the three Hidatsa donor figures who created the world; the others are Lone Man and First Creator. Interestingly, in stories subsequent to the Creation, First Creator becomes Coyote (see Beckwith 1930) – thus the world was made by a male, a female, and a trickster figure, a triad not unlike the men, women, and *miati* of traditional Hidatsa culture. After Lone Man and First Creator made the land and the male animals,

a mysterious or holy woman named Village–Old–Woman living in the southland learned of this new land. She resolved to create females of each species . . . in order to perpetuate life, and to give the people female creatures to worship.

(Bowers 1992: 323)

One of the deities she created is Woman Above. Woman Above is a cannibal whose other activities include 'eating' the dead with her brother the Sun (the Hidatsa practiced scaffold burials), arranging battles in order to have victims on which to feed, and rousing hot winds to destroy crops. She is described as jealous and vindictive, essentially a negative analog to Village–Old–Woman's benevolent nature. To protect them from Woman Above, Village–Old–Woman gave the people the Holy Women Society and the Women Above Spirit Bundles as means for preventing the 'misfortunes such as miscarriages, premature births, insanity, and paralysis' (1992: 330) associated with Woman Above. The Holy Women Society comprised older women and berdaches, and was among the most active of all groups of ritual specialists, while the Woman Above Spirit Bundles were cared for by Bundle Guardians as described earlier.

According to Bowers, berdaches were metaphorically captured by Village–Old–Woman:

The customs of the berdache were based on native concepts that for a man to dream of Village–Old–Woman or a loop of sweetgrass was an instruction to dress as a woman and to behave as a special class of 'females'. It was believed that when a man saw a coil of sweetgrass in the brush he should look away, otherwise the Village–Old–Woman or the female deities whom she created would cause his mind to weaken so that he would have no relief until he 'changed his sex'.

(1992: 326)

By virtue of their calling, Hidatsa Two Spirits became members of the Holy Women, a group of about twenty women and berdaches who represented Village–Old–Woman's deities and were the only people authorized to participate in every Hidatsa ritual. Two Spirits' physical strength relative to the other Holy Women made them integral participants in many important ceremonies, where they 'performed many tasks otherwise too difficult for the women, such as raising the posts for the NaxpikE ceremony' (Bowers 1992: 326). This ceremony required setting large tree trunks upright into holes in the ground. I believe Hidatsa berdaches were also integral to house-building ceremonies, thereby mediating the differences between the feminine earth and masculine sky as they raised the main supporting posts of the earthlodge (see Prine 1997).

Bowers seems conflicted about the community's reception of berdaches. He reports that they were both pitied and respected:

A mother taught a son early in life to play boys' games, to dress like boys, to be brave, and at all times to avoid female avocations lest he be 'blessed' by one of the female deities and become a berdache.

(105)

Those who made the change and assumed feminine attire and activities were pitied by others. The people would say that he had been claimed by a Holy Woman and therefore nothing could be done about it.

(326)

They were treated . . . as mysterious and holy . . . Inasmuch as the organization of Holy Women was considered to be a benevolent group, doing much to assist the people in time of starvation, berdaches were well thought of although pitied.

(326–27)

Since the berdaches were viewed as mystic possessors of unique ritual instructions secured directly from the mysterious Holy Woman, they were treated as a special class of religious leaders . . . The berdaches comprised the most active ceremonial class in the village. Their roles in ceremonies were many and exceeded those of the most distinguished tribal ceremonial leaders.

(167)

It is difficult to say why becoming a berdache was something to be avoided, precisely how berdaches were perceived by other Hidatsas, or even whether a consensus about those perceptions existed. 'Losing' a child to a deity against whom one had no recourse may have been cause enough for concern, and Bowers does describe the path to Two Spiritedness in metaphors of raiding and kidnapping. Because of their prevalent roles in rituals, berdaches moved in and out of liminal states more frequently than other members of Hidatsa society, which may also have caused concern. It is possible that Two Spirits' central, highly public roles in ritual life simply accrued more difficult personal and public responsibilities than was common; certainly analogous situations often elicit pity and respect in American culture today. However, I suspect that the concern Bowers heard was more a result of colonial pressures than of worry over *miati* social or spiritual liminality or responsibilities. Bowers' fieldwork was conducted during the 1920s, and his informants related that the last Hidatsa berdache 'had fled to the Crow Agency when the government agent forcibly stripped him of his feminine attire, dressed him in men's clothing, and cut off his braids' (1992: 315). Such disturbing treatment is a most obvious cause for concern; it also indicates that *miati* were seen as a threat to U. S. federal policies – or at least to those charged with their enforcement.

Perhaps the threat arose from Hidatsa berdaches' power within their communities. Becoming a *miati* implied a certain amount of prominence, and in Hidatsa communities, men's prominence traditionally arose from leadership in ritual and military exploits (e.g. Bundle Guardianship and raiding). Two Spiritedness implies an alternative route to power, and one that might have been sought on at least two accounts.

First, Bowers' informants asserted that only the brothers and sons of a Woman Above or Holy Woman Bundle Guardian were eligible to become *miati* (1992: 167). For the moment let us presume that Bowers' informants referred strictly to consanguinal relationships (as discussed below, affinal connections may also have been seen as legitimate in this context). An examination of Hidatsa kinship indicates that being related to an appropriate Bundle Guardian would not have been so restrictive a prerequisite for aspiring *miati* as it appears to be at first glance: the Hidatsa classify 19 of the 38 possible consanguinal categories for males related to a male ego, as ego's father or brother (Bowers 1992: 80–103). Given this kin classification system, it is possible that a significant number of young men would have been eligible for *miati* status via consanguinal connection to the Guardians of the Woman Above and Holy Woman Bundles.

Because the people's well-being depended in very real ways on the Guardian's skill in, and devotion to, his duties, Bundle Guardians were very prominent members of the community. According to Maxidiwiac, herself the daughter of a Bundle Guardian, the Guardians' prominence also accrued in some sense to their families (Wilson 1934); we might assume that at least some of their children would also possess or seek to acquire high degrees of spiritual power and/or social prestige. Yet as an outlet for spiritual power or as a path to prestige, Bundle Guardianship was also a very scarce 'resource': each Bundle could have only one Guardian at a time. Spirit Bundles were passed from a man to one of his sons or brothers; thus, becoming a *miati* might have been an alternative route for the expression of great spiritual power, or for attaining social prestige, for those young men of prominent families who knew they were unlikely to inherit a Bundle Guardianship.

Other young men might have acquired the necessary connections through affinal relations. Although one's wife's sister's husband was the only marital affine referred to as brother, and this relation would not have obtained for *miati* (Bowers 1992: 84), ritual adoption between adults presented another opportunity for creating kin relations:

> 'Adoption' rites were of common occurrence. All men of distinction, and some women as well, adopted 'sons' from clans and lineages not otherwise closely related . . . As far as it is possible to determine, all council leaders had established, by means of the

adoption ceremony, 'father–son' or 'friend–friend' relationships with a number of distinguished men from other tribes.

(Bowers 1992: 91)

This raises the possibility that families with sons who were experiencing visions of sweet-grass or Village–Old–Woman might have made arrangements to become related to an appropriate Bundle Guardian through adoption.

Some young men might have chosen to become *miati* for reasons other than the possession or pursuit of social or spiritual power. One of Bowers' informants suggests that young men had incentive to be called by Village–Old–Woman:

> Wolf Chief described the training of the young men as equivalent to a wagon drawn along a deeply rutted road; there was no way to get out of the road except by going forward in the same path as others had done before – one could make no progress backing up, and the depth of the ruts prevented one from taking a different course. A young man, according to Wolf Chief, got along very well as long as he performed in exactly the same way as his elders had; he was destined to be very unhappy if he attempted to stray the least bit from the beaten path. The only effective alternate was to become a berdache.
>
> (Bowers 1992: 220)

Thus Two Spiritedness may have provided an alternative 'vocation' for young men who were disinclined to take either of the more common male routes to adulthood.

Whatever the cause for 'leaving the rutted road', it is clear that Hidatsa berdaches were important members of their villages. Bowers's informants recalled either two or four *miati* from the latter half of the nineteenth century; in earlier times as many as fifteen to twenty-five were thought to have lived at any given time (Bowers 1992: 167). Plains ethnologists generally agree with Hanson's (1983) Knife River area population estimates, which place about 5,000 Hidatsa people in the three major villages during the late eighteenth century. When combined with Bowers's informants' estimates of *miati* resident in the villages, we derive a proportion of approximately one miati per 200 to 300 people. Given this degree of representation and the fact that *miati* participated very actively in public life, we can presume that they would have been a rather strong element within Hidatsa society.

The *miati* were especially powerful in the ritual–spiritual realm; Bowers notes that their hallmark was innovation. They were not

> bound as firmly by traditional teachings coming down from the older generations through the ceremonies, but more as a result of their individual and unique experiences with the supernatural, their conduct was less traditional than that of the other ceremonial leaders.
>
> (1992: 167)

Given that all of the Hidatsa behavioral codes were related in some way to ceremonial wisdom, berdaches' penchant for individual self-expression as it related to ritual is significant. Nonetheless, berdaches' domestic lives were apparently in close accordance to those of other Hidatsa families. They typically formed a marital household with an older divorced or widowed man, adopted children captured on raids (a common practice in traditional Plains cultures), and, like berdaches in other parts of North America, were 'industrious individuals working harder than the women of the village and exceeding the women in many common activities' (Bowers 1992: 167).

Interestingly, the Hidatsa, like several other Plains tribes, used ritual sexual intercourse as a means for transferring power from one person to another (Kehoe 1970). Power from an older man was transferred to a younger man's wife through coitus, then transferred in turn from the woman to her husband. Berdaches are not discussed in the Plains literature on ritual sex, but their strong presence in a variety of rituals suggests that they may have had yet another role to play. Given their aptitude for innovating in ritual contexts, one might ask whether, as William Clark suggested in 1804, sexual behavior was within the scope of *miati* innovation (Clark in Moulton 1993: 486; Ronda 1988: 130–31).

PLACING FIGURES IN THE SCENE: SEEING *MIATI* IN THE PAST

The section above lays out the cultural contexts for *miati* life; how do we move from these contexts to archaeological research? Hidatsa berdaches were differentiated from their age and sex cohorts in six ways: (1) in adolescence they changed their gender; (2) they were either born into or acquired kinship with a Woman Above or Village–Old–Woman Bundle Guardian; (3) their communities accorded them an unusual amount of respect and concern; (4) they created households that focused on a same-sex relationship; (5) they were highly productive; (6) they had a strong propensity, and the social latitude, to innovate.

Most of these distinctions might be associated with particular forms of archaeological evidence – 'openings' in the archaeological data that might allow us to 'see' a past as diverse as our present. For instance, burial contexts might illuminate the gender transition by unearthing a male body with female grave goods (cf. Roscoe 1991; Whelan 1991). Kinship and community respect might also be traced from grave goods, through clan insignias, genetic analysis, and markers of rank. Berdache households were said to have fewer people than mixed-sex households (Bowers 1992: 167), and the architectural remains of berdache households might therefore be expected to be proportionally smaller. Two Spirits' high productivity might be expressed through richer household assemblages. Finally, we might expect *miati* homes and burials to exhibit innovative uses of traditional and/or trade materials.

Mortuary studies are not a feasible research mode within Hidatsa archaeology; household archaeology, however, has been extensive. Most Hidatsa archaeological data arose from the Missouri River Basin subdivision of the Smithsonian Institution River Basin Surveys (SIRBS; for an overview, see Lehmer 1971). SIRBS teams excavated numerous Plains villages prior to their inundation by the six Pick-Sloan Plan dams constructed on the Missouri River. The teams varied to some extent in their field techniques, but were consistent in emphasizing speed and extensive recovery in the face of rising flood waters; excavations regularly used heavy equipment to remove overburden, were generally completed via shovel scraping (albeit with some trowel work), and avoided screening (Lehmer 1971: 13–20). Many of the SIRBS excavation reports were published as volumes in the *Bureau of American Ethnology Papers* (Cooper 1958; Lehmer 1954; Roberts 1960; Wedel 1947, 1948, 1953) or as stand-alone publications (Lehmer 1971; Smith 1972); others can be found in doctoral dissertations (e.g. Hartle 1960). Although the excavation and reporting standards of the era do limit these reports' utility for research,[2] the assembled works provide architectural data for a range of Plains sites that is remarkable in both geographic and chronological breadth. As no Hidatsa earthlodges have been fully excavated in recent years, the remainder of this chapter focuses on the SIRBS data.[3]

A survey of SIRBS publications elicited a total of 23 circular earthlodges excavated at two confirmed Hidatsa sites, Rock Village (32ME15; see Hartle 1960) and Like-a-Fishhook village (32ML2; see Smith 1972). All but one of these homes (95.7%) conform to classic Plains earthlodge characteristics, including a sheltered entryway, four main supporting posts arranged around a central hearth, and a single series of secondary supporting posts arranged in circular fashion beyond the main supports.

A variety of evidence suggests that the unusual lodge might have belonged to a *miati*. This home, Feature 72 at Rock Village, had an architectural detail that stands in striking contrast to all the other lodges: seven of its nine secondary support posts were 'doubled' (see Figure 11.2; posts one and nine, marking the transition from entryway to lodge, were single). I will refer to this lodge as 'Double Post'. Hartle describes Double Post in his doctoral dissertation, a culture-historical excavation report on the site, noting that 'the "double" supporting post holes in this lodge were unique for all lodges excavated' (Hartle 1960: 82). This is intriguing, as one might wonder whether the double-spirited identity reported for *miati* might have been expressed through the material medium of the posts. Certainly architectural production was one of the most important duties of Hidatsa berdaches (e.g. as in raising NaxpikE and earthlodge posts); because home construction was heavily ritualized, it would have been a likely forum for *miati* innovation and self-expression.

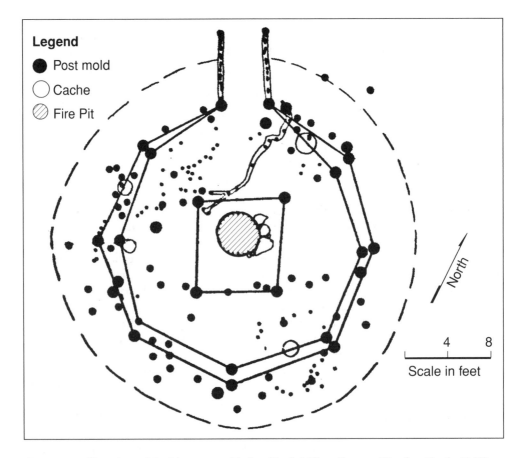

Figure 11.2 Plan view of double post earthlodge (Rock Village Feature 72; after Hartle 1960).

The number four has special significance for Hidatsa people, as it does for many other Native American groups. The Hidatsa count four cardinal directions, typically have four stages of entry to each ritual and ceremony, and traditionally believed that each person had four souls (Bowers 1992). It is possible that Double Post's four main supporting posts were left in typical earthlodge formation because a heavy symbolic load prevented innovation in that part of the structure. The secondary posts apparently carried no such constraint, as the home's builder(s) altered their number from the more typical eleven or twelve single posts to nine supporting loci (e.g. there were eighteen posts at the nine secondary support locations). This doubling might have signified the doubling resulting from the *miati* life path: while an individual *miati* would continue to use the four main posts to represent his four souls, he might show his 'doubled' nature by changing the configuration and number of the secondary posts of his earthlodge.

The differences between Double Post and other homes at Rock Village go beyond impressionistic details of architectural construction. Double Post was by far the smallest earthlodge excavated at the site, with a maximum diameter of only 34 ft. The next largest lodges were 42 ft. in diameter (n = 2), and the overall average for all the site's homes was 43.7 ft.[4] In fact, Double Post is significantly small for Rock Village: it is nearly four standard deviations off the mean when compared to summary data for the rest of the lodges excavated there.[5] Yet Double Post was a substantial dwelling, with over 900 sq. ft. of interior floor space. It was far too large to have been the home of an old childless couple, or an elder living alone, as Bowers (1992: 165) describes their homes as 'much smaller one[s] built on a four-post foundation *without the peripheral posts*' (emphasis mine). However, Double Post's unusual size may reflect the significantly smaller households attributed to Hidatsa berdaches, comprising just one adult couple and their children rather than the more customary three generations with their in-marrying spouses (Bowers 1992: 167).

Rock Village's general site contexts also lend credence to the hypothesis that Double Post was a Two Spirit's lodge. Rock Village is the only post-contact Hidatsa village site in close proximity to the Grandmother's Lodge site (32ME59; a village site inhabited *c.* 1450–1550; see Lehmer 1971: 96–97). Rock Village and Grandmother's Lodge were located only a few miles apart. Grandmother's Lodge is both the northernmost Plains Village site on the Missouri and the only habitation site the Hidatsa explicitly associate with Village–Old–Woman. After Rock Village, the next closest post-contact village site lies about fifty miles downriver. That the residents of Rock Village would travel to such lengths to create a home so near to the deity who 'captures' Hidatsa berdaches is certainly suggestive. Interestingly, Hartle suggests that the village was established in the late eighteenth century (1960: 200) – a time locus immediately following the severe smallpox epidemic of 1780–1781, in which an estimated 50 to 68 percent of the Missouri villagers died (Hanson 1983: 107–110).

The sampling contexts of which Double Post is a part are also interesting. It has become an archaeological maxim that sampling provides an approximate analog of the spatial and typological distribution of given material types, whether sites, architecture, or artifactual materials (Binford 1964; Plog 1976; Redman 1975, 1987; Wobst 1983). In this case, Hartle's estimate of approximately 200 residents in Rock Village (1960: 202) coincides with the ratio of 200 to 300 Hidatsa to each berdache suggested by combining Bowers' informants' reminiscences of *miati* with Hanson's ethnohistoric projections for the Knife River villages' populations (see discussion on p. 208; also Bowers 1992, Hanson 1983).

What of the proportion of potential *miati* residences to the overall number of earthlodges excavated under the SIRBS program? Hanson (1983) and other ethnohistorians (e.g. Wood and Thiessen 1985) presume eight to twelve residents for each Hidatsa earthlodge; given Bowers' description of smaller *miati* families, a berdache earthlodge might have had four or five residents. If we consider the proportion of homes associated with *miati* versus those associated with non-*miati* (i.e. four to five people per *miati* earthlodge and eight to twelve people per non-berdache earthlodge) and combine it with the overall proportion of *miati* to the population (1:200 to 1:300), we derive a figure indicating that between 1.4 and 6.3 percent[6] of all Hidatsa homes might have been *miati* residences. In fact, of the 43 late Plains Village earthlodges excavated by SIRBS (e.g. from villages associated with the protohistoric or historic Hidatsa, Mandan, or Arikara), 2.3 percent (n = 1, Double Post) displayed the small size and architectural innovation that might suggest a berdache residence. If we narrow the scope of the study to include only earthlodges from confirmed Hidatsa villages (n = 23), 4.3 percent of the sample (again n = 1) consists of potential berdache homes. Thus both the intersite and intrasite samples fall well within the hypothesized range for late Plains Village *miati* homes.

CONCLUDING THOUGHTS: ON SEEING MULTIPLE SEXUALITIES IN THE PAST

Although we cannot definitively state that Double Post was a *miati* home, the evidence is strong. Double Post is a highly unusual earthlodge; it is clearly different from its neighbors in terms of the number and grouping of its structural elements and in its size. Hidatsa Two Spirits were known to maintain relatively small households; as cultural–ritual innovators and earthlodge builders, we might expect them to have expressed innovation through changes in the size and the internal design of the structures which they built for their own use.

In addition, Double Post is part of a site that is notable as the closest post-contact village to the mythic–historic home of Village–Old–Woman, the creator (or captor) of *miati*. It was established at a point in time, the late eighteenth century, when the Hidatsa were experiencing heightened psychological, physical, and cultural stress in the wake of a massive smallpox epidemic. Proximity to this primal donor figure may well have been seen as a way to boost the efficacy of ceremonial practices designed to heal and prevent those 'misfortunes such as miscarriages, premature births, [and] insanity' that are associated with smallpox and that the protohistoric Hidatsa may well have associated with Woman Above (Bowers 1992: 330).

Finally, inter- and intrasite sampling indicate that the data correspond to the hypothesized proportion of berdache versus non-berdache homes in contact period Plains Villages generally, and Hidatsa villages specifically. The proportions of berdache residences at late Plains Village sites and at confirmed Hidatsa sites (2.3 and 4.3 percent) fall well within the range hypothesized from a close reading of the historical and ethnographic records (1.4 to 6.3 percent). Furthermore, population and architectural data from Hartle's excavations at Rock Village coincide with the Bowers–Hanson ratio of one berdache to 200 other residents. While sampling ratios cannot provide positive associations between home types and their residents' sexuality (or any group of artifacts and their cultural meanings), in this case, at least, sampling strongly suggests an association. If we have not 'found' a berdache household, Double Post certainly has allowed us a frame in which to 'see' one.

The routine, intense, polysemic use of abstract symbols is just one of several characteristics that mark humans as distinct from other species. Anthropologists have long recognized that culture provides innumerable methods and forms for attaching meaning to the routine and the extraordinary. This volume focuses on ways archaeologists might engage with one facet of culture, sexuality, and explore its content and meanings for past groups. Although it is unlikely that we will find any index artifact that consistently 'marks' sexuality for all cultures (or even for a few cultures, or one), archaeologists can and should peruse larger cultural patterns and seek ripples in their fabric – spaces which we might tease apart so that we may see a culture's underlying structures. Viewed through the lens of myriad archaeological, ethnographic, and historical data, we can see the archaeological evidence with new eyes, eyes which are open to diversities we have not previously considered.

I close this chapter with questions rather than concrete answers. Were there berdaches in Hidatsa proto- and prehistory? This I can answer with a definitive yes. Will we ever 'find' berdaches and other transgendered individuals, with consistency and reliability, throughout prehistory and in all cultures of which they were members, as we have grown accustomed to 'finding' toolmakers? Perhaps. Keeping in mind that archaeologists 'find' no real people in the past, but only the remnants of their behavior – and this is as true for the flintknapper as it is for the berdache – the archaeologist's mission must be to marshal evidence that increases our understandings not only of cultural processes, but also of the rich cultural tapestries of past life. Sexuality is a strong but elusive pattern running through those tapestries, and given its enormous influence on human behavior is one well worth investigating.

ACKNOWLEDGEMENTS

My thanks go first to the editors of this volume, Barb Voss and Rob Schmidt, for inviting me to contribute to the text and for their gentle good humor and excellent suggestions throughout the creative process. I thank Ray Wood for his thoughtful reading of the chapter during our work on the Menoken Archaeology Project; his suggestions reflected both his long experience in Plains archaeology and ethnohistory and his willingness to foster innovative studies in the region. I am grateful to Erik Pauls for our many productive discussions focusing on this chapter; he knows more than anyone the leaps and twists this piece has taken, and proved to be an invaluable compass throughout the work. Finally, I thank those members of the Three Affiliated Tribes who have tolerated (and I think occasionally even welcomed) my presence in their lives. Without such a myriad of people, this piece would not have been written; of course, all errors of thought and fact remain my own.

NOTES

1   I will use these two terms interchangeably. My intention is to respect the wishes of Native peoples, who seem to prefer the term 'Two Spirit', while avoiding the awkward constructions that would result from abandoning the currently preferred anthropological term, 'berdache'.

2   For instance, these reports commonly summarize artifacts only by raw counts. Little descriptive information is included beyond these counts; even minimum numbers of individuals or species are generally lacking. This is the case with Hartle's (1960) Rock Village report as well as with numerous others, and was a major consideration as I undertook the present research.

3   The National Park Service testing and inventory program at the Knife River Indian Villages has been excellent, however (see Ahler and Swenson 1985; Ahler and Weston 1981; Ahler et al. 1980; Thiessen 1993a, 1993c, 1993d).

4   For the thirteen lodges Hartle excavated, the minimum internal diameter = 34, maximum = 48, mean = 43.69, median = 43, standard deviation = 3.86; all measurements in feet (see Hartle 1960).

5   In this case, Double Post is 3.97 standard deviations from the mean; n = 12, minimum internal diameter = 42, maximum = 48, mean = 44.5, median = 43, standard deviation = 2.65; all measurements in feet (see Hartle 1960).

6   These percentages derive from the following presumptions: minimum proportion of 4 residents of *miati* homes to 296 residents of other homes (1.4 percent); maximum proportion of 5 residents of *miati* homes to 195 residents of other homes (2.6 percent). Alternatively, a minimum of one *miati* home to 37 other homes (2.7 percent; e.g. 296 people not residing with berdaches at 8 people per residence) and a maximum of one *miati* home to 16 other homes (6.3 percent; e.g. 195 people not residing with berdaches at 12 people per residence).

REFERENCES

Ahler, S. A. and A. A. Swenson (1985) *Test Excavations at Big Hidatsa Village (32ME12), Knife River Indian Villages National Historic Site*, Grand Forks: Department of Anthropology and Archaeology, University of North Dakota. Excavation report submitted to the US National Park Service in compliance with Section 106 of the Historic Preservation Act.

Ahler, S. A., T. D. Thiessen and M. K. Trimble (1991) *People of the Willows: The Prehistory and Early History of the Hidatsa Indians*, Grand Forks: University of North Dakota Press.

Ahler, S. A. and T. Weston (1981) *Test Excavations at Lower Hidatsa Village (32ME10), Knife River Indian Villages National Historic Site*, Grand Forks: Department of Anthropology and Archaeology, University of North Dakota. Excavation report submitted to the US National Park Service in compliance with Section 106 of the Historic Preservation Act.

Ahler, S. A., T. Weston and K. D. McMiller (1980) *Cutbank Profiling and Test Excavations at Sakakawea Village (32ME11), Knife River Indian Villages National Historic Site*, Grand Forks: Department of Anthropology and Archaeology, University of North Dakota. Excavation report submitted to the US National Park Service in compliance with Section 106 of the Historic Preservation Act.

Albers, P. (1993) 'Symbiosis, Merger, and War: Contrasting Forms of Intertribal Relationship Among Historic Plains Indians', in J. H. Moore (ed.) *The Political Economy of North American Indians*, Norman: University of Oklahoma Press.

Beauchemin, M., L. Levy and G. Vogel, (1991) *Two Spirit People* (video), Berkeley: Gender on a Stick Productions.

Beckwith, M. W. (1930) *Myths and Hunting Stories of the Mandan and Hidatsa Sioux*, Poughkeepsie, NY: Vassar College Press.

Bender, B. (1992) 'Theorising Landscapes and the Prehistoric Landscapes of Stonehenge', *Man* 27, 4: 735–55.

—— (1993) 'Stonehenge – Contested Landscapes (Medieval to Present-Day)', in B. Bender (ed.) *Landscapes: Politics and Perspectives*, Providence: Berg: 245–79.

Binford, L. R. (1962) 'Archaeology as Anthropology', *American Antiquity* 28, 2: 217–25.

—— (1964) 'A Consideration of Archaeological Research Design', *American Antiquity* 29, 4: 425–41.

—— (1967) 'Smudge Pits and Hide Smoking: The Use of Analogy in Archaeological Reasoning', *American Antiquity* 32, 1: 1–12.

—— (1978) *Nunamiut Ethnoarchaeology*, New York: Academic Press.

Bourdieu, P. (1977) *Outline of a Theory of Practice*, New York: Cambridge University Press.

—— (1984) *Distinction: A Social Critique of the Judgement of Taste*, Cambridge: Harvard University Press.

Bowers, A. W. (1948) 'A History of the Mandan and Hidatsa', unpublished doctoral dissertation, University of Chicago.

—— (1950) *Mandan Social and Ceremonial Organization*, Chicago: University of Chicago Press.

—— (1992) *Hidatsa Social and Ceremonial Organization*, Lincoln: University of Nebraska Press. First published in 1965 by the Smithsonian Institution, Bureau of American Ethnology, Bulletin No. 194, Washington, DC.

Callender, C. and L. M. Kochems (1983) 'The North American Berdache', *Current Anthropology* 24: 443–56.

Chardon, F. A. (1932) *Chardon's Journal at Fort Clark, 1834–1839*, A. H. Abel (ed.), Pierre: State of South Dakota Department of History.

Conkey, M. (1991) 'Contexts of Action, Contexts for Power: Material Culture and Gender in the Magdalenian', in J. M. Gero and M. W. Conkey (eds) *Engendering Archaeology: Women and Prehistory*, Oxford: Basil Blackwell.

Conkey, M. W. and J. M. Gero (1991) 'Tensions, Pluralities, and Engendering Archaeology: An Introduction to Women and Prehistory', in J. M. Gero and M. W. Conkey (eds) *Engendering Archaeology: Women and Prehistory*, Oxford: Basil Blackwell.

Conkey, M. W. and J. Spector (1984) 'Archaeology and the Study of Gender', in M. B. Schiffer (ed.) *Advances in Archaeological Method and Theory, 7*, New York: Academic Press: 1–38.

Conkey, M. W. with S. H. Williams (1991) 'Original Narratives: The Political Economy of Gender in Archaeology', in M. di Leonardo (ed.) *Gender at the Crossroads of Knowledge: Feminist Anthropology in the Postmodern Era*, Berkeley: University of California Press: 102–39.

Cooper, P. L. (1958) 'Archaeological Investigations in the Heart Butte Reservoir Area, North Dakota', Inter-Agency Archaeological Salvage Program Papers 9–14, Bureau of American Ethnology Bulletin 169: 5–40.

Crabtree, D. E. (1974) 'Experiments in Replicating Hohokam Points', *Tebiwa* 16, 1: 1–36.

Culbertson, T. A. (1952) *Journal of an Expedition to the Mauvaises Terres and the Upper Missouri in 1850*, J. F. McDermott (ed.) Smithsonian Institution, Bureau of American Ethnology Bulletin 147.

Dobres, M. A. and C. R. Hoffman (1994) 'Social Agency and the Dynamics of Prehistoric Technology', *Journal of Archaeological Method and Theory* 1, 3: 211–58.

Dobres, M. A. and C. R. Hoffman (1999) (eds) *The Social Dynamics of Technology*, Washington, DC: Smithsonian Institution Press.

Dorsey, J. O. (1894) 'A Study of Siouan Cults', in J. W. Powell (ed.) *Eleventh Annual Report of the Bureau of American Ethnology, 1889-'90*, Washington, DC: Smithsonian Institution, Government Printing Office.

Epple, C. (1998) 'Coming to Terms with Navajo *nadleehi*: A Critique of Berdache, "Gay", "Alternate Gender", and "Two-spirit"', *American Ethnologist* 25, 2: 267–90.

Falk, L. (ed.) (1991) *Historical Archaeology in Global Perspective*, Washington, DC: Smithsonian Institution Press.

Ferguson, L. (1992) *Uncommon Ground: Archaeology and Colonial African-America*, Washington, DC: Smithsonian Institution Press.

Foucault, M. (1970) *The Order of Things*, New York: Vintage Books.

—— (1977) *Discipline and Punish*, New York: Pantheon.

Frederickson, G. M. (1981) *White Supremacy: A Comparative Study in American and South African History*, New York: Oxford University Press.

Fulton, R. and S. W. Anderson (1992) 'The Amerindian "Man–Woman": Gender, Liminality, and Cultural Continuity', *Current Anthropology* 33: 603–10.

Gero, J. M. and M. W. Conkey (eds) (1991) *Engendering Archaeology*, NewYork: Basil Blackwell.

Giddens, A. (1979) *Central Problems in Social Theory: Action, Structure, and Contradiction in Social Analysis*, London: Macmillan.

—— (1984) *The Constitution of Society*, Berkeley: University of California Press.

Gilman, C. and M. J. Schneider (1987) *The Way to Independence: Memories of a Hidatsa Indian Family, 1840–1920*, St. Paul: Minnesota Historical Society Press.

Goodbird, E. (1914) *Goodbird the Indian: His Story Told by Himself to Gilbert L. Wilson*, New York: Fleming H. Revell Company. Reprinted in 1985 by the Minnesota Historical Society Press, St. Paul.

Gould, R. A. and P. J. Watson (1982) 'A Dialogue on the Meaning and Use of Analogy in Ethnoarchaeological Reasoning', *Journal of Anthropological Archaeology* 1: 355–81.

Hall, M. (1995) 'The Architecture of Patriarchy: Women and Slaves in the Eighteenth-Century South African Countryside', in M. E. D'Agostino, E. Prine, E. Casella and M. Winer (eds), *The Written and the Wrought: Complementary Sources in Historical Anthropology*, special thematic edition of the *Kroeber Anthropological Society Papers*, 79: 61–73.

Hanson, J. R. (1983) 'Hidatsa Culture Change, 1780–1845: A Cultural Ecological Approach', unpublished doctoral dissertation, University of Missouri at Columbia.

Harrod, H. L. (1995) *Becoming and Remaining a People: Native American Religions of the Northern Plains*, Tucson: University of Arizona Press.

Hartle, D. D. (1960) 'Rock Village: An Ethnohistorical Approach to Hidatsa Archaeology', unpublished doctoral dissertation, Columbia University.

Hauser, R. E. (1990) 'The *Berdache* and the Illinois Indian Tribe during the Last Half of the Seventeenth Century', *Ethnohistory* 37, 1: 45–65.

Hawkes, C. (1954) 'Archaeological Theory and Method: Some Suggestions from the Old World', *American Anthropologist* 56: 155–68.

Hodder, I. (1982) (ed.) *Symbolic and Structural Archaeology*, New York: Cambridge University Press.

—— (1985) 'Postprocessual Archaeology', *Advances in Archaeological Method and Theory* 8: 1–26.

Johnson, M. (1989) 'Conceptions of Agency in Archaeological Interpretation', *Journal of Anthropological Archaeology* 8: 189–211.

—— (1991) 'Enclosure and Capitalism: The History of a Process', in R. W. Preucel (ed.) *Processual and Postprocessual Archaeologies: Multiple Ways of Knowing the Past*, Carbondale: Center for Archaeological Investigations, Southern Illinois University.

—— (1993) *Housing Culture: Traditional Architecture in an English Landscape*, Washington, DC: Smithsonian Institution Press.

—— (1996) *The Archaeology of Capitalism*, Washington, DC: Smithsonian Institution Press.

Kehoe, A. (1970) 'The Function of Ceremonial Sexual Intercourse Among the Northern Plains Indians', *Plains Anthropologist* 15, 48: 99–103.

Kestler, F. R. (1990) *The Indian Captivity Narrative: A Woman's View*, New York: Garland Publishing.

Kolodny, A. (1975) *The Lay of the Land: Metaphor as Experience and History in American Life and Letters*, Chapel Hill: University of North Carolina Press.

Larpenteur, C. (1933) *Forty Years a Fur Trader on the Upper Missouri: The Personal Narrative of Charles Larpenteur [1833–1872]*, Chicago: R. R. Donelly and Sons. Reprinted in 1989 by University of Nebraska Press, Lincoln.

Lehmer, D. J. (1954) *Archaeological Investigations in the Oahe Dam Reservoir Area, South Dakota, 1950–51*, Smithsonian Institution, Bureau of American Ethnology Bulletin 158, Inter-Agency Archaeological Salvage Program Paper no. 7.

—— (1971) *Introduction to Middle Missouri Archaeology*, Washington, DC: National Park Service, US Department of the Interior.

Leone, M. P. (1982) 'Some Opinions About Recovering Mind', *American Antiquity* 47, 4: 742–60.

—— (1984) 'Interpreting Ideology in Historical Archaeology: Using the Rules of Perspective in the William Paca Garden in Annapolis, Maryland', in D. Miller and C. Tilley (eds) *Ideology, Power, and Prehistory*, New York: Cambridge University Press: 25–35.

Markell, A., M. Hall and C. Schrire (1995) 'The Historical Archaeology of Vergelegen, an Early Farmstead at the Cape of Good Hope', *Historical Archaeology* 29, 1: 10–34.

Matthews, W. (1877) *Ethnography and Philology of the Hidatsa Indians*, Washington, DC: USGS Miscellaneous Publications no. 7. Reprinted in 1971 by the Johnson Reprint Corporation, New York.

Maxidiwiac (1921) *Waheenee: An Indian Girl's Story Told by Herself to Gilbert L. Wilson*, Saint Paul: Webb Publishing Company. Reprinted in 1981 by Minnesota Historical Society Press, St. Paul.

Maximilian, Prince of Wied-Neuwied (1996 [1843]) *Travels in the Interior of North America*, reprinted in R. G. Thwaites (ed.) *Early Western Travels, 1748–1846*, vols 22–24, New York: AMS Press.

McGinnis, A. (1990) *Counting Coup and Cutting Horses: Intertribal Warfare on the Northern Plains, 1738–1889*, Evergreen, CO: Cordillera Press.

McGuire, R. H. and R. Paynter (eds) (1991) *The Archaeology of Inequality*, Cambridge: Basil Blackwell.

Meyer, R. W. (1977) *The Village Indians of the Upper Missouri: The Mandans, Hidatsas, and Arikaras*, Lincoln: University of Nebraska Press.

Miller, D. and C. Tilley (eds) (1984) *Ideology, Power, and Prehistory*, Cambridge: Cambridge University Press.

Moore, H. (1986) *Space, Text, and Gender*, Cambridge: Cambridge University Press.

Moser, S. (1992a) 'Visions of the Australian Pleistocene: Prehistoric Life at Lake Mungo and Kutikina', *Australian Archaeology* 35: 1–10.

—— (1992b) 'The Visual Language of Archaeology: A Case Study of the Neanderthals', *Antiquity* 66: 831–44.

Moulton, G. (ed.) (1993) *Journal of the Lewis and Clark Expedition*, vol. 4, Lincoln: University of Nebraska Press.

Owsley, D. W. and R. W. Jantz (eds) (1994) *Skeletal Biology in the Great Plains: Migration, Warfare, Health, and Subsistence*, Washington, DC: Smithsonian Institution Press.

Plog, S. (1976) 'Relative Efficiencies of Sampling Techniques for Archaeological Surveys', in K. V. Flannery (ed.) *The Early Mesoamerican Village*, New York: Academic Press.

Prine, E. P. (1996) 'Who Paid for This Information? Power and Influence in Historical Ethnography', paper presented at the 95th Annual Meeting of the American Anthropological Association, San Francisco.

—— (1997) 'The Ethnography of Place: Landscape and Culture in Middle Missouri Archaeology', unpublished doctoral dissertation, University of California, Berkeley.

—— (1998) 'Home and Away: Using Lithics to Elucidate Household Connection in the Northern Plains', paper presented at the 63rd Annual Meeting of the Society for American Archaeology, Seattle.

Raab, L. M. and A. C. Goodyear (1984) 'Middle-Range Theory in Archaeology: A Critical Review of Origins and Applications', *American Antiquity* 49(2): 255–68.

Redman, C. (1987) 'Surface Collection, Sampling, and Research Design: A Retrospective', *American Antiquity* 52, 2: 249–65.

—— (1975) 'Productive Sampling Strategies for Archaeological Sites', in J. W. Mueller (ed.) *Sampling in Archaeology*, Tucson: University of Arizona Press.

Roberts, F. H. (ed.) (1960) *Historic Sites Archaeology on the Fort Randall and Garrison Reservoirs and the Oahe Dam*, Smithsonian Institution, Bureau of American Ethnology Bulletin 176, Inter-Agency Archaeological Salvage Program Papers, nos. 15–20.

Ronda, J. P. (1988) *Lewis and Clark Among the Indians*, Lincoln: University of Nebraska Press.

Roscoe, W. (1991) *The Zuni Man–Woman*, Albuquerque: University of New Mexico Press.

—— (1998) *Changing Ones: Third and Fourth Genders in Native North America*, New York: Saint Martin's Press.

Schiffer, M. B. (1972) 'Archaeological Context and Systemic Context', *American Antiquity* 37: 156–64.

Smith, G. H. (1972) *Like-a-Fishhook Village and Fort Berthold, Garrison Reservoir, North Dakota*, Washington, DC: National Park Service, US Department of the Interior.

—— (1980) *The Explorations of the La Verendryes in the Northern Plains, 1738–43*, Lincoln: University of Nebraska Press.

Smith, V. (1990) 'Split Affinities: The Case of Interracial Rape', in M. Hirsch and E. Keller (eds) *Conflicts in Feminism*, New York: Routledge, Chapman, and Hall.

Tabeau, P. A. (ed.) (1939) *Tabeau's Narrative of Loisel's Expedition to the Upper Missouri*, A. H. Abel (ed.) Norman: University of Oklahoma Press.

Thiessen, T. D. (ed.) (1993a) *The Phase I Archaeological Research Program for the Knife River Indian Villages National Historic Site, Part I: Objectives, Methods, and Summaries of Baseline Studies*, Lincoln, NE: National Park Service, Midwest Archaeological Center Occasional Studies in Anthropology, no. 27.

—— (ed.) (1993b) *The Phase I Archaeological Research Program for the Knife River Indian Villages National Historic Site, Part II: Ethnohistorical Studies*, Lincoln, NE: National Park Service, Midwest Archaeological Center Occasional Studies in Anthropology, no. 27.

—— (ed.) (1993c) *The Phase I Archaeological Research Program for the Knife River Indian Villages National Historic Site, Part III: Analysis of the Physical Remains*, Lincoln, NE: National Park Service, Midwest Archaeological Center Occasional Studies in Anthropology, no. 27.

—— (ed.) (1993d) *The Phase I Archaeological Research Program for the Knife River Indian Villages National Historic Site, Part IV: Interpretation of the Archaeological Record*, Lincoln, NE: National Park Service, Midwest Archaeological Center Occasional Studies in Anthropology, no. 27.

Tringham, R., G. Cooper, G. Odell, B. Voytek and A. Whitman (1974) 'Experimentation in the Formation of Edge Damage: A New Approach to Lithic Analysis', *Journal of Field Archaeology* 1: 171–96.

Watson, P. J. (1984) *Archaeological Explanation: The Scientific Method in Archaeology*, New York: Columbia University Press.

Watson, P. J., S. A. LeBlanc and C. L. Redman (1971) *Explanation in Archaeology: An Explicitly Scientific Approach*, New York: Columbia University Press.

Wedel, W. R. (1947) *Prehistory and the Missouri Valley Development Program in 1946*, Smithsonian Institution Miscellaneous Collections 107, 6.

—— (1948) *Prehistory and the Missouri Valley Development Program in 1947*, Smithsonian Institution Miscellaneous Collections 111, 2.

—— (1953) *Prehistory and the Missouri Valley Development Program in 1948*, Smithsonian Institution, Bureau of American Ethnology Bulletin 154, River Basin Survey Paper no. 1.

Whelan, M. K. (1991) 'Gender and Historical Archaeology: Eastern Dakota Patterns in the 19th Century', *Historical Archaeology* 25, 4: 17–32.

Whitehead, H. (1981) 'The Bow and the Burden Strap: A New Look at Institutionalized Homosexuality in Native North America', in S. Ortner and H. Whitehead (eds) *Sexual Meanings: The Cultural Construction of Gender and Sexuality*, Cambridge: Cambridge University Press.

Wilson, G. L. (1917) *Agriculture of the Hidatsa Indians: An Indian Interpretation*, Minneapolis: University of Minnesota, Studies in the Social Sciences, No. 9. Reprinted as *Buffalo Bird Woman's Garden: Agriculture of the Hidatsa Indians*, by the Minnesota Historical Society Press, St. Paul.

—— (1924) *The Horse and Dog in Hidatsa Culture*, The American Museum of Natural History *Anthropological Papers* 15: 127–311.

—— (1928) *Hidatsa Eagle Trapping*, The American Museum of Natural History *Anthropological Papers* 30: 99–245.

—— (1934) *The Hidatsa Earthlodge*, in Weitzner, B. (ed.), The American Museum of Natural History *Anthropological Papers* 33: 340–420.

Wobst, H. M. (1983) 'We Can't See the Forest for the Trees: Sampling and the Shapes of Archaeological Distributions', in J. A. Moore and A. S. Keene (eds) *Archaeological Hammers and Theories*, New York: Academic Press.

Wood, W. R. (1974) 'Northern Plains Village Cultures: Internal Stability and External Relationships', *Journal of Anthropological Research* 30, 1: 1–16.

—— (1980) *The Origins of the Hidatsa Indians: A Review of Ethnohistorical and Traditional Data*, Lincoln, NE: National Park Service, Midwest Archaeological Center, reprinted in Lincoln: J & L Reprint Company.

Wood, W. R. and T. D. Thiessen (eds) (1985) *Early Fur Trade on the Northern Plains: Canadian Traders Among the Mandan and Hidatsa Indians, 1738–1818*, Norman: University of Oklahoma Press.

Wylie, A. (1982a) 'An Analogy by Any Other Name Is Just as Analogical: A Commentary on the Gould–Watson Dialogue', *Journal of Anthropological Archaeology* 1: 382–401.

—— (1982b) 'Epistemological Issues Raised by a Structuralist Archaeology', in I. Hodder (ed.) *Symbolic and Structural Archaeology*, New York: Cambridge University Press.

—— (1985) 'The Reaction Against Analogy', in M. B. Schiffer (ed.) *Advances in Archaeological Method and Theory*, New York: Academic Press: 63–111.

—— (1991) 'Gender Theory and the Archaeological Record: Why Is There No Archaeology of Gender?', in J. M. Gero and M. W. Conkey (eds) *Engendering Archaeology: Women and Prehistory*, Oxford: Basil Blackwell.

—— (1992a) 'Feminist Theories of Social Power: Some Implications for a Processual Archaeology', *Norwegian Archaeological Review* 25, 1: 51–68.

—— (1992b) 'On Skepticism, Philosophy, and Archaeological Science', *Current Anthropology* 33, 2: 209–13.

Chapter Twelve

Shamans and northern cosmology: the direct historical approach to Mesolithic sexuality

Robert A. Schmidt

INTRODUCTION

In this chapter I interrogate the social organization and practice of sexuality in a deep prehistoric context. With the term 'deep prehistory' I refer to human societies whose temporal and/or geographic settings are remote from any direct written sources. The archaeological context discussed in this chapter is the late Mesolithic of northern Europe *c.* 5000–3000 BC, a period that clearly meets the definition of this term.

Probing sexuality in such circumstances is an undertaking fraught with difficulties. The most obvious of these will in general be the relative paucity of available evidence from these remote contexts, in comparison with more recent archaeological contexts. Another difficulty emerges from the recognition that the meanings of 'sexuality' itself, as a discursive category of human experience, are historically and culturally contingent, such that the contours of our contemporary category may not 'map' cleanly or conveniently onto emic systems of meaning in the past (see Voss and Schmidt, Chapter 1; and Meskell, Chapter 14). Thus we must take care that our etic categories do not unnecessarily obliterate emic patterns and nuances of meaning.

Moreover, sexuality is an aspect of human experience whose center of gravity lies within the compass of a combination of our physical and emotional lives. Kus (1992) has described this combination of the physical and emotional with the term 'sensuous', and at first glance there would seem to be little that archaeologists could do to recreate and understand the sensuous experiences of lives lived in prehistory. Yet, as other authors in this volume (e.g. Voss and Prine) argue, practice theory provides a convenient tool for modeling sensuous experience and behavior in general, and sexuality in particular, because it demonstrates that meaning can be produced and maintained through repetitive patterns of activity, and because such meaningful patterns may be discerned in the archaeological record (Bourdieu 1977; Kus 1992; Moore 1986). My goal in this chapter is the evocation of an archaeology of sensuous, lived human experience, including sexuality but by no means limited to sexuality, and upon the articulation of sensuous human experience with other facets of experience. Just as this volume deliberately sets a course into an uncharted area of archaeological interpretation, sexuality, so do I remind myself and my readers that the experience of the sexual cannot be understood in containment or isolation from other aspects or qualities of our lives. As with any embodiment of the sensuous, sexuality is inextricably entwined with multiple aspects of human experience. My purpose below is to sketch an outline of specific conditions of and contexts for manifestations of sexuality in the Mesolithic period of northern Europe.

Following this introduction, I briefly address theoretical issues regarding sexuality, gender, and sex through a consideration of relevant terminology. Next I touch briefly upon research into Mesolithic societies in order to provide a context for my subsequent argument. I go on to outline a hypothesis which employs the direct historical approach in order to trace ideological and ritual connections between northern Eurasian ethnographically described societies and Mesolithic societies across northern Europe. I summarize ethnographically known aspects of Siberian sexuality, including both sexual practices and the ideological belief systems within which sexual practices are embedded, and hypothesize that the organization of sexuality in the European Mesolithic may have resembled the ideological and social organization of sexuality among ethnographically described peoples from northern Eurasia. I conclude with a consideration of some of the implications of this argument for various interpretations of Mesolithic societies, and for the investigation of archaeologies of sexuality generally.

COMING TO TERMS: SEXUALITY AND 'SEX/GENDER SYSTEMS' IN PREHISTORY

As with other parts of human experience, the analytical isolation of sexuality as an object of knowledge must be pursued with an appreciation for the interconnections of sexuality with other aspects of societies. Thus the investigation of sexuality in the past may best be undertaken through recognition of the historically variable social contexts within which sexuality operates. Throughout this chapter I employ the terms 'sex/gender systems' and 'sex/gender' as referents for sexuality and its variable social contents and contexts, and especially for the interrelationships of sexuality with the social categories of sex and gender. Use of these terms refers by implication to debates regarding the emic existence of multiple sex and/or gender statuses, including third, fourth, and more genders, as well as various nonbinary biological sex statuses, i.e. sexual categories which do not unambiguously conform to the boundaries of either of our etic categories of male and female. Because of these debates, and because what I mean by these terms differs from their original usage, I must summarize their intellectual heritage.

The term 'sex/gender system' was introduced by Rubin (1975), who pointed out that gender identity is not a straightforward and inevitable product of sex assignment, but that social systems – sex/gender systems – produce gender. Thus the elements of gender and the mechanisms of gender production may vary in differing social contexts and between societies. Subsequent theorists, most prominently Judith Butler (1990, 1993), have extended this insight by arguing that biological sex, too, is a constructed set of categories which are not a 'natural' given, but are, like gender, a set of categories which are socially produced and regulated. Roscoe (1998: 127) conveniently summarizes these two arguments by identifying 'sex as a category of bodies, and gender as a category of persons'. For fuller discussions of the complexities involving the conceptualization of sex and gender in many societies, see the works cited above, as well as Herdt (1994a, 1994b), Roscoe (1994), and the contributions to Jacobs, Thomas and Lang (1997).

I suggest that the terms 'sex/gender category' and 'sex/gender systems' are both convenient and appropriate for drawing together the range of variability relating to sex, gender, and sexuality in prehistoric social systems, especially when much of the variability remains uncharacterized, or if lack of evidence does not currently permit resolution between these constituent elements. The variability between sex/gender systems can be enormous, as evidenced by the characterizations of some societies such that sex but not gender would constitute a relevant emic category, for others that gender but not sex would be a relevant emic category, and for still others that both sex and gender constitute distinct emic categories (Roscoe 1998). The usage I propose for this terminology is apposite as well if 'sex/gender' and 'sex/gender systems' are taken to mean that the constituent analytic elements, sex, gender, and sexuality, may be inextricably entwined with each other. Although Rubin (1984: 307) later argued that gender and sexuality must be analytically distinguished in Western industrial societies, she explicitly exempts 'tribal organizations' from this argument.

Of course I do not mean to suggest that sexuality and/or other aspects of sex/gender systems should not be distinguished from one another, if the evidence to do so exists and such a distinction would be analytically appropriate. For example, gender has been a very productive analytical category since Conkey and Spector (1984) originally drew attention to it in archaeological contexts (see Voss and Schmidt, Chapter 1), and it will continue to be in the future. Rather, my use in this chapter of terms such as 'sex/gender system' or 'sex/gender category' is meant to reflect both the common threads by which sex, gender, and sexuality are interwoven, and the difficulties involved in resolving between these potentially distinct but interrelated categories in many prehistoric contexts. The archaeological context discussed below illustrates the utility of these terms as I define them, for the sake of their brevity of expression, convenience, and accuracy.

THE MESOLITHIC OF NORTHERN EUROPE

Generally defined as the interstitial period between the end of the Paleolithic period, and the adoption of food production techniques in the subsequent Neolithic period, the Mesolithic ('Middle Stone Age') period was the unwanted stepchild of European prehistory for over a century.[1] The reason for this disregard was the widely-held view that the Mesolithic was a period of relative stagnation sandwiched between the cultural heights of the Paleolithic, wherein the hunters of Ice Age megafauna created the spectacular cave art which has justifiably impressed Europeans in the twentieth century; and the cultural innovation of the Neolithic, a period which saw the invention and spread of the technological basis of our own civilization: agriculture (Zvelebil 1996). In the last generation, however, this perspective has been substantially challenged, and research on the Mesolithic period has flourished (e.g. Bonsall 1989; Kozlowski 1973; Price and Brown 1985; Vermeersch and Van Peer 1990; Zvelebil 1986; Zvelebil, Domanska, and Dennell 1998).

Although interest in and appreciation of the lives of Mesolithic peoples has increased recently, much of this has focused not so much upon the Mesolithic for its own sake, but upon the Mesolithic/Neolithic transition, i.e. the reasons why and mechanisms by which hunter-gatherer peoples adopted, or in some cases delayed the adoption of, agricultural/pastoral subsistence economies. Not surprisingly, relatively little work has been done to investigate relations of gender or sexuality among Mesolithic populations. In general, the only variable relating to sexuality which has been seriously examined for the northern European Mesolithic in particular (e.g. Jacobs 1995; Newell and Constandse-

Westermann 1988), and for deep prehistoric contexts more generally, has been the characterization of mating networks in terms of population size and geographic extent. Gregg's (1988) and Zvelebil's (1998a) speculative, yet plausible suggestions regarding mechanisms for the possible exchange of mates across foraging/farming frontiers in prehistoric Europe, and upon some of the social consequences of such exchanges for the Mesolithic/Neolithic transition, represent interesting variations of this theme. Yet the Gregg and Zvelebil examples too focus upon potential interactions between Mesolithic and Neolithic populations, and do not explore the pre-contact situation.

Given the history of early and sustained interest in archaeology in Scandinavian countries, it is not surprising that northern Europe has been one of the regions where Mesolithic research has been most actively pursued. Here, too, a principal focus of research has been the Mesolithic/Neolithic transition as it occurred in the southerly latitudes of Denmark and southern Sweden *c.* 3000 BC. Due to the influence of environmental constraints, the spread of aspects of Neolithic agricultural technologies from the south into more northerly areas of Europe was not uniform, in either a geographic or chronological sense. In general, agriculture becomes increasingly impractical and unprofitable in areas of climatic extremes, such that the penetration of aspects of agricultural subsistence methods tended to be impeded the further north and the further inland these methods were taken. This environmental resistance to the adoption of agricultural subsistence has implications which will be explored below.

A DIRECT HISTORICAL CONNECTION TO THE NORTHERN EURASIAN MESOLITHIC

Recent work has opened an intriguing potential avenue for the exploration of sexuality among Old World Mesolithic peoples of northerly latitudes. Zvelebil has linked observations of aspects of material culture continuity of thousands of years duration across northern Eurasia with a broad corpus of ethnographic data on ritual and ideology of recent hunting-gathering peoples of the circum-boreal zone (Zvelebil 1993a, 1998b). Based upon this linkage, he has suggested the existence of a generalized continuity of ideological and cosmological belief systems for many millennia throughout this region. In effect, Zvelebil argues that it is appropriate and reasonable to make inferences about societies in this region from the Mesolithic to the modern period – a period of some seven to eight thousand years – based not solely upon ethnographic analogies with recent anthropological observations of these societies, but also based upon a direct historical linkage between successive periods throughout the Holocene occupation of this region. It is by no means unprecedented to suggest such a continuity of religious, ideological, and cosmological belief systems across many millennia. Other scholars have made the same argument for circumpolar groups generally (Hultkrantz 1981; Lowie 1934), as well as for specific groups. For example, Hultkrantz has asserted that the 'precursors' of contemporary 'Saami cultural and religious variations' are to be found in 'the Circumpolar culture of the Paleolithic and Mesolithic and its derivatives' (Hultkrantz 1994: 347). Nevertheless, the scope of Zvelebil's claim for continuity merits a closer examination of his argument, because the argument can inform an examination of Mesolithic sexuality.

Zvelebil uses Ingold's (1986: 243–76) abstraction of circum-boreal (Siberian and North American) ethnographic data on religious ideology, as well as the work of Anisimov (1963) and Vasilevitch (1963), to summarize elements of a generalized 'boreal foragers' belief system' (Zvelebil 1993a: 57). These include a tripartite division of the universe into sky, earth, and underworld, which are linked by a feature such as a 'cosmic pillar' or 'cosmic river', often symbolized by a tree placed in the center of a shaman's tent. Humans and animals are similarly divided into three elemental substances: the physical body, the body-soul and the free-soul. Humans partake of all three elemental substances, but not all animals do so: only animals such as bears, who are seen as masters or guardians of wild animals as well as mediators between animal beings and human beings, also possess all three substances. Elk (or other ungulates) and waterfowl also play roles as guardians of other animals and as channels of communication with other, non-terrestrial worlds (Zvelebil 1993a: 58).

After noting that care must be taken when mapping the ethnography of modern hunting-gathering peoples onto the past without careful scrutiny of the archaeological evidence (Wobst 1978), Zvelebil asserts that

> in the hunter-gatherer prehistory of Northern Europe, the symbolism of rock-carving sites, of carved objects in the material culture and of ritual contexts of burials clearly relates to the boreal system of beliefs. Material representations include sculpted terminals of wooden household utensils, such as spoons, bowls and ladles, zoomorphic figurines, axes and maceheads, rock carvings and zoomorphic ornamentation on pottery. Elk, bear and waterbirds are the most common designs. Within this symbolic context, the meaning[.] of ritual sites can be comprehended by reference to this ideology[.] (1993a: 58).

The fundamental basis for Zvelebil's assertion of cultural continuity between Mesolithic and modern hunting-gathering societies rests upon the fact that agricultural social systems were slow to make incursions into far northern environments, for the obvious environmental reason that the domesticated species at the heart of Neolithic technologies could not flourish in the increasingly harsh climatic conditions which prevailed as they were taken north. Thus according to this line of thought, it is feasible to argue for ideological and cultural continuities between prehistoric and modern hunting-gathering groups where conditions prevailed such that there were no Neolithic-induced subsistence or social transformations were limited in scope.

MESOLITHIC CEMETERIES

In his 1993 discussion of the applicability of the direct historical approach[2] to the Mesolithic of northern Eurasia, one of Zvelebil's explicit goals is to provide a spatio-temporal context for the large Mesolithic cemetery of Oleneostrovski mogilnik in Karelia in western Russia, radiocarbon-dated to *c.* 7500 BP (Zvelebil 1993a: 61). With 170 individuals recovered, Oleneostrovski mogilnik is certainly the largest Mesolithic cemetery uncovered to date in northern Europe; moreover, it is estimated that the site originally contained more than 400 or 500 individuals, most of which were destroyed by quarrying operations prior to excavation in the 1930s (Jacobs 1995; O'Shea and Zvelebil 1984). Other than some small lithic scatters nearby, the lack of evidence of human occupation in the vicinity seems to mark this cemetery as a purely ritual location. Oleneostrovski mogilnik has been interpreted very differently by various researchers: by Soviet archaeologists Ravdonikas and Gurina (before radiocarbon dates were available for the site) as a point along the unilinear sequence of Marxist social evolutionary development, specifically as an early Neolithic site because of its sheer size, and despite the absence of ceramics (explained as a ritual prohibition) (Jacobs 1995; O'Shea and Zvelebil 1984; Zvelebil 1993a:

61); as evidence that the peak or climax of hunter-gatherer occupation in this region occurred during the Mesolithic occupation, with a maximum density of population and maximum social complexity, compared to which more recent hunter-gatherer occupations represent but a pale reflection (O'Shea and Zvelebil 1984); and in the most recent (re)interpretation, the cemetery was seen as serving as a ritualized central place for small-scale dispersed hunter-gatherers to maintain an integrated social and mating network, an interpretation which explicitly rejects O'Shea's and Zvelebil's argument for the existence of social complexity (Jacobs 1995).

Despite these widely differing interpretations of the site, however, observers seem to be in general agreement about the significance of the mortuary treatment of four individuals (two females and two males) excavated at Oleneostrovski mogilnik. Due to their unique style of interment ('shaft' burials with more nearly vertical positions of interment, and an orientation facing west rather than east), by which they are set apart from all the other interments in the cemetery, as well as by the relatively high levels of grave good wealth provided to three of the four, these individuals have been identified as shamans or ritual specialists of similar standing by Gurina, as well as O'Shea and Zvelebil (O'Shea and Zvelebil 1984: 6), with Jacobs more recently offering a cautious and conditional consent to this interpretation (Jacobs 1995). The recovery of six beaver mandibles from one of these graves strengthens the identification of these individuals as shamans, as mandibles form a part of shaman's outfits among some Siberian groups, and the beaver has often been seen by many boreal peoples as possessing ritual and medicinal properties (O'Shea and Zvelebil 1984: 6).

After Oleneostrovski mogilnik, the site of Skateholm on the southern Baltic coast of Sweden constitutes the next largest body of mortuary evidence from this period reported to date in northern Europe, with more than eighty individuals in two chronologically distinct Mesolithic cemeteries. In the first volume of the site report (Larsson 1988), Newell and Constandse-Westermann (1988) discuss the significance of the site to the wider context of European Mesolithic archaeology. In order to compare the Skateholm site with other Mesolithic sites, they discuss 'gender identification and determination' of individuals from Skateholm, employing data derived from both associated grave goods and physical anthropological examinations of skeletal remains done by various researchers. Regarding one individual from Skateholm II they write:

> Grave XV has been labelled male by the Persons, Alexandersen and Frayer, while Constandse-Westermann takes no firm stance. Culturally it fits with neither the males nor the females. Both the composition and the quantity of the grave accoutrements set this person very much apart from the rest of the samples. As the physical data weigh more heavily, this person has been regarded as a male, but with a culturally unique identity.
>
> (Newell and Constandse-Westermann 1988: 165)

This evidence echoes the mortuary evidence from Oleneostrovski mogilnik which was interpreted to identify individuals treated in a similar fashion as shamans, and thus strongly suggests the possibility that this individual from Skateholm could have been a shaman or ritual specialist of similar standing. Thus the two largest Mesolithic cemeteries in northern Europe contain evidence pointing to the presence of shamans in these societies.

NORTHERN EURASIAN SHAMANS AND SEXUALITY

If Zvelebil's assertion of cultural continuity has merit, then given the widespread occurrence of the phenomenon of the shaman in present-day circumpolar societies, the social category of shaman would very likely have a time depth extending back into the Mesolithic. As described above, this inference appears to be supported by mortuary evidence suggesting the presence of shamans at Oleneostrovski mogilnik and Skateholm. This reasoning begs the question of the role of shamans in these societies.

Shamans have long fascinated outside observers. Descriptions of shamans by western European travelers proliferated during the age of discovery and resulted in a considerable body of accounts circulating in western Europe beginning in the seventeenth century and expanding greatly during the eighteenth century (Flaherty 1992). The literature on shamans has continued since that time, and is voluminous, contentious and on-going.[3] Even the definition of the term is highly contested (Pentikäinen 1996a). Although many scholars as well as popular writers today include religious and ritual specialists from all corners of the world within the category of shaman, this inclusionary movement remains controversial. The social phenomenon of the shaman was identified by Western observers among Siberian peoples (Hultkrantz 1993), and the word 'shaman' itself was taken from the Tungus language of Siberia (Clottes and Lewis-Williams 1998, Flaherty 1992). For the purposes of this chapter I choose to use a quite restrictive definition, by which the term 'shaman' is understood to include religious and cultural specialists from indigenous societies in northern Eurasia, and in far northern North America.[4] Even very similar social roles among indigenous groups in other cultural and geographic areas such as temperate North America are excluded by this definition. The definition used here is even further removed from the recent rise of contemporary self-styled 'practitioners of shamanism' who lift the methods and accouterments of shamans from their indigenous contexts in order to offer them to Euro-American audiences 'as a universal means of penetrating into the depths of the human conscience' (Pentikäinen 1996a: 6). I employ a narrow definition of the term 'shaman' in order to particularize my argument to the Mesolithic of northern Eurasia.

Scholarly positions on shamanism vary widely. Shamans have frequently been characterized by anthropologists as physicians or medical specialists in Eurasian societies, i.e. they use their abilities to connect with energies available in other realms of existence to cure the sick (e.g. Rogers 1982). Others have seen the shamanic role as being designed for individuals afflicted with psychopathological disease; in fact, this question of whether the shaman is a disturbed individual (neurotic, psychotic, or schizophrenic) or is on the contrary a gifted, balanced and perfectly well-adjusted person, constitutes one of the oldest of all anthropological debates (Kennedy 1973: 1,149–52; Pentikäinen 1996a: 6–7). Mircea Eliade's influential view points to the ecstatic experience of the shaman as the defining characteristic of the role (Eliade 1972). In Eurasian societies that incorporate the role of shaman, Eliade asserts that 'the ecstatic experience is considered the religious experience par excellence'; while shamans do not usurp all religious activity in these societies, they are nevertheless considered 'the great masters of ecstasy' (1972: 4).

Without taking a position with regard to the above debates, I focus in this chapter upon the intersection between aspects of the sensuous bodily experiences of shamans, and the role of the shaman as a bridge between various levels of existence. Shamans, as the Sakha (Yakut) curer, and widely reputed shaman, Vladimir Kondakov told Mandalstam Balzer (1996: 164), 'should be able to balance and mediate energies within multiple levels of cosmological worlds'. How is this accomplished? It requires the harnessing of both male and female sexual potential. For many, this means having male shamans accept female spirit helpers as guides, and vice versa, incorporating their power and even their gendered essence in trance and during seances. It can involve tapping the gendered spiritual force of a tree, for instance the female birch, to cure a male patient. And in a particularly dramatic form, the greatest shamans, even if they are males, are able to themselves give birth to spirit animals.

(Mandelstam Balzer 1996: 164)

One of the most common outward manifestations of a shaman's ability to harness sexual potentials was the phenomenon of transvestism (Mandelstam Balzer 1996). In addition to this, many shamans would give up the tools associated with their pre-shamanic sex/gender status and begin to use the tools associated with male occupations if they had been female, and vice versa. In some Siberian cultures, the shamanic use of sexual power and symbolism could manifest as a transformation of a male shaman into a female, whether for particular shamanic seances, or more permanently (Mandelstam Balzer 1996: 165). According to the turn-of-the-century Russian exile-ethnographer, Waldemar Bogoras, certain particularly revered and feared male Chukchi shamans who had changed their sex/gender status were referred to as 'soft men' or 'similar to a woman', while esteemed and feared female shamans who had transformed their sex/gender were referred to as 'similar to a man' (Bogoras 1975). Transformed shamans among the Chukchi were considered especially powerful because of their transformations, and were dreaded even by untransformed shamans, as they were perceived to have spirit protectors who could and would retaliate for slights (Bogoras 1975).

Transformed or not, outside observers have reported that in many Siberian societies, assuming the shamanic identity was a change that could be dreaded. Among many groups a person could be called to become a shaman at any time during his or her life. Moreover, despite the power and prestige associated with the role of shaman, many reportedly resisted the call. Especially feared and resisted was the call to become a transformed shaman (although reports claiming to characterize emic attitudes toward aspects of societies relating to sexuality may be unreliable – see below). Even a married person with children could be called by spirits to change or transform him or herself in this way (Mandelstam Balzer 1996).

Transformed shamans might have sexual relations with either normative men or women, including partners of their own pre-transformation sex/gender status. 'A true "soft man" enters into sexual competition with women for young men ... chooses a lover and takes a husband' (Mandelstam Balzer 1996: 166).

> They cohabit in a perverse way, *modo Socratis*, in which the transformed wife always plays the passive role ... some 'soft men' are said to lose altogether the man's desire and in the end to even acquire the organs of a woman; while others are said to have mistresses of their own in secret and to produce children by them.
>
> (Bogoras 1975: 451)

Given the explicit moral judgments, e.g. 'cohabit in a perverse way', expressed by various early ethnographers of sexuality (for a discussion of some of the problems with early ethnographic descriptions of non-heterosexual sexual practices, see Roscoe 1995), not to mention their lascivious attention towards forms of sexual expression which violated their own moral codes, it is legitimate to question the reliability of aspects of Bogoras' characterization of sexuality among the Chukchi. For instance, there is really no way that he could be certain that 'the transformed wife always plays the passive role' in sexual relations (see Wobst 1978 for a discussion of failings of ethnographic accounts), especially if the 'soft man' might also be concurrently begetting children with a woman. Nevertheless, among the Chukchi and other groups, some shamans, especially some of the most powerful, reportedly engaged in varieties of sexual expression which, again reportedly, were not widely engaged in by most members of Siberian societies. Even though we must, for a number of reasons, treat such characterizations of sexuality and sexual activity with skepticism, sufficient evidence does exist to confirm that the sexual lives and experiences of shamans differed from the sexual lives and experiences of non-shamans.

Some researchers have argued that the power of sexuality, and sex/gender transformation, constituted a key ingredient of the shamanic ability to act as an intercessor between human beings and the spirit realm (see references to the work of Bernard Saladin d'Anglure and Leo Sternberg in Mandelstam Balzer 1996: 168–9). To the extent that this was true (and this is a contentious issue – see Mandelstam Balzer 1996: 168), then the ability and necessity to freely manipulate sexual energy in various forms is an element at the heart of the phenomenon of Siberian shamanism. Moreover, shamanism is not the only aspect of Siberian cultures wherein manipulation of sexual energies plays a role. In the widespread Siberian religious complex known as the bear ceremony, non-shamans enjoy license to partake of the sacred by ritually acting as, dressing as, and/or taking the names of another sex/gender status (Mandelstam Balzer 1996: 169–74).

Thus a broad northern Eurasian cultural pattern emerges, wherein sexual energies comprised a crucial element within and link between the various levels of existence in the cosmology and world-view of indigenous societies. The ability to fluidly move between sex/gender categories, and act congruently with different aspects of these categories as needed, was highly valued and sometimes feared throughout northern Eurasian indigenous societies, due to the connection with the realm of the sacred. Because sexual expressions were at least potentially associated with the sexual aspects of the sacred, sexuality constituted a social arena explicitly affected by the cultural work of the manipulation of sexual energies. Considerable variability existed between different societies regarding the particulars of how patterns of sexual expressions may have manifested as products of this cultural work, but the broad outlines of this pattern hold across the region. As cultural specialists of the sacred, empowered in part through their control of sexual energies, shamans in general enacted the widest range of sexual expressions among their fellows.

THE DIRECT HISTORICAL APPROACH TO MESOLITHIC SEXUALITY

In light of the above analysis, how might one characterize sexuality among northern European Mesolithic peoples, including those who buried their dead at Oleneostrovski mogilnik, Skateholm, Vedbaek, and other cemeteries in the region? Two principal lines of evidence support the view that the sex/gender systems of recent northern Eurasian societies are directly historically related to, and are not dissimilar in broad outline from the sex/gender systems of Mesolithic societies of the region: (1) the evidence that Zvelebil has adduced regarding continuity of ideological/cosmological belief systems, in the form of material culture manifestations in the archaeological record which are consistent with features of ethnographically documented belief systems; and (2) the evidence at Oleneostrovski mogilnik and at Skateholm for the presence of shamans. In addition to these lines of evidence, it may also be appropriate to cautiously give some weight to the truism that religious/cosmological belief systems tend to be among the most conservative elements of human culture (but see further discussion below). Moreover, this truism is more likely to retain its relevance in the absence of dramatic social change, as may accompany the introduction of a new subsistence technology such as farming. As indicated above, while Neolithic agricultural subsistence systems were indeed adopted in some of the more southerly, ecologically favorable areas under discussion, including southern Scandinavia as early as 5,000 years ago, the spread of agricultural subsistence technologies and agriculturally-based societies in other parts of northern Eurasia has been patchy, and dependent upon local ecological and social conditions (Dolukhanov 1986; Zvelebil 1998a). In fact, the subsistence economy and ways of life in the most northerly areas have only in recent centuries been dramatically altered from the pattern which obtained during the Mesolithic.

Having established an argument for continuity in ideological/cosmological beliefs from the Mesolithic to the recent past in this region, to propose an outline of the features of northern Eurasian Mesolithic sexuality is straightforward. This endeavor proceeds from the ethnographic evidence for the widespread belief in northern Eurasian societies of the central cosmological importance and sacredness of sexual energies. These ideological features manifest in ethnographically described societies through the social role of the shaman and through the character of the bear ceremony and other ritual occasions wherein sex/gender categorical boundaries become permeable. I suggest that Mesolithic societies enacted versions of Mesolithic cosmological beliefs through similar institutions, particularly including the role of shaman.

To put it concretely, I suggest a pattern of marriage and/or socially recognized sexual liaisons in the Mesolithic which would include, in addition to marriages and liaisons between women and men, socially recognized sexual relations between untransformed shamans and partners of 'opposite' sex/gender identities, and socially recognized sexual relations between transformed shamans and 'same' sex partners, referring here of course to the shamans' pre-transformation sex/gender identities. I suggest that these socially validated and recognized sexual relations both reified and enacted the sexualized cosmology which, I have argued, comprised part of the ideological heart of these societies. Other sexual relationships almost certainly would have taken place from time to time, such as the type mentioned above in which some Chukchi 'soft men' reputedly had children by mistresses, or same-sex contacts between non-shaman women, and between non-shaman men. The status of these 'other' sexual expressions remains unclear, not only due to a lack of data that could address the issue, but because we cannot uncritically rely upon the accuracy of historical and ethnographic reports that purport to convey emic evaluations of these behaviors.

Further research that would examine sexuality within the contexts of specific Siberian groups could be very helpful. Such detailed investigations could enrich understanding of the range of variability of patterns of sexual expressions within recent groups. Moreover, comparisons between such deep contextual analyses could further illuminate widespread Siberian patterns of sexuality. Both the narrowly focused and the comparative cross-cultural research could characterize, more precisely than I have been equipped to do here, the elements comprising the sex/gender systems of these societies (e.g. do the elements of the shamanic role within a specific group warrant designation as a third or fourth sex/gender role?), and could further provide useful new analogies for archaeologists of north Eurasian sexualities.

IMPLICATIONS, COMPLICATIONS AND SPECULATIONS

If the argument presented here has any congruence with the actual lives of Mesolithic peoples, then this chapter will have served the important function of marshaling evidence for a range of sexual variability deep into prehistory. Moreover, the Mesolithic range of sexual variability would have resembled modern ranges of variability in that its shape was a manifestation of, and a response to a particular ideology of sexuality. In other words, a corollary of the argument presented here is that by at least 7,000 years ago, human sexuality was being shaped by social and cultural influences in a fashion similar to the ways we see it being shaped in the present, and was not a function of an essentialized biology.

However, using the direct historical approach through multiple millennia is a perilous analytical strategy, and it is important to face the questions and challenges which arise in connection with its use. First, do both Zvelebil and I lump past and present hunter-gatherer societies together as a single, fundamental ahistorical category of the 'Other?' In other words, does the claim for long-term ideological continuity reify a patronizing and colonialist view of hunter-gatherers as static and unchanging? Such a critique is undermined by the evidence that suggests ideological continuity over a great period of time. It is further undermined through a recognition of the ecological constraints outlined above that support the argument for social continuity. Given that such continuity has been hypothesized, it would be pointless to ignore the implications for understanding Mesolithic sexuality. Moreover, Zvelebil has been one of the strongest and most consistent champions of the position that European Mesolithic hunter-gatherer groups were not helpless victims of a monolithic historical process of Neolithization, but that different hunter-gatherer groups participated as knowledgeable actors in differing ways in a variable and nuanced process which depended upon local environmental and social conditions (Zvelebil 1978, 1986, 1989a, 1989b, 1993b, 1995, 1996, 1998a). I entirely agree with this position. Aspects of ideological and social stability in far northern Eurasia can thus be appreciated in the context of the unique historical and environmental circumstances which made them possible.

Second, by invoking shamans and shamanism, I risk a variety of possible misreadings of my argument. By stressing the presence of shamans in northern European Mesolithic societies, and their association with a particular ideology, I do not intend to support arguments for the universality of the institution of shamanism, or for the presence of shamans within any other social context,[5] whether in other Mesolithic societies, or in hunter-gatherer or pre-state level societies generally. Nor is this chapter intended as support for the view that modern circumpolar peoples preserve elements of the adaptations and lifestyles of Eurasian Paleolithic societies.[6] Although I argue for some aspects of ideological and social continuity throughout most of the Holocene for a particular geographic region, I do not argue or assume that this ideology originated in the Paleolithic. To summarize, my argument here is dependent upon, and a reflection of concrete evidence for ideological and social continuities in a particular area throughout a specified time-span, and should not be extended beyond the limits of that evidence.

Moreover, it is clear that, even with the specified time-span and place within which Zvelebil argues for elements of social stability, substantive changes did occur in far northern Eurasian societies between the Mesolithic and modern periods, such as the inclusion of small-scale reindeer-herding pastoralism within the hunting-gathering subsistence economy by groups such as the Khanty (Pentikäinen 1996b). In light of this recognition of change, it is interesting to reconsider the analysis of O'Shea and Zvelebil (1984) in relation to the issue of diachronic change in the sex/gender systems of northern Eurasian societies.

Recall that O'Shea and Zvelebil (1984) asserted that the group who buried their dead at Oleneostrovski mogilnik, and by extension at least some other Mesolithic northern Eurasian groups as well, may have had greater population densities, and been more socially complex, than their successor societies (but see the critique of this position by Jacobs 1995). O'Shea and Zvelebil argue that, because 'the modern Boreal zone cultures of Siberia seem relatively simple', the most convincing ethnographic parallel to Oleneostrovski mogilnik society, 'and indeed to the late Mesolithic of Karelia as a whole, might well be the complex cultures of the American North-west Coast' (O'Shea and Zvelebil 1984: 35). Echoing the suggestions of others (e.g. Lee and DeVore 1968; Sahlins 1972), they attribute the inadequacy of modern Siberian groups as ethnographic analogs to bias in the recent hunter-gatherer ethnographic sample, because most ethnographically described hunter-gatherers have been pushed into marginal environments, and so could not sustain social organization based upon economic ranking and inequality. Therefore our ethnographic analogies may be too simple to reflect a past richness of internal differentiation which it is now difficult for us to imagine.

Newell and Constandse-Westermann (1988: 170–71) have in fact asserted that evidence from Skateholm mortuary practices suggest the existence of a three-tiered hierarchy of ascribed status at this site, in contrast to the evidence from many other European Mesolithic cemeteries, where the evidence points to ranking based upon earned status. Instead of the traditional, flattened view of Mesolithic social differentiation, in which status would invariably be individually earned, this evidence suggests that variation may have existed between Mesolithic groups with regard to the means by which status could be acquired. To put it another way, 'Mesolithic society' may not have been a unitary phenomenon with respect to ranking, but one with a range of variation. If so, then the characterization of Mesolithic sex/gender systems presented in this chapter may be considered as a foundation or starting point, with various groups evolving elaborations upon this sex/gender substrate depending upon the development of hierarchies of rank and upon other particular circumstances.

CONCLUSION

In this chapter I have attempted to say something beyond the trivial about the sex/gender system of a society in 'deep' prehistory. The argument presented in this chapter is intended as a starting point for understanding the expression and social regulation of sexuality in the Mesolithic. My intention has been to begin to complicate a previously static and flat view of sexuality in deep prehistoric contexts. I have suggested that sexuality in the Mesolithic was about more than mating networks. As instantiations of a sexualized cosmology, meaningful patterns of sexuality shaped how people lived and experienced their lives. For men and women, for shamans and transformed shamans, and for the sexual partners of all of these, sexuality was an element in the construction of social identities.

Perhaps even more important than the specific conclusions regarding Mesolithic sexuality are several points that I hope this chapter has demonstrated. First, it has underscored the assertion made in the introduction to this volume that investigators of sexuality must be willing to experiment with novel and innovative approaches. The application in this chapter of that special case of ethnographic analogy, the direct historical approach, to a social context 7,000 years in the past, constitutes an example of such experimentation. The second point that I hope this chapter has demonstrated is how inextricably sexuality is bound up with other axes of analysis, particularly in small-scale societies. As we have seen, discussions of sexuality among northern Eurasian Mesolithic peoples must implicate issues of gender and cosmology/ideology. Finally, I hope that this chapter has demonstrated that the exercise of prudence in archaeological interpretation is good, that the exercise of imagination is better, and that the exercise of both is best of all.

ACKNOWLEDGEMENTS

This chapter has greatly benefited from the generous support and editorial acumen provided by my co-editor of this volume, Barb Voss, with whom it has been absolutely wonderful to work. As always, Meg Conkey has provided important guidance throughout the writing of this chapter. I very much appreciate the critical input on earlier drafts from Will Roscoe and Marek Zvelebil, which were crucial for improving the chapter. All errors, of course, remain my own.

NOTES

1 Definitions of the Mesolithic, and distinctions between the Mesolithic and the preceding and subsequent periods, have been problematic (Rozoy 1989; Zvelebil 1995). For discussions of the problematic place of the Mesolithic in the history of European prehistoric research, see Clark (1978, 1980) and Zvelebil (1986, 1993b, 1995, 1996, 1998a) among others.
2 Zvelebil does not use the phrase 'the direct historical approach' to describe the connection between Mesolithic societies and ethnographically described boreal societies; this identification is my own. Zvelebil (1993a) structures his argument in terms of differing concepts and scales of time.
3 For example, a new journal devoted to shamanistic studies (*Shaman*) began publication in 1993 (see Hultkrantz 1993).
4 In the twentieth century the role of shaman was vigorously suppressed by Soviet authorities. With the end of the Soviet state, a revitalization of shamanic traditions has been occurring (Mandelstam Balzer 1996).
5 When broadly defined, the institution of shamanism may be found in many ethnographic and archaeological contexts. For example, Lewis-Williams associates shamanism with rock art from all over the world, spanning thousands of years, including southern Africa (Lewis-Williams and Dowson 1989) and Upper Paleolithic south-west Europe (Clottes and Lewis-Williams 1998). Without commenting upon Lewis-Williams' work in this area, the definition of shamanism used here is deliberately narrow and would preclude its application in these contexts.
6 See de Laguna (1994) for an interesting recounting of some of the intellectual history of proposed links between Paleolithic peoples of south-west Europe and modern Eskimo cultures.

REFERENCES

Anisimov, A. F. (1963) 'Cosmological Concepts of the Peoples of the North', in H. N. Michael (ed.) *Studies in Siberian Shamanism*, no. 4, *Anthropology of the North: Translations from the Russian Sources*, Toronto: University of Toronto Press for the Arctic Institute of North America.

Bogoras, W. (1975) *The Chukchee*, reprint of the 1904–1909 edition, *The Jesup North Pacific Expedition: Memoir of the American Museum of Natural History Volume VII*, New York: AMS Press, Inc.

Bonsall, C. (ed.) (1989) *The Mesolithic in Europe: Papers Presented at the Third International Symposium Edinburgh 1985*, Edinburgh: John Donald Publishers.

Bourdieu, P. (1977) *Outline of a Theory of Practice*, Cambridge: Cambridge University Press.

Butler, J. (1990) *Gender Trouble: Feminism and the Subversion of Identity*, New York: Routledge.

—— (1993) 'Imitation and Gender Insubordination', in H. Abelove, M. A. Barale and D. Halpern (eds) *The Lesbian and Gay Studies Reader*, New York: Routledge.

Clark, J. G. D. (1978) 'Neothermal Orientations', in P. Mellars (ed.) *The Early Postglacial Settlement of Northern Europe*, Pittsburgh: University of Pittsburgh Press.

—— (1980) *Mesolithic Prelude*, Edinburgh: Edinburgh University Press.

Clottes, J. and D. Lewis-Williams (1998) *The Shamans of Prehistory: Trance and Magic in the Painted Caves*, New York: Harry N. Abrams, Inc.

Conkey, M. W. and J. D. Spector (1984) 'Archaeology and the Study of Gender', in M. B. Schiffer (ed.) *Advances in Archaeological Method and Theory*, vol. 7, New York: Academic Press: 1–38.

de Laguna, F. (1994) 'Some Early Circumpolar Studies', in T. Irimoto and T. Yamada (eds), *Circumpolar Religion and Ecology*, Tokyo: University of Tokyo Press.

Dolukhanov, P. M. 1986. 'The Late Mesolithic and the transition to food production in Eastern Europe', in M. Zvelebil (ed.) *Hunters in Transition: Mesolithic Societies of Temperate Eurasia and their Transition to Farming*, Cambridge: Cambridge University Press.

Eliade, M. (1972) *Shamanism: Archaic Techniques of Ecstasy. Bollingen Series LXXVI*, Princeton: Princeton University Press.

Flaherty, G. (1992) *Shamanism and the Eighteenth Century*, Princeton: Princeton University Press.

Gregg, S. A. (1988) *Foragers and Farmers: Population Interaction and Agricultural Expansion in Prehistoric Europe*, Chicago: University of Chicago Press.

Herdt, G. (1994a) 'Introduction: Third Sexes and Third Genders', in G. Herdt (ed.) *Third Sex, Third Gender: Beyond Sexual Dimorphism in Culture and History*, New York: Zone Books.

—— (1994b) 'Mistaken Sex: Culture, Biology and the Third Sex in New Guinea', in G. Herdt (ed.) *Third Sex, Third Gender: Beyond Sexual Dimorphism in Culture and History*, New York: Zone Books.

Hultkrantz, Å. (1981) 'North American Indian Religions in a Circumpolar Perspective', in P. Hovens (ed.) *North American Indian Studies: European Contributions*, Göttingen: Edition Herodot.

—— (1993) 'Introductory Remarks on the Study of Shamanism', *Shaman* 1: 3–14.

—— (1994) 'Religion and Environment among the Saami: An Ecological Study', in T. Irimoto and T. Yamada (eds) *Circumpolar Religion and Ecology: An Anthropology of the North*, Tokyo: University of Tokyo Press.

Ingold, T. (1986) *The Appropriation of Nature: Essays on Human Ecology and Social Relations*, Manchester: Manchester University Press.

Jacobs, K. (1995) 'Returning to Oleni' ostrov: Social, Economic, and Skeletal Dimensions of a Boreal Forest Mesolithic Cemetery', *Journal of Anthropological Archaeology* 14: 359–403.

Jacobs, S., W. Thomas and S. Lang (eds) (1997) *Two-Spirit People: Native American Gender Identity, Sexuality, and Spirituality*, Urbana and Chicago: University of Illinois Press.

Kennedy, J. G. (1973) 'Cultural Psychiatry', in J. J. Honigman (ed.) *Handbook of Social and Cultural Anthropology*, Chicago: Rand McNally College Publishing Company.

Kozlowski, S. K. (ed.) (1973) *The Mesolithic in Europe*, Warsaw: Warsaw University Press.

Kus, S. (1992) 'Towards an Archaeology of Body and Soul', in J.-C. Gardin and C. S. Peebles (eds) *Representations in Archaeology*, Bloomington: Indiana University Press.

Larsson, L. (1988) *The Skateholm Project I: Man and Environment*, vol. 1, Lund, Sweden: Royal Society of Letters at Lund.

Lee, R. B. and I. DeVore (1968) 'Problems in the Study of Hunters and Gatherers', in R. B. Lee and I. DeVore (eds) *Man the Hunter*, Chicago: Aldine Publishing Co.

Lewis-Williams, J. D. and T. Dowson (1989) *Images of Power: Understanding Bushman Rock Art*, Johannesburg: Southern Book Publishers.

Lowie, R. H. (1934) 'Religious Ideas and Practices of the Eurasiatic and North American Areas', in E. E. Evans-Pritchard, R. Firth, B. Malinowski and I. Schapera (eds) *Essays Presented to C. G. Seligman*, London: Kegan Paul, Trench, Trubner.

Mandelstam Balzer, M. (1996) 'Sacred Genders in Siberia: Shamans, Bear Festivals, and Androgyny', in S. P. Ramet (ed.) *Gender Reversals and Gender Cultures: Anthropological and Historical Perspectives*, New York: Routledge.

Moore, H. L. (1986). *Space, Text, and Gender: An Anthropological Study of the Marakwet of Kenya*, Cambridge: Cambridge University Press.

Newell, R. R. and T. Constandse-Westermann (1988) 'The Significance of Skateholm I and Skateholm II to the Mesolithic of Western Europe', in L. Larsson (ed.) *The Skateholm Project I: Man and Environment*, vol. 1, Lund: Royal Society of Letters at Lund.

O'Shea, J. and M. Zvelebil (1984) 'Oleneostrovski mogilnik: Reconstructing the Social and Economic Organization of Prehistoric Foragers in Northern Russia', *Journal of Anthropological Archaeology* 3: 1–40.

Pentikäinen, J. (1996a) 'Introduction', in J. Pentikäinen (ed.) *Shamanism and Northern Ecology*, Berlin: Mouton de Gruyter.

—— (1996b) 'Khanty Shamanism Today: Reindeer Sacrifice and its Mythological Background', in J. Pentikäinen (ed.) *Shamanism and Northern Ecology*, Berlin: Mouton de Gruyter.

Price, T. D. and J. A. Brown (1985) *Prehistoric Hunter-Gatherers: The Emergence of Cultural Complexity*, Orlando: Academic Press, Inc.

Rogers, S. L. (1982) *The Shaman: His Symbols and His Healing Power*, Springfield, IL: Charles C. Thomas Publisher.

Roscoe, W. (1994) 'How to Become a Berdache: Toward a Unified Analysis of Gender Diversity', in G. Herdt (ed.) *Third Sex, Third Gender: Beyond Sexual Dimorphism in Culture and History*, New York: Zone Books.

—— (1995) 'Strange Craft, Strange History, Strange Folks: Cultural Amnesia and the Case for Lesbian and Gay Studies', *American Anthropologist* 97: 448–53.

—— (1998) *Changing Ones: Third and Fourth Genders in Native North America*, New York: St. Martin's Press.

Rozoy, J.-G. (1989) 'The Revolution of the Bowmen in Europe', in C. Bonsall (ed.) *The Mesolithic in Europe: Papers Presented at the Third International Symposium Edinburgh 1985*, Edinburgh: John Donald Publishers.

Rubin, G. (1975) 'The Traffic in Women: Notes on the "Political Economy" of Sex', in R. R. Reiter (ed.) *Toward an Anthropology of Women*, New York: Monthly Review Press.

—— (1984) 'Thinking Sex: Notes for a Radical Theory of the Politics of Sexuality', in C. S. Vance (ed.) *Pleasure and Danger: exploring female sexuality*, Boston, London, Melbourne and Henley: Routledge and Kegan Paul.

Sahlins, M. D. (1972) *Stone Age Economics*, Chicago: Aldine.

Vasilevitch, G. M. (1963) 'Early Concepts about the Universe among the Evenks (Materials)', in H. N. Michael (ed.) *Studies in Siberian Shamanism*, no. 4, *Anthropology of the North: Translations from the Russian Sources*, Toronto: University of Toronto Press for the Arctic Institute of North America.

Vermeersch, P. M. and P. Van Peer (eds) (1990) *Contributions to the Mesolithic in Europe: Papers Presented at the Fourth International Symposium 'The Mesolithic in Europe', Leuven 1990. Studia Praehistorica Belgica 5*, Leuven, Belgium: Leuven University Press.

Wobst, H. M. (1978) 'The Archeo-ethnology of Hunter-Gatherers or the Tyranny of the Ethnographic Record in Archaeology', *American Antiquity* 43: 303–09.

Zvelebil, M. (1978) 'Subsistence and Settlement in the north-eastern Baltic', in P. Mellars (ed.) *The Early Postglacial Settlement of Northern Europe*, Pittsburgh: University of Pittsburgh Press.

—— (ed.) (1986) *Hunters in Transition: Mesolithic Societies of Temperate Eurasia and their Transition to Farming*, Cambridge: Cambridge University Press.

—— (1989a) 'Economic Intensification and Postglacial Hunter-Gatherers in North Temperate Europe', in C. Bonsall (ed.) *The Mesolithic in Europe: Papers Presented at the Third International Symposium Edinburgh 1985*, Edinburgh: John Donald Publishers.

—— (1989b) 'On the Transition to Farming in Europe, or What was Spreading with the Neolithic: a Reply to Ammerman', *Antiquity* 63: 379–83.

—— (1993a) 'Concepts of Time and "Presencing" the Mesolithic', *Archaeological Review from Cambridge* 12: 51–70.

—— (1993b) 'Hunters or Farmers? The Neolithic and Bronze Age Societies of North-East Europe', in J. Chapman and P. Dolukhanov (eds) *Cultural Transformations and Interactions in Eastern Europe*, Aldershot, UK: Avebury.

—— (1995) 'Hunting, Gathering, or Husbandry? Management of Food Resources by the Late Mesolithic Communities of Temperate Europe', *MASCA Research Papers in Science and Archaeology* 12: 79–104.

—— (1996) 'Farmers our Ancestors and the Identity of Europe', in P. Graves-Brown, S. Jones, and C. Gamble (eds) *Cultural Identity and Archaeology: The Construction of European Communities, Theoretical Archaeology Group (TAG)*, London: Routledge.

—— (1998a) 'Agricultural Frontiers, Neolithic Origins, and the Transition to Farming in the Baltic Basin', in M. Zvelebil, L. Domanska and R. Dennell (eds) *Harvesting the Sea, Farming the Forest: The Emergence of Neolithic Societies in the Baltic Region*, Sheffield, UK: Sheffield Academic Press.

—— (1998b) 'Hunter-Gatherer Ritual Landscapes: Questions of Time, Space and Representation', paper presented at the European Association of Archaeologists Annual Meeting, Gothenburg, Sweden.

Zvelebil, M., L. Domanska and R. Dennell (eds) (1998) *Harvesting the Sea, Farming the Forest: The Emergence of Neolithic Societies in the Baltic Region*, Sheffield, UK: Sheffield Academic Press.

Chapter Thirteen

Constructing utopian sexualities: the archaeology and architecture of the early Soviet State

Victor Buchli

The cultural project of an archaeology of sexuality is not in itself an entirely new thing. A similar moment occurred in the Soviet Union of the 1920s and 1930s, though with unexpectedly different results which have not been fully appreciated, even to the present day. Between these current and past cultural projects there is a certain continuity, in the form of a common genealogy. The common elements can be found in the problematization of gender, early feminism, and social reform, all of which strove to radically rethink sexuality and archaeology as many researchers in the present have done, and some of those represented in this volume. However, the sexuality in question in this earlier project was that of traditional early twentieth-century opposite-sex relations firmly situated within what Judith Butler would call the dominant 'heterosexual matrix' of the time. Same-sex relations were not really imaginable and formed the abject 'constitutive outside' (Butler 1993: 38–39) that provided the defining contours of the social problems surrounding heterosexuality at the time. Thus, Frederick Engels, the theoretical father of this project, could clearly show how one formed the other. Engels imaginatively linked same-sex relations to misogynist abuse and sexual and social inequality: 'but the degradation of women recoiled on men themselves and degraded them too, until they sank into the perversion of boy-love, degrading themselves and their gods by the myth of Ganymede' (Engels 1972: 74).

Within this framework founded on Marxian materialism, Engels could thus frame one of the key problems of social reform: the subordinate role of women within opposite-sex relations and society: 'In the family, he is the bourgeois; the wife represents the proletariat' (Engels 1972: 81–82). Determining this, the first fundamental social inequality upon which the dominant heterosexual matrix was founded, was the key to restructure society according to socialist principles to achieve industrialization, modernization, and the eventual realization of communism: 'It will become evident that the first premise of the emancipation of women is the reintroduction of the entire female sex into public industry; and this again demands that the quality possessed of the individual family of being the economic unit of society be abolished' (82). Feminism and the reconstitution of opposite sex relations were thus integral to the realization of Marxist revolution and the creation of an industrialized communist society.

However, social revolution is, to state glibly, a very complicated affair that involves the restructuring of society and the negotiation of many conflicting visions of diverse groups and interests. I would like to emphasize here a point which at times is not understood sufficiently in relation to the Soviet experience – that the pursuit of this project of social restructuring, as with most social works, had an overtly cultural performative aspect by various individuals and groups. Through enacting and reproducing the evolving and contested terms of Soviet society, individuals and groups had a decisive role in the real-ization of this project. Their performances were geared towards the most perfect realization of the principles of Enlightenment-era modernization; that is, the total obviation of the contradictions of industrialized society, which was the defining work and purpose of the Russian Revolution. As Zygmunt Bauman has stated '. . . the communist system was the extremely spectacular dramatization of the Enlightenment message' (Bauman 1992: 221). However, this project resulted in an inexorable slippage with devastating conse-quences – from the total obviation of societal contradictions towards the totalitarian project.

The Marxist revolution of 1917 in Russia had two primary objectives: the liberation of the working class and the liberation of women. These formed the dominant cultural strug-gles which legitimated the Soviet State. Engels' book *The Origin of the Family, Private Property and the State* (1972 [1884]) provided the theoretical guide to this cultural work by historicizing the changing structures of the family and sexuality. This was based on Lewis Henry Morgan's foundational text *Ancient Society* (1877), which was brought to the attention of Engels and Karl Marx by the nineteenth-century Russian ethnologist Maksim Kovalevsky (Engels 1972: 8). Armed with this text, Engels criticized restrictive notions of nineteenth-century romantic heterosexual love within the nuclear family, based on male control of female sexuality. He rejected it in expectation of the creation of a new sexually-egalitarian classless and industrialized society imagined from Morgan's primordial images of early human society. Engels, citing Morgan, said that this would 'be a revival, in a higher form, of the liberty, equality and fraternity of the ancient gentes' (Engels 1972: 22) and a return to the promiscuity of Bachoffen's Mother Right, where paternity was uncertain, lineage was reckoned only through the mother, and women's power, both sexu-ally and socially, was equal, if not superior, to that of men.

Marx, Engels, and early Soviet commentators were uncertain as to what shape these ancient forms of sexual and social egalitarianism took, as well as what shape they might take in an industrialized socialist future. However scant the evidence might have been, ethno-graphy and archaeology provided the means by which to imagine such formations; in particular the archaeology of the Upper Paleolithic, which corresponded to Morgan's original phase of 'savagery'. The 1920s, therefore, was a period of intense speculation. New forms of architecture and material culture were being explored with which to reconfigure opposite-sex relations towards new reformed egalitarian heterosexualities under formation within a rapidly industrializing society. Soviet family law in the 1920s worked to realize these new forms, simultaneously making real the idealizations of ethnographic descriptions. This is exemplified in Engel's admiring observations from Arthur Wright's ethnography of Seneca Iroquois longhouses: 'Usually the female portion ruled the house; the stores were in common; but woe to the luckless husband or lover who was too shiftless to do his share of the providing. The house would be too hot for him; and he had to retreat to his own clan; or, as was often done, go and start a new matrimonial alliance in some other' (Engels 1972: 61). Thus in the Soviet Union, divorce and abortion were available on demand. Homosexuality was decriminalized and opposite-sex relations were free and unencumbered – like 'drinking a glass of water' as the slogan of the time went.

Inspired by these primordial visions, various new forms of communal living were pursued. These forms attempted to restructure traditional heterosexual female roles, and bring them out of the oppressive capitalist and patriarchal nuclear family into the public realm of socialist construction. In the more radical established communes, children were raised communally and sometimes given matronymics and their mother's surnames (Stites 1989). Communards shared sexual partners and even pooled clothing. In material terms, Communal Houses (Dom Kommuny) were conceived and built specifically to facilitate these new forms of heterosexuality, based on egalitarian public roles for women in a rapidly industrializing society (Buchli 1998; Cooke 1995; Bliznakov 1993). At times, specially designed communal houses attempted to realize the communal spatiality of Morgan's Iriquoisian longhouse. Throughout, imagined prehistoric and ethnographic models of pre-class society pervaded these undertakings. Such models were imaginatively linked in other architectural circles, both within and outside Russia. Thus, Le Corbusier's exploration of the archaeological La Tene culture of his native Switzerland served as an inspiration for imagining elemental and revolutionary architectural forms (Vogt 1998).

These new communalistic designs were built to a very limited degree, despite being the putative standard for all new state-sponsored housing in the Russian republic (Cooke 1995; Buchli 1998, 1999). Only within a fully industrialized society could these new architectural forms be built and the services provided that could displace the domestic economy of the nuclear family. The inequalities of opposite-sex relations and women's roles would be overcome, eventually transforming Soviet citizens into communal-living socialists. Despite a slowly emerging industrial infrastructure, these new social forms were seriously pursued in other ways: through the cooperative housing movement which reconfigured existing housing stock (Buchli 1999); the agitational work of the women's section of the Communist Party (Zhenotdel, see Goldman 1992); as well as the more prosaic reforms of housework according to Taylorist efficiency principles. These palliative measures would ease women's domestic burdens, until the time when an industrial infrastructure was in place which could realize new egalitarian forms of opposite-sex relations independent of the exploitative domestic economy of the nuclear family. Only then could the objective of an ethically-socialist heterosexuality be realized (Buchli 1999).

However, within this new emerging public realm of socialism, the masculine – as constructed within the dyads of opposite-sex relations – was understood as the norm. Moreover, the masculine was not seen to be in need of reconstitution, except in its exploitative relation to its opposite female sex. It was the 'deformed' feminine suffering from false consciousness which was problematic, and the focus of reform. Make-up, non-rational ornamental clothing, and elaborate hairdos were denounced as counter-revolutionary and petit-bourgeois at the height of the Cultural Revolution and industrialization drive of the First Five-Year Plan (1928–1932). Women were encouraged to shed the artifice of bourgeois propriety and become rationalized, literally stripped down, towards a more authentic elemental state; to be, in short, primordial, true, and void of the deforming frippery of bourgeois artifice.

Thus the primordial women imagined in prehistoric 'pre-clan' societies could provide the models for future forms of opposite-sex relations and a redeemed ethical heterosexuality. The discovery of Upper Paleolithic figurines associated with hearths suggested to early Soviet archaeologists the exalted (if not equal) position enjoyed by women in the past that the new Soviet woman was just attempting to realize in the near future (Efimenko 1934). Archaeology offered another hopeful representation of women's social power that could reconfigure the image of women from radically new perspectives. But as we shall see, these representations could work both ways; at once asserting primordial feminine equality and power, while also naturalizing feminine roles within opposite-sex relations, and thus determining the subordinate roles of women within the relations of economic production.

Since the nineteenth century, Russian archaeologists had a vital role to play in imagining social reform along with its alternative visions of opposite-sex relations (see Howe 1980 and Soffer 1985). Given the importance placed on pre-clan societies by Morgan, Marx, and Engels, the Upper Paleolithic held pride of place amongst radicalized archaeologists for very obvious reasons. Fedor Kondrat'evich Volkov excavated the first Upper Paleolithic sites discovered in Russia at the site of Gontsy between 1873 and 1874. Volkov was an ardent Narodnik, a political group closely linked with anarchist groups that hoped to realize an egalitarian, stateless, communalistic society; could be imagined with the discovery of Upper Paleolithic sites. His student Efimenko was to become one of the most important archaeologists of that period in Soviet times (see Soffer 1985 and Howe 1980), and the author of one of the canonical texts of Soviet archaeology.

Thus the contours of Upper Paleolithic society – its material culture as constituted by Soviet archaeologists with their implied social formations and sexualities – had immense significance for a society groping to find the material and social terms with which to imagine new communistic social formations, identities, and sexualities. Archaeologists had an unprecedented and urgent mandate to determine the 'origins' and nature of primeval communism, just as architects were entrusted to determine and create its 'future' forms.

In the West the study of Paleolithic dwellings was virtually ignored (Childe 1950: 4), while it was the subject of intensive debate among Soviet archaeologists. The constitution of the communalistic dwellings of the Upper Paleolithic past was subject to controversy; just as were the plans being conceived by architects for the communistic future, alternating between individual huts or cells to large communal structures (see Willen 1953; Bliznakov 1993; Cooke 1974, 1995; Hudson 1994; Buchli 1998, 1999). These forms were highly contested as both disciplines attempted to understand the material terms of egalitarian communism (see Vogt 1998). The examples here of two different individual 'dwelling' types, one futuristic (Figure 13.1) and one prehistoric (Figure 13.2), are apposite. Both 'discoveries' from the beginning of the Cultural Revolution were of similar size (approximately 5 m in diameter) and were used to imagine new forms of egalitarian opposite-sex relations. Figure 13.2 is the plan of an Upper Paleolithic dwelling at Gagarino, Ukraine, discovered by Zamiatnin in 1928–1929. The grand man of Paleolithic archaeology,

Figure 13.1 Green City, Nikolai Ladovskii (1929).

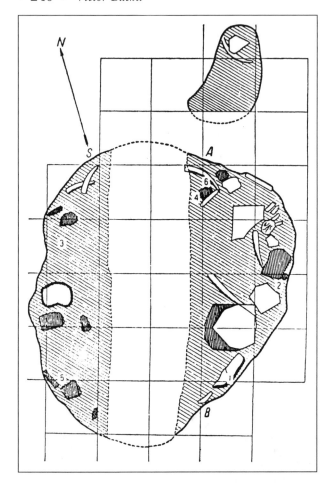

Figure 13.2 Dwelling plan, Gagarino, from Efimenko (1934).

Efimenko, described this smaller 5.5 m long dwelling as being of a 'somewhat different type' ('*pravda, neskol'ko inogo tipa*') (Efimenko 1934: 291), for not conforming to the communal Iroquoisian longhouse type he associated with the Paleolithic, as derived from Morgan (Efimenko 1934: 291). The Gagarino dwelling, according to ethnographic analogies taken from North American Eskimos, suggested to Efimenko a collective of several such dwellings based on communal relations of production (Figure 13.3). Three positively-identified female figurines found along the periphery were interpreted as evidence of matriarchy, and evidence of a profoundly different and decidedly more egalitarian heterosexual matrix at the beginning of human social evolution (Efimenko 1934: 292). Similarly, architects such as the dis-urbanist Ladovskii, exploited similarly ethnographic forms (not unlike Le Corbusier, see Vogt 1998) (see Figure 13.4) to invoke an original 'primitive hut' (see Rykwert 1989), with which to construct a similar image of communality and mobile flexibility (Figure 13.1). Like ethnographic and Paleolithic dwellings of mobile nomadic social groups, these new buildings could also be collapsed and built again anywhere on the territory of the Soviet Union, exploiting communalized industrialized technologies.

Significantly, these new structures accommodated flexible opposite-sex productive and reproductive relations, founded on the equality of the sexes and liberated from the oppressive heterosexual matrix of the pre-Revolutionary capitalist era. Couples, especially women, freed from marital monogamy and the shackles of the domestic economy of the hearth, could link up if they so chose with opposite-sex partners in these dwellings and break up and move on whenever they wanted, thereby reimagining the original freedom of heterosexual relations in 'pre-clan' and 'savage' societies, described in Engels and Morgan and facilitated by recent Soviet family law reforms. More specifically, during this period of Paleolithic research, opposite-sex relations could be seen as segregated from economic relations of production, rather than determinate of them, as Engels had originally suggested (Howe 1980: 147–49). Thus it would follow that the Revolution's radical reworking of economic relations, and the obliteration of any economically-based distinctions within opposite-sex relations suggested a radical reworking of heterosexuality, unprecedented since the primeval beginnings of human social history. Heterosexuality could be conceived again as independent of relations of economic production, just as radical thinkers in the late 1920s and early '30s were attempting to rethink contemporary Soviet heterosexuality in similar terms. As we shall see, this factoring out of heterosexuality from relations of economic production was to have a highly conflicted and controversial impact on Soviet debates across a wide spectrum of Soviet disciplines, requiring a re-evaluation of the role of biology over economics as the final expression of revolutionary socialism reached its peak with the establishment of Stalinism in the early 1930s (Howe 1980: 151, 204–205).

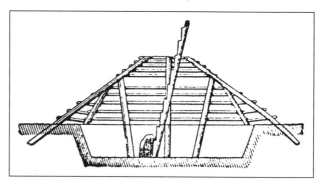

Figure 13.3 Section of a winter dwelling of Tomson River Indians, from Efimenko (1934).

How Paleolithic dwellings were understood in primordial, more egalitarian times, was just as contentious in archaeological circles (as evidenced by Efimenko's awkward handling of the Gagarino dwelling) as which housing type architects thought was appropriate for the egalitarian communist near-future. Pits discovered at sites such as Kostenki could be interpreted as large pit houses comprised of multiple hearths forming a large communal longhouse, reminiscent of Morgan's Iroquoisian longhouses (Efimenko 1934); in later years, others such as Bibikov (Bibikov 1959 in Grigor'ev 1993) suggested that these very same pits were actually individual oval dwellings focused on segregated hearths, such as those suggested by Efimenko at Gagarino. Even later, other scholars argued for a new version of the longhouse on the basis of these pits (Grigor'ev 1993: 59). In his 1972 book *Hunters, Gatherers, Fishermen*, Grigor'ev saw these same ovoid dwellings as supporting the nuclear family, demonstrating it as the basic social unit of Upper Paleolithic society (Soffer 1985: 12). As Grigor'ev himself observed in 1993 after the fall of the Soviet Union, those scholars who argued for large longhouses saw them as signs of communal social organization, while those who insisted on individual dwellings

Figure 13.4 An African dwelling, from *Zhilishche*, M. Ginzburg (1934).

saw small segregated families as the basic social unit (1993: 59). Others, such as the American archaeologist Lewis Binford, saw these same pits as facilities for meat storage (Binford 1983 in Grigor'ev 1993: 59). That these pits should even be interpreted as dwellings seemed, according to Grigor'ev (1993), more a function of how the individual researcher interpreted the bone assemblages within; as having exhibited a certain intentional order as a consequence of either being a collapsed dwelling on one hand, or of the deposition of large and awkwardly shaped bones within oval pits on the other hand. Thus these enigmatic pits, including those at Kostenki, served as a kind of Rorschach test of the socialist realist imaginary. Researchers interpreted evidence according to which social formations and heterosexualities were to be desired and imagined from the Paleolithic material: from individual houses with individual (nuclear) families all the way along the spectrum to communal houses with large communal domestic units.

During the Soviet period, the chronology of these interpretations almost seems to follow exactly similar imaginings within architectural circles (see Buchli 1999, 1998). That this might appear to be a specious coincidence is belied by what we shall see later as the logic of socialist realism and the foundationalist totalizing cultural project that was the construction of socialism, along with the historically shifting terms of its performative realization. Thus what might appear as frustratingly contradictory is entirely consistent with the shifting terms of socialist performance and what Boris Groys has called the 'total art' of the socialist state (Groys 1992). Alexei Kojevnikov has described the ritual 'games' of Stalinism in scholarly, political, and social life, where 'in their theoretical views about science, Soviet Marxists tried to combine adherence to objective scientific truth with the idea of an inseparable relationship between knowledge and social values' (Kojevnikov 1998: 38).

Architects, like archaeologists, were preoccupied with how to imagine these communalistic formations at yet another level. This was to have a lasting impact on the development of twentieth-century urban planning, and also heightened an already existing concern with the primordial forms of human social organization. This echoed and reinforced Le Corbusier's work with even greater impact. In the late 1920s and early 1930s, architects heatedly debated the virtues of communards living in communal houses or segregated individual housing for nuclear families. In the end, segregated family dwellings won favor with the less radically-minded, but more numerous and politically ascendant cadres of Stalinism. The famous debates of urbanism versus dis-urbanism (Buchli 1999, 1998; Cooke 1995, 1974; Bliznakov 1993) attempted to determine whether linear concentrated cities (imagined along the lines of the Iroquoisian longhouse), or dispersed settlements of individual dwellings (not unlike those ovoid pit houses of the Paleolithic), should prevail. Like their archaeological colleagues, architects exploited ethnographic analogies for the creation of new industrialized architectural forms for the near future.

Very quickly, however, an alternative vision of the ideal socialist family emerged with the rise of Stalinism. As the gains of liberal family law benefiting women were gradually eroded under Stalin, there was a return to more familiar pre-Revolutionary norms of heterosexuality, based on nuclear families living within enclosed segregated spaces (Buchli 1999). The segregation of heterosexuality from the realm of production was unsettling to these ascendant Stalinist elites whose notions of social propriety and subjectivity were predicated on more traditional and economically embedded notions of heterosexuality. Such a shift also made a virtue of existing shortcomings. It acknowledged the increasingly evident inability of the industrialization drive to provide the economic infrastructure which would permit the development of a heterosexuality segregated from relations of production. Thus opposite-sex relations were refigured to form a distinctly Stalinist heterosexuality which envisioned women as economically and ontologically tied to the domestic sphere. There, women served as the guardians of the now socialist and communal (as opposed to the individual) hearth of Stalinist society (see Buchli 1999). Towards this end, heterosexuality had to be defined again in reference to biologically-embedded and determinate roles structuring opposite-sex relations. Not until the 1960s was the debate reopened, with a plurality of conflicting interpretations of the primordial origins of egalitarian society, and with a re-evaluation of heterosexuality as segregated from biologically-determined economic roles.

It becomes clear that the archaeological record being constituted reflected these changing attitudes as well. During the Cultural Revolution of the late 1920s, archaeological and ethnographic debates on human origins stressed the primacy of economic relations of production over biology in the very beginnings of human social evolution in the Upper Paleolithic (Howe 1980). This echoed work in other cultural spheres such as law and architecture, and demonstrated that the primeval contours of opposite-sex relations defined a heterosexuality independent of relations of production. Ethnographers working in the early 1930s such as Zolatarev and Tolstov, as well as the pre-eminent archaeologist of the Upper Paleolithic, Efimenko, saw kinship in 'primitive' society as fundamentally based on relations of production that were 'unavoidably clothed in "natural" forms' (Howe 1980: 148–49). Opposite-sex relations eventually evolved into monogamous 'pairing-families' or nuclear families which grew to be distinct from the productive economic unit of the 'gentes' or clan. The result was an individual, segregated sphere of economic relations based on opposite-sex pairs forming independent units whose interests were at odds with the collective, thereby sowing the seeds of future societal contradictions (Howe 1980).

However, with Ravdonikas' text of 1934 'Marx-Engels and the Fundamental Problem of Pre-Class Society' (Howe 1980), and with Stalin's purge of the archaeological establishment complete by 1935 (Miller 1956), Stalinist orthodoxy was ushered into archaeology as within other spheres of cultural work. Ravdonikas' text 'offered a scheme logical and simple enough to satisfy the requirements of propaganda and the elimination of heterodox viewpoints' (Howe 1980: 157), thereby establishing a form of archaeological Socialist Realism for prehistory. Within this scheme, biology replaced production as determinate of primeval human social organization. Ravdonikas argued for the primacy of biologically-determinate opposite-sex relations in establishing relations of production. Thus, segregated male and female spheres with separate economic roles were clearly defined within this primeval heterosexual matrix: men hunted, and women gathered, reared young, and tended the domestic hearth. Matrilineality and matriarchy were established as the primeval state of human social organization, in keeping with the nineteenth-century views of Engels, and contrary to, then recent, writings of ethnographers such as Zolatarev and Tolstov in 1932 and Efimenko in 1931 (Howe 1980). In this fashion, archaeology was brought in line with other areas of cultural work, reconfiguring opposite-sex relations towards a heterosexuality firmly embedded within and determinate of economic relations. This was in keeping with the aspirations towards a different heterosexual order with the rise of the Stalinist totalitarian state. Just as Grigor'ev's later representation of the patriarchal nuclear family was to eventually prevail as the essential unit of the decidedly communalistic society of the Upper Paleolithic, so too would the nuclear family and conventional heterosexuality prevail in other spheres of Soviet life many years later. The totalizing logic of Stalinist science and modernity required that such issues be coordinated across the scholarly and political body of socialist society (Kojevnikov 1998). As terms of socialist development shifted with the rise of a new elite and a new vision, new archaeological myths were required towards the continued formation of the Stalinist state (see Conkey 1991: 86 and Tomášková 1997: 280–81 regarding archaeology and myth-making).

The sexually egalitarian vision held by earlier Soviet social reformers during the Cultural Revolution began to crumble. The terms of socialist performance and the cultural work that was required of archaeology changed as much as it did in other spheres of cultural work, such as architecture, with direct consequences for the development of a new hetero-sexual ethic within Soviet society. The terms of social performance shifted with the rise of Stalin. A new elite was being groomed, culled from the greater mass of Soviet citizens at the expense of the urban pre-Revolutionary liberal intelligentsia of the Bolshevik revo-lution. It was, after all, in the name of these new men and women rising up from the ranks under Stalin that the Revolution was waged (Fitzpatrick 1979). These men and women had a vision radically different from their predecessors of the socialist good life and of the social theories and archaeological myths needed to sustain it. In architecture, the social radicalism of the Bolshevik elite gave way to what has been called Socialist Realism. On the surface this seemed to be a repudiation of the earlier Bolshevik project. However, as Boris Groys has pointed out, Stalinist Socialist Realism was the ultimate expression of the total project of the modernist avant-garde. It was a politico-aesthetic project of long standing within the Enlightenment tradition, but with unexpected, yet inexorable and devastating consequences (Groys 1992: 30–37; Bauman 1992). The prin-ciple of 'democratic centralism' characterized party as well as cultural and scholarly life: a plurality of opinions was tolerated until which time a final position could resolutely prevail and form the 'general line'. These 'final positions' thus provided the foundations with which to realize the total socio-cultural project which was the Soviet Union (Buchli 1999; Kojevnikov 1998).

In architecture, the absolute resolution of the conflicts between two generations of archi-tects came in the guise of Stalinist classicism and the return to pre-Revolutionary bourgeois norms in housing. In particular, this meant the abolition of the founding principles of communal homes and the entire project for the reform of daily life based on the oblit-eration of women's oppression in the domestic realm. The Stalinist cadre's vision of the socialist good life and social propriety was based on more traditional, non-elite under-standings of heterosexual femininity. This femininity involved the cultivation of the domestic sphere, the nuclear family, and the joys of the hearth; the benefits of this revi-talized domestic sphere were enjoyed by the male cadre, in return for unswerving devotion to the more populist and inclusive socialism which Stalin created. This male cadre had a vision of the socialist good life that was in stark contrast to more established and austere Bolshevik predecessors. This development set into motion two completely different enactions of socialism, one of which, according to the modernist logic of the time, had to prevail, with Stalin as the ultimate judge of which was the better performance.

As in every other sphere of social, political, and scholarly life, the historical science of archaeology was not immune to the changing terms of socialist performance, particularly in relation to the restructuring of opposite-sex relations. The purging of the archaeolog-ical establishment towards the realization of these understandings was quite devastating, according to figures provided by Mikhail Miller, especially in comparison with the archi-tectural establishment which experienced only one purge-related death (see Hudson 1994: 147–65). Old pre-Revolutionary archaeologists such as Efimenko, the student of the first Paleolithic archaeologist, Volkov, continued his work on the Paleolithic. His insights into pre-clan society were fitted into the evolving Marxian schema of the Stalinist period. Thus according to observers of the period, such as Mikhail Miller, Efimenko managed to preserve his life and professional status by adequately playing the evolving and high-risk ritual games of Stalinist legitimacy (Kojevnikov 1998). In the end, a large number of archaeologists who did not adapt to the political and cultural requirements of the profession were invariably arrested, with many perishing in labor camps (Miller 1956; Howe 1980). By 1934 all contact with archaeologists from capitalist countries had ceased, trips abroad were canceled, subscriptions to foreign journals were strictly controlled, and Soviet scholarship was not published abroad.

After 1935 the purge of the archaeological profession ceased. And as could be expected, the sociological dimension of archaeological work relevant to recent reconsiderations of socialist heterosexuality had also ceased to be as significant. The polemical literature of 1930–1934 was denounced as extreme, as it no longer corresponded to the needs of the time. As Groys has pointed out in other cultural fields, the bitter conflicts, denunciations, and recriminations within professions, of which archaeology was no exception (see Miller 1956), were geared to realize the true and objective terms of socialist work. Virulently competitive factionalism eventually required the intervention of the Party for guidance to break the stalemate. Plurality was not a virtue (Kojevnikov 1998; Buchli 1999). It was on par with parliamentary democracy and inimical to Soviet principles (Groys 1992: 37). Thus, the objectivizing enterprise had to be resolved and arbitrated by Party authority. To assert an independent and contradictory authority against this intervention was to infringe on the authority of the state in the construction of socialist society, and contravene the foundationalist logic of the socialist project. Together with professional bodies, the regime ruthlessly opposed those who might intervene in this process. Thus, some of the most vocal exponents of the Cultural Revolution, such as archaeologists describing a radically refigured heterosexuality, were the first victims of Stalin's creative resolution of this Enlightenment-era project. As Groys observed in other spheres of cultural work, 'it was no accident, therefore, that the triumph of the avant-garde project in the early 1930s should have coincided with the final defeat of the avant-garde as an established artistic movement' (1992: 35).

Some archaeologists, however, were skilled in the performative requirements for enacting socialism under Stalin and the rules of its ritual games (see Buchli 1999 and Kojevnikov 1998). Individuals such as Ravdonikas were more adept performatively, and could play the high-stakes games of Stalinist ritual and maintain their revolutionary vanguard positions through this intense and brutal period of cultural and social restructuring (see also Kotkin 1995). To say that such individuals were merely political and venal opportunists is to misunderstand the nature of cultural work during this period: the unified and totalizing foundationalist Enlightenment-era project that found perfect and terrifying expression in the Stalinist state (Bauman 1992). The process reached its final peak with Ravdonikas' second major work, *History of Primitive Society* (*Istoriia Pervobytnogo Obshchestva, vol 1*) in 1939, where he updated Engel's *Origin of the Family, Private Property and the State* in light of recent archaeological discoveries, and the cultural and political work of the time. Ravdonikas' book became the handbook for undergraduate students, who until then had to rely on Engels' text for the study of human prehistory (Miller 1956). Ravdonikas' canonical work firmly established Stalinism and rationalist unity in archaeology over the cacaphonous and competitive radicalism of the preceding years (Ravdonikas 1939, 1947; Miller 1956). By the eve of World War II, a certain 'normal' science resumed amongst Soviet archaeologists. A significant segment of the archaeological establishment was purged, and new practitioners took their place. The Enlightenment-era demiurge of the Leninist intelligentsia was replaced by a more populist demiurge, practiced by newly empowered

Stalinist cadres and the new architects and archaeologists of the Stalin era. Thus, a final and more perfect expression of the total socialist project of the earlier avant-garde (Groys 1992) was found. Archaeology on the eve of World War II worked again to provide a truly coherent body of origin myths, valorizing anew a familiar, less destabilizing heterosexual ethic. Biological sex was determinative of men's and women's roles complementing each other in different spheres of activity: women as cultivators of the socialist hearth, and men working outside in the public sphere of socialist labor.

It may be argued that the archaeology of the Soviet era, whether related to sexuality or other interpretive topics, was not 'true' in that it did not follow the trajectory of an objective science. What ensued during this period was 'illustrative' of whatever the regime required: it helped to provide the required myths with which to perpetuate the legitimacy of the prevalent order and its attendant forms of heterosexuality. To do otherwise was hazardous under the peculiar conditions of the Soviet Union under Stalin (as Miller's figures eloquently testify) and afterwards. This, however, ignores the larger totalizing cultural logic involved in the realization of the foundationalist Enlightenment-era principles that so attracted Gordon Childe initially and then repulsed him later (McGuire 1992: 69).

Considering the larger scope of cultural work in which Soviet scholars such as archaeologists, architects and others were involved, it seems appropriate to discuss parallels between early Soviet archaeology and 1980s' anglophone feminist archaeology, when it reconsidered the role of women and the origin myths of traditional Western patriarchy. This latter cultural and professional critique (see for example, Conkey and Spector 1984; Gero and Conkey 1991) tried to reimagine alternative heterosexualities based on different social divisions and relations, and re-examined the cultural work of archaeology in the reproduction of patriarchal traditions in the West. Similarly, feminist archaeologies of the 1980s problematized biology and economic relations of production (Moore 1991: 408) as did their Soviet predecessors much earlier. For if anything, the experience of Soviet archaeology is that of a mirror held up, focusing, more perfectly than any other European project to date, the experiences and aspirations of Enlightenment-era rationality and foundationalism to reveal a terrifying, grotesque, and 'vulgar' image. That archaeology should perform the sort of cultural work it did during the early Soviet period is not unique, as we know from Western feminist observations of the discipline which have always emphasized the political relevance and significance of the cultural work of archaeology (Gero and Conkey 1991). Under Stalin, archaeological work was subject to the same requirements as other fields to participate in the construction of Stalinist socialism, and in the most perfect and total realization of modernity and the Enlightenment-era project. By its own inexorable logic, such a total project clearly required an 'author' in the guise of the ultimate demiurge, Stalin himself, the ultimate architect, artist, novelist, linguist, and archaeologist (Groys 1992: 56–57). An independent, 'high scientific' professional body concerned with the very origins of the socialist project was inimical to the resolute logic of the cultural project of Stalinism. Such a project simultaneously required adherence to a totalizing objectivity of knowledge, but was lashed to the Party (in the spirit of 'democratic centralism') and to the caprices of the demiurge Stalin, and towards the realization of the socialist state (Groys 1992). For two competing objectivizing projects ('Science' and the 'Party') to be at odds with each other was inimical to the common realization of this Enlightenment-era foundationalist social project – which to be realized totally required the leading role of the Party to prevail (Groys 1992; Kojevnikov 1998; Buchli 1999).

Thus, as the preceding discussion of sexual politics in early Soviet archaeology suggests, the 'vulgarization' of Soviet archaeology is far more complex and less 'vulgar' than it may appear to be, especially when considered in light of the larger cultural project of which it was a part. Soviet archaeologies of sexuality were certainly no less 'vulgar', theoretically, than the cultural work done by European and American archaeologists to support the myths underlying the inequalities of the dominant heterosexual matrix, and the exclusionary practices and cultural costs involved. Feminist scholarship in archaeology has amply demonstrated this point. Yet, there has been a tendency by archaeological observers across a broad spectrum of theoretical positions (Soffer 1985; Trigger 1989; and Childe in McGuire 1992) to view this cultural work, either Soviet or European/American, as incidental to archaeology; in fact, to view it as the circumstances that archaeology and the pursuit of true science (Soffer 1985) or true Marxism (Trigger 1989; Childe in McGuire 1992: 69) were to overcome to create 'enduring' work, despite the social context and avowed cultural project in which it functioned. But as we have seen, to ignore or miss this key element of the development of Soviet archaeology and its cultural work is to miss the entire logic of the period. To do so at once discounts the very real suffering of individuals caught within this terrifying project, and precludes the possibility of learning from their experience by dismissing the entire process as abject and 'monstrous', thereby preserving the contours that shape the hopes and sanctity of the foundationalist modernist project. In any period and place, archaeology inevitably performs cultural work. To disavow this through an adherence to a transcendent foundationalism (either processualist as in Soffer and Praslov 1993: 7–8; Soffer 1985; or an ever purer Marxism as in Trigger 1989) is to render oneself unable to assess and account for the cultural work done, and thus to act responsibly.

To say that Soviet archaeologists 'got it wrong' about sexuality, or about any other topic, or to dismiss their work because they were manipulated, venal, or victimized, is to miss out on the complexities and poignant contradictions of social and cultural life under which individual men and women labored and lived during the Stalinist period. It is also to minimize the demiurgic cultural project which was Soviet socialism and its terrifying realization of Western modernity.

Russian and Soviet archaeology was, from its radical beginnings in the nineteenth century, intimately implicated within larger cultural projects – theorizing about the origins of human societies, the family, human sexuality, and sexual inequalities. Doing archaeology was a key element in the radical cultural work of social reformers in the late nineteenth and early twentieth centuries; in this respect this historical science, as it was considered in Russia, was very much a political and social art (Howe 1980). To differentially construct socialism for competing group interests from the remains constituting the archaeological record was just as much a culturally constructive act towards the creation of a future past, as the creation of different, and at times competing, architectural visions of the future present (see Vogt 1998). This new social vision, which was predicated on a reformed and ethically-socialist heterosexuality, required new cultural work and origin myths. This does not mean that these different stories or myths were any less true because of the cultural work they attempted to perform. But what may be said without controversy is how much these stories, and the cultural work they were to perform while realizing different heterosexualities, cost in order to be 'true' (Foucault in Butler 1993: 93). In other words, we can measure the price of archaeological cultural work by observing who gets excluded, disenfranchised, and hurt (Butler 1993). In this respect, we are always at risk of 'getting it wrong' now and at any other time (Butler 1993; Smith 1988; Mouffe 1993). Should this not be a point of academic responsibility rather than 'chagrin' (Smith 1988 and Rorty 1991: 19)? Perhaps what seems in the end to be 'vulgar' is wanting to 'get it right' at any cost. The nomothetic urge run rampant and so cynically manipulated by the modernist cultural logic of Stalinism, which uninhibitedly followed the logical course of Western foundationalism, demonstrates this point, but is not the only example. It is too easy to dismiss the Soviet experience as 'aberrant' and perverse towards the calculation of a socially disengaged 'objectivity'. We must not forget how to calculate the 'cost' of such cultural work, both then and especially now. The Soviet case reminds us to consider the very important and vital 'costs' of our own work as we try again to participate in a larger cultural project and constitute new inclusions and as yet unimagined exclusions, which, like the Soviet example, is focused on the problem of sexuality.

ACKNOWLEDGMENTS

I am very grateful to Barbara Voss and Robert Schmidt for their invitation to contribute to this volume and to the 1998 Society for American Archaeology session in Seattle, Washington, 'Archaeologies of Sexuality' where I gave the original paper on which this chapter was based. Meg Conkey provided very thoughtful direction while Olga Soffer very kindly pointed out Jovan Howe's extraordinary doctoral thesis and offered generous criticism early on. However, despite the very kind assistance of those mentioned, all omissions and errors are mine alone.

REFERENCES

Bauman, Z. (1992) *Intimations of Postmodernity*, London: Routledge.

Binford, L. (1983) *In Pursuit of the Past*, London: Thames and Hudson.

Bliznakov, M. (1993) 'Soviet Housing During the Experimental Years, 1918 to 1933', in W. Brumfield and B. Ruble (eds) *Russian Housing in the Modern Age: Design and Social History*, Cambridge: Cambridge University Press.

Buchli, V. (1998) 'Moisei Ginzburg's Narkomfin Communal House in Moscow: Contesting the Social and Material World', *Journal of the Society of Architectural Historians* 57, 2: 160–81.

—— (1999) *An Archaeology of Socialism*, Oxford: Berg Publishers.

Butler, J. (1993) *Bodies that Matter: on the Discursive Limits of Sex*, London: Routledge.

Childe, V. G. (1950) 'Cave Men's Buildings', *Antiquity* 24: 4–11.

Conkey, M. (1991) 'Contexts of Action, Contexts of Power: Material Culture and Gender in the Magdelenian', in J. M. Gero and M. W. Conkey (eds) *Engendering Archaeology*, Oxford: Basil Blackwell.

Conkey, M. and J. Spector (1984) 'Archaeology and the Study of Gender', in M. Schiffer (ed.) *Advances in Archaeological Method and Theory*, Vol. 7, New York: Academic Press.

Cooke, C. (1974) 'The Town of Socialism', unpublished Ph.D. thesis, Cambridge University.

—— (1995) *Russian Avant-Garde: Theories of Art, Architecture and the City*, London: Academy Editions.

Efimenko, P. P. (1934) *Dorodovoe Obshchestvo*, Moscow/Leningrad: OGIZ.

Engels, F. (1972 [1884]) *The Origin of the Family, Private Property and the State*, New York: Pathfinder Press.

Fitzpatrick, S. (1979) 'Stalin and the Making of a New Elite, 1928–1939', *Slavic Review* 38, 3: 377–402.

Gero, J. and M. Conkey (eds) (1991) *Engendering Archaeology*, Oxford: Basil Blackwell.

Ginzburg, M. (1934) *Zhilishche*, Moscow: Gosstroiizdat USSR.

Goldman, W. (1992) 'The Utopianism of the Zhenotdel', *Slavic Review*, 51, 3: 485–96.

Grigor'ev, G. (1993) 'Kostenki-Avdeevo Culture', in O. Soffer and N. Praslov (eds) *From Kostenki to Clovis*, New York: Plenum Press.

Groys, B. (1992) *The Total Art of Stalinism: Avant-Garde, Aesthetic Dictatorship and Beyond*, Princeton: Princeton University Press.

Howe, J. (1980) 'The Soviet Theories of Primitive History: Forty Years of Speculation on the Origins and Evolution of People and Society', unpublished Ph.D. dissertation, University of Washington.

Hudson, H. (1994) *Blueprints and Blood: The Stalinization of Soviet Architecture, 1917–1937*, Princeton: Princeton University Press.

Kojevnikov, A. (1998) 'Rituals of Stalinist Culture at Work: Science and the Games of Intraparty Democracy circa 1948', *Russian Review* 57, January: 25–52.

Kotkin, S. (1995) *Magnetic Mountain*, Berkeley: University of California Press.

McGuire, R. (1992) *A Marxist Archaeology*, San Diego: Academic Press.

Miller, M. (1956) *Archaeology in the USSR*, London: Atlantic Press.

Moore, H. (1991) 'Epilogue', in J. M. Gero and M. W. Conkey (eds) *Engendering Archaeology*, Oxford: Basil Blackwell Press.

Morgan, L. H. (1877) *Ancient Society*, New York: Henry Holt and Company.

Mouffe, C. (1993) *The Return of the Political*, London: Verso.

Ravdonikas, V. (1939) *Istoria Pervobytnovo Obshchestva, vol. 1*, Leningrad: Izdanie Leningradskogo Gosudarstvennogo Universiteta.

—— (1947) *Istoriia Pervobytnogo Obshchestva, vol. 2*, Leningrad: Izdatel'stvo Leningradskogo Gosudarstvennogo Ordena Lenina Universiteta.

Rorty, R. (1991) *Essays on Heidegger and Others*, Cambridge: Cambridge University Press.

Rykwert, J. (1989) *On Adam's House in Paradise*, Cambridge: Cambridge University Press.

Smith, B. H. (1988) *Contingencies of Value*, Cambridge, MA: Harvard University Press.

Soffer, Olga (1985) *The Upper Palaeolithic of the Central Russian Plain*, Orlando, FL: Academic Press.

Soffer, O. and N. Praslov (eds) (1993) *From Kostenki to Clovis*, New York: Plenum Press.

Stites, R. (1989) *Revolutionary Dreams*, Oxford: Oxford University Press.

Tomášková, S. (1997) 'Places of Art: Art and Archaeology in Context', in M. W. Conkey, O. Soffer, D. Stratman and N. G. Jablonski (eds) *Beyond Art: Pleistocene Image and Symbol*, Memoirs of the California Academy of Sciences, no. 23, San Francisco: California Academy of Sciences.

Trigger, B. (1989) *A History of Archaeological Thought*, Cambridge: Cambridge University Press.

Vogt, A. (1998) *Le Corbusier, the Noble Savage: Toward an Archaeology of Modernism*, Cambridge, MA: MIT Press.

Willen, P. (1953) 'Soviet Architecture in Transformation', unpublished M.A. thesis, Columbia University, New York.

PART IV

The sexual gaze: representation and imagery

Chapter Fourteen

Re-em(bed)ding sex: domesticity, sexuality, and ritual in New Kingdom Egypt

Lynn Meskell

INTRODUCTION

Drawing on recent theorizing in the study of sexuality, I investigate the complex construction of sexuality in an ancient Egyptian context. Inspired predominantly by the later work of Michel Foucault, I argue that, in fact, sexuality did not exist as a discursive category in New Kingdom Egypt, unlike its recent European formulation. The ancient Egyptians had no word for sexuality nor specific terms which defined people on the basis of their sexual predilections. Neither did they appear to have public marriage ceremonies which are common to many cultures. One might posit that sexual relationships were entered into in more fluid and private ways, and could just as easily be dissolved in the same manner. To uncover the contextually specific experience of sexual life, I turn to the settlement data of the New Kingdom, primarily the well-preserved houses at the site of Deir el Medina (*c.* 1500–1100 BC). Here the archaeology, iconography, and textual data reveal that sexual life was deeply involved in other significant spheres, such as domestic life and ritual practice. Sexuality imbued these other aspects of life to such a degree that the separation of sexuality as a discrete category (as is the case in the modern West) appears meaningless. Moreover, the experience of sexuality was linked to moments in time and to particular groups in ways which modern interpreters might find unthinkable – for instance, to the circumstances of birth, nursing, and death, and to children of all ages, most notably girls. The disjunctures between ancient Egyptian sexuality and sexuality as we experience it within our own culture impel us to rethink the bounded fixity of sexuality, which we have created, and to recognize that there are other ways of being. By examining other cultural contexts, whether ancient or contemporary, we might free ourselves from the narrow constrictions and confinements of our own judgments and refigure sexuality in its myriad possibilities.

THE HISTORICAL BACKGROUND

At the outset I'd like to make several comments about the study of gender in Egyptian archaeology. Scholars of ancient Egypt have been slow to take up the challenges of gender and feminist research, and somewhat slower to acknowledge a position of reflexivity in their constructions of Egypt (Meskell 1997). Gender analysis has been largely construed as the study of women in ancient Egypt. The pioneering work of Gay Robins (1993, 1994–1995, 1994, 1996) is a notable exception amongst the surfeit of popular books which seek to glamorize or suburbanize the women of Egypt (e.g. Watterson 1991; Tyldesley 1994). Not surprisingly there are no substantive studies of men, or any works that consider gender in more complex relational ways. Gender has thus become a study of women, by women. This is a problematic position both politically and academically, since it ghettoizes gender studies and concomitantly renders men an unproblematic, untheorized category. Only through broadening the discussion can more complex, contextual analyses of sex and sexuality be undertaken (Meskell 1997, 1999).

Studies of women in Egypt have primarily targeted elite individuals, for whom the best iconographic and textual evidence remains. As is often the case in Mediterranean studies, 'woman' becomes the signifier for concepts revolving around the body – most often seen in studies of iconography, dress, adornment, posture, and hairstyles. Egyptologists have failed to refigure the body in any nuanced sense, opting instead to focus on female exteriority in the most literal manner. Because of this, the body and sexuality are thus read straight from the iconographic sources with little consideration of the social construction, much less embodied reality, of specific gendered or sexually-demarcated groups. So if the body is an absent area of analysis, then embodiment and experience are similarly overlooked (full discussion in Meskell 1997). 'Woman' is reduced to a visual spectacle, and female sexuality is construed normatively through male-oriented artistic representations or literature (e.g. love poetry). To date, only a handful of writers have engaged with contextual constructions of sex, gender and the body using the rich suite of data that Egypt provides (Parkinson 1995; Meskell 1996, 1998a; Montserrat 1996, 1998; Robins 1996; Wilfong 1998).

From the modern viewer's perspective, ancient Egyptian sexual categories derived from artistic or literary sources focus primarily upon women, which may not be surprising given that only men were trained as scribes, painters, etc. Women's largely illiterate position has impeded our knowledge of complementary discourses on the sexual beauty of men: love poems supposedly penned by women probably had a man behind each papyrus. It is possible that erotic genres depicting men also existed, but that the subtleties of the Egyptian system simply elude us. Or perhaps the young, muscular bodies we witness in Egyptian art were sufficient to signify male sexuality.

However, at least one illustrated papyrus, the Turin Papyrus, intentionally shows men with enlarged genitalia, engaged in a series of sexual activities with young women. Images of men on this papyrus do not conform to the bodily perfection of conventional Egyptian art; by comparison, the men depicted on the Turin Papyrus are scruffy, balding, short, and paunchy. Conversely, the young women depicted are nubile, slim, and associated with canonical erotic imagery: lotus flowers, convolvulus leaves, Hathoric imagery, sistra, and monkeys (see Manniche 1987). This purposive opposition of the respective representations of males and females is unlike formal Egyptian art. The narrative scenario presented, a series of sexual encounters between couples, may be satirical or may actually refer to a series of known incidents, possibly even a brothel. Perhaps this represents a more vernacular expression of male sexuality and desire. Unfortunately, there is no exact provenience for this papyrus, although it was alleged to have been found in a domestic context, possibly from the site of Deir el Medina.

The Turin Papyrus illustrates the variety of sexual representations in ancient Egypt. But just as sex and gender studies have been limited to the study of women in Egyptology, the entire subject of sexuality has either been largely avoided or treated as an extension of normative modern European categories. In general, Egyptologists have posited a connection between women and sexuality. It seems from textual evidence that there existed a whole aura of sexuality around female professions like musicians, dancers and entertainers, and adolescent serving girls (Robins 1996). These groups of women were sometimes represented on tomb walls or on various items of material culture, most often toiletry objects. These erotic genres are well known in the Egyptian context as are the informal sketches on ostraca[1] which show sexualized women or scenes of sexual intercourse. Representations of sexuality are usually interpreted as heterosexual, whilst there is strong documentary evidence in mythology and didactic texts that same-sex relations existed (Parkinson 1995, 1997). One might postulate that sexuality as a dominant characterizing force was not recognized as such in the ancient world: sexual preferences were acknowledged, but only as one would recognize someone's taste in food without characterizing that person as a member of a subspecies of humanity (Parkinson 1995: 59). Sexuality in ancient Egypt was a practice rather than a discourse or a label with which one designated people. In the hieroglyphic language there was no term for either homosexual or heterosexual, rather a variety of practices could be described within a fluid sexual system. The Egyptian verb *nk* refers to having penetrative sex, and has no particular overtones, positive or negative. But the word *nkw* has been used as a term of abuse and implies a passive role (Parkinson 1995: 62). Yet these words relate to the practices, rather than to categories of individuals. Moreover, interrogating ancient Egyptian sexuality should not simply provide a forum for studying sexual practices deemed non-normative in modern times. We should also study the social construction of heterosexuality. If left untheorized, heterosexuality, like masculinity and the body, becomes normative, unproblematic, and given. In fact, part of any social analysis of sexuality should be to deconstruct 'naturalism', and examine how actions are given their meaning and significance through social practices (Weeks 1997: 7).

Because the evocative images of Egyptian iconography seem so familiar to us now, very little new work has attempted to re-signify them or re-embed them in their original context. Because of the obvious hermeneutic pitfalls, I want to suggest that we have misread Egyptian sexuality and cast it in our own experience. We have analytically separated out sexuality as a socially constructed sphere, much as it exists in our own society: a Foucauldian category which is the outcome of specific cultural and historical processes. Sexuality is a constantly changing category in modern society, one that is undergoing continued monitoring and negotiation. Blurred boundaries seep into other social and legal categories, and modern sexuality itself is a slippery and fluid entity at the close of the millennium. Some 3,500 years ago, the Egyptians had no word for sexuality. But there certainly existed a culturally contextual experience of sexual life in Pharaonic Egypt. Perhaps sexuality did not exist as a category then, but rather assumed different roles and permutations within certain contexts. Sexuality infused so many aspects of ordinary life that it would have been unthinkable to isolate it. Specifically, I would argue that the sexual and the religious/ritual were united in ways which would be inconceivable from a twentieth-century Judeo-Christian perspective. That the *sexual* and the *religious* could exist harmoniously in Pharaonic Egypt suggests that we are witnessing real cultural difference.

For example, in New Kingdom tomb scenes, sexual images of women served to revive the male tomb occupant in the next life: the sexual self was an integral component of the living, embodied individual. Famous examples of these can be found in the tombs of elite men such as Nebamun and Rekhmire on the West Bank of modern-day Luxor (Baines and Málek 1982: 206). These images are not sexually explicit by modern standards;

however the message would have been clear to the Egyptian viewer. The scenes traditionally depict naked serving girls attending women who are wearing diaphanous gowns, heavy wigs, floral collars, and holding *menat*-necklaces – all imagery which is indicative of Egyptian eroticism (Brunner-Traut 1955; Derchain 1975; Robins 1994). Additionally, tomb iconography indicates that dances of a sexual nature were performed at funerals in the hope of sexually rejuvenating the deceased. Following from this, the 'Underworld Books' show the newly resurrected dead in a state of sexual arousal (Pinch 1993: 153). Here, I simply want to suggest that sex/sexuality and religion/ritual should not be viewed as mutually exclusive categories and that in ancient Egypt the situation was far more complex, or alternatively, far less theorized.

ARCHAEOLOGICAL CONTEXT

To explore this further, I want to consider a specific and well-documented archaeological context, the houses at the New Kingdom settlement of Deir el Medina (Figure 14.1). The site is situated on the West Bank of modern-day Luxor and remains in a remarkable state of preservation. It was originally founded to house the workers who constructed the royal tombs, along with their families, in close proximity to the Valley of the Kings. The substantial archaeological remains of Deir el Medina encompass not only the enclosed village, but scattered dwellings beyond the walls, silos, and storage facilities, some 400 tombs scattered in various necropolis, chapel complexes and the Hathor temple. The first settlement was probably constructed at the outset of the eighteenth Dynasty, under the Pharaoh Tuthmosis I (*c.* 1504–1492 BC). It was expanded during the nineteenth and

Figure 14.1 The settlement of Deir el Medina.
Photograph by the author.

twentieth Dynasties when the team of workers was increased in line with the changing dimensions of the royal tombs. The official role of the village came to an end during the reign of Ramesses XI (*c.* 1098–1069 BC), when the occupants gradually deserted the site due to civil unrest (Valbelle 1985: 125). However, the site continued to be an important religious and mortuary locale over the following centuries into Christian and Islamic times (Montserrat and Meskell 1997).

There are some sixty-eight houses for which a varying amount of detail is preserved, specifically fixtures, painting, decoration, and material culture. These were recorded in some detail in the 1930s by Bernard Bruyère and the French Institute (1939). It is primarily the first room of these houses from which we derive the majority of wall paintings and fixtures. These spaces were notionally female-oriented, centered around elite, married, sexually potent, fertile females of the households at Deir el Medina (Meskell 1998b: 217–29). They were loaded with what we would describe as sexual and ritual images. Yet the first rooms may also have been similarly used for sleeping, eating, and general domestic duties for many hours of the day. In this section I examine how Egyptian domestic spaces and iconography have been read, suggesting that the present-day discursive separation of spheres of sexuality from other spheres has restricted a fuller, contextual understanding of Egyptian renderings of sexuality as an embedded sphere. This is a potent example of how unreflexive archaeological scholarship can reify rather than analyze contemporary assumptions about the segregation of experiences such as sexuality from other relevant domains, be they social life, familial activities, or ritual practice. I argue that our own naturalized domains (see Yanagisako and Delaney 1995) should not be conflated with past cultural constructions, and I hope to offer an alternative reading.

The first room of the majority of houses at Deir el Medina has usually been designated the room of the enclosed bed (the so-called *lit clos*) (Figure 14.2). The majority of houses within the village have conclusive evidence of this bed-like structure in this first room. The *lit clos* dimensions are roughly 1.7 m long, 80 cm wide, and 75 cm high (Friedman 1994: 97). In house SE5 the *lit clos* was plastered, with molded and painted Bes figures, the male deity associated with women, sexuality, fertility, music, and magic (Pinch 1994: 43, 116). Bes predominates in the first room throughout the site. House C5 has a *lit clos* with an associated Bes painting, and in the house of the woman Iyneferty, SW6, there are also Bes decorations. In sum, the enclosed bed was associated with a constellation of features: white walls, paintings, moldings, niches, Bes decorations, cultic cupboards, shrines, etc. (Meskell 1998b: 223–25).

These structures were first termed 'enclosed beds' (*lit clos*) in the 1930s by Bernard Bruyère (1939), and the concept of the bed, primarily the birthing bed, has been a pervasive explanation ever since. Although it meant something very specific in his native French culture, Bruyère's notion of the bed has had a pervasive impact on Egyptological interpretations of the *lit clos* ever since (Friedman 1994: 97). Given the size of these structures, the feasibility of sleeping one or two people cannot be ruled out. It may have also acted as a ritual place for sexual intercourse and/or conception. However, there are inherent problems with this theory. For instance, there is ample evidence, in the form of illustrated ostraca from the site (Vandier d'Abbadie 1937), for the traditional birthing apparatus being a stool (or bricks) rather than a bed. Birth arbors shown in these representations might be specially constructed outdoor buildings; their temporary nature has precluded archaeological discovery. Other scholars have suggested that they may have been constructed on rooftops (Loose 1992: 23). These representations do not resemble the *lit clos*.

Figure 14.2 An example of a *lit clos* from house NE2 at Deir el Medina.
Photograph by the author.

These illustrated ostraca represent a genre of post-birthing representations which incorporate an erotic component, through motifs such as grooming, wigs, hip girdles, and nudity. There are also ceramic models showing a female or couple reclining in association with a child (Pinch 1993) (Figure 14.3). Such sexual overtones do not appear to be hampered by the presence of a child. The majority of these infants are shown to be male, as evidenced by a pronounced penis. In fact, age seems no barrier for the most part to representations with sexual overtones, as we have seen with the genre of the adolescent serving girl. This association between children and sexuality is something which scholars have not clearly set in its wider social setting. Just as sexuality may not have been a category constituted in a way we would find familiar, I would suggest that we need to rethink the whole category of children in Egypt and to acknowledge that 'childhood' in the modern sense is probably a misnomer. Just as children were expected to *work*, so perhaps they were expected to *play* in ways not dissimilar to adults. Irrespective of this issue, such data challenges the singular notion that the *lit clos* was exclusively a birthing bed; a broader cultic interpretation is more plausible.

Archaeological evidence for linking cultic practices with the *lit clos* can be found in individual houses at Deir el Medina, and also at the New Kingdom site of Amarna (Robins 1996: 29–30). In house NE11 at Deir el Medina, Bruyère excavated a *lit clos* containing several items: a limestone headrest, part of a statue, and a fragment of a female statuette in limestone. In front of this *lit clos* was an offering table. A similar situation was present in house C7. In house NE15 the *lit clos* was built with an associated cultic cupboard, as it was in Iyneferty's house, SW6. These objects suggest a more generalized cultic function. Although the first room has been associated with women, a number of finds name men of the house; associated limestone offering tables or stelae often bear a male name, rather than a female name. Assemblages from the first rooms consist primarily of ritual artifacts: stelae, shrine busts, offering tables, and statues. Taken together, this evidence warrants the general conclusion that a household cult, centered around mature females, was focused in the front rooms of Deir el Medina houses. More practically, these spaces could have been utilized on a daily basis for domestic activities, since troughs and mortars were also located in houses NE14 and SW1.

It is important to also contextualize the associated wall paintings located in the first room. The extant data suggest that the front rooms were heavily decorated, having whitewashed walls with female-oriented paintings, scenes of nursing or grooming, and deities pertaining to women's lives. In house SE1 there was a wall painting showing a woman breast-feeding; in house C7 a scene of a female grooming with her attendant; and in house NW12 a person on a papyrus skiff, probably female. These wall paintings show vernacular images, scenes which also appeared on items of everyday material culture. In house SE8, workman Nebamun must have commissioned a mural, either for himself or his wife, of a nude female musician with a tattoo on her upper thigh (Figure 14.4). She plays a double flute and is surrounded by convolvulus leaves, which the Egyptians considered symbolically erotic. While the erotic features of this representation would have been immediately obvious to

Figure 14.3 A ceramic bed model, showing woman and child. Photograph courtesy of the British Museum, inv. EA 2371.

Figure 14.4 Wall painting from the house of Nebamun, SE8.
Drawing by the author.

anyone entering the house, how it was received by various groups has not been considered. We must ask how the Egyptians viewed these ritual and sexual images, especially ones which might be interpreted as signifying 'prostitution'. My sense is that they were not separate spheres. Messages of religiosity and sexuality exist side-by-side, but should not be viewed as sexual in a pornographic sense. Our sense of sexuality is a highly articulated category, with a well-developed attendant discourse.

This is not to argue that sexuality in Egypt was not informed by moral codes. In fact, sexual codes were set out in dream books and didactic texts (Guglielmi 1996). I think we have to find another way of viewing Egyptian experience. One avenue is obviously via comparative ethnography. For example, the contradictory nature of sexual perceptions and attitudes is illustrated in many cultures, especially in terms of women's sexuality in the Middle East today (Atiya 1984; Attir 1985: 122). Instead of emphasizing contradiction, we might consider that sexuality existed in a broader social system, and because of this fluidity, it enabled a certain cross-cutting of other domains such as religious life, private life, cosmology, etc., in a way that modern Judeo-Christian traditions constrain.

ANCIENT SEXUALITY

In a sense, I am attempting to read Egyptian sexuality as more ordinary and more embedded within the social fabric of life. It seems that sexuality was inextricably linked to domesticity and ritual: to procreation, childbirth, nursing, various life stages, death, and even beyond to the afterlife. The archaeology of the *lit clos* demonstrates the ambiguity which coheres to discrete taxonomies such as ritual, domesticity, private life, and sexuality. The domestic data from Deir el Medina also challenge us to rethink the social categories as we apply them to the archaeological record. In particular the concept of 'childhood' should be refigured. From an anthropological perspective, Marilyn Strathern (1988: 92) states that amongst the Hagen there is 'no concept of childhood prolonged through continued dependency, because there is no equation between adulthood and independence'. In the West the 'sacred' category of childhood must be rigorously monitored and controlled with regard to sexuality, although this has been a relatively recent development. Only in the nineteenth century did the West witness the separation between 'grown-ups and children, the polarity established between the parents' bedroom and that of the children . . . the relative segregation between boys and girls, the strict instructions as to the care of nursing infants . . .' (Foucault 1978: 46). There are manifold sexualities which can certainly extend to children (Foucault 1978: 47; Foucault in Kritzman 1988: 113) and while this appears to be a taboo subject in a contemporary context, we should consider the possibilities of cultural difference when analyzing the past.

As this chapter suggests, sexuality was linked to so many facets of Egyptian culture that it should not and cannot be fetishized as sexuality has been fetishized in our own society. As Foucault reminds us, it was only during the seventeenth century that sex became clandestine, circumscribed, and policed, and that its discourse became coded. After that time, European societies have experienced a period of taboo, non-existence, and silence around sexual matters. From the eighteenth century onwards 'sex was driven out of hiding and constrained to lead a discursive existence' (Foucault 1978: 33). We should not assume that this was how the ancients perceived sexuality and we should not conflate those experiences – I suggest that in Egypt sex was a practice rather than a discourse. Jeffrey Weeks (1997: 15) has sensibly argued that we should 'define 'sexuality' as an [*sic*] historical construction, which brings together a host of different biological and mental possibilities – gender identity, bodily differences, reproductive capacities, needs, desires and fantasies – which need not to be linked together, and in other cultures have not been'. Ancient Egypt is a case in point. Finally, I'd like to recenter Foucault's famous insight (1978: 35) that 'what is peculiar to modern societies, in fact, is not that they consigned sex to a shadow existence, but that they dedicated themselves to speaking of it *ad infinitum*, while exploiting it as *the* secret'.

ACKNOWLEDGMENTS

This paper was written while I was Research Fellow at New College, Oxford. My participation at the conference was generously funded by the Oriental Institute at Oxford University. I owe both institutions a great debt of gratitude. All the usual suspects have been supportive and inspirational: John Baines, Ian Hodder, Dominic Montserrat, and Richard Parkinson. A special thanks to Rosemary Joyce for her careful reading of the text, her many insights and for all our discussions over e-mail.

NOTE

1 Ostraca is the name given to potsherds or chips of limestone with illustrations or writing painted on their surface. Many thousands of these have been discovered at Deir el Medina.

REFERENCES

Atiya, N. (1984) *Khul-Khal: Five Egyptian Women Tell Their Stories*, Cairo: American University Press.

Attir, M. O. (1985) 'Ideology, Value Changes, and Women's Social Position in Libyan Society', in E. W. Fernea (ed.) *Women and the Family in the Middle East: New Voices of Change*, Austin: University of Texas Press.

Baines, J. and J. Málek (1984) *Atlas of Ancient Egypt*, Oxford: Equinox.

Brunner-Traut, E. (1955) 'Die wochenlaube', *Mitteilungen des Instituts für Orientforschung* 3: 11–30.

Bruyère, B. (1939) *Rapport sur les Fouilles de Deir el Médineh (1934–1935)*, Cairo: Imprimerie de l'Institut Français d'Archéologie Orientale.

Derchain, P. (1975) 'La perruque et le cristal', *Studien zur Altägyptischen Kultur* 2: 55–74.

Foucault, M. (1978) *The History of Sexuality*, vol. 1, London: Routledge.

Friedman, F. A. (1994) 'Aspects of Domestic Life and Religion', in L. H. Lesko (ed.) *Pharaoh's Workers: The Villagers of Deir el Medina*, New York: Cornell University Press.

Guglielmi, W. (1996) 'Der Gebrauch rhetorischer Stilmittle in der ägyptischen Literatur', in A. Loprieno (ed.) *Ancient Egyptian Literature: History and Forms*, Leiden: E. J. Brill.

Kritzman, L. D. (1988) *Michel Foucault. Politics, Philosophy, Culture: Interviews and Other Writings 1977–1984*, New York: Routledge.

Loose, A. A. (1992) 'Woonhuizen in Amarna en het domein van de vrouwen', *Phoenix* 38, 2: 16–29.

Manniche, L. (1987) *Sexual Life in Ancient Egypt*, London and New York: Kegan Paul Inc.

Meskell, L. M. (1996) 'The Somatisation of Archaeology: Institutions, Discourses, Corporeality', *Norwegian Archaeological Review* 29, 1: 1–16.

—— (1997) 'Engendering Egypt: a Review Article', *Gender and History: Body and Gender in the Ancient Mediterranean* 9, 3: 557–602.

—— (1998a) 'The Irresistible Body and the Seduction of Archaeology', in D. Montserrat (ed.) *Changing Bodies, Changing Meanings: Studies on the Human Body in Antiquity*, London: Routledge.

—— (1998b) 'An Archaeology of Social Relations in an Egyptian Village', *Journal of Archaeological Method and Theory* 5, 3: 209–43.

—— (1999) *Archaeologies of Social Life: Age, Sex, Class Etc. in Ancient Egypt*, Oxford: Blackwell.

Montserrat, D. (1996) *Sex and Society in Graeco-Roman Egypt*, London: Kegan Paul International.

—— (ed.) (1998) *Changing Bodies, Changing Meanings: Studies on the Human Body in Antiquity*, London: Routledge.

Montserrat, D. and L. M. Meskell (1997) 'Mortuary Archaeology and Religious Landscape at Graeco-Roman Deir el Medina', *Journal of Egyptian Archaeology* 84: 179–98.

Parkinson, R. B. (1995) '"Homosexual" Desire and Middle Kingdom Literature', *Journal of Egyptian Archaeology* 81: 57–76.

—— (1997) *The Tale of Sinuhe and Other Ancient Egyptian Poems*, Oxford: Clarendon.

Pinch, G. (1993) *Votive Offerings to Hathor*, Oxford: Griffith Institute, Ashmolean Museum.

—— (1994) *Magic in Ancient Egypt*, London: British Museum Press.

Robins, G. (1993) *Women in Ancient Egypt*, London: British Museum Press.

—— (1994–1995) 'Women and Children in Peril: Pregnancy, Birth and Infant Mortality in Ancient Egypt', *KMT* 5, 4: 24–35.

—— (1994) 'Some Principles of Compositional Dominance and Gender Hierarchy in Egyptian Art', *Journal of the American Research Center in Egypt* 31: 33–40.

—— (1996) 'Dress, Undress, and the Representation of Fertility and Potency in New Kingdom Egyptian Art', in N. B. Kampen (ed.) *Sexuality in Ancient Art*, Cambridge: Cambridge University Press.

Strathern, M. (1988) *The Gender of the Gift: Problems with Women and Problems with Society in Melanesia*, Berkeley: University of California Press.

Tyldesley, J. (1994) *Daughters of Isis: Women of Ancient Egypt*, London: Penguin.

Valbelle, D. (1985) *'Les Ouvriers de la Tombe': Deir el Médineh à l'époque ramesside*, Cairo: Institut Français d'Archéologie Orientale.

Vandier d'Abbadie, J. (1937) *Ostraca figurés de Deir el Médineh*, Cairo: Imprimerie de l'Institute Français d'Archéologie Orientale.

Watterson, B. (1991) *Women in Ancient Egypt*, Stroud: Allan Sutton Publishing.

Weeks, J. (1997) *Sexuality*, London: Routledge.

Wilfong, T. (1998) 'Reading the Disjointed Body in Coptic: from Physical Modification to Textual Fragmentation', in D. Montserrat (ed.) *Changing Bodies, Changing Meanings: Studies on the Human Body in Antiquity*, London: Routledge.

Yanagisako, S. and C. Delaney (eds) (1995) *Naturalizing Power: Essays in Feminist Cultural Analysis*, New York: Routledge.

Chapter Fifteen

A Precolumbian gaze: male sexuality among the ancient Maya

Rosemary A. Joyce

> *All* practice, insofar as it engages the senses, lays the body open to the world and to others
> . . . no one learns (or unlearns) anything – a gender or a sexuality or an identity or even
> a meaning – except through some process of physical modeling, sensuous experimentation,
> and bodily play. In the least perception, we are perpetually crossing over and becoming
> entangled, finding and losing the self, making and dissolving the world.
>
> (Lancaster 1997: 565)

INTRODUCTION

Ramón Gutiérrez summarizes one scholarly view of the social significance of sexual relations between males in Native American societies, writing of early colonial New Mexican
Pueblos that

> bachelors were residentially segregated in kivas until they married, ostensibly to master
> male esoteric lore, but also to minimize conflicts between juniors and seniors over
> claims to female sexuality that adult married men enjoyed. Sex with a berdache served
> a personal erotic need and a religious (political) end. So long as bachelors were having
> sex with the half-man/half-woman, the social peace they represented was not beset
> with village conflicts between men over women. This may have been why the Spaniards
> called the berdaches *putos* (male whores). European prostitutes initiated young men
> to sexuality and gave married men a sexual outlet without disrupting family, marriage,
> or patrimony.
>
> (1991: 35)

Gutiérrez is extremely sensitive to the central role of the sexual attitudes of Franciscan
missionaries in our reception of early reports about Pueblo sexual practices, including
descriptions of Two Spirits (formerly *berdache*). Yet this awareness is not sufficient to
avoid the appearance of his accepting a description of these individuals as being made
'use' of, as required not to 'deny' sexual advances by 'any one who offered her pay'
(Gutiérrez 1991: 35). Nor does he avoid a mechanistic notion that society – Spanish and
Puebloan – *required* a release of phallic sexuality otherwise sure to disturb social order.

At their worst, similar characterizations, founded in European and Judeo-Christian ideologies, may simultaneously derogate same-sex desire and opposite sex desire, by presenting male-male sexuality as founded in a rejection of the feminine. Absent from Gutiérrez' account, and from many much less nuanced visions of the early Spanish colonial Americas, is a consideration of sexuality conceived of as the play of desire, its realization in another, and the production through such realization of pleasure.[1]

In this chapter, I would like to approach Classic Maya male sexuality not as a utilitarian value, harnessed in the service of state procreative policies (although I believe there is a strong argument to be made that Classic Maya states attempted to foster procreative ideologies), nor as a socially disturbing physical manifestation that required a safe release. Instead, I explore here suggestions of a visual and textual discourse that celebrated the male body as an object of a male gaze, a celebration at some points realized in the sexual relations between males, but also realized in the sexual desire of women for the aestheticized male body.

MASCULINITY IN CLASSIC MAYA SOCIETY

Elsewhere I have argued that imagery of adult male gender in Classic Maya society is strongly tied to sexuality, and particularly to display of the male body (Joyce 1996b). In scenes painted on pottery vessels and the interior walls of buildings, and even in more formal and visible carved stone images (Figure 15.1), male bodies are exposed by elaborate costuming that leaves arms, legs, and chests uncovered (Joyce 1992, 1996a). Male figures wear loincloths with long hanging ends that draw attention to male genitalia as much as they conceal them. What little clothing is worn is primarily adornment of the body: cuffs and anklets depicting beads, probably of jade or shell; helmets or headdresses incorporating the heads, tails, or hoofs of animals, ornamented with feather panaches; and massive belts, pendants, and ear ornaments, also likely depicting jade.

The male figures whose bodies are displayed and ornamented in these scenes commonly appear in groups engaged in all-male pursuits where physical strength and skill were required. Battles, ball games, ritualized deer hunts, and dance performances, some involving body piercing, are common settings of all-male socialization repeatedly depicted in Classic Maya art (Figures 15.2 and 15.3). The display of the male body was central to these all-male settings. The bodies shown in these performances are highly idealized, presented in a timeless young adulthood. The exposed chests, arms, and legs of these figures are solid, rounded, and marked to suggest musculature that is equally implied by the ease with which the figures move in their sometimes massive ornaments. The occasional display of facial hair is unique to these all-male scenes, emphasizing both age and sex, embodying a particularly pointed physical masculinity.

Internally, these multi-figure compositions engage their male subjects in visual hierarchies directed at male viewers within the scene: the dancers in the third Bonampak mural, about to begin the twirling motion which will drive blood from their pierced genitalia outward by centrifugal force to pattern white cloth strips in red, perform at the base of a stairway from whose highest point a male lord observes them (see Schele and Miller 1986: 180–81, 193 for the link between this dance and bloodletting). Paired athletes competing for control of the rubber ball on a polychrome cylinder vase are the focus of the regard of other male figures that encroach on each edge of the playing field (for example, Schele and Miller 1986: Plates 95, 96). And scenes of capture in battle painted at monumental scale on the walls of Bonampak, and pictured as moments of single combat

Figure 15.1 Portrait of Classic Maya noble man and woman, showing the exposure of the male body and contrast to the concealed female body. Yaxchilan lintel 24.
Courtesy of Ian Graham, Copyright President and Fellows of Harvard College.

Figure 15.2 Bonampak mural showing idealized battle scene in which elaborately costumed male warriors engage in hand-to-hand combat. Painted on the wall opposite the doorway of a room located on a raised platform, most likely a reception hall like those represented on contemporary pottery vessels.
Photograph by Hillel Burger, detail of a copy painted by Antonio Tejeda. Courtesy of Peabody Museum, Harvard University, Copyright President and Fellows of Harvard College.

on countless stone monuments throughout the Maya world (Figure 15.3), present defeated male warriors under the hand and the eye of their richly adorned male captors (for example, Yaxchilan Lintel 8, Piedras Negras Stela 12; Schele and Miller 1986: Figure V.3, Figure V.8).[2] Contemporary understandings of the ownership, circulation, and use of the polychrome vessels that provide the most abundant corpus of all-male multi-figure scenes suggest that they were produced for noble male patrons (Reents-Budet 1994). If this is accurate, the internal visual relationships of these vessels reflexively invoke the objectification of male bodies as subjects of the gaze of noble males, patrons of artists, and owners of these elaborate objects (Figure 15.3).

Figure 15.3 Male lord gazing down toward a noble man he has captured. Yaxchilan lintel 45. Courtesy of Ian Graham, Copyright President and Fellows of Harvard College.

CLASSIC MAYA MASCULINITY AND SEXUALITY

I infer a sexualization of this aesthetic delight in the male body, and of the settings in which it was displayed, from a marginalized aspect of some Classic Maya art: the representation of the erect penis. Especially noted for very late Classic period settlements of northern Yucatan (*c.* AD 750–950), depiction of erections has been dismissed as anomalous: a trait putatively introduced by less civilized invaders from non-Maya societies located to the west (e.g. Spinden 1913: 200; Tozzer 1957: 111; Thompson 1970: 319).

The number of Maya sites where explicit sexual imagery is found is in fact quite extensive: at least twenty-two have been identified.[3] Unfortunately, most examples were found out of their original context. Notable exceptions exist at Chichen Itza, the largest late Classic site in northern Yucatan, which can serve as a model for understanding the distribution of this imagery. Tozzer's (1957: 111) data for Chichen allow the identification of two architectural settings of explicit male sexual imagery.

The building known as the House of the Phalli at Chichen Itza (Structure 5C14) consists of a series of at least ten interconnected rooms, with three-dimensional phalli projecting from the interior end walls of five rooms. This building forms part of a cluster of twenty-five buildings, raised on a common platform, that is exemplary of some of the most elaborate house compounds at the site (see Lincoln 1990: 429–47 for the most recent description). A formal entry to the group was defined on the north-east by a vaulted gateway. Entry through this gateway leads immediately past a prominent raised temple, located on the east side of an open court that is flanked by specialized buildings: the House of the Phalli on the south, a smaller temple (Structure 5C3) on the west, and a raised hall on the north. Groups of buildings with typical residential features, including water storage facilities, occupy the areas north-west, east, and south of this specialized entry court. Structure 5C3 featured two anthropomorphic figures supporting the vaults; these had their clothing 'pushed aside, revealing the genitals', a posture Tozzer (1957: 111) described as lewd. The rooms in the House of the Phalli are the size and shape of those typical of residential buildings throughout the site, including built-in benches below the phallic sculptures. It is connected to an unusual colonnaded courtyard that is not typical of other residential buildings.

Lincoln (1990: 629–34) argued that buildings with floor plans like the House of the Phalli were palaces that symbolically represented male lines of descent and military power.[4] He contrasted these buildings with a second architectural form, the 'gallery-patio structure', which he suggested represented the maternal line and the symbolically female action of ritual bloodletting. While his sociological argument is not entirely compelling, Lincoln has accurately characterized the distribution of gendered imagery between buildings of these two types at the site. The House of the Phalli, and other buildings like it, are sites of the display of masculine sexuality, especially by figures adorned as warriors.

The second example of localization of imagery of male sexuality at Chichen Itza is distinct. Tozzer (1957: 111) identified a single-room building, Structure 6E6, in which a stone carving of a penis was set upright in the center of the floor. On the original map of Chichen Itza, this building is shown as an isolated construction south of two larger clusters of buildings. The northernmost platform in this area was comparable in scale and elaboration to the platform that supported the House of the Phalli, but lacked a comparable palace-plan building (Lincoln 1990: 518–32). Unfortunately, Lincoln did not investigate Structure 6E6 so that its integration with the other buildings in this area remains uncertain.

Single room buildings at Chichen Itza generally are identifiable as locations of ritual activities, so that if the original report of the building is accurate, it provides a second architectural context for male sexual imagery at Chichen Itza: shrines or temples. Tozzer (1957: 111) suggests that a narrative pictorial image from the main ceremonial architectural group at the site depicted a 'phallus in connection with a worshipful Toltec'. While his comment is maddeningly vague, recent drawings of these low reliefs, interpreted as visual records of the ceremonies of burial of one ruler and investiture of the next (Wren and Schmidt 1991; Wren 1994), include a scene in which what appears to be a monumental scale phallic sculpture is the focus of ritual action by some of the male participants (Figure 15.4).

Both types of abstraction of erect male genitalia from the body for use in architecture are identifiable at other sites. The use of three dimensional sculptures of the erect penis as waterspouts characterizes the Temple of the Phallus at Uxmal (Pollock 1980: 263). Like its counterpart at Chichen Itza, this building is located in an outlying elaborate

Figure 15.4 At the left hand side of the upper register, a standing male figure with an exposed penis faces a monumental image of a phallus. Located on the interior ceiling of the North Ballcourt Temple at Chichen Itza, this image is part of a suite of architectural sculpture and murals surrounding the single largest ballcourt ever constructed in Meso-America, a probable location of all-male ceremonial performances.
Drawing by Linnea Wren after Marvin Cohodas, reproduced by permission.

residential neighborhood. Graham (1992: 4–83) shows this structure as a multi-room building of the same type as the Chichen palace, on a platform incorporating other less elaborate buildings and multiple water-storage facilities, typical of residential groups. As many as five monumental sculptures of phalli were also reported from Uxmal, regrettably without known original locations (Pollock 1980: 267).

Many other sites include either or both kinds of architectural settings of phallic sculpture. Chacmultun Structure 1, a palace-plan building, was ornamented with phallic drain spouts (Pollock 1980: 364). At Labna a monumental phallic sculpture 0.9 m long (Figure 15.5) was originally reported in association with another such sculpture and stelae, south of a temple decorated with frescoes of ball-game playing (Pollock 1980: 36–38, 51). Acanmul Miscellaneous Sculpture 1, a stone phallus 0.96 m long, was located in a courtyard delimited on the east by a small temple, and on the north by a colonnaded palace-plan building with carved images of elaborately dressed male dancers (Pollock 1980: 541).

The palace-plan buildings, ornamented with phallic imagery at Chichen Itza, Uxmal, and Chacmultun, and presumably similar buildings originally the context of identical architectural sculptures from sites like Kanalku and San Pedro, are *generally* residential in their plans, settings, and built-in features, but are not necessarily *generalized* residences with a full range of evidence for household economic activities. They tend to have more rooms and less differentiation of space, and are uniformly located adjacent to more open, public spaces than the enclosed courtyards of generalized residences. They may be better compared to specialized houses described for the early colonial Yucatec Maya, where young men lived together apart from their families of birth (e.g. Landa 1959: 54). At Chichen, the class of buildings to which the House of the Phalli belongs are also the sites of other imagery which emphasizes all-male group activities, including warfare, ball-game playing, and dancing, leading to Lincoln's (1990) identification of them as sites symbolic of masculinity. Similar elaborate palace-plan buildings with imagery of warriors, dancers, and ballplayers are located adjacent to the monumental freestanding phallic sculptures at sites

Figure 15.5 Monumental sculpture of a phallus from Acanmul. Multiple examples, most out of original context, were recorded in sites from northern Yucatan.
Photograph Carnegie Institution of Washington. Courtesy of Peabody Museum, Harvard University, Copyright President and Fellows of Harvard College.

like Labna and Acanmul (Figure 15.6). These activities overlap with those described as typical of the life of young men who lived in the centrally located men's houses within sixteenth-century Yucatec Maya towns.

Far from representing a late and aberrant introduction into Classic Maya society from some less civilized society, however, the celebration of male sexuality and male beauty for apparently exclusively male audiences was already present earlier in the Late Classic, although in different spatial settings. The cave of Naj Tunich includes among its ninety-four images (dated to between AD 692 and 771) scenes that have plausibly been described as representing exaggerated male sexual arousal (Stone 1995: 194–97). These include images of simulated or real masturbation (Figure 15.7). They also include a unique image in which two nude figures stand face-to-face. The left-hand figure displays an exaggerated

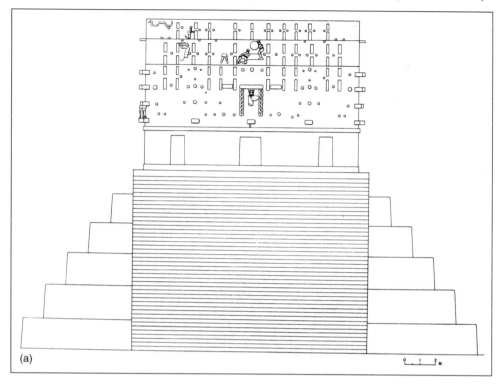

Figure 15.6 Images ornamenting buildings associated with possible young men's houses at Labna and Acanmul, northern Yucatan.

(a) The stucco relief of ball-game players from a temple in the courtyard at Labna, the building closest to a monumental sculpture of a phallus at the site, depicts one of the typical activities of young men in the sixteenth century. This courtyard also included a set of buildings similar to residences, but was located at a distance from the main palace compound, to which it was linked by a raised walkway.

Reproduced with permission from Pollock (1980: figures 65 and 907b), Copyright 1980 by the President and Fellows of Harvard College.

erect penis. The right-hand figure was originally described as female, although it has no definitive sexual characteristics. Andrea Stone (1995: 143–46) suggests that this image, previously regarded as a depiction of heterosexual intercourse, in fact involves two males, one marked by hairstyle and ornament as socially female. Stone emphasizes the apparent lack in the texts and images documenting visits to these caves of any identifiable female persons (Stone 1995: 117, 145, 183–84, 239). She suggests that Classic Maya caves such as Naj Tunich constituted an arena for all-male socialization during which, among other things, sexuality was openly subject to verbal and physical play, as it is in some performative settings among modern Highland Maya.

Here Roger Lancaster's (1997: 568–70) discussion of the relationships between play, practice, and the social construction of gender is illuminating. Lancaster describes play as

a special genre of practice – that form most perfectly aligned with what Marx calls 'sensuous practice', or 'practice as sensuous activity'. It embodies practice at its freest and

most creative. In this engagement of body and the world, we test the plasticity of the world against the dexterity of the body.

(1997: 569)

It is precisely this sense of play and of testing the dexterity of the (male) body that is foregrounded in the imagery of all-male socialization in Classic Maya art. The players strain to meet the motion of the ball, the warriors turn their bodies towards their opponents, the hunters reach out to capture and subdue the magical deer: through these activities, and through their re-presentation for the contemplation of patrons and viewers of the artworks that commemorate them, the male body engaged in sensuous activity is presented as something beautiful. The participants in all-male gatherings, like those memorialized in Naj Tunich Drawing 18, were engaged in just such tests of their bodies against 'the world', but as Lancaster notes, the creativity of social-practice-as-play is not unlimited:

The freedom of play is meaningful, and faculties are reshaped by its exertions, precisely because both the body and world are encountered as obstacles, resistances, counterforces … Huizinga's heuristic origins stories aside, we are never in the position of the first to play. We thus play our games freely, but we are not free to play them just any way we choose.

(1997: 569)

Lancaster explicitly links his analysis to Judith Butler's (1993) arguments about the social construction of 'bodies that matter'. I suggest that the 'obstacles, resistances, and counterforces' to play that result in limiting the way actors 'play our games' include the citational precedents that Butler argues gendered performances seek to repeat (1993: 12–16, 101–119). I have elsewhere suggested that the visual representation of specific aspects of bodily existence and specific, highly stereotyped and repeated actions in Classic Maya inscriptional media constituted social production of citational

Figure 15.6 (b) Low-relief sculpture of a male dancer, one of a series on the door jambs of a residence in a similar architectural group at Acanmul, the site of another monumental sculpture of a phallus.

precedents for gendered performance (Joyce 1996b). If Stone's argument that Naj Tunich Drawing 18 presents male transvestist sexual performance is correct, this and other all-male performances – whether held in the confines of caves or in other locations within settlements – would have provided settings for male citational gender performance, constructing Classic Maya male sexuality through a male gaze on male sex.

The images from Naj Tunich provide what Whitney Davis (1998) would call 'an erotic history' for the display of male sexual arousal that has been marginalized in discussions of Classic Maya art as an aberrant practice of northern Yucatec sites of the very late Classic period. Naj Tunich stands firmly within the canons of Classic Maya art in graphic style, the use of Classic Maya script, calendar system, and references to known political centers. While these images are remarkable, sexualization of the Classic Maya male body is equally evident in Classic Maya text, a medium of discursive representation which addressed a narrower audience than the more accessible visual imagery it accompanied (Figure 15.8).

A sign in the Maya writing system (T703) that is read today as the syllable *xib*, meaning both young man and penis in Yucatec Maya, represents a profile view of a body with a detailed image of a penis replacing the head (Bricker 1992). A pictograph of male genitalia was also used as a personal title from the Late Preclassic through the Late Classic Periods (*c.* 100 BC to AD 830), and was widely distributed, from Copan in the eastern Maya area (Figure 15.8) to Bonampak in the western Maya borderlands (Lounsbury 1989; Justeson 1984: 356; Schele and Miller 1986: 83, 151; Thompson 1962: 361–62). While not displayed in a state of arousal, this pictographic title constituted a decisive display of male sexual status in a writing system and language that did not otherwise provide a clear means to differentiate the sex or gender of the subject of texts. The apparent discursive place of titles, including this one, in Classic Maya texts is a

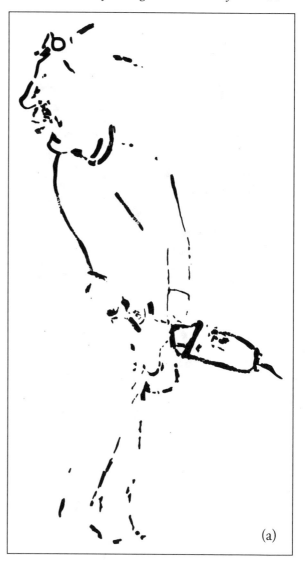

(a)

Figure 15.7 Paintings located in one section of Naj Tunich cave.

(a) Drawing 17 showing standing figure possibly engaged in masturbation. (b) Drawing 18 showing possible male-to-male embrace with exaggerated phallic image (see over). (c) Drawing 20 showing squatting figure masturbating (see p. 275). A short undeciphered text that forms part of this drawing is not reproduced here.
Figures 6–12, 6–28, and 6–16 from *Images from the Underworld: Naj Tunich and the Tradition of Maya Cave Painting* by Andrea J. Stone, Copyright 1995. By permission of University of Texas Press.

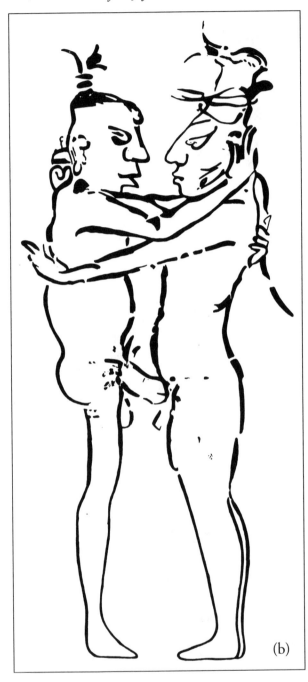

(b)

Figure 15.7 (*continued*)

part of the recounting of personalized claims to legitimate political authority by male rulers. This discourse draws on the same range of all-male activities that are represented visually in settings like the Naj Tunich caves and the palace-plan buildings of Chichen Itza that were settings of masculine imagery. Rulers described themselves as initiated in battle, as distinguished ballplayers, and as participants in dance-dramas. The audience with whom this persuasive discourse engaged presumably was neither the general population (presumed to be nonliterate and with restricted or non-existent access to these inscriptions), nor the political counterparts of rulers at other sites, but rather the rivals and peers among whom these Maya lords grew to adulthood, the men of their own cohort.

Scholars have de-emphasized the sexual nature of the display of male genitalia in a noble title by linking it to ritualized perforation of the penis for bloodletting. But the prominence of imagery of manipulation of the penis in ritual contexts in Classic and Postclassic Maya sources also contributed to a sexualization of masculinity through shared experience of the male body. The explicit or implicit site of male bloodletting in Classic Maya art is the penis (Joralemon 1974; Schele and Miller 1986; Stuart 1984, 1988). Andrea Stone (1988: 75) suggests that 'this particular method of shedding blood conceptually transformed the male genitalia into a doubly potent agent of fertility, capable of shedding two life-giving fluids: semen and blood'. Bloodletting from the penis is repeatedly depicted as a group male activity. J. Eric S. Thompson's original identification of the practice as the subject of a polychrome painted vessel from Huehuetenango, Guatemala, concerns such a multi-figure bloodletting scene (Thompson 1961; see Schele and Miller 1986: 193, Plate 72). The dancers in the third Bonampak mural are considered to be engaged in a final stage of a similar multi-person bloodletting ceremony (Schele and Miller 1986: 180–81). A painted polychrome vessel from the Dumbarton Oaks collection shows a principal male figure engaged in piercing the penis attended by another male, whose costume and ornaments suggest he is also of noble status, also engaged in bloodletting (Schele and Miller 1986: 192, Plate 68). An early page of the Postclassic Yucatec Codex Madrid (Figure 15.9) shows multiple male actors joined by a rope run through their pierced genitals (Codex Tro-Cortesianus 1967: 19).

Lancaster writes that

> in the absorption of observation, subject/viewer and object/viewed are momentarily fused. We lose ourselves in finding the object, only to recover ourselves among objects – which become extensions of our own limbs, 'encrustations in our own flesh' . . . we are always entangled with others, with objects, with the world; . . . by its very nature, the body locates itself only by going beyond its place of standing; . . . we find ourselves and lose ourselves in the same gesture, the same glance.
>
> (1997: 564)

The homosocial performances that are foregrounded in Classic Maya art involved identification between the men they involved that was not intellectualized, but experienced in the perception of the other as engaged in 'the same gesture, the same glance'.[5]

MALE SEXUALITY IN COLONIAL YUCATAN

We can trace the celebration of the male body, male sociality, and male-male sexual desire into the records of the European encounters with Yucatan and use the archaeological interpretation to reorient our reading of these sources.[6] Early colonial religious sources commented on the prevalence in Yucatan of the practice of male genital bloodletting, implying the late continuation of body practices that foregrounded the male body in sexually segregated settings (e.g. Landa 1959: 49, 58).

The same sources downplay or deny the existence of male-male sexual relations. Landa comments in his description of young men's houses:

> Although I have heard that in other parts of the Indies they practice in such houses the black sin, in this country I have not found that this was done, nor do I believe

(c)

Figure 15.7 (continued)

Figure 15.8 Classic Maya titles of a Late Classic ruler of Copan, Honduras, with penis title at the extreme right. Temple 26, Copan.

that they did it because they say that those given to this pestilential misery are not friendly to women as were these, who brought prostitutes to those places and used them there, and the poor women that certainly had this role among this people, notwithstanding that they received payment from the young men, were so much resorted to by them that they were taken to the point of exhaustion and death.[7]

(1959: 54)

Here Landa not only speaks from his own position as a member of a sixteenth-century Spanish society that insisted on imposing narrowly envisaged sexual and gender identities on human possibility (Burshatin 1996), but also reflects the deliberate selection by his unacknowledged noble Maya informants of the knowledge they offered to him. Bishop Landa was inspired to write his account to defend himself in Spain against charges stemming from his overly zealous pursuit of Maya idolatry. As Inga Clendinnen (1987) has demonstrated, the Yucatec Maya produced for their inquisitors confessions of the kinds of transgressions those authorities wanted to hear; equally, we may presume, they learned what topics were literally unspeakable for the Spanish. Will Roscoe (1991: 170–76) discusses the effects of repression of alternative sexualities in the Spanish colonial period, noting that by 1552 López de Gómara could list as one of the benefits of conquest the eradication of sodomy. Diego de Landa, chronicler of Yucatan, arrived there only in 1549, about twenty years after the date Yucatec Maya writers recorded as the effective beginning of colonization; he wrote his account of pre-conquest Maya practices two decades later still.[8]

Other colonial texts, written in Yucatec Maya using the newly introduced roman alphabet, by contrast, have been interpreted as referring to male-male sexual relations (for example, Edmonson 1982). The texts in question, collectively known as 'Books of Chilam Balam', were locally written post-colonial revitalization prophecies and histories. Individual copies were held within Yucatec Maya communities until the nineteenth century, when they were removed or copied during the antiquarian researches of European and American scholars.

Yucatec Maya vocabularies for sexual activities provide a sense of the range of sexual activities that were current in sixteenth-century communities.[9] Two different roots are glossed in these vocabularies as referring to anal sex. One (*kuchpach tan, kuchpach k'eban*) specifies the position as 'reversed', regardless of whether the participants were both male or male and female. The other (*top chun, top it*) employs the same verb root as for male-female sex (*top*), but specifies the site of penetration as the 'base' of the body or the anus.

Figure 15.9 Male actors joined by a rope through the penis. The black-painted figure at lower left and the similar light-painted figure at upper right show the conventional wrench-shaped image of the penis, with the rope passing behind. The light-colored figure at upper left is rotated so that the rope is shown passing through the tip of the penis. Drawing from Postclassic Yucatec Codex Madrid, page 19.

Neither term differentiates sexual activity on the basis of the sex or gender of the partners; instead, the relevant variability captured is in positions.

The vocabularies also provide a diverse lexicon for masturbation, the form of sexual activity that is explicitly depicted in Classic Maya images, an activity that did not correspond to the sixteenth-century colonial Spanish definition of sodomy and hence would not have been construed as the 'black sin'. Glosses for two of these terms (*baxalba*, *kol ach*) explicitly refer to mutual masturbation, including among more than two people: *baxala'antanba*, glossed as 'some touching others improperly', is a multiple plural form. The root form, *baxal*, primarily refers to play, and is the verb used in references to group amusements by young men: *baxal u ka'ah palalo'ob*, 'the boys are playing'; *baxal ok'ot likil yok'ol k'in tio'ob*, 'they place themselves in the sun, playing and dancing'. *Baxal* was also defined in Maya lexicons with the terms for games of chance (*bulah*) and ball-game playing (*pok'ah pitsah*), the diversions of youths in the young men's houses.

Notably, none of these terms is associated with the rich colonial Yucatec Maya moral vocabulary glossed by the Spanish commentators with the term 'fornicar', and otherwise specified as dealing with 'lewdness' and excessive sexual activity; these terms are based on the root *ko'*: daring or shameless, lacking judgment. Excessiveness and lack of balance are the emphases of the glosses employing this term, and the root in fact is equally used for other kinds of behavior, including madness, extreme anger, and quarrelsomeness. The only moral judgments recorded in the vocabulary of sexual acts come from the use in some combinations of the term *k'eban*, pressed into service by the Spanish clerics for 'sin'. The core sense of this root, 'disquiet', allowed it to be used to express the Spanish Catholic notion of sin as a disturbance of conscience, and it appears in the dictionaries primarily in glosses from catechisms, strongly suggesting it does not reflect an indigenous notion of moral sanction.

The Yucatec Maya colonial vocabularies emphasize sexual actions, not sexual identities. Most nominal forms are agentive compounds of verbal roots: *ah top chun*: the one who carries out the action of penetrating at the base of the body, glossed as 'sodomite'. Thus, the few terms that reflect sex/gender identity stand out: *ch'upal ol*, literally 'maidenly heart', glossed as 'effeminate man', and *ch'uplalhal ol*, 'to make oneself effeminate'. Before 1898, this is the only term in the Yucatec Maya dictionaries reflecting sex/gender identity. When modern Yucatec Maya vocabularies expanded in the twentieth century to create terms to label homosexuality *as an identity* (just as Euro-American languages were concretizing the concept of homosexuality through a parallel process), they returned to the male body for their distinctive signifier: *x-ch'upul xib*, *xibil x-ch'up*: maiden with a penis, young man/penis who is maidenly.

IMPLICATIONS

Absent from colonial texts for the most part, and completely obscured in later commentaries on them, is the sensual context of male-male sexual practices. The sexual encounters recorded in Naj Tunich cave present an image of sensual connection. Classic Maya images of all-male groups glamorize the display of the male body to male peers in the context of physical contests between warriors from different polities, between hunters and their prey, and between ballplayers contending for control of the rubber ball at play in the courts that were ubiquitous in Maya archaeological sites. The same celebratory display of ornamented, youthful, powerful male bodies marks all-male ritual processions and dances, which may also have had an aura of competition between men.

The presence of a 'phallic cult' in Late Classic and Postclassic Yucatec Maya society, while distasteful to the early twentieth-century students of the Maya, was nonetheless acknowledged. Explanations for this imagery, however, were thoroughly imbricated with Anglo-American cultural attitudes that assumed that male homosexual relations were immutably about effeminacy and the exercise of domination, requiring the creation of an abjected male sexual object. Spanish colonial accounts of sexual practices and attitudes, which denied that the Yucatec Maya engaged in any same-sex sexuality, were used to reinforce desexualized archaeological assessments of imagery that suggested otherwise. Similar assumptions have continued to distort more recent analyses, which compare male-male sex to burlesques of women or project onto Classic Maya men mysogynistic attitudes by linking masturbation to rejection of women.

To echo Roger Lancaster,

> theorizing these capers proves no less problematic, for theory, too, would put before us a set of dreary options . . . with such options, we are invited to choose sides, to pick a team, and to play a game whose outcome is already decided . . . But what if a dramatic moment *en cours* is overwhelmed by nuance and ambiguity?
>
> (1997: 560)

As Susan Bordo (1994: 284–85) has suggested in a consideration of contemporary North American imagery of the male body, same-sex desire may be viewed as involving an identification with the similarity of the other, rather than a dis-identification with the difference of an other. If we can be allowed to extend this psychological characterization to a society as different from the contemporary United States as that of the ancient Maya, then we might be able to suggest that the depiction of the male body as an object of desire for male viewers both within and outside the visual field was accompanied by identification with the desired one.

One outcome of such identification by men with the performance of other beautiful, powerful male bodies might have been desire for the male body inscribed in Classic and Postclassic Maya visual and textual representations. As Lancaster puts it,

> every act of attention, every empathic power of the flesh, involves a kind of crossing-over, a loss and recovery of the self . . . Because we are social creatures, 'self' is always found in an 'other'. And because our sociability is carnal in its very nature, the desire for another, the desire to be another, is part of the fundamental magnetism the world exerts on us.
>
> (1997: 564)

NOTES

1 While Gutiérrez (1991: 227–28) does explicitly consider the personal importance of one emotion – love – in colonial New Mexico, it is also as a force disruptive of social arrangements in marriage. I am explicitly concerned in this paper with desire and pleasure, rather than love. That desire was a social fact in Puebloan societies might be taken as a given; Gutiérrez provides support for this in his summary of the Hopi Marau society dances (held in January and September) in which,

> dancing naked in a circle with their backs to the community, the women would fondle clay phalluses and taunt the men with lewd songs to the clouds (rain, semen) and lightning (penis)

[of the sky], repeatedly bending over to expose their genitals to the men. 'Iss, iss, iss,' the men would cry excitedly. 'I wish I wish, I wish I wish!' – wishes the women satisfied at the dance's end, cooling the passion of the men through intercourse . . .

(1991: 19)

The text immediately preceding this passage – 'Throughout the next two days the women danced to awaken the sky's (men's) desires so that it would pour forth its rain (semen)' – and the gloss added at the end of the passage – 'cooling the passion of the men *through intercourse, the symbol of cosmic harmony* (emphasis added)' – demonstrate the utilitarianism of Gutiérrez' approach to this dance. Regardless of the assumed functional goals of this ritual the dance itself, as a social practice, enacts desire and male–female sexual attraction. For the purposes of this paper, this is a reminder not to ignore the sensual dimensions of activities of the Postclassic and Classic Maya not necessarily described in those terms either by Spanish colonial authorities or subsequent anthropological commentators.

2   While this characterization is accurate for the main battle scene in Bonampak Room 2, the scene on the opposite wall, the 'judging of the prisoners', is distinct. Although prisoners are arrayed on the steps leading down from the vantage point of the central frontal male figure, he makes no visual or physical contact with them. Instead, his gaze is directed towards a line of standing profile warriors who can be equated with figures in the battle scene. This engagement is mirrored by the female figures at the right of the scene, including one who is posed centrally. The presence of these female figures marks this scene as distinct from the all-male settings under discussion here; visually, the pyramidal arrangement of prisoners on the steps, some in direct contact with captors, is distinct from the interaction shown as occurring on the upper platform. The naked male prisoner at the top of this pyramidal arrangement looks upwards towards the face of the central male figure, but his glance is not engaged. This contrasts with the similar composition on Piedras Negras Stela 12, where the seated frontal male captor who forms the apex of the pyramid gazes down at the uppermost of the captives displayed on the steps before him. The interpretation of the Bonampak scene as a 'judgment' or other engagement of the victorious rulers with their captives seems ill-founded; instead, the focus here is on the relations within the victorious group.

3   Tozzer (1957) lists Chichen Itza, Uxmal, Labna, Chacmultun, Kabah, Xkichmook, Xul, Nisucte, Telantunich, Pustunich, Sayil, and Cumpich as including either phallic images, male nudity, or 'lewdness' (*sic*). Thompson (1970: 319) adds Nohcahcab, San Pedro, Xkoben Haltun, Xkonchen, and Hampopol as other locations of what he called a phallic cult. Pollock (1980) lists Nohpat, Almuchil, San Pablo, Kanalki, and Acanmul as having freestanding phalli, and cites Oxkintok and Santa Maria as having figures with phallic emphasis. The image from Santa Maria does not exhibit any clear evidence of genitalia, instead having a carved depression, and I exclude it from this discussion. Pollock specifically rejects the identification by others of phallic sculpture at Xkichmook, and I have therefore not included it in the total given for sites with this imagery. These authors merge together all images that show male genitalia; I do not include in my discussion nude figures lacking signs of sexual arousal, most of whom are captives.

4   The word 'palace', as used by Lincoln, implies both that the buildings involved were used for daily life and that residence was restricted to members of noble families. While I use the term throughout this paper to distinguish buildings of similar plan, I explicitly regard the question of the social status and kinship relations of those using palace-plan buildings as open issues.

5   The *same* performances provided a foundation for male realization of female desire for the admired Classic Maya male body in male–female sex. Rather than presenting a derogatory burlesque of heterosexuality, the cave painting at Naj Tunich enacts this attraction in a way that is visually celebratory of both the male and (transvestic) 'female' bodies. The comparison Stone (1995) draws to contemporary public performances in Highland Chiapas in which men cross-dress as women in comic sexualized displays, is ultimately problematic. While helpful in opening the possibility of reconceptualizing the Naj Tunich image, it ignores the colonial European background of the modern Maya Catholic ceremony that frames this performance, which participates in what Patricia Zavella (1997) characterizes as the 'Catholic-based discourse' of sexuality that is part of modern Mexican nation-building. The analogy undercuts the crucial importance of the Naj Tunich cave as a setting for homosocial gatherings, fundamentally unlike the mixed gender public setting of modern Maya ceremonies.

6 I am consciously reversing the expected direction of interpretation which would lead from European texts to Precolumbian archaeological remains, denoted by the term direct historic approach, in order to illustrate the potential that exists for a historicized reading that proceeds from the earlier state to the later, and as an expression of my belief that the material testimony of the physical settings and objects used to frame experience is a powerful resource for alternative discourses.

7 My translation. The original Spanish is:

> Y dado que he oído que en otras partes de las Indias usaban en tales casas del nefando pecado, en esta tierra no he entendido que hiciesen tal, ni creo lo hacían porque los allegados de esta pestilencial miseria dicen que no son amigos de mujeres como eran éstos, que a esos lugares llevaban a las malas mujeres públicas y en ellos usaban de ellas, y las pobres que entre este gente acertaba a tener este oficio, no obstante que recibían de ellos galardón, eran tantos los mozos que a ellas acudían, que las traían acosadas y muertas.
>
> (Landa 1959: 54)

8 See Restall (1995), Sigal (1995), and Restall and Sigal (1992) for discussions of colonial Yucatec Maya attitudes toward sexuality. I thank Susan Kellogg for these references.

9 I compiled these terms using the authoritative edition of colonial and modern vocabularies of Yucatec Maya, the *Diccionario Maya Cordemex* (Barrera Vasquez 1980). Not all terms related to sexuality are presented here.

REFERENCES

Barrera Vasquez, A. (ed.) (1980) *Diccionario Maya Cordemex: Maya-espanol, Espanol-maya*, Merida, Yucatan, Mexico: Ediciones Cordemex.

Bordo, S. (1994) 'Reading the Male Body', in L. Goldstein (ed.) *The Male Body: Features, Destinies, Exposures*, Ann Arbor: University of Michigan Press.

Bricker, V. (1992) 'A Reading for the "Penis Manikin" Glyph and its Variants (Una interpretación del glifo "maniquí-pene" y sus variantes)', *Research Reports on Ancient Maya Writing/Informes Sobre Investigaciones de la Antigua Escritura Maya* 38, Washington DC and Mexico DF: Center for Maya Research and Instituto Nacional de Antropología e Historia.

Burshatin, I. (1996) 'Elena alias Eleno: Genders, Sexualities, and "Race" in the Mirror of Natural History in Sixteenth-century Spain', in S. P. Ramet (ed.) *Gender Reversals and Gender Cultures: Anthropological and Historical Perspectives*, London and New York: Routledge.

Butler, J. (1993) *Bodies that Matter: On the Discursive Limits of 'Sex'*, New York: Routledge.

Clendinnen, I. (1987) *Ambivalent Conquests: Maya and Spaniard in Yucatan, 1517–1570*, New York: Cambridge University Press.

Codex Tro-Cortesianus (1967) *Codex Tro-Cortesianus (Codex Madrid). Museo de América, Madrid*, Graz: Akademisches Druck u Verlagsanstalt.

Davis, W. (1998) 'The Site of Sexuality', paper presented at the Annual Meeting of the Society for American Archaeology, Seattle, WA.

Edmonson, M. (trans. and ed.) (1982) *The Ancient Future of the Itza: The Book of Chilam Balam of Tizimin*, Austin: University of Texas Press.

Graham, I. (1992) *Corpus of Maya Hieroglyphic Inscriptions, vol. 4, part 2: Uxmal*, Cambridge, MA: Peabody Museum of Archaeology and Ethnology, Harvard University.

Gutiérrez, R. (1991) *When Jesus Came, The Corn Mothers Went Away: Marriage, Sexuality, and Power in New Mexico, 1500–1846*, Stanford: Stanford University Press.

Joralemon, D. (1974) 'Ritual Blood-Sacrifice Among the Ancient Maya, part 1', in M. G. Robertson (ed.) *Primera Mesa Redonda de Palenque, part 2*, Pebble Beach, CA: Robert Louis Stevenson School.

Joyce, R. A. (1992) 'Dimensiones simbólicas del traje en monumentos clásicos mayas: la construcción del genero a traves del vestido', in L. Asturias de Barrios and D. Fernández García (eds) *La indumentaria y el tejido mayas a través del tiempo*, Guatemala City: Museo Ixchel del Traje Indigena de Guatemala.

—— (1996a) 'The Construction of Gender in Classic Maya Monuments', in R. Wright (ed.) *Gender in Archaeology*, Philadelphia: University of Pennsylvania Press.

—— (1996b) 'Negotiating Sex and Gender in Classic Maya Society', in C. Klein (ed.) *Recovering Gender in Precolumbian America*, Washington, DC: Dumbarton Oaks, in press.

Justeson, J. S. (1984) 'Appendix B: Interpretations of Mayan Hieroglyphs', in J. S. Justeson and L. Campbell (eds) *Phoneticism in Mayan Hieroglyphic Writing*, Albany: Institute for Mesoamerican Studies, State University of New York.

Lancaster, R. N. (1997) 'Guto's Performance: Notes on the Transvestism of Everyday Life', in R. N. Lancaster and M. di Leonardo (eds) *The Gender/Sexuality Reader: Culture, History, Political Economy*, New York and London: Routledge.

Landa, D. de (1959) *Relación de las cosas de Yucatan*, 10th edition, Mexico, DF: Editorial Porrua, SA.

Lincoln, C. E. (1990) *Ethnicity and social organization at Chichen Itza, Yucatan, Mexico*, Ann Arbor: University Microfilms International.

Lounsbury, F. (1989) 'The Names of a King: Hieroglyphic Variants as a Key to Decipherment', in W. Hanks and D. Rice (eds) *Word and Image in Maya Culture*, Salt Lake City: University of Utah Press.

Pollock, H. E. D. (1980) *The Puuc: An Architectural Survey of the Hill Country of Yucatan and Northern Campeche, Mexico, Memoirs of the Peabody Museum, vol. 19*, Cambridge, MA: Peabody Museum of American Archaeology and Ethnology, Harvard University.

Reents-Budet, D. (1994) *Painting the Maya Universe: Royal Ceramics of the Classic Period*, Durham and London: Duke University Press.

Restall, M. (1995) '"He Wished it in Vain": Subordination and Resistance among Maya Women in Post-Conquest Yucatan', *Ethnohistory* 42: 577–94.

Restall, M. and P. Sigal (1992) 'May They Not Be Fornicators Equal to These Priests: Postconquest Yucatec Maya Sexual Attitudes', in L. Sousa, *Indigenous Writing in the Spanish Indies*, Los Angeles: UCLA Historical Journal, Special Issue.

Roscoe, W. (1991) *The Zuni Man-Woman*, Albuquerque: University of New Mexico Press.

Schele, L. and M. E. Miller (1986) *The Blood of Kings: Dynasty and Ritual in Maya Art*, Fort Worth: Kimbell Art Museum.

Sigal, P. (1995) *Maya Passions: Colonial Yucatecan Ideas of Sexuality, Gender and the Body*, Ann Arbor: University Microfilms International.

Spinden, H. J. (1913) *A Study of Maya Art: Its Subject Matter and Historical Development*, Cambridge, MA: Peabody Museum of American Archaeology and Ethnology, Harvard University.

Stone, A. (1988) 'Sacrifice and Sexuality: Some Structural Relationships in Classic Maya Art', in V. Miller (ed.) *The Role of Gender in Precolumbian Art and Architecture*, Lanham, MD: University Press of America.

—— (1995) *Images From the Underworld: Naj Tunich and the Tradition of Maya Cave Painting*, Austin: University of Texas Press.

Stuart, D. (1984) 'Royal Auto-Sacrifice among the Maya', *Res: Anthropology and Aesthetics* 7 and 8: 6–20.

—— (1988) 'Blood Symbolism in Maya Iconography', in E. Benson and G. Griffin (eds) *Maya Iconography*, Princeton: Princeton University Press.

Thompson, J. E. S. (1961) 'A Blood-drawing Ceremony Painted on a Maya Vase', *Estudios de Cultura Maya* 1: 13–20.

—— (1962) *A Catalogue of Maya Hieroglyphs*, Norman: University of Oklahoma Press.

—— (1970) *Maya History and Religion*, Norman: University of Oklahoma Press.

Tozzer, A. M. (1957) *Chichen Itza and Its Cenote of Sacrifice: A Comparative Study of Contemporaneous Maya and Toltec*, Cambridge, MA: Peabody Museum of American Archaeology and Ethnology, Harvard University.

Wren, L. (1994) 'Ceremonialism in the Reliefs of the North Temple, Chichen Itza', in M. G. Robertson and V. M. Fields (eds) *Seventh Palenque Round Table, 1989*, San Francisco: Pre-Columbian Art Research Institute.

Wren, L., and P. Schmidt (1991) 'Elite Interaction during the Terminal Classic Period: New Evidence from Chichen Itza', in T. P. Culbert (ed.) *Classic Maya Political History: Hieroglyphic and Archaeological Evidence*, Cambridge: Cambridge University Press.

Zavella, P. (1997) '"Playing with Fire": The Gendered Construction of Chicana/Mexicana Sexuality', in R. N. Lancaster and M. di Leonardo (eds) *The Gender/Sexuality Reader: Culture, History, Political Economy*, New York and London: Routledge.

Conclusion

Chapter Sixteen

Meanwhile, back at the village: debating the archaeologies of sexuality

Margaret W. Conkey

In his classic book, *The Early Mesoamerican Village*, Flannery (1976) engaged archaeologists with some of the major issues of the time through the creative dialogue between several characters: The Skeptical Graduate Student, The Real Mesoamerican Archaeologist, and The Grand Synthesizer. These were characters perfectly suited to the debates and posturings that personified the heat of the New Archaeology. While that kind of passionate, but in Flannery's hands not uncritical, acclaim for a single 'school' of archaeological theory and practice is nowhere to be found in these times of multiplicities, the dialogue approach from *The Early Mesoamerican Village* can be rejuvenated.

More than two decades later, I will frame my comments about Archaeologies of Sexuality through variants of these Village characters, though there's little chance that this will be as well crafted as Flannery's original. However, I do sort of like the idea of what Flannery might think about his characters being brought back to address a topic such as archaeologies of sexuality!

However, there must be some character shifts: today, it is the establishment archaeologist who is the skeptic, so we have the Skeptical Establishment Archaeologist; it is the graduate student who is real-world, or the Real World Graduate Student; and the grand synthesizer is today more of a Grand Sympathizer. A beginning dialogue might be as follows:

Skeptical Establishment Archaeologist: What?! Ten years ago, you start insisting that archaeologists must think about gender as well as status in our analyses and interpretations of prehistory and of the past, and *now* you think *sexuality* is not only important, but doable? Most of us still don't think you can 'see' gender, much less 'sexuality,' and besides, isn't all this getting a bit personal? After all, archaeology is the objective, scientific approach to the archaeological record, not some post-modern, situational identity politics.

Real World Graduate Student: Come now, you have to admit that many archaeologists have come to understand all sorts of new things about past labor, space, technology, art, and iconography – to name just a few – by taking gender and social personae into consideration. After all, you can't possibly deny that there were, in the past, at least what *we* consider to be biological males and biological females, which is probably all the more reason for considering sexuality as much as, if not in conjunction with, the myriad cultural versions of sex/gender systems.

Besides, you don't have to be a post-processualist – if there even is such a thing – to admit that archaeology is a culturally- and historically-contingent practice. While we may strive for empirical depth, analytic rigor, and grounded interpretations, we cannot proclaim archaeology as a purely objective endeavor. All sciences are social, and I might add, it is precisely because we have deeply held, usually masked, or undiscussed cultural understandings of sexuality, sex, and gender – such as the sex-negativity discussed here by Voss and Schmidt and originally by Rubin (1984) – that to take up these issues in archaeology is important and fruitful in many cases, as can be seen in this edited volume. After all, many scholars (e.g. Lloyd 1993) have shown how, for example, our conflation (in today's dominant society) of female sexuality with reproduction has led to some very problematic and downright incorrect scenarios for human evolution; this has influenced our understanding of all sorts of things, such as the images of females in prehistoric art, and for interpreting archaeological materials that may be as ordinary as lithics! And, if you took the time to read – instead of prematurely dismiss – the chapters in this volume, you might see, for example in Buchli's chapter, exactly how, as he puts it, 'archaeology is inevitably cultural work'. Even this work with gender and sexualities is very much a set of culturally-informed and motivated projects; but this does not make the research and the analyses any less valid, particularly since much of it recognizes this aspect, unlike many archaeologies that proclaim their way is *the* right way, and that they have most certainly 'got it 100 percent right'.

Grand Sympathizer: Well, I agree with you both. For example, I can see how it is probably important to decouple our ideas about female sexuality and reproduction, but I myself was skeptical – at least before reading many of these papers – that sexuality is something that can be taken into account in our archaeological studies. I must admit, I'm not yet convinced that we have an agreed upon definition, or better yet, a conceptual framework for what we mean by sexuality, especially for archaeological purposes. I mean, I hate to be old-fashioned, but how do we 'measure' sexuality? How do we, to use Binford's terms, 'monitor the variability'? But then again, certain papers in this volume have begun to define rather creative contours of what this might be and how this might be done.

For example, there is Voss's point about the architectural constraints and sexual geographies of post-contact sexual relations, which reinforces the idea that it is often in such situations of cultural change that archaeologists can best 'see' certain phenomena that might otherwise be less remarkable, if not downright ignored. Also, there is Hollimon's continuing work with Chumash ethnography, ethnohistory, and material culture, offering a more complex conceptualization of 'genders' as an intersection with, and of, sexual practices. I have begun to get the impression that even those who have been grappling with an archaeology of gender have begun to understand that there is no single notion of 'gender', even among analysts from modern Western countries (e.g. Demoule and Coudart 1997; del Valle 1993: 2), so that we must from the start entertain the notion that when we talk about 'sexuality', it is at least as equally diverse and mutable a concept. Whoever thought, as Meskell argues here, that the ancient Egyptians, for example, did not take 'sexuality' as a separate category of life, the way we in the West now do? How can one even study 'it' (sexuality) if it's not even a separate category? Or, if it is something we can barely imagine?

Other chapters here are a real challenge in this regard. For example, in Gilchrist's essay, she details a notion of a personal sexual identity that is not even predicated upon an intimate sexual activity with another animate individual! And Joyce's paper proposes that even in a state-level society, sexuality can be considered in ways other than as utilitarian and/or for state procreative power. Suddenly, there are perhaps even too many ways of conceptualizing 'sexuality'!

The 'how-tos' are as challenging as having a viable conceptual framework. But again, there are tantalizingly effective approaches here. Davis really 'wows' us with his expansive use of multiple, but converging lines of evidence, and his use of such concepts as 'opticality', activity, and even the idea of bringing forth an 'erotic history'. Both Meskell and Joyce, in their respective papers, which deal with two different cultural repertoires of representation, show the real potential of a topic – representation – that archaeology as a field has been reluctant to take up, yet is one that will be crucial to 'jump starting' these studies of gender and sexuality, especially when in such creative, and yet such cautious analytical hands as those of these two authors. And many other authors show how all sorts of new – albeit perhaps not yet really solid – ideas pour forth once one allows oneself to 'think' sexuality, or something like it, is 'at work'.

Skeptical Establishment Archaeologist: Listen, here you have studies of sexual practices, like prostitution, which are documented in historical texts and which we all know about; even if one admits that perhaps some historical archaeologists have overlooked some evidence for prostitution because they have not opened their minds to this as a possible account for their evidence. And Davis's study of Beckford's architectural and representational world as a 'site' of sexuality is also so enmeshed in textual support that it is no wonder that, for prehistory, where we have none of these texts, Binford (e.g. 1983) told us to forget ever accessing even ethnographic facts of life, much less these kinds of historically enriched and enabled 'peep holes'!

Now, I know that the editors of this volume are quite clear on the importance of text-aided approaches, as was good old Christopher Hawkes (1954) long ago, especially for 'these' kinds of social phenomena, though surely Hawkes never imagined that something like 'sexuality' was among the features of past human life we would even think of accessing. He must be turning over in his grave, poor old guy!

Sure, you can make the case that with the use of historical narratives – especially of situations that are 'closer' to our own experience and understanding, where we can perhaps have greater understanding, connectivity, and relationship to the situation – one can see clearly the tension and dialectic (did I really use *that* term?) between sexual ideologies and sexual practices, especially in a colonial context of *new* power relations. But, wait a minute, I see that you have gotten me into a different vocabulary and mindset. I bet that one should be critical of sexuality studies from both sides of the issue – why does everything have to be discussed these days in terms of 'power', and why isn't the all-important notion of 'power' used in more nuanced and refined ways?

Although I personally am still not convinced that we can find the all-important (yes, they are still *the* all-important!) material correlates for past sexuality, especially without textual anchors, you may have a point that we ought to think about our assumptions about our archaeological research problems. After thinking about it over the past decade – admittedly only once or twice – I thought that to study gender, we only had to think about the sexual division of labor, making gender another variant of status, and finding gender attributes in the archaeological record. After all, now that gender archaeology has come along, we can agree that there were women in the past and that 'they' can sometimes be documented, too.

Real World Graduate Student: Well, clearly you have *not* been reading the important critiques of the feminist research in anthropology and other fields: just as there is no homogenous essentialized entity such as 'women' or 'men'. In all times and all places, there are, intimately tied up with the performance of what we would call 'gender roles', localized conceptions of sexuality that are widely variant. That is, what these papers show is that we can *not*, in fact, merely transpose such processes as the conflation of sexuality and sexual behavior with power negotiation that has come to dominate in the recent history of much Western social life *onto* past societies, or even onto other segments or sections of historically known societies and contexts. The particular notion of the social construction of gender that you may now begin to admit into your limited imagination is itself problematic and complex. For example, it shares some basic criteria that enable, if not promote, racism, ethnocentrism, and Western sexuality; namely, this social construction of gender has nonetheless promoted the formation of *ideal models* or types, and the consequential exclusion of those that do not fulfill or adhere to them.

This can be extended to our understandings and approaches to 'sexuality': without coming to grips with the ways in which ideals of or for sexuality and sexual behaviors and ideologies are promulgated such that they too enact and enforce conforming, and thus are limited and constraining roles and practices, we are perhaps more like pawns in systems of social control rather than the scholarly pursuers of diversity and comparison that we hold ourselves to be. Recall the point made in Prine's chapter that, even when you have the ever-tantalizing textual references, those who recorded such historically known sexual practices and identities usually had a stake in controlling and exploiting them, so even with textual sources, the task is not straightforward and certainly not neutral.

Grand Sympathizer: I see: you are suggesting that in addition to a more embodied knowledge about our past people as socially constituted subjects, the archaeological consideration of sexuality is another lesson in how our reconstructions or representations of past societies and people are and can be ethnocentric, paternalistic, and used for the implementation of certain conceptions of power and control; how archaeology is drawn into producing knowledge that is controlling, more than knowledge that leads to understanding.

While I am sympathetic to the idea that *limited* conceptualizations and limited accounts of the past are likely to be both limiting and exclusionary, I am still stymied by how we can ever 'know' about past sexuality; especially if it is something that is so local and contextual, and even in flux, or at least ever-fluid. For many of us, furthermore, to admit that we want to know about past sexuality goes against our ingrained upbringings and cultural mores! I must admit archaeology was much simpler when we assumed ideal, stereotypic categories, and, because it made sense in contemporary life, archaeology was really archaeo-*logical*!

Skeptical Establishment Archaeologist: Well, you'll never convince me that I need to think about sexuality when I am measuring potsherd rims in order to define cultural horizons; besides how can I possibly tell the local Boy Scout troop that the archaeology of sexuality is relevant for their archaeology badge requirements?! I can't even think about sexuality in general without getting all red and embarrassed. I have to admit, though, that some of these papers in this volume have been rather interesting, especially when they show what we might have missed or misunderstood if the notion of sexuality is not taken into account; such as the distribution of those 'illicit' artifacts in the Tasmanian women's prison (Casella, this volume), or what *might* – and I only will say 'might'! – have been going on in the one Hidatsa house (Prine, this volume) with the 'double posts', even if the tried and true methods of sampling and average house size are part of the argument Prine makes.

Real World Graduate Student: Well, none of us ever said that *all* archaeology has to take sexuality into explicit account in our work, but perhaps you ought to have a conversation with yourself about your own assumptions about such things, given that they inevitably have some impact on your conceptions of yourself in your life and work. Remember Meskell's quotes from Foucault that show your attitudes and 'comfort levels' are themselves part of very specific historical contexts that, however, have not inhibited archaeologists from undermining their own abilities to understand *very* alien worlds of the past. Rather, these inquiries into sexuality that are here in this volume make the point very forcefully that we ought to question all sorts of agreed-upon assumptions, and more importantly, we alone may have unique perspectives to bring to bear on some very prevalent – and I won't say universal – aspects of human life, such as sexuality! Just look at the way that standard things for archaeologists – like certain clusters of artifacts (as in Wilkie's, Costello's, Casella's or other chapters) – take on new and even more vibrant potential meanings when considered in the light of social and sexual practices! Even Flannery long ago (1972) recognized the problem of having reconstructions that were so one-sided that some prehistoric people only seemed to be eco-robots and others only cognitive maestros.

While archaeologists have always drawn on relevant theory (whether doing environmental reconstruction or social agency), these chapters in this volume remind us that relevant theorists (such as Butler (1990, 1993) or Herdt (1994)) are *only* thinking about the contemporary world. Butler, for example, can only or primarily imagine that the performance of gender and its relation to sexuality is central to everyday existence in the here and now, while this may not be the case for many situations in the recent or deep past. However, she has provided us a framework – as shown, for example, in Joyce's work (e.g. 1998) – not so much for confirming this centrality, but for seeing and showing both the limits of this view and the possibilities of, or for, alternatives. As Joyce's paper in this volume shows, one can take some of the Butler notions and expand them – in this case to consider the dimension of 'play', as elucidated by Lancaster (1997) – and yet show a certain salience in a historical and cultural setting that such theorists have hardly imagined.

Indeed, as the papers in this volume proclaim, it is up to the individual situational analyses and inquiries by archaeologists to do this, which is archaeology's important (albeit not yet readily recognized) contribution to bodies of theory and to the human sciences.

Skeptical Establishment Archaeologist: Oh come on, who cares about archaeology contributing to bodies of theory (or to theories of body, for that matter)? After all, where's the archaeology? Where's the basic excavation, the solid analysis of geology, ecology, material remains? What is all this, some 'kind of bungee-jump into the Land of Fantasy' (Flannery and Marcus 1993: 261)?

Real World Graduate Student: Now, you come on – if you have read these papers you have to see there is not only plenty of archaeology here, but plenty of implications for not just archaeological interpretation, but for the very way in which one *does* one's archaeology – what to look for, or what kinds of evidence might be useful in expanding our archaeological understandings. After all, in a discipline (like archaeology) that basically destroys its data as it recovers them, we don't have a chance to go back and redo it, so if these inquiries into the archaeologies of sexuality provide us with some ways of getting even more information from our archaeological contexts, that alone is good reason to consider taking it up! Furthermore, lots of so-called 'real' archaeological data – things like burial practices, grave goods, wall murals, stuff from under floorboards, in abandoned wells, building remains, and so forth – are actually explained or understood better when aspects of sexuality are taken into account.

Look again! For example, how does one account for the 'illicit items' that Casella's excavations – yes, real excavations – recovered? Does one argue that these imprisoned women in the solitary cells drank alcohol because of some nutritional deficiencies? How does one account for the kaolin pipes that are almost always otherwise the artifacts of men? Are these just more cultural deviations from imprisoned and therefore culturally-deviant women? And with the burials that both Schmidt and Hollimon discuss, there are 'unexpected' sets of grave goods. How does one account for such constellations of attributes? Do we simply revert to the kinds of 'it must be ritual' accounts that archaeologists often give if they can't explain something? Or do we go through some contortions, as Winters (1968) did in his attempt to explain why females in burials in Indian Knoll (US Midwest) were quite frequently interred with so-called 'male' artifacts, such as atlatl components? Remember that Winters thought they must have been purely ceremonial inclusions; the women couldn't have possibly used them, given a stereotypic *a priori* notion of what men and women 'did'. If they did use them to hunt, Winters had to postulate a 'platoon of Amazons' was part of the culture!

With the kinds of views that Hollimon and Schmidt bring to their respective archaeological examples of some burials – the Chumash of California and the far northern (European) Mesolithic – one is tempted to go back to the Hopewell burials – those men with 'women's' grinding stones and those women with 'men's' atlatl components – and reconsider the possible sex/gender implications! Who knows what might have been going on in Indian Knoll culture?!

Grand Sympathizer: Well, on the one hand, many of these papers have convinced me that, in some cases, there are some things that can be better understood if we think that sexual identities and roles – really, just a variant of social roles – might have been part of why certain burials were made, why certain artifacts are found in a single-sex prison or in a well attributed to a midwife, why a certain house differed from others in its architecture and contents, or that certain new and imposed architectural forms might have impacted on people's ways of 'getting together'. On the other hand, I don't see how you could begin to formulate a scientific hypothesis that would be testable; how could you ever get funding from a respectable agency to carry out research that would demonstrate that, for example, Maya images of men were part of a homoerotic culture or that the cultural settings of the ancient Egyptians at Deir el Medina were permeated with what *my* mother would consider to be downright pornographic and suggestive imagery and artifacts?

I know, I know, I can step back and be the anthropologist of myself; I can see how my own notions and presumptions are getting in the way of perhaps a more

expansive and even liberating approach to not just archaeology, but to the understanding of our past subjects as living meaningfully constituted lives in all domains,
including the sensuous, the physical. Believe you me, if it weren't for the studies in
this volume, I would have never thought it possible; I would not have been able to
imagine how one could even go about 'seeing' sexualities 'at work' in the past –
even in historically documented contexts. So I have to admit I have learned something, even if I am not likely to undertake such work myself.

Skeptical Establishment Archaeologist: Well, I am not so sanguine as you, my dear colleague,
that archaeologists should be spending their time on such fleeting, personal, and
historically situational topics as 'sexuality' – yes, for once I found a good use for
that faddish term, 'historically situational'. I could turn around the claim about the
way in which we destroy our archaeological data as we recover them, to say that it
is a waste of time and resources to speculate about 'sexualities' when we could be
saying something substantive about the long-term macro processes that shaped the
course of the human career. Now, *that* is anthropological archaeology, and is as
objective as we can possibly be. In fact, many of us have dedicated out entire careers
to refining the methods for researching such things!

Real World Graduate Student: I would be the first to admit that the decades of work that
has been done before I got interested in archaeology has been enormously fruitful
and that we have learned a great deal about cultural ecology, subsistence systems,
settlement patterns, how to do regional survey, and the like. But, as I mentioned
before, it is not a new idea to suggest that there is indeed more to human life. What
your generation has provided is a solid knowledge-base of information that in fact,
can be, and is, used as a platform onto which new ideas can be added. There is
research to be done at different scales of analysis, and there are many new sides of
past humans to be 'seen' if we view them as knowledgeable participants in the
cultural worlds of their own making, which is quite different from viewing them as
merely adapting to external exigencies.

While the archaeologies of sexuality presented here may indeed yield all sorts of
tantalizing insights into specific case studies, and may also show that sexualities are
something to be considered, no one is proposing to do a Kinsey Report for the
Chumash, the European Mesolithic, the Hidatsa, or the Egyptians; or that we need
to make an inventory of prehistoric and historic sexual practices. Rather, to undertake the archaeologies of sexuality, it seems to me, is a way to show just how very
rich our archaeological data are; how important it is to consider a multiplicity of
approaches to understanding even the most 'ordinary' of archaeological evidence;
how crucial our own theories are to our interpretations; and how exciting a field
archaeology is – not content to continue uncritically with both tried and true ways
of interpreting and with some of the more recent approaches, such as gender archaeology. Yes, we can now say something about what we take to be 'sexuality' in a
number of contexts, but above all, these studies show that documenting sexualities
per se is not *the* single aim of these studies; rather, they show that our archaeologies – the careful recovery and analysis of the material worlds of the human past –
must be even more nuanced, careful, and yet rigorous, than we ever imagined, and
that we must learn to think even more creatively than ever before.

The Grand Sympathizer: If I am correct in assessing the debate between you two, I would
have to say that it is agreed that your generation – and those before you, dear Skeptic
– has left a rich legacy, but also a challenge. To undertake the Archaeologies of

Sexuality is but one of a number of responses to that challenge, and one that, at least based on the studies in this volume, has great promise; and, for a first attempt, shows gifted imaginations at work, both in conceptualizing the topic and in the handling of 'real' archaeological data and situations. I couldn't have imagined any of this myself, but, hey, now that you have shown me some ways to think about it, I might just go back to rethink some archaeological data; perhaps to those Indian Knoll burials, or maybe, what about those so-called men's tools and male-related features, and women's tools and female-related features in the households in the Mesoamerican Village (Flannery and Winter 1976: 42–45)?

REFERENCES

Binford, L. R. (1983) *Working at Archaeology*, New York: Academic Press.

Butler, J. (1990) *Gender Trouble: Feminism and the Subversion of Identity*, New York: Routledge.

—— (1993) *Bodies That Matter: On the Discursive Limits of 'Sex'*, New York and London: Routledge.

del Valle, T. (1993) 'Introduction', in T. del Valle (ed.) *Gendered Anthropology*, London and New York: Routledge.

Demoule, J -P. and A. Coudart (1997) 'Les archéologues au pays de Mickey Mouse', *Les Nouvelles de l'Archéologie* 57: 43–45.

Flannery, K. V. (ed.) (1976) *The Early Mesoamerican Village*, New York: Academic Press.

Flannery, K. V. (1972) 'The Cultural Evolution of Civilizations', Annual Review of Ecology and Systematics 3: 399–426.

Flannery, K. V. and J. Marcus (1993) 'Viewpoint: Cognitive Archaeology', *Cambridge Archaeological Journal* 3, 2: 260–70.

Flannery, K. V. and M. Winter (1976) 'Analyzing Household Activities', in K. Flannery (ed.) *The Early Mesoamerican Village*, New York: Academic Press.

Hawkes, C. (1954) 'Archaeological Theory and Method: Some Suggestions from the Old World', *American Anthropologist* (n.s.) 56: 155–68.

Herdt, G. (ed.) (1994) *Third Sex, Third Gender: Beyond Sexual Dimorphism in Culture and History*, New York: Zone Books.

Joyce, R. A. (1998) 'Performing the Body in Pre-Hispanic Central America', *RES: Anthropology and Aesthetics* 33: 147–65.

Lancaster, R. N. (1997) 'Guto's Performance: Notes on the Transvestism of Everyday Life', in R. N. Lancaster and M. di Leonardo (eds) *The Gender/Sexuality Reader: Culture, History, Political Economy*, New York and London: Routledge.

Lloyd, L. (1993) 'Pre-theoretical Assumptions in Evolutionary Explanations of Female Sexuality', *Philosophical Studies* 69: 201–15.

Rubin, G. (1984) 'Thinking Sex: Notes for a Radical Theory of the Politics of Sexuality', in C. S. Vance (ed.) *Pleasure and Danger: Exploring Female Sexuality*, Boston: Routledge and Kegan Paul.

Winters, H. (1968) 'Value Systems and Trade Cycles of the Late Archaic in the Midwest', in S. R. Binford and L. R. Binford (eds) *New Perspectives in Archaeology*, Chicago: Aldine.

Index